"I DIDN'T DO IT! I WANNA GO HOME!"

Serena was huddling on the bare cement floor of a six-by-eight room of concrete blocks carved with graffiti. A bed, molded out of concrete, was covered with a thin vinyl mat. One woolen blanket. A small, dirty window. An open white and chrome toilet and a small sink.

"I loved Mallory," Serena sobbed raggedly. "You know I could never hurt her!"

Tears flooded Sharri's eyes and she drew her daughter close. "Yes, I do know," she whispered. "I do, I do."

They rocked together until the cell door swung open. "Time to go."

Fresh tears spurted down Serena's cheeks. "Mom!"

"Stay seated," warned the attendant. "You must stay seated as your visitor leaves."

A QUESTION OF INNOCENCE

BRANDILYN COLLINS

AVON BOOKS ⬖ NEW YORK

For Mallory
She dances with the angels

A QUESTION OF INNOCENCE is a journalistic account of an actual murder investigation for the 1992 death of Mallory Moore in Fremont, California. The events recounted in this book are true, although some of the names have been changed. The scenes and dialogue have been reconstructed based on tape-recorded formal interviews, police department records, and published news stories. Quoted court testimony has been taken verbatim from trial transcripts.

AVON BOOKS
A division of
The Hearst Corporation
1350 Avenue of the Americas
New York, New York 10019

First Avon Books Printing: November 1995

Acknowledgments

MY THANKS TO all those who granted me their time for interviews, in particular, attorneys Shelley Antonio, Matt Golde, Doug Horngrad, and Penny Cooper. A special thanks to defense attorney Horngrad for his perusal of all legal aspects in this book. Any errors in that vein most certainly are mine.

I also greatly appreciate my discussions with Sergeant Allen Holm of the Fremont Police Department and with the Moores' numerous friends. And, of course, Sharri, Michael, and Serena Moore, who forced themselves to relive many traumatic moments in order to make events come alive for me.

I must add here a hearty "mugs-up" to the folks at San Carlos' Coffee Club Too, who kept me fueled with mochas as I toiled over bringing those events to life in my manuscript.

To my editor, Tom Colgan, goes expressions of deep gratitude for his support and professionalism.

And I'm forever grateful to my dear friend Niwana Briggs for her no-holds-barred editorial perceptions as she read and reread the manuscript.

Most important, I thank my husband, Mark, and children, Brandon and Amberly, for indulging and enduring the sometimes tumultuous forces of creativity.

—Brandilyn Collins
Redwood City, California

A false witness will not go unpunished, and he who pours out lies will not go free.

Foreword

IF THIS BOOK were fiction, I doubt it would have been published. "Too farfetched," editors would say, "overly reliant on coincidence." So many extenuating circumstances could not occur in one trial—the puzzling death, the mentally unstable teenager, the zealous Deputy D.A. and the defense team that, according to a judge, "fell below the required [legal] standard."

The old adage holds fast. Truth is, indeed, stranger than fiction.

I first attended the trial in *The Matter of Serena M.* during its third and final week. Media reports of the case had been both bizarre and sensational, mixing descriptions of Serena's diary confession to murder with tales of her dysfunctional home. That day, the defendant was on the stand, looking at times uncomfortable, at others, oddly detached. More mystifying was the evidently supportive presence of her parents, who sat stoically silent as attorneys on both sides accused them of child abuse. Why weren't they defending themselves? I wondered. Were they indeed child abusers? Was Serena Moore guilty of murdering her little sister? And *why,* if the Moores believed their daughter innocent, had they given her diary to police in the first place?

Continuing to attend the trial that week, I began to realize that something was wrong. Underneath all the rhetoric there lay an untold story, one that I soon found myself driven to uncover.

This story twists again and again to form a labyrinthian journey mapped, by various people, with winding tunnels of conjecture. Amidst the many heartfelt, uncompromising opinions to which they cling, I have done my best to be fair. The final legal conclusion of the "Diary Girl's" guilt or innocence was hard-won, built in large part upon evidence that never came to light in her first trial.

But I push ahead of my tale.

In this account of pride and passion, humiliation and heartbreak, I have allowed you, the reader, an omniscient view of the rapid-fire events with little interjection on my part. The record, as they say, speaks for itself. All quoted letters have been printed verbatim, errors included. Newspaper articles have been reprinted with permission from the *San Francisco Chronicle, Almeda Newspaper Group,* and the *San Jose Mercury.*

Friends and family members of the Moores did not ask to be placed within the vortex of these events, and have been granted anonymity through pseudonyms, with the exception of Sharri, Michael, and Mallory. The defendant's name has been changed in compliance with court order, issued because she is a juvenile. All professionals connected with this case have retained their true identities.

Prologue

On August 18, 1992, in Fremont, California, four-year-old Mallory Moore died, inexplicably, in her sleep.

Her death would become a sore point for investigating officers. In law enforcement, the unexplained demise of any person raises a cynical eyebrow. When the victim is a child, that cynicism hardens into a bullet spray of righteous anger seeking a defined target. A grim determination to punish the perpetrator sets in.

Dr. Paul Herrmann performed an autopsy on Mallory at 9:15 A.M., August 19. Observing the little girl's face and neck, he saw a few "petechial hemorrhages"—small bursts of blood vessels near the skin. In her lungs, Dr. Herrmann found "clinical and microscopic evidence of asthma." Cause of death, he reported, was "traumatic asphyxia, mechanism undetermined." In layman's terms, something asphyxiated Mallory, but the cause was unknown. It looked like a homicide to the coroner, but he couldn't prove it. Disposition on the case remained "open."

Dr. Herrmann's findings set in motion a series of events that would all but destroy the Moore family.

As Sergeant Allen Holm, then supervisor for Fremont's Crimes Against Persons Unit, explained, "This case hinged primarily on the coroner's determination that Mallory did not die of natural causes, but that she died at the hands of another."

The autopsy conclusions sent Fremont police scrambling. Believing that Mallory Moore died of natural causes, officers at the scene had taken no fingerprints or photos and had made no diagrams. Detective Greg Whiteley, assigned to the case, began an investigation by questioning Mallory's parents,

Sharri and Michael Moore; her half sister, Serena, and a few of the family's friends. Most interesting were the statements of one woman and her teenage daughter. Tragically, their fingers pointed to fourteen-year-old Serena. A sizable stack of police reports indicated that Serena was unstable and prone toward sensational, attention-gaining lies and schemes. Could Mallory's murder have been one of them? Or was jealousy a motive?

After a second interview with the parents, the case ground to a halt. The investigation was "suspended," as Holm called it, not "just put away and forgotten," but detectives "had exhausted all their leads." Whiteley was left with an "unattended death" that was suspicious but lacking enough evidence for an arrest.

Before the case could be solved, Whiteley began preparing to transfer from detective duty back to the streets. This was a typical rotation within the Fremont Police Department, in which cops change jobs every two to three years. The system was established partly to reduce job burnout, but mostly to produce well-rounded officers. In effect, it replaced the "good buddy" routine of making friends and influencing people in order to move from pavement to wooden desk.

The Moore case was handed to Detectives John Anderson and Bob Davila, who could do little to move it forward. Any pressure they may have felt to crack the case, Sergeant Holm maintained, would have come from within. "These detectives are highly motivated and take pride in their work," he said. "When they can't clear a case immediately or not at all because there are no leads, they become frustrated."

With such little information to go on, the two detectives faced a brick wall. They needed something to seize upon, needed it mightily. A new lead—a neighbor's statement, a piece of evidence. A confession. Something, *anything* placed in their hands to help them prosecute the perpetrator of this heinous crime.

They were about to get their wish.

PART I

Blind Faith

December 1992–April 1993

If somebody loves somebody, they want them close to their hearts forever.

—SERENA MOORE TO CONNIE CHUNG

One

WHEN IT CAME to her daughter's diary, Sharri Moore was a snoop.

And with good reason, she thought, eyeing Serena's blue-flowered journal as it lay on the desk. Buried among the fantasies, the teenage yearnings, the diatribes against snotty schoolgirls who flaunted their friendship like candy dangled beyond a baby's reach, lay occasional nuggets of gold. Glints of the real Serena.

Sharri hoped to find more than glints this particular night. What she needed was hard evidence. It was a Saturday in December 1992, one day after Christmas and half an hour after Serena had stormed out of the house headed for who-knows-where.

"If you guys are gonna argue, I'm leaving!" she'd yelled, slamming the door behind her for effect. Which was frustrating to begin with, because they hadn't really been arguing. Sharri would call it more of a heated discussion. She, Michael, and Serena had managed to survive their first Christmas since Mallory's death, flinging themselves through a celebration with family in Carson City, Nevada. Now, just after returning home, they faced a letdown. At the moment, her and Michael's dammed-up tensions were threatening to overspill their carefully constructed barriers. That was all.

Sharri guessed the last few days had been too much for Serena. Here she was, acting out again, running off in a sudden temperamental snit. On some distant, rational level, Sharri understood that Serena's sorrow over Mallory's death was as wretched as her own, that such intense emotions were far overplayed on a psychologically unstable fourteen-year-old. But rational understanding was hard to come by these days. Sharri was too tired.

Plunked momentarily on her daughter's bed, she stared at the journal. The backs of her legs registered warmth emanating from an electric blanket. That was strange. Either Serena had been preparing for bed before she split or it had been left on for three days, since before they'd left for Carson City. Throw the coin, call heads or tails—either scenario would fit. Serena was just as apt to forget taking care of details as she was to blitz from one mood to another.

Regardless, Sharri was left to pick up the pieces.

That wasn't going to happen tonight if she could help it. Sharri had already tried to cut this episode short, cruising three miles of dark streets in hopes of finding Serena in case she was headed to the house of her boyfriend, Troy. No luck. She'd hurried home, spilled the news to Michael, then skittered into Serena's room to see what she could find. Beyond that, Sharri hadn't known where to look. Now, drumming impatient fingers soundlessly on her daughter's quilted bed, she realized she *did* know where.

The diary.

Jumping to her feet, Sharri swiftly crossed the small bedroom to pluck it from Serena's desk. It felt smooth and stiff, unlike the tattered edges of Serena's white journal in her desk drawer. Serena had used that volume for three years, cumbersomely filling its lines mostly in her large, open print, occasionally in cursive. Now that it was full, she had begun this new blue-flowered diary.

Picking up the blue diary, Sharri remembered the last time she'd looked in Serena's diary, searching for clues to her insolent behavior. One entry had caught her eye, all right. According to Serena, then eleven, she'd been raped by a boy at school and was pregnant. Another of her wild tales. Sharri prayed she wouldn't read any more entries like that one. But maybe she'd find *something*—plans of a tryst, perhaps—that could point to where Serena might have run one hour before midnight.

She flipped through the pages. Serena had only written one entry. She skimmed the final lines. Nothing of interest. In irritation, she looked back at the beginning of the entry. Her eyes narrowed as they blipped side to side, down the left page, flicked up, then down the right. Still nothing. She tossed the blue journal back on the desk in disgust.

A television droned in the condo's living area, on the other side of Serena's bedroom wall. Doubtless, Michael was still parked in front of it on the couch, trying to lose himself in a program. It was his way of escaping the sharp-toothed worry that nipped at his stomach every time his stepdaughter ran away.

This time Sharri and Michael were surprised at Serena's sudden flight. She had settled down, been almost cooperative, for the last month. In the lull, they had let themselves believe that, finally, Serena was learning to deal with her little sister's death.

Sharri ran nervous fingers through her long hair. It had grown scruffy since Mallory died last August. Still, she couldn't bring herself to cut it. Mallory used to grab hold of its reddish brown strands. Somehow, Sharri felt, cutting her hair would be like cutting away part of her little girl.

She glanced downward at the thought, as if to avoid staring sorrow in the face. As she did, her green eyes fell on Serena's new diary, also lying on the desk, the one she'd just received for Christmas. Sharri had bought it for her on impulse, even though she really didn't need it. Its cover design was feminine. Green stripes alternated with white ones, the latter serving as backdrop for a pattern of delicately stemmed roses and leaves. To the right was a dainty lock with flowers, raised in bronze. Not a bad deal for $1.99. And small enough to fit into Serena's stocking.

Out of vague curiosity, Sharri reached for it. Not that she expected to find anything. This was a year-long diary, allowing only one thin-leafed page for each day, starting January 1. There was no reason for Serena to have started it yet. But it wouldn't hurt to check.

Her fingers ran over the soft cover, picked it up. The diary was locked. Sharri frowned. Maybe Serena *had* used it. Carefully, trying not to break the thin cardboard, Sharri bent back the cover. She gazed at the first page on the right. It was blank. She tilted the diary and peeked at the left page, directly underneath the cover, then blinked in surprise. She could see

Serena's familiar round print, pushing against the top and bottom of each narrow line.

What was it, Sharri would later ask herself, the cosmic force culpable for urging her on? Fate? The darker side of God's will? Or was she to blame, solely—for her own prying fingers?

She pulled the cover harder until it strained its lock, raised the diary close to her face. She peered inside. As far as she could tell, the page was full, but she could only read half of it.

That was enough to send Sharri Moore's world spinning.

Dear Diary,

Well, it's New Years so I'm gonna start telling you everything dearest to me. I have to get something off my back. I killed my little sister. . . .

A bolt of white-hot lightning shot through Sharri, sizzling her nerves. Dazed, she smacked the diary shut and pressed it between her palms. For a moment she could not move. Then, mind reeling, she staggered across the room and sank onto Serena's bed as her knees caved in. Far, far away her legs again registered warmth radiating from the pink electric blanket. Or was that heat emanating from her own burning body? She felt her chest constrict, forcing her to suck each breath in ragged catches.

What was she going to do?

I don't want to know this, I can't know this! she screamed to herself. How could Serena write something like this? How could she *do* this?

A gush of bile rose suddenly, sickeningly, in her throat. With a small cry, Sharri pushed herself to her feet and rushed for Serena's bathroom. Awkwardly, she fell to her knees on the cold tile and slammed back the toilet lid. Leaning over its gaping mouth, she didn't think to fling back her hair until it fell into the water below. Her jaw slacked and she heaved, then heaved again. Her stomach was churning, churning, but no vomit would come. The initial rush of heat drained from her head, leaving her goose-pimpled and shivering.

She could not know how long she hung there, throat spasming in dry, gasping clutches. Time had suspended her in a void all her own. Somewhere far below, she sensed her right hand gripping itself into a cramp, then realized why.

Serena's green and white diary still lay clenched in her fingers.

TWO

SHARRI ROSE SHAKILY and stood over the toilet, the diary still in her hand. Dizziness surged like a violent tide pulling her out to sea, its force sucking away each breath. She shook her head but could not clear it. Blindly, she groped with her left hand for the tile counter and clung to it, white-knuckled, as she slowly raised her head. Another retch threatened to explode from within at the sight of herself in the bathroom mirror. Her face was chalk white, each skeletal-like cheekbone sticking out above dark hollows. Both eyes disappeared into her skull.

I'm dead, she thought.

She felt her eyes blinking rapidly of their own accord. Her right hand let go of the diary momentarily to raise itself and rub across her face. Were those her own fingertips? The hand lowered itself, came to rest against smooth cardboard, its little finger sensing a small metallic square. Sharri's eyes rolled their line of vision toward the hand. Between its fingers she saw the blurred rectangular design of stripes and roses, flowing around a bronze lock.

How could she tell Michael? The question blew through her like a cold wind. Did she dare tell him what Serena had written? No, she couldn't; it was asking too much. Through all the fights and struggles, all the wild claims from Serena, he had clung to his grim determination to help his stepdaughter. But this was the ultimate. Mallory was Michael's world; she was his everything. How could Sharri face him while in her hands lay the confession that her own sick daughter had murdered his precious little girl?

Sharri knew this was just another of Serena's fantasies, an

outpouring of her guilt over Mallory's death. But would *he* believe that? Even if he didn't believe her words, wouldn't he fly into a rage, strangle her for even writing—so blithely— about the moment that took away his life?

No. She could not tell him.

Sharri's chin came up. Once again she faced her own stark reflection. She couldn't tell him, but she must. She knew she could not face this alone; she hadn't the strength. What little reservoir she had left after Mallory's death had long since dried up in the heat of battle over Serena, leaving a lake bed inside her that was cracked and brittle. Her mind was chaotic, her thoughts driven here and there like sand in a swirling wind. Her body felt depleted.

A force beyond herself turned Sharri away from the mirror and propelled her through the bathroom door.

Michael was still on the couch. How odd, thought Sharri, that he would sit there so long. Some corner of her brain signaled a reminder that she had just left him—had it only been five minutes ago? A surreal sensation hovered over her, like dense fog at the end of a time warp tunnel. She'd left her husband only moments before, had returned to find him just the same, while she had traveled miles, flashing through insanity and back again.

Sharri crossed the living room on wobbly legs and dropped to her knees before Michael. She opened her mouth, struggling to tell him, but no sound came. He looked at her stricken face.

"What's wrong?"

She felt a staccato sound erupt from her throat. "I, I—"

Michael's eyes widened. *"What?"*

"I, Serena—" Sharri faltered. Her mouth seemed made of wood, her tongue parched. "Serena wrote something in her diary."

"What is it?"

"It's—something about how Mallory died."

Michael stared at her, an unreadable expression flickering across his brow. "Something that she knows about it?"

Sharri felt a quaking deep within, fought to keep it under control. "Yes. That she—I could only see the first—that she had something to do with it."

Michael's face contorted. "What do you mean?" Shooting

out a hand, he grabbed the diary from Sharri's fingers. When the lock fought to keep the diary's secrets, he slapped a hand on either cover and ripped it open with one twist. Vaguely, he sensed his wife shrinking back as his eyes tore across the rounded print.

Dear Diary,

Well, it's New Years so I'm gonna start telling you everything dearest to me. I have to get something off my back. I killed my little sister Mallory! I went into her room, got her and took her into my room. I told her I loved her and covered her mouth and sufficated (sic) her. Then I took her back into her room and put her back into bed. You're the first person I have ever told this to. Well I feel better.

Love Always, Serena

Michael read the entry a second time, allowing the words to sink into his consciousness. Not daring to ask what was on the rest of the page, Sharri knelt silently at his feet, hands over her mouth. Michael looked away then and stared at the far wall, his mathematical mind working to find a reasonable explanation for this illogical equation.

A minute ticked by, one that would remain forever etched in Sharri's mind.

Quietly, Michael placed the diary on the coffee table. "She didn't have anything to do with it." His voice was flat.

Relief washed over Sharri, leaving her giddy in its wake.

"But how could she do this? How could she write something so *awful?*"

Michael shrugged. "You know she feels guilty. Mallory wanted to sleep with her that night and she wouldn't let her."

Sharri reached for the diary and read the last few lines. "God," she choked, "how could she write this!? To even *think* these words! Do you think she really feels she had something to do with it?"

"Who knows?" Michael sounded almost flippant. "Who knows why Serena says the things she says or does the things she does."

The statement hit hard.

He's been more damaged than I realized, Sharri thought.

Serena had burned him so many times that *this* could not even faze him. Her fear for Michael gained momentum, then spread to her daughter. Suddenly, she remembered that Serena was out there—alone—in the cold of midnight. What must she be thinking? What kind of deep, inner pain could have driven her to write such a warped confession?

"We have to find her," Sharri blurted. "Maybe she's hurting herself. If she's feeling guilty, she could be out there somewhere, trying to cut her wrists again or standing in front of a train! We have to call the police!"

"No way," Michael shot back. "What if they believe it? What do you think they'll do then?" He looked at her like she'd lost her mind. "They'll take her away from us. Wait until she comes home. Then we'll get her help."

"What if she doesn't come home? Besides, they won't believe it. They *can't*. They know all she's been going through; they know all of her lies. It's in their reports."

Michael shook his head.

"They said they'd help us, Michael," Sharri pleaded. "They have to know her mental state, otherwise they won't even look for her. What if she's *hurt?*"

Confused, unable to act, they talked in circles. With each passing moment, Sharri grew further afraid of what Serena might do. Michael was more concerned about the police—what *they* would do with a "confession" in their hands. He'd already lost one little girl. He wasn't about to risk losing his only other child—the stepdaughter he'd helped raise from age eight.

Finally, the Moores agreed to call Doug Evans, their pastor. They needed his wisdom. They needed a friend to tell them what to do.

The streets of Newark were quiet, brightened by occasional Christmas lights resolutely blinking in the chilled air of midnight. Pastor Doug rolled to a stop at an intersection, squinting at its street sign as Michael's directions played soddenly through his head, like a tape player on low batteries. Doug had been asleep when the phone rang. Eleven o'clock was early for him to retire, even when his alarm would signal Sunday morning, with its full schedule of preaching two services and teaching Sunday school in between. But that night a feverishness and grating cough from the flu had settled over his body. No matter that his associate was slated to lead tomorrow's services; Doug still was expected to read the liturgy. He had gone to bed early, hoping that when he woke up, he'd have a voice.

Doug had never visited the Moores' new rented condo, and was still unfamiliar with many of the thoroughfares connecting Fremont with its smaller sister city of Newark. He had only lived in the San Francisco Bay Area a little over four months, having uprooted his willing wife and teenage daughter to accept the senior pastorship at the First Presbyterian Church of Newark after over twenty years of serving in the Pittsburgh area. His older daughter, finally settled down with a husband and new baby, had remained back East.

Doug took a wrong turn, realized his mistake and doubled back. The Moores' condo was close to Mowry Avenue. That, he knew, was a busy road that headed east toward Mission Boulevard, which ran north and south along the foothills. A newcomer couldn't get *too* lost in Fremont, considering those hills bordered the city's eastern side and the San Francisco Bay lapped its edges to the west. Doug knew also to look for a cornfield, backed up eccentrically beside the condo and its urbanized surroundings, the result, no doubt, of a determined farmer holding out against citification of his anciently fertile land.

When Doug had last visited the Moores, they were living in their four-bedroom home on Lucia Street. They still owned that house, but now were renting it out, no longer able to bear living within its memory-filled walls.

The call from Lucia Street bearing the news of Mallory's death was another one that Doug would not forget. He and his family had been unpacking from their move when Michael's brother Ben phoned on behalf of the grief-stricken parents, who were reaching out in natural trust to the new pastor they had not met.

Doug had visited Sharri and Michael that evening. Serena had come home while he was there, very upset, needing her mother to calm her down. Through the interaction, Doug could tell that Serena struggled with a rebellious nature.

In the next few days before conducting Mallory's funeral, Doug met with Sharri and Michael several times, learning about their short years with Mallory. She had wanted to be a ballerina, Sharri recounted. She and Serena often danced together, Mallory crawling up on their long coffee table for height as she swayed in her sister's arms, eyes closed, mouth spread in a blissful smile. The last night of Mallory's life, she had been tucked into bed, excited, counting the hours until she could sign up for dance lessons the next day.

But she never woke up.

In the months following Mallory's funeral, Doug had talked often with Sharri and Michael, offering support between services or in phone calls. Intermittent in their previous attendance, the Moores began coming to services every week, eventually joining the church the first Sunday in December. On that day, Serena and Michael were baptized; Sharri had already been through the ritual. Serena started attending the church's youth group, joining the twenty or so teenagers in weekly meetings and outings. Her attendance throughout the fall, however, was sporadic, marred by bouts of her running away from home.

Naturally, it was a difficult time for Sharri and Michael, but seemed more so for Serena. Doug knew that she had been hospitalized twice for psychiatric care. Beyond that was the running away or "splitting," as Sharri called it. Numerous times, Sharri had phoned the church, asking for prayer as she and Michael searched for their daughter. Doug's heart ached for them. He'd had problems with his eldest daughter when she was a teenager, and could point to gray hairs to prove it. He couldn't imagine facing that on top of the death of a child.

As Serena began making friends in the youth group, Doug had found himself in an odd position. She always wanted to be the center of attention, whether it came from him, the youth leader, or the teenagers themselves. That was all right by Doug; he could understand her needing extra care after her sister's death. But her schemes for attention didn't stop with mere effusiveness. Serena, to put it bluntly, was a chronic liar. She had the kids believing, among other things, that she was seventeen, had been engaged numerous times, and had undergone two abortions.

A number of the teenagers came to Doug, asking him questions about Serena. In response, he had to play it very carefully. He was new to the church, and had not had much time to build a strong relationship with the youth. He wasn't sure if they'd trust him enough to follow his lead. But he gave it a try, asking them to accept Serena. He reminded them that she was still grieving over her sister's death in August. She had a problem, he told them, and she needed their friendship. At the same time, they need not accept everything she said as the gospel truth. It was a difficult balancing act, pleading with them to be Serena's friends when one of the most important components of friendship—trust—was missing. Doug was pleased that the kids had been able to do so.

In December, Serena had calmed a little. Then two weeks before Christmas, she bounced into church, ecstatic, waving around a "pre-engagement ring" on her finger, bubbling on about how her boyfriend, Troy, had bought it for her. That much, Doug learned, was true. He hadn't met Troy, but knew Serena's parents disapproved of the relationship. Evidently, many of the times that Serena ran off were stolen opportunities to be with him.

Which, Doug figured as he made a final turn down the Moores' street, was probably why she'd written such a wild entry in her diary. This was more than just another lie. This was a blatant confession to an act she could not have committed. Serena was trying to get kicked out of the house. She must have decided, with the twisted reasoning of a disturbed fourteen-year-old, that if she wrote such an ugly statement, her parents would finally reach their fill of her antics and show her the proverbial door. Then she'd be free to live with Troy.

This sick "confession" also reflected to Doug the severity of Serena's mental instability. Without question, the child required further psychiatric care.

Three

AT NEARLY 2:00 A.M., business was winding down at Mowry Lanes bowling alley. Two late-night patrons plunked down multicolored rented shoes on the long front counter and sauntered off, flexing their fingers. Sudden laughter burst from the bar, separated from a snack table area by wide swinging doors covered in maroon vinyl. The chink-chink of video games was now audible, now indistinct amidst the rhythmic pattern of extended ball rolls before sudden crashes of wood, repeated like some futile telegraphic message.

Serena Moore hunched over a small round wooden table, sipping a Coke between drags from a cigarette. Across from her in a white plastic chair, Troy Cole was stubbing out a smoke, gesturing with his chin.

"Let's go."

Serena eyed him coolly. To her, his skin and hair were striking, their darkness, so she had been told, harkening back to Filipino ancestry on Troy's father's side. His hair, shoulder-length, thick, and wavy, was combed straight back, leaving a bare forehead that emphasized eyes of bitter chocolate. His was a hardened countenance for seventeen years, though Serena didn't view it that way.

"Not that he looked really mean," Serena's best friend, Mary Corren, would later say of him, "but you could just tell that he had that way about him."

Abrasive, domineering, Troy treated Serena as his personal possession and servant. When they stayed at his house, she had to fetch the drinks, the snacks, the cigarettes. When he wanted to go somewhere, they went; if he wanted to stay, they stayed. If he had to pull hair or shove her around to keep her in line, that was okay by him. She didn't fight it much.

Serena had not always been that way. She'd had countless boyfriends since her precocious introduction to puberty in the fifth grade. All of them were "really nice, clean-cut guys" who treated her well, as Mary put it. But Serena's volatile alliance with Troy since the past spring had molded her into a new stance—the self-effacing pose of a ready and willing victim. Not a surprising position, perhaps, for a teenager who, as a young child, had watched her mother endure countless beatings at the hands of a drunken husband.

As Serena saw it, she was simply falling into the pattern that fate had designed.

"If there was a room full of nice guys and one jerk," she would later declare, "I'd pick the jerk, without even knowing." It ran in her genes, she said, flowing from Grandma Tessie to Mom and into her. Her mom, sick of that kind of life, had finally broken the cycle for herself when she married Michael.

That night at Mowry Lanes, Serena rationalized her decision to repeat that cycle. She was "hella in love" with Troy. If he mistreated her, well, she'd live with it. Somewhere in a black crevasse within her mind a sniggering voice echoed that whatever he dished out, she most likely deserved.

"I said let's go."

Serena pushed herself to her feet, pressing both lips around a cigarette while she shrugged into the black wool veteran's flight jacket she'd just received for Christmas. It hung loosely over her jeans, all but covering a dark shirt underneath. She stopped to pull her long brown hair out from under its collar.

Serena was well developed for her years, her only drawback a chunky waist. By the sixth grade, her breasts had already reached and surpassed thirty-six inches. Her figure may have belied her age, but her face did not, with its youthful pudginess and spatter of pimples. Her hazel eyes were deep set and pretty, almost transparent. Her naturally pink lips were generous, spreading wide across her face when she smiled.

Dutifully, she followed Troy into the parking lot. An overhead light turned their faces to paste and tinted the low-slung salmon-colored stucco and brick building a nondescript shade of mud. Set back from the street, tucked behind other businesses, the bowling alley offered Serena and Troy a perfect meeting place. They'd hung around Mowry Lanes long enough for Troy's parents to be asleep. As was their custom, Troy would bang through the front door to let his mom and stepfather know he was home—if they happened to be around. Once in his bedroom at the front of the house, he'd slide open a window and Serena would slip through.

It was a plan that had worked dozens of times before.

Serena caught Troy's arm as they walked in the clear night toward his Ford Blazer. Across Mission Boulevard the foothills hulked like brooding monsters, their haunches separating the lit streets of Fremont from the dark valley beyond. It seemed colder to Serena than three hours ago, when she'd raced the few blocks from home to meet Troy. She knew her parents would be ticked as hell that she split, but she didn't care.

Not that Serena didn't love her mother and stepfather. Hers was not a conscious desire to inflict pain on them, but rather the narrow-visioned compulsion of a teenager bent on having things her way at all costs. Since her sister's death, that compulsion had turned to obsession, driving her into a frenzy of destructive behavior that was beyond both her control and understanding.

This night's spontaneous tryst with Troy was for Serena one more misdirected attempt at diversion from her grief. Her despair had abated earlier in December. Then the dreaded holiday had hit, like a slap in the face. Christmas at Grandma Tessie's had been weird, the family shrieking in wild laughter one moment and crying the next. She knew Christmas had been difficult for her mom and dad. For her, it had been overwhelming.

So, after arriving home, she had escaped as she so often did, banging out into the night in an ill-fated flight from her pain and guilt, not thinking, never *dreaming,* of the consequences.

Wrapped in a jacket, Michael leaned against the railing of their condo's deck, prepared to wave Pastor Doug in as he searched for their place in the dark. At five-foot-ten, Michael carried a few more pounds than he would have liked. His full head of brown hair was beginning to gray, as was his well-trimmed mustache. He was dressed in one of his ever-present pairs of casual pants and a long-sleeved cotton shirt. Even if the situation required it, Michael felt ill at ease dressed up.

Sharri flitted about the kitchen in a losing battle to control her nervous energy, making coffee, wiping down the tile, smoking a cigarette.

Doug gave them a quick hug when he stepped through their door. "We don't believe this now, do we?"

Michael and Sharri sank down on their textured beige couch, Doug, on the matching love seat. The pastor shook his head over the diary. There was no way Serena could do this, he said. From everything he'd heard, she loved her little sister too much.

Frantic, Sharri filled in details of the last few months. Serena had not only been hospitalized twice, she'd also tried suicide. She'd gone berserk at a friend's house, tearing apart a soda can and aiming its jaggedness at her wrist. Four friends had jumped her, fighting against Serena's surprising strength in a battle to save her from her own madness.

Sharri sprang up, skirted the coffee table, and began pacing, her five-foot-four-inch frame exuding an almost-palpable apprehension. The intensity of her expression magnified her high cheekbones and sharply defined jaw. What's more, she rattled on, Serena had run away so many times that the police wouldn't even look for her now. Running away in California wasn't against the law. If the cops spotted her, they'd try to pick her up, but that could be *days* from now.

"Call the police," Doug urged. "Right now." Serena could be suicidal; she needed immediate care.

Underlying Doug's response was an unconscious transference of past experiences. He had total trust in the police. In Pittsburgh, he'd witnessed numerous crises with church members, and the police had always been supportive. He'd seen authorities play every possible angle to rectify situations between parents and children. Incarceration was the last resort. When you called the police, he believed, they were supposed to help.

Sharri grabbed onto Doug's certainty and hung on. Michael was still reticent. Turning over that diary meant placing the situation out of their control, he argued. What if the cops made a bad decision somewhere down the road? What would happen to Serena? God, they couldn't afford to make a mistake. She was the only child they had left.

"But what about Serena's safety now?" Doug argued. They had to force the police to search for Serena immediately. The only way to do that was to show them the diary to emphasize her fragile state of mind. They'd *have* to look for her, with a possible suicide on their hands.

"I don't know; I just don't know." Michael ran a hand across his forehead. "I want her safe. But I'm still afraid of what they'll do."

"We've got to do *something,*" Sharri insisted, anxiety pinching her face. If they didn't call the police, what was the alternative? Go to bed? Sleep while Serena was out there—maybe hurting herself? For all they knew, she could be dying right now!

That's what happened to Mallory.

The remembrance stopped Sharri cold.

Sharri had been in bed with an earache, selfishly upset that she couldn't sleep, while just on the other side of the wall, her little girl suffocated. Feeling her throat tighten, Sharri berated herself for the millionth time for not doing something. Mommy was so close, but Mommy failed Mallory. She died alone.

Sharri swiveled toward her husband. "Michael, we've got to do this *now*."

Michael gazed out the window, as if looking for an answer in the black night. Sharri and Doug were probably right, he thought. Serena's behavior was too unpredictable. They couldn't sit back while she might be in danger.

"Okay," he said. "Let's do it."

The ghost of a premonition struggled, then, to raise a wispy hand in warning. Neither he nor Sharri could make the phone call.

"If I dial," Sharri asked Doug, "would you talk to them for me?"

Doug accepted the phone, heard the ringing in his ear. He, too, felt a sudden foreboding. What would be the repercussions of their call? There was still time to change their minds. He held the receiver away, looking at Sharri. "Are you sure this is what you want?"

His question hung in the air, weighted by indecision. Sharri hesitated as their eyes locked.

The next few seconds would sear in the Moores' fate as surely as a branding iron sizzling on their skin.

She nodded.

Far away, Doug heard someone answer. "Fremont police."

He pressed the phone to his ear. "I'd like to report a possible crime," he heard himself say.

The dispatcher asked what crime.

"Murder," he replied.

That got her attention.

Officer John Morillas responded to the dispatch, logged in at 1:47 A.M., December 27. As calls went, this was one of the wilder ones. Some guy wanted to report a murder, the dispatcher said, but not really a murder. There was no body now—the death had occurred four months ago. No crime was committed, you see, but someone had just confessed. And that someone was a kid.

Like Doug, Morillas was waved into the house by Michael, who was keeping an outside watch for the police car, a blue-and-white.

Sharri vaguely recognized Morillas's stocky build, probably from one of her frequent police contacts about Serena, she thought. She launched immediately into their story. Why she'd looked in the diary. How upset their daughter must be. When she paused for a breath, Michael filled in the gaps. Doug, feeling the growing effects of sleeplessness and the flu, spoke occasionally between coughs.

The Moores told Morillas about their daughter's death, that its investigation had been suspended, and that he might want to talk to the detectives handling the case for further information.

Without compunction, they handed over the diary.

Morillas seemed to take it in stride, listening intently. If he knew details of the pending case on Mallory, he gave no indication.

"He was very pleasant," Doug later remembered. "As helpful, courteous and understanding as he could be. Then, *bingo*."

Morillas asked the Moores what they wanted him to do when Serena was found—bring her home or take her to a psychiatric hospital?

Doug, Michael, and Sharri exchanged glances in silent consensus. You call the shots, they encouraged, depending on how she seems. Most likely, she would need to be hospitalized.

Morillas offered assurances. They'll probably call in a psychologist to talk to her, he said, just to make sure she's okay. Then he left, promising to phone as soon as Serena was found. He took the diary with him.

Morillas wasted no time contacting Javier Marquez, one of the few detectives from the Crimes Against Persons Unit on call during the Christmas holiday. That unit, Morillas knew, would have been handling the investigation of Mallory Moore's death.

By all means, look for Serena, Marquez told Morillas, and pick her up as an incorrigible.

"Oof!" Troy grunted as he fell, a deadweight, on top of Serena.

"Ow, I can't breathe!" she protested. "Get off me."

Troy took his time planting a wet kiss on her mouth, then rolled off. Shivering in the sudden absence of his warmth, Serena sat up to reach for the covers.

"Boom, boom, boom!" She froze at the sound of loud knocks on the front door. A moment of silence, then more pounding.

Serena knew that knock. In the middle of the night, with that kind of force, it could only mean one thing. "Shit! It's the cops." She grasped the covers and pulled them up to her chin.

"Aw, Christ," Troy moaned. "Wait a minute." The sheets rustled. "You stay here, I'll go check."

Sliding out of bed, he bent over to grope his way around the floor in search of his jeans. Serena heard the chink of pocket change as he thrust them on, then the slight metallic whir of a zipper.

"Your dad's up," she whispered at the sound of footsteps in the hall. She scrunched further under the sheets.

"I'll be right back." Troy skulked across the room, willing his eyes to get used to the darkness. Quietly, he unlocked the bedroom door and clicked it open, furtively leaning his head into the hallway.

"Is Serena Moore here?" he heard a man ask. A muffled, sleepy answer from his stepfather, then footsteps approaching his room.

Troy slid back his head and closed the door. "Get up, Serena!" His voice was low, tight. "They're coming."

Within seconds, the room was filled with light. Serena snapped her eyes shut, then blinked them open, nerves tingling at the sight of a policewoman pushing Troy out the door. Serena huddled, her face hardening.

The woman commanded her to get dressed. She was under arrest.

Serena felt a jolt of anger shoot through her limbs. "What the hell am I being arrested for?"

"Just get dressed." The officer stepped purposefully toward the bed as if to pull the covers away from Serena.

"Okay, okay! Just would you turn around at least."

"I can't turn around. You may have contraband."

Serena raised up on her elbows and glared. "What do you think this is? I don't have any 'contraband,' " she hissed. "Turn around!"

The woman held her eyes, then shrugged. It wasn't worth an altercation. She swiveled slowly to face the far wall.

Serena flung back the sheets and slipped into her underwear. Then, one leg in her jeans, she stopped to light a cigarette. She took a long, deep drag. Something told her it would be a while before she enjoyed another one.

The officer looked over her shoulder. "Put that out."

Serena flicked a smoldering gaze in the cop's direction and inhaled again.

"I said put it out. You're not old enough to smoke." She turned to face Serena, hands on her hips.

"What are you arresting me for?" Serena challenged again, smoke puffing from her mouth.

"Would you put that cigarette out!"

Serena rolled her eyes to the ceiling. "Just answer my question," she yelled. "Who cares about the goddamn cigarette! I wanna know why I'm being arrested!"

Moments that followed blurred amidst the chaos in Serena's head. Somehow she finished dressing, somewhere she stubbed out her cigarette. A male officer was in Troy's room then, patting her kindly on the back, telling her everything would be explained. She heard Troy call "I love you," heard herself reply the same. Felt the clamminess of cuffs on her wrists, sensed the hallway flowing as she moved toward the front door, shivered at a rush of cold winter air. A hand pushed her head down and she stumbled, mouthing a curse, into the backseat of a blue-and-white. A motor started and Troy's house began to fade away.

She would not see her boyfriend again.

Four

SHORTLY AFTER 3:00 A.M., Javier Marquez, hearing from Morillas of Serena's arrest, responded to police headquarters. While Morillas booked Serena for homicide on the first floor of the station, Marquez mounted steps to the offices of the Crimes Against Persons Unit to search for information on the investigation regarding Mallory Moore's death. Detective Greg Whiteley had handled the case, then it had been reassigned to Robert Davila and John Anderson, neither of whom was on duty that night. Marquez located the file and thumbed through it, searching for the coroner's statement. He blinked. There it was. The autopsy report termed the cause of death "traumatic asphyxia, mechanism undetermined." It fit with the teenager's diary confession of having suffocated her sister.

Marquez called Morillas. Bring Serena up to the investigator's room, he advised, and leave her there until she can be interviewed. Morillas led Serena to the third floor and shut her in the closetlike room, then turned the diary over to Marquez. The detective reached for the phone again. Anderson might not be in town, but at least he could wake up Davila. Together, they would question the teenager who'd written that she had killed her little sister.

The Moores' phone was ringing. Michael was in bed, trying to catch some sleep before his wake-up time at five-thirty. Doug had gone home, hoping for a few hours' rest before eight-thirty church services. Sharri grabbed for the receiver. The caller identified himself as Officer Cortez, then told her they'd found Serena and were at the police station. They were going to have her talk to a detective about the diary.

Sharri was not alarmed. The police were just checking Serena out as Morillas had promised. "We'll come right down."

Cortez demurred, telling her to wait until the detectives talked to Serena.

Now that Serena was safe, Sharri felt anger pricking at her skin, a release of pent-up fear. She hesitated. Maybe a talk with police officers would do her daughter some good. Maybe that was just the dose of reality she needed—a solid, hard consequence for making up another lie. God knows she'd told enough in her lifetime.

"Okay. But *please* call us."

Sharri wondered, as she hung up the phone, if the police didn't want her and Michael there for fear they would influence how Serena answered questions. Maybe, she thought, they'd let Doug see Serena. Quickly, she dialed his number. He hadn't yet reached home. She left word with his wife.

A few minutes later, Doug's wife was meeting him at their door, giving him Sharri's news. He was instantly alarmed. Police had taken Serena to the station? What for? That was not at all what they had discussed.

Immediately, he climbed back into his car and headed for the station. Surely, they'd let a fourteen-year-old girl arrested for the first time see her pastor.

Serena dropped tiredly onto an old couch, the only piece of furniture in the detectives' interview room. She didn't notice the video camera. She waited, then waited some more. She had no idea of the time, but it seemed an eternity. Leaning against the couch's armrest, with her head in one hand, she tried to doze.

At 6:00 A.M., two men entered the room. They brought chairs with them and placed them a few feet apart, facing the couch. Marquez also held an Admonition and Statement form, from which he read Serena her Miranda rights. "Having these rights in mind, do you wish to talk to us now?"

Serena had talked to policemen lots of times. It didn't bother her. "Sure." She wiped her runny nose and pushed back her hair. Airily, she waived her rights to the presence of a lawyer and her parents by signing the form.

Serena did not realize the trouble she was in. She had been arrested, and thought she was about to be questioned, for running away. But she had been booked for homicide. The Miranda ruling states that a person has the right to remain silent and have an attorney present during an interview with police, but may waive this right provided the waiver is made "voluntarily, knowingly, and intelligently." In not explaining current charges against her, Davila and Marquez apparently allowed Serena to waive her rights without understanding the purpose of the interview. No alleged Miranda error, however, would be argued in her trials.

With videotape running, the detectives began their questioning. "The reason we want to talk to you," Marquez said, "is some information has come to us regarding the death of your sister. Plus, you were also picked up for being incorrigible."

"Yeah." Serena sat cross-legged and cracked her knuckles.

Marquez questioned Serena about her family and Troy, then turned to the morning of August 18.

"I've already told everything I knew to the other big detective dude," Serena replied, sniffing.

"Detective Whiteley, the guy with the mustache?"

"Yeah, he's big, chubby."

"Yeah."

"I told everything I know to him. I mean this was four months ago."

Serena told the detectives, without emotion, how she had gotten up about seven-thirty on August 18, gone into her sister's room, and was unable to wake her. "I couldn't wake her up so I ran into my mom's room and I told my mom I couldn't wake her up. My mom was waiting for her already, too, to come in and wake her up and I said mom I can't wake her up and she got up, went in there, and she couldn't wake her up either and she ran down the hallway and I asked her what was wrong and I was all crying and screaming and asked her what was wrong and she said Mallory's dead and I dropped to the floor, started crying, and then when I heard her say that her four-year-old was dead on 911, I ran out of the house."

Davila asked Serena how she got along with her half sister.

"Oh gosh, we were so, we were like that, you know." She pressed two fingers together. "We were like, I mean, you know, she had her times, she came in my room, I'm like get the hell out of my room, but that's like normal. You know, but we like, we were really close. I mean, she was like—''

''And Michael,'' Davila interjected, ''her father, is your stepfather?''

''Yeah.''

''Where does your real father live at?''

''Uh, he's in jail.''

''He's in jail?''

''Yeah.''

''When he's not in jail did you used to visit him at all?''

''No, I haven't seen him in about ten years.''

''So as far as you're concerned, Michael, I guess, is your father.''

''No.''

''Do you call him—''

''No.''

''Michael—you don't consider him your father?''

''I don't consider any of the people she marries my father. Um, she married Kevin, I called him Dad, it didn't work out, they broke up. Divorced. I called Michael Dad for a while. I don't think of him as even remotely part of my family.''

''How long have they been married?'' Marquez shifted in his chair.

''Six years.''

''Now before your current stepfather and your mom got married how was your relationship with your mom?''

''Oh, we were close.''

''Real close?''

''Yeah.''

''How close?''

''We were like really close.''

''Uh-huh.''

''I mean I was like eight years old and we were like really close.'' Serena yawned.

''How about when Mallory came?''

''We were still close.''

''You were still close to your mom?''

''Uh-huh. I had no jealousy against Mallory and my mom had no jealousy about me and Mallory being so close. I mean, I used to hold that baby all the time. I used to, I mean, I still, before she died I used to hold her like a baby.''

"Was there any competition between you and her?"

"No."

"As far as with your mom and stepdad?"

"No. We had our little, we had our quirks, you know, you know, I mean, arguments, but nothing about Mallory, you know."

"Uh-huh."

"We used to get in fights sometimes you know, I think like three fights, physical fights, me and my mom got in physical fights 'cause we're so much alike that we both want the same things out of each other and it doesn't work. She wants me to realize how much she's hurting and I want her to realize how much I'm hurting and we go back and forth on that."

"Uh-huh."

"She calls me selfish, I call her selfish. It's no big thing so, you know, it doesn't work out. We got into big old physical fights but we haven't got into a physical fight in a long time. I haven't, I haven't hit her I think in, I don't know how long. She hasn't hit me in I don't know how long. Michael hasn't hit me in about a year and a half, two years, you know. It's been awhile."

"So you and Michael, how, what about your relationship with Michael?"

"Oh, um, I like him sometimes and sometimes I can't stand him." Serena gave a little laugh.

"But he hasn't hit you for about a year and a half now?"

"Um, like if I was arguing with my mom, I'd tell him shut up and then we'd start hitting each other and then Michael would rip me off my mother and, you know, like bat me around, you know, don't hit your mother and I'd hit him back and he'd hit me back and—"

"Sort of a mutual thing."

"Yeah, but one time he got a little bit too far and he got me on the ground and punched me in the stomach."

"How long ago did that happen?" Marquez.

"Oh, about a year ago."

What kind of relationship did Mallory and Michael have? Davila wondered. Serena said it was "pretty good," that "they got along." She didn't like it when Michael spanked

Mallory, though; she "didn't like anybody hitting" her little sister.

Davila changed the subject. "Did you ever tell anybody that you were, ah, the one responsible for killing Mallory?"

"Uh-uh."

"Did you ever write anything, write a letter to anybody or write anything saying that you were the one responsible for killing her?"

Serena was suddenly frightened. She laid both hands in her lap and eyed the detective. "No, not that I know of."

"So I mean you didn't tell anybody that or write anything to that effect or tell anybody that at all?"

"Uh-uh. Uh-uh."

"Do you keep any journals or anything?"

"I have one journal in my room but I haven't written in it in a while." She sniffed.

"When's the last time you wrote in it?"

"Oh, man, it's a blue journal my mother got for me awhile ago before my baptism—"

"What kind of things do you write in it?"

"I wrote like, you know, I miss Troy and I talk, I, most of those pages I talked about Troy in it."

Serena played with her fingers as the detectives kept at it. This was the only journal she had, she insisted, but, oh yeah, there was the new one she just got for Christmas.

Davila and Marquez exchanged glances. "Okay," Marquez indicated. Davila got up and left the room.

Serena sighed. "What time is it?"

Marquez checked his watch. "It's six thirty-five."

"Am I going home?"

"I don't know. We're going to call your parents and see because, because leaving home, you know you're only fourteen years old."

"The other dude said that my mom was going to come pick me up."

"Oh, I don't know. We've got to call her up and let her know."

"Have you guys called her yet?"

"No, I haven't."

Serena was irritated. She'd already been here three hours. "You guys haven't even talked to her yet?"

"I haven't talked to her yet. Another officer talked to her."

"Who?"

"The officer that brought you in."

"Oh." Serena yawned.

Davila returned, holding Serena's diary. "Is this the diary here, the one your mom gave you?"

Serena felt another stab of fear. "That seriously does not look familiar."

"Doesn't look familiar at all?"

"No, it doesn't actually."

Davila sat down. "Is that your handwriting?" he asked, pointing to the entry.

"No."

"That's not your handwriting?"

"It's not even my handwriting. That's not even my handwriting. This is a long entry."

Davila offered her the diary. "Why don't you read that aloud."

"I want to read it to myself." She held it close to her face, laboring purposefully over each word. "Interesting," she said, slowly. "I can tell you I did not write this."

"You didn't write that?"

"No way, not." Serena's voice grew louder.

"What does that say?" asked Detective Davila.

"It says I killed her. I did not."

"So this isn't your diary?"

"It does not look familiar."

Serena could feel her heart beating. The room was chilly and her nose wouldn't stop running. Detective Davila read the entry aloud in a stumbling monotone. No, she said again, she did not write that.

Davila leaned forward. "Why would somebody write that?"

"I have no idea but I did not write that and I'm like in deep shock now."

"I think," Davila countered, "maybe you need to start being honest with us, okay. This was found in your house and Officer Morillas told me that your mom had given it to him or to some patrol officers. I don't think you're being totally up-front and honest with us."

"I am being up-front," Serena insisted. "I did not write that." She played with her hair.

Her denials continued. She hadn't written the entry, hadn't gotten the diary for Christmas. Marquez left the room.

"Okay," Davila said, flexing his arms. "So your mom and dad aren't going to say this is your diary?"

"I don't know what they're gonna say. I'm not even gonna consider her my mother anymore because if she'd pull something like this on me, she is really out there. This is like the last straw 'cause I'm like pissed off now!"

"But this is in your handwriting though, right?"

"No, it's not!"

"This is the first time you've ever seen this diary?"

"Yeah." Serena opened her mouth in a bored yawn.

Davila thumbed through the diary. "And you have absolutely no idea why somebody would write that and sign your name on it?"

Serena shook her head. "Uh-uh. I am so mad." Her voice was matter-of-fact, quiet.

Marquez returned. "Serena," he said, taking a seat, "you say it's been about a year and a half ago since Michael and you have been in a fistfight or anything?"

"Yeah, about that. Quite a long time ago."

"A long time ago. Then why is there, there's a report on file that you filed back in September of this year that you all had been involved in an altercation and a fistfight."

Serena stretched out her legs, crossed her ankles, and wiggled a foot. "That might have been it. I'm not real good with like months and years and stuff."

Marquez pointed to the diary. "Have you ever seen this book before?"

"That book?"

"Yeah."

"Nope. Today's the first day."

"Don't you have another diary or a journal at home?"

"Yeah."

"Where's that kept?"

"On my bed stand."

Davila stared at his hands, then looked at Marquez. "Don't you think it's pretty weird that somebody would put that in your room?"

"I don't know; I'm just really mad."

"Who are you mad at?"

"I'm trying to think of who in the hell would do that 'cause it's starting to really piss me off 'cause I know that's not my handwriting." She rubbed an eye hard.

"And you told Detective Marquez and myself that you didn't get any kind of diary for Christmas at all?"

"Nope. My mom already knew I had one."

Both detectives rose. "We'll be right back."

Serena waited for about fifteen minutes, playing with her hair and picking at her fingernails until Davila returned. She was growing impatient. "How long is it gonna be?"

"It'll be awhile, a little bit. We're gonna have you write some things."

Serena got up tiredly. "Okay." She followed the detective through the door.

A few minutes later, Serena was copying her diary entry in both cursive and print as Marquez read the words aloud. "I never write in cursive," she complained, "and I don't even remember how." Marquez told her to do the best she could.

In his report about the session, he noted:

> Every time she wrote out the statement, Serena never showed any emotion as to what the statement said. The only thing she would complain about was that her hand was getting tired and that she could not write in cursive. It appeared to me that Serena would deliberately try to change the style of her natural writing on the cards.

After Serena completed ten cards, Marquez requested permission to search her bedroom for other materials. She said "okay," signing a Consent To Search statement, which allowed the detectives to "take from [her] premises and/or vehicle any letters, papers, materials or other property which they may desire."

While they paid a visit to the Moore home, she would be taken to juvenile hall.

The police station was quiet, save for occasional officers coming and going. Doug sat heavily in a wooden chair, his coughs echoing through the entryway. He raised tired eyes now and then to numbly record the time from a large clock hanging over the dispatcher's desk. By 5:15 A.M., there was still no word, except that Serena was still waiting to be questioned.

Footsteps heralded someone's approach. Doug raked his gaze in their direction. Officer Morillas was on his way out. "Are you here to see her?" he asked.

Doug nodded.

He might as well go home, Morillas responded, he wouldn't get to see Serena.

Doug wanted to know why.

"I don't understand it," Morillas said, spreading his hands. "But I think they're going to charge her with murder."

Five

TEN IN THE morning, December 27. Michael had gotten little sleep the previous night; Sharri had never been to bed. Their minds felt fuzzy as they faced the two detectives in their home.

"We need you both to write it ten times," one of them was saying.

Sharri stared, uncomprehending, at Davila. Her body ached with fatigue. They had dealt with so many policemen and detectives the last few months. Had she seen this man before? She couldn't remember. "You mean what Serena wrote in her diary?"

He nodded.

"*Why?*"

Writing exemplars, he explained. The police needed to compare their handwriting against the entry since Serena was claiming she hadn't written it.

Michael exchanged a horrified look at his wife. Two thoughts shot laserlike through his brain. First, that Serena must be very, very afraid in order to deny writing the entry. His second thought hit him like a punch in the gut. Those sickening words about his little girl's death would have to flow once again, this time from his own hand.

First, Marquez wanted to see Serena's other journals, showing them her signed consent form. Declaring her belief that Serena's entry was false, Sharri led him to Serena's bedroom. There, lying on her desk, was the blue-covered journal. Sharri was quick to pull from Serena's top drawer the completely filled white journal, its entries beginning October 15, 1989, and ending September 14, 1992. Flipping through it, Marquez noticed that Serena's handwriting changed styles numerous times, switching from print to cursive.

Sharri impatiently grabbed the journal from Marquez's hands and pointed out an entry toward the end. "See here," she exclaimed, "this shows you we know she didn't do anything. This talks about the morning she found her sister."

Marquez's eyes blipped over the entry dated August 23, 1992, five days after Mallory's death:

> *sorry I haven't written in a while! well, i got tuns to tell you. you remember my little sister Mallory she was 4! well on Monday night between midnight Mon. and 7:00 Tues., she died. i woke up, went in there and something was wrong. she wouldn't move or breath or anything. so i went into my mom's room and told her so she went in there and she was dead.*

Serena then remembered Mallory's funeral:

> *and the funeral was yesterday and all my friends and family were there it was a beautiful sermon. . . . it was a little pink coffin and everyone cryed. . . . I had to get up in front of about 75 people and do a speach and it was so hard to do!*

With incongruous sequence, the entry continued with references to Serena and Troy having sex.

Marquez's report would record the time—around 10:00 A.M., December 27—when Serena's white journal, months later to be known as "Diary #1," was placed in his hands, noting in particular the entries about Mallory and her funeral. Serena's account of finding her little sister's body, Marquez would point out in his report, was "similar to that of the statement she gave to Ofc. Sischka," who had responded to the 911 call the morning of August 18. The blue journal also was taken as evidence, although it would prove to be of little significance.

So it was just seven hours after Serena's arrest, Fremont police had in their possession *two* diaries containing entries about Mallory's death—one with a dramatic, "I-centered" entry written four months after Mallory died, and one with a quiet report of her death and funeral, written concurrently with those events. The sensational "Confession Diary" would remain in the forefront. Eventually, police would turn the white journal, "Diary #1," over to Serena's attorneys.

Sharri showed Marquez a couple of letters written by Serena that he would take as further handwriting samples. Then, as Marquez began searching Serena's room, Davila sat down with the Moores at their kitchen table. Numbly, they followed the detective's instructions, writing letters and numbers, then the diary's chilling words over and over again—until each sentence had burned a permanent scar into their memories. After six times, the detective told them they could stop.

Marquez emerged from Serena's bedroom with her blue and white journals, the letters, and a set of keys, found in her jewelry box, that fit the "Confession Diary." One more thing, he mentioned to the Moores, he wanted to check Serena's bed—the one she slept in the night Mallory died.

"We gave Serena's bed away," Sharri told the detective. She could hear her own voice quivering. No one had asked to see Serena's bed before. "I'm sorry." Serena had so wanted to get rid of her bed. It reminded her too much of the nights she had slept with her little sister, she had told them. Sharri and Michael, grasping at anything to help ease her pain, had agreed to buy a new one.

"We do have her pillows," Michael cut in.

The detective swung his gaze in his direction. "Can we take those?"

"Yes."

Marquez disappeared around the corner again, then returned, pillows in hand.

The phone rang. It was an Officer Uhler, asking for Marquez. The detective accepted the receiver, listened intently, then thanked the policeman for his information.

Sharri was pleading again to Davila that Serena be given

psychiatric help, reminding him that her police reports would indicate how many problems she had. Davila tried to reassure her, pulling out a recorder as he talked. They could make a formal statement on tape if they so desired.

While the tape rolled, Sharri and Michael reiterated their certainty that Serena was innocent, that she loved her little sister dearly, and wrote the diary entry only because she was overwhelmed with guilt over Mallory's death. The detective listened quietly, nodding occasionally until their words trickled to a stop. He lifted his eyebrows at them questioningly, then leaned over to click off the recorder.

Soon the detectives were hurrying away, arms filled with Serena's pillows, the "Confession Diary" and its keys, the other two journals and letters, plus their own tape recorder and the Moores' handwriting samples. Marquez would later note in his report that "the Moores were very cooperative and were willing to assist in any way."

If only Serena would be as cooperative. Now, with all her journals in hand and after the phone call Marquez had just received, they'd have to pay her another visit.

Serena was dead-dog tired. Her head pounded and her chest felt heavy under the weight of a near-sleepless night. All that time at the police station. Then she'd had to write that stupid diary entry ten times. Now she was being ushered to private quarters at juvenile hall. Lord knew what fate awaited her there. Chinese water torture. Maybe the rack.

She had given the cop who was driving her to juvenile hall an earful, leaving no doubt in his mind as to how she felt about the two detectives who interviewed her. "If I run, would you shoot me?" she had asked as Officer Uhler led her through the police station parking lot to his car. He had tried to calm her, saying he was only there as a driver; he had nothing to do with the detectives or anything she had gone through that night. So let's just have a nice, quiet ride. As the car began to roll, Serena rambled on, asking questions about juvenile hall and claiming that she had been in the getaway car after a shooting in the nearby town of Oakland. Officer Uhler listened in silence.

Suddenly, Serena felt exhausted. She laid her head against the car seat and closed her eyes. "God," she pleaded silently, "don't let them take me to juvenile hall. I promise I'll never run away again. Just let me go home."

Serena could well imagine her mom finding the diary; she'd snooped many times before. But why had she and Michael given the diary to the police? Were they just mad because she split? Serena couldn't allow herself to think her worst fear. What if her parents really believed that diary, just like the cops?

Frustrated and angry, Serena turned toward the window and mumbled to herself. Her voice was matter-of-fact.

"What? What did you say?" Behind the wheel, Officer Uhler tilted his head back in her direction. He would soon call Detective Marquez with information about her reply.

Serena glared at him. "I said my little sister's better off in heaven," she said evenly. "This is a crummy place to grow up."

Little did she know how that statement would come back to haunt her.

After leaving the Moores', Davila and Marquez stopped by Troy's house for a talk. His information wasn't helpful. He knew little about Mallory's death, he said, and Serena had never said anything to him about killing her sister.

At four P.M. that afternoon, the two detectives paid Serena a second visit, this time in a grungy, cold cell called "intake" at Alameda County Juvenile Hall. In his report, Marquez detailed that interview:

I asked Serena if she was still aware of her rights and if she was still willing to talk to us. Serena said she was aware of her rights and did wish to talk to us. I advised Serena that we had searched her room and that I had found letters, journals and a diary with handwriting that matched that of the confession showed to her earlier.

Serena continued to deny that she wrote that statement in the diary. I then told Serena that I had found the keys to her new diary in her jewelry box. Here Serena began to change her story. She said that she could not remember getting the diary as a Christmas gift or not. She said she got very drunk on Christmas Eve and cannot remember what had happened from the time she left Carson City to the time she got back home.

We again asked Serena if she had written that confession in the diary. Again Serena said she could not remember if she had or not. Serena was asked what reason would anyone have to write such a statement if it wasn't true. Serena said that she did not write the statement, but her opinion would be that maybe that person was being asked several times what happened to Mallory and that they wrote it to stop people from asking.

Even when confronted with the similar handwritings Serena continued to deny writing the confession. Serena was asked what would the results be if she were to take a lie detector test. She said that she heard they were not reliable, but that she thinks it would say she was telling the truth, that she did not kill her sister, Mallory. Det. Davila and I then concluded the interview.

Six

IN A BLEAK county building a stone's throw away from juvenile hall, John Poppas returned to his hole-in-the-wall office Monday morning, December 28, 1992, after spending a much-needed Christmas weekend with his family. His friendly visage and easygoing manner belied the fact that he had been a prosecutor for twenty-four years, having "worked juvenile" in Alameda County for the past thirteen.

That Monday, children would be foremost on Poppas's mind. Specifically, one dead four-year-old and her older sister, still a "little girl" in his eyes, arrested for her murder. After being apprised of Serena Moore's arrest, Poppas felt the weight of the case on his shoulders. The decision of whether or not to charge the juvenile now was up to him. Even though the girl had made what in precise legal terminology was an "admission," of guilt, he still faced the legal issue of establishing a *corpus delicti*—objective proof that a crime has been committed, in this case, homicide. The law, however, required only a *prima facie,* or "on first appearance," standard for accepting an admission.

Poppas reviewed the autopsy report. Coroner Paul Herrmann's cause of death was listed as "traumatic asphyxia, mechanism undetermined." Something had caused Mallory to stop breathing, but was the coroner certain that the "something" was not accidental? The coroner's report apparently had been long in coming. Although Dr. Herrmann had performed the autopsy on August 19, his investigator, Frank Gentle, had not informed Fremont police of final conclusions until September 22. Even then, the death was only "considered unnatural" since "the pathologist could not prove homicide."

Phoning Fremont police, Poppas spoke with numerous officers, including Detective John Anderson, explaining that he had questions about the medical findings. He requested that Anderson ask Dr. Herrmann to reevaluate the case, searching for any sign that the death might have been from natural causes. Poppas also gleaned information about the scene of Mallory's death as noticed by responding officers and paramedics. Had there been any sign of forceable entry to the house, which could point to an outside perpetrator? Or had a chest of drawers or something heavy fallen on the little girl, causing the asphyxia?

Negative answers to these questions helped establish the *corpus delicti.*

Dr. Herrmann had performed Mallory Moore's autopsy on August 19, 1992, the day after she died. Since 1970, when he founded the Institute of Forensic Sciences in Oakland, he had been contracting his services to Alameda County, performing autopsies as well as testing blood for drugs or poisons in the institute's toxicology lab. Autopsies were routine in cases such as Mallory's, in which the cause of death was unknown.

At first, Mallory Moore's death had not seemed suspicious. Policemen called to the scene had found nothing untoward. No broken windows, overturned furniture, or signs of forced entry that would indicate an intruder. Officer Frank Gentle from the county Coroner's Bureau, who had also investigated the scene, noted in his report that Mallory had suffered from asthma, but had "not had any serious problems in the last few months." (Gentle's report was correct; however, Mallory had undergone a midnight asthma attack five months previously that would have been labeled as "serious.")

In examining Mallory's body externally, Dr. Herrmann was interested in a "group of petechial hemorrhages on the right side of the neck" and others near each eyelid, on the forehead and below the left side of the nose. These small, red patches of burst blood vessels indicated to him that blood had been unable to leave the head and flow back into the chest.

Before proceeding, Dr. Herrmann phoned Fremont police, who connected him with Detective Whiteley. He possessed little information on the case, Dr. Herrmann informed the detective, but his initial observations of the deceased had "yielded petechial hemorrhages," which made him suspicious. Whiteley advised Dr. Herrmann that he would be en route to his office to view the autopsy.

As Whiteley watched, Dr. Herrmann made the Y incision on Mallory and began examining each organ. He stopped from time to time to jot down notes that would become the basis of his report. Most of what he saw rendered an "NR"— not remarkable. In his notes, under "Lungs" he indicated "congestion, large bronchi show changes of chronic asthmatic bronchitis. . . . The large bronchi show little mucus but at least one shows plugging. The smaller bronchi are less involved." These notes would vary somewhat from his written report, prepared over a month later, in which he stated that "the bronchi show a very small amount of thin, clear mucus" and cut sections of the lungs showed "no mucus plugging anywhere" but were "diffusely congested." In the chest, the report noted there was "no evidence of trauma" and ribs were "intact."

Months later in Serena's trial, "mucus plugging" would be an important topic.

Externally in the genitals, Herrmann wrote that he saw "no abnormalities." The anus was "relaxed and dilated" with "no foreign material around" it and "no evidence of acute trauma." Or, as his notes at time of autopsy read, "No fresh trauma." He did see, however, what looked like scars inside the anus, and took some slide cuttings for further examination. On those slides, he later saw what he termed "healed tears."

His "anatomical diagnoses," then, listed among their major findings the petechial hemorrhages; edema, or swelling in the brain; congestion of the lungs; "dilatation and healed tears" of the anus; and "clinical and microscopic evidence of asthma." Swelling in the brain, he knew, was consistent with asphyxia. The petechial hemorrhages were of even more significance. Given the absence of any other signs of trauma, such as strangulation marks, the hemorrhages could only have occurred, he believed, if the chest had been compressed.

The following morning, August 20, Dr. Herrmann further discussed his findings with Detective Whiteley. As the detective later reported, "Dr. Herrmann said that there were 'signs that suggest' this death was other than by natural causes. He stated that he had done all the microscopic examinations, and that was about all he could do. His disposition on the death was still open."

In further investigation, Poppas reviewed police reports on the case. He also learned indications of Serena Moore's mental condition from statements made by Valerie Wood, a therapist in Carson City, Nevada, who had seen Serena weekly from May through August 1991, while Serena was living with her grandmother, Tessie Dornellas. There had been sexual abuse allegations, Wood had indicated, referring to an incident in which "Serena had taken the family vehicle, claiming to protect her and Mallory from a molesting Michael." (Wood apparently was repeating what she had heard secondhand from an unknown source about this event, since she had stopped counseling Serena before the incident.) Wood described Serena as having "oppositional behavior" and "almost viewing Mallory as her own daughter." Further, the girl had many fantasies, nightmares of a sexual nature, and "personality splitting." She often detached from emotion. The therapist mentioned that Serena had once threatened to burn down her office. Wood did not think Serena capable of hurting Mallory. However, she hadn't seen Serena in over a year.

Sharri and Michael spent frantic moments on the phone that Monday, begging authorities for information. Paula Galoegos, the juvenile hall probation officer, couldn't tell them anything.

"Surely they're not going to charge her," Sharri insisted, taking a ragged pull on her cigarette. "We don't understand why we can't see her."

Paula didn't know "what was happening." Poppas hadn't told her what he was going to do. She *did* know that he only had until 5:00 P.M. Tuesday to make up his mind, and that he must inform her of his decision. In the meantime, Sharri could see Serena during the regularly scheduled visiting hour that afternoon. Galoegos promised to call the Moores with any further news.

Stubbornly, Sharri clung to her blind faith in the system. Michael wasn't so sure. The way things were going—how logical was it to think they'd let Serena come home?

"God, Michael, the police *know*," Sharri fumed. "How could they think she did it when she's told so many lies?" She strode around the coffee table and plopped into their couch only to pop up seconds later. "All her fantasies, all her false reports. I just can't believe they'd keep her this long."

Her heart broke at the thought of Serena in jail. What was she feeling? Did she think her parents had coldly turned her in to the police? Serena was in such turmoil over losing Mallory; now she couldn't even have her mom.

"She must be so scared," Sharri lamented. Michael put his arms around her as she leaned against him and cried. "She's the only kid I have left. I have to know what's happening. I *have* to see her."

Seven

SAN LEANDRO STRETCHED for miles underneath a gray sky as Sharri drove west on Interstate 580 that Monday afternoon. The hills on her right, brown during the Bay Area's rainless summers, had now turned to a pleasant green in the winter months.

Not that she noticed.

Her mind was a stupor of sleeplessness and emotion as she wound her way through traffic, looking for the Fairmont exit. At the sight of a small green sign printed with the name "Juvenile Hall" and a white arrow pointing ahead, she knew she was on the right track.

The road to 2200 Fairmont was wide, its lanes separated by a large median filled with flowering bushes and eucalyptus trees. On the right loomed a mustard yellow building with a dark red roof. JOHN GEORGE PSYCHIATRIC PAVILION, the sign read.

My daughter should be in that kind of place, thought Sharri, *getting help.*

Juvenile hall was suddenly on her right. She braked at a row of reddish brown wood signs with arrows pointing in various directions for Los Cerros boys' camp and other county facilities.

Her destination was a rambling building of dirty beige concrete blocks. A long ramp led to the visiting area, advertising easy access with the federal blue handicapped sign. A line of people stretched from the bottom of the ramp and out onto the sidewalk.

"Your pass, please."

"Oh." Sharri's eyes fell to the red line painted at the bottom of the ramp—VISITORS STOP HERE.

"I—I don't know. I don't have it. I thought it was supposed to be here; I've never been here before."

"Name?"

"Sharri Moore."

The black man consulted a list. "Here it is. Give this to the desk inside." He handed her a rectangular piece of paper, labeled "Alameda County Juvenile Hall Visiting Permit" and asked her to sign on its blank line, across from the issuing officer's scrawled signature. She flipped the card over and was shuffling forward, reading the short list of visiting hours on the back, when a woman stopped her.

"Spread your arms, please." The woman held a flat black box in her hand. Underneath her feet, Sharri noticed a painted yellow strip that read "scanning area." She lifted her arms, feeling the hair on them rise at the personal affront. The woman ran her scanner quickly up and down Sharri's back and legs. "Now turn around and spread them again." Numbly, Sharri obeyed. The black box raced across her front. "Thank you."

Sharri stepped forward through a black grill gate that led to a small courtyard covered with a carportlike ceiling, painted beige with brown trim.

"Sign here, please, your name and your child's name."

Scanning the long white pages, she hesitated, hating to write Serena's name along with the others. Penned there in black ink, it screamed the stark reality of Serena's fate. Swallowing hard, she signed.

An employee unlocked a glass door and let her into a foyer big enough for only four to five people. "You must place your purse in one of these lockers, ma'am. You're not allowed to take anything inside." Rows of various-colored lockers lined the room. She put her purse inside one, locked it, and dropped the key into her pocket. The foyer exit was through another locked door. Just beyond, to the right, loomed a big yellow desk, striped white by a row of visiting passes placed end to end. Three employees on the other side were busily making phone calls. "Send down Mack Carter," one intoned. "Send down Malcolm Ruiza .. Send down Laura Phan ... Anthony Berezetti ... Celeste Crane...."

Past the desk lay a visiting room, filled with gaudy rows of green, yellow, blue, and orange plastic chairs. A TV was mounted high on a wooden platform on the back wall. Twenty or more square plaques painted in colorful Indian designs hung on the right.

The room was quickly filling as parents claimed chairs, small children playing at their feet. Juveniles filed in slowly, clad in khaki jeans, oversize blue sweatshirts and slip-on denim shoes. The kids looked cocky, resigned, bored. The noise level in the room, although not yet full, assaulted Sharri's ears.

"Serena Moore," a man behind the desk was saying. "She's new. That would be intake."

"Intake?"

"To the left."

Serena wasn't with these other children. Sharri didn't know whether to feel relieved or frightened. She stepped anxiously through the doorway and looked around.

"This way, please," an attendant chirped. Sharri found herself following a guide into a corridor lined on the right by chain-link fencing. Through the fence, she saw another small courtyard area. It looked unused. She shivered. It was so cold. Was Serena in a warm place? Was she in a different building? Maybe a nicer one, with fewer people and less commotion. A left turn, and she found herself facing two more attendants behind desks lined with monitors. She fixed her eyes on a screen, feeling her jaw go slack at the sight of a teenager moving ghostlike in a solitary confinement cell.

Oh, God, she thought. Not here. Not my daughter.

"She's down there" the attendant was saying. "First on the left. I'll have to lock you in. I'll be back when time's up."

Sharri gazed, petrified, at a long row of cells painted institutional green. Each was locked by a heavy metal door with one small window offering a view of what lay beyond. Fumes of Lysol and bleach hung in the frigid air. Her guide stopped abruptly, unlocked a door, and swung it open.

No, Sharri protested silently, *I'm not ready for this.* Head beginning to spin, she took in the scene in one horrified glance. It was about a six-by-eight-foot room of concrete blocks, carved with graffiti. A bed, molded out of concrete that jutted from the wall, was covered with a thin vinyl mat. No sheets. One woolen blanket. A small dirty window above the bed looked out at empty sky. Across the gray-painted shiny floor was an open white and chrome toilet and a small sink. Was Serena supposed to use that for a bathroom, and in front of a camera?

Serena was huddling on the bare cement floor beside her bed in a thin white hospital-type gown and cotton duster, crying. At the clank of the door opening, her head snapped up. Her mouth opened, a gasp gurgled from her throat. Before Sharri could walk three steps across the floor, Serena scrabbled on both knees to throw herself at her mother's feet.

"I didn't do it!" she sobbed raggedly. "I didn't *do* it. I wanna go *home.*"

Sharri sank to the floor and clung to her daughter, her throat aching with grief. Serena was so cold. Quickly, Sharri pulled her up on the hard bed and hugged her close, trying to warm her limbs. Her first thought was to grab Serena and run. Run, run anywhere. How could they throw her in here like an animal?

Fleetingly, Sharri remembered why Serena was there and pulled away. "Serena, look at me. Look me in the eyes." Serena raised her blotched face. "Is it true?"

Serena stared at her, panic-stricken, like a deer caught in headlights. "No," she wailed. "No, I swear!"

Tears flooded Sharri's eyes and she drew her daughter close once again. "Then *why*," she asked, rocking back and forth, "why did you write it?"

"Because I knew you'd read it," Serena moaned. "You'd see it and we'd talk about it. And you'd stop asking why. I wanted you to know how much your questions *hurt*. It hurt so much."

Sharri pressed Serena's head against her chest. "But you ran out. You left me. I didn't know."

"That was just to see Troy." Serena's voice choked. "I loved Mallory! She meant more to me than anybody. You know I could never hurt her."

"Yes, I do know, I do," whispered Sharri. "I do, I do, I do." Holding Serena, she prayed to God the police knew it, too.

Slowly, Serena's tears subsided. Her arms seemed a little warmer after Sharri chafed them with the palm of her hand. "You ask them for another blanket. And don't worry; everything will be all right. If you tell the police the truth, you'll be out of here and back home soon. Tell them you wrote the diary; tell them you said you didn't at first because you were scared. Will you do that, can you tell them the truth?"

Serena nodded.

They rocked together again until the cell door swung open. "Time to go."

Fresh tears spurted from Serena's cheeks. "Mom—"

"Stay seated," warned the attendant. "You must stay seated as your visitor leaves."

Sharri buried her face in her daughter's hair. She couldn't leave, not like this. What if Serena had to face another lonely night on that cold, hard bed? Sharri's shoulders bore lead weights, her feet were cement as she struggled to rise. "It *will* be all right," she said again. "We love you. We'll see you soon." Gently, she released her hold. Backing toward the door, she reached, trembling, to grasp for Serena, stretching her arm as far as possible, Serena doing the same, until their fingers could no longer touch. Somehow, she knew not from where, Sharri found the strength to turn and walk away.

She shuddered at the sound of Serena's sobs as the metal door clanged behind her.

Eight

FOR THE THIRD time, Serena faced two detectives—Bob Davila again, and a new face, John Anderson. She was now ready to talk. The men brought chairs into her small cell and a tape recorder.

In a long interrogation she admitted ownership of the diary and confessed to having written that she killed her sister. However, she repeatedly denied having hurt Mallory.

Bob Salladay tapped a pencil as the phone rang in his ear. It was noon on Tuesday, December 29, time for his "daily check" for information. In his four months as crime reporter for the *Argus,* Salladay had created a rapport with the Fremont police captain of Patrol Services, who also served as media spokesman for the police department. And a good four months it had been after Salladay's two-year stint as a copy editor for the *Alameda Newspaper Group.*

The phone stopped ringing. "Captain Lanam."

"Hi, it's Bob Salladay." He shifted his tall, lean frame forward, poised to write. Lanam's next statement commanded his full attention.

"I might have something good for you."

Salladay's pencil scratched as Lanam gave background details of a diary confession and possible homicide. Be careful and wait until you hear from Poppas, Lanam warned. We're not sure yet whether the girl's being charged. Salladay noted that the captain hadn't told him to hold the story, only to check with the D.A. first.

The *Argus* editor *did* tell Salladay to hold—he wasn't willing to run a story on a juvenile's mere arrest. Wait and see if she's charged, he said.

Another anxious day of waiting had rubbed the Moores' nerves raw. Tuesday afternoon was ticking by, and Paula Galoegos still had no word. Sharri could not force the picture of Serena in that cold cell from her mind. *She'll be home soon,* Sharri repeated to herself. *Serena will be home soon.* The police would not charge her daughter.

"They won't believe that diary," she insisted to Michael for the hundredth time. "They know how much she *lies.*"

Detective Anderson was hurriedly typing his report about Dr. Herrmann's reevaluation of the case on Mallory Moore. It was 4:30 Tuesday afternoon.

> Dr. Herrmann had received the medical history of Mallory Moore from Detective Whiteley and it was his belief that there was no pre-existing medical condition that contributed or led to the death. Dr. Herrmann was aware that Mallory Moore suffered from asthma and he ruled this out as a contributing cause of death. Dr. Herrmann advised that cause of death was via asphyxia, and that the petechial hemorrhaging documented in the autopsy report occurred as a result of the constriction of blood flow. Dr. Herrmann indicated that this constriction could occur from the body being squeezed and/or pressed during the asphyxiation, such as from weight being applied to either the chest or back area, and that this pressure would not by itself leave bruising or internal injuries.

(Anderson's first sentence was factually correct, but misleading. Dr. Herrmann had received Mallory Moore's medical records, but not until *after* he had written his autopsy report.)

Poppas spoke with Dr. Herrmann, who confirmed Anderson's paraphrase of his conclusions. They also briefly discussed the anal dilation and tears on Mallory, Dr. Herrmann noting how he believed they were caused. The conversation remained in precise terms—Herrmann's responsibility was only to state the medical findings; Poppas's responsibility was to decide if those findings supported bringing charges against the suspect in custody. Until then, Serena's fate had teetered precipitously on a sharply defined legal brink. Dr. Herrmann's adherence to death by traumatic asphyxiation would push it over the edge. The D.A. now had a clear *corpus delicti*—a little girl, apparently dead at the hands of another, and her sister's uncoerced, written admission.

Serena Moore would be charged with homicide.

Time was running out. Hastily, Poppas gave the necessary paperwork to his secretary to type, who quickly called the court clerk in their building for a case number. After typing, Poppas's secretary ran her papers to the clerk to be filed and "stamped in." The charges against Serena Moore were now official.

As was routine, Poppas did not directly call Paula Galoegos with the news of Serena's being charged, knowing she would see the "log sheet" that would be sent to her. Apparently, however, she had gone home for the day.

When Bob Salladay called after five asking for the final decision, Poppas told him the case had been filed. Frances Dinkelspiel, a reporter from the *San Jose Mercury,* also had heard of the arrest, and phoned Poppas with inquiries. For the two newspapers, the story was a "go."

With no word Tuesday evening from Galoegos, Sharri called Carson City. She desperately needed her mother's support. Tessie was appalled. How could you have given that diary to the police? she demanded. Why couldn't Sharri have taken Serena to a psychologist, get her some help? Now she was stuck in that awful place because of her own mother.

Sharri couldn't convince Tessie they'd done what they thought was best. Four days after Christmas, and she and her mother were back to the years-old argument: Sharri could do no right. Neither did Sharri find solace in a call to her sister. "I don't want to tell you what *I* think," Roxanne remarked.

Nausea nipped at Sharri's stomach as she hung up the phone. So much for help from her family.

Tuesday night dragged by. Sharri slept in fitful starts, her slumber scarred with nightmares of concrete cells, locked doors, and monitors. Exhausted by early morning, she did not wake when Michael rose at five-thirty. He, too, had managed little rest. Numbly, he drank two cups of coffee, drove the twenty minutes to work, and headed for his office at Raychem, a large engineering firm in Menlo Park. He'd worked at Raychem since graduating from high school twenty-one years earlier, his longevity broken only by a three-year stint in the army during his early twenties. Now, without a college degree, he'd risen about as far as he could in the company as a plastic technician. His salary was $52,000 a year including benefits, a respectable, but not high sum, considering that rental or mortgage payments on a basic three-bedroom home in the Bay Area could run $2,000 per month. When he arrived at work, he faced a desk cluttered with lab reports detailing plastics specifications such as maximum heat, cold, and stability under pressure; shrinkage potential; tensile, strength, and elongation requirements. He tried to read, but numbers blurred on the page. Distractedly, he rubbed a hand over his face.

"Hey, Michael." Guy Fletcher's voice shot through his frazzled nerves. "I thought—" His boss hesitated. "I didn't know if you had seen this." Silently, he laid the morning's edition of the *San Jose Mercury* on Michael's desk.

Somewhere inside Michael's head, a bell went off. He stared at Guy, dread rolling through his intestines, then snapped his head down. His eyes flew like magnets to the large front-page headline:

"I Killed My Little Sister"
Diary Entry Leads Fremont Police To
Charge Fourteen-Year-Old

Nine

BY WEDNESDAY MORNING, Captain Lanam's line was ringing off the hook with calls from newspaper reporters and television stations. Serena's tiny green-and-white-striped diary was an instant sensation. Bob Salladay put it mildly when he commented, "This is probably the biggest media case they'd ever seen in Fremont."

For Fremont police, who in 1992 faced four unsolved homicides out of the year's six, including the case on Mallory Moore, the positive publicity of pumping a stalled investigation into high gear may have been welcomed. As Salladay wrote his second story, he sensed that the police "felt they had cracked the case" even though he "didn't hear the detectives crowing over it." Had they done so, crime reporters would have known better. "It really wasn't detective work," Salladay explained. "It was luck, because the diary was handed to them."

If the police didn't "crow" about the case, they perhaps puffed their feathers. Lanam hastily scheduled a press conference for Wednesday afternoon, checking first with Poppas regarding what information to give out. Scenes of the conference, run on news shows that evening, were fraught with a sense of incongruousness. The dainty diary, small enough to lie in Lanam's large hand, was put on display, as Sharri Moore would comment, "with all the fanfare of a blood-drenched murderer's ax." Photographers battled for close position, shutters clicked and television cameras rolled as the dark-haired, handsome Lanam read the contents of Serena's diary, then posed it at optimum angle.

Diary #1 was not mentioned.

"That press conference was ridiculous," Deputy District Attorney Matt Golde, who later would prosecute Serena, declared. "The police made it look like they'd just seized twenty thousand tons of heroin and captured Pablo Escobar."

Lanam's response would be that the session was not held to "glamorize or publicize," but merely to handle the deluge of media phone calls with "efficiency."

The conference wasn't the only draw Wednesday in the quickly dubbed "Diary Girl" murder case. Salladay missed the press conference to dash to San Leandro Juvenile Court, where Serena was being arraigned before Referee Ted Johnson. Sharri and Michael, dazed at the sudden onslaught of publicity, had their first taste of dodging cameras and microphones as they hurried to and from that hearing, at which Serena was ordered held in custody.

Salladay's front-page article on Thursday, December 31, was wrapped around a small picture of Lanam's hand holding the diary and a large photo of the Moores descending the courthouse steps, flanked by Sharri's cousin, Tom Hallinger; Ted Navell, Michael's friend and best man at his wedding; and Marietta Wilson, Ted's girlfriend. At sight of the *Argus*'s photographer, Sharri and Marietta ducked. By the time the *San Jose Mercury* photographer caught up with them, the women were running toward the Moores' car, Marietta firmly clutching Sharri's arm. The camera recorded only their retreating backs.

Although they found the press and cameras "despicable," Sharri and Michael soon fell victim to their own morbid curiosity, devouring every newspaper article they could find about their daughter's case. "One moment we were nobody," Sharri remembered, "and the next, our faces and names were splashed everywhere—look at the parents of a teenage killer! As much as I hated reading it and watching on TV what they were saying about us, I was like a moth to flame. I didn't want to know; I *had* to know."

A New Year's Day article in the *Chronicle,* however, gave them some reason to hope. Reporter Catherine Bowman, who would continue to cover the "Diary Girl" case, teamed up with her East Bay Bureau colleague, Bill Wallace, to write the story. That article would, in time, make a significant difference in the lives of the Moores.

Experts on law enforcement and psychology say the Fremont teenager charged this week with murdering her little sister might have been lying when she allegedly confessed to the slaying in her new diary.

The experts warned that police and prosecutors should investigate the possibility that she did not commit the murder, despite the fact that police have publicly said they believe she did kill her sister. . . .

Elizabeth Loftus, a professor of psychology at the University of Washington, said there are at least three possible explanations of what might have occurred.

"One is that she really did it and it (the diary passage) is a general confession. Two is it's a deliberate lie and she knows it . . . and three is it's not true but she honestly thinks it is. . . ."

"Hopefully, police won't assume that only one hypothesis is the one to investigate," she said.

Although Loftus said she would have to know a great deal more about the child before reaching any conclusions, she said the teenager's decision to leave her diary in a prominent place in her bedroom may support her assertion that she was trying to get attention.

"A lot of times kids do feel some responsibility when people close to them die," Loftus said. "Maybe the guilt got translated into a false memory. There's certainly a long history of people who confess to things they didn't do. . . ."

Sharri emphatically read the quote from professor Loftus to Michael. This woman saw the diary as they did! Sharri immediately phoned the University of Washington and tracked down the professor. Upon hearing Sharri's story, she referred the Moores to San Francisco defense attorney Art Wachtel. Sharri phoned Wachtel and, since he was out of the office, spoke with his partner, Douglas Horngrad.

Horngrad was interested in the case, he told Sharri, and his fee could be paid over time, an option he offered many of his clients. Problem was, he *did* need upfront money for expert witnesses such as other coroners to dispute Dr. Herrmann's findings. A case this serious could not afford to be underfunded when the need for such witnesses was so crucial. Sharri, not knowing how she and Michael could come up with his estimation of $5000 to $7000 for the experts, didn't want to assume a debt they could not pay. She reluctantly ended the conversation.

A few days later, a friend mentioned San Francisco attorney Melvin Belli. Word was, sometimes he took cases for free. The Moores jumped at the chance. *Everybody* knew who Belli was; he was *famous,* for God's sake! No less than three people ended up calling the Belli firm on behalf of the Moores—Sharri's mother, Tessie Dornellas; the realtor handling the sale of their house on Lucia Street; and their friend, Marietta Wilson.

Tuesday, January 5, 1993, not quite a week after Serena's arraignment. Shelley Antonio was staring with growing excitement at a phone message as she sat in a borrowed office in the "Belli Building," a square-shaped, redbrick landmark in the heart of San Francisco's financial district. Melvin M. Belli, Attorney-at-Law, the "King of Torts," housed his firm there at 900 Montgomery. The firm that Antonio had just joined on December 28—Belli, Belli, Brown, Monzione, Fabbro and Zakaria—was about to split wide open, creating two enemy factions hurling accusations, threats, and lawsuits at each other. Antonio had sensed from her first day that her hiring had been "controversial," a unilateral decision made by an increasingly independent Belli. Evidently, it had not been approved by the other partners. She hadn't counted on being in the vortex of the firm's bitterly disputed breakup.

What she *had* counted on, in joining Belli and his sixty-plus years of law experience, was the chance to "fight for justice" and "make a difference." Some of her colleagues from Stanford Law School, she felt, had lost their original, fresh-faced notions of changing the world and now cared only for making money, but she had not. She had a different agenda. At the same time, her career goal was "to be a famous woman trial attorney." Current best-known lawyers, such as Belli, Gerry Spence, and Tony Serra, were men. She hoped to change that, too.

Admittedly, Antonio had little experience. She'd graduated from Stanford in 1982, but didn't take her bar exams until 1984. She had yet to be involved in any trial proceedings. After cofounding a sexual harassment clinic in San Francisco, she served as its director, supervising attorneys for women who had filed sexual harassment complaints. When that lost its excitement, she considered various offers, but felt the one from Belli was a "godsend."

And so, she would come to believe, was the message now lying in her hand.

It wasn't even intended for her. Almost magically, she was the first attorney to see it, merely because she was sitting at the desk of the intended recipient—Tom Kaster.

"This is going to be *pro bono*," said the person who'd taken the call, "but it's the kind of case the boss likes. Why don't you take a look at it, then give it to Tom."

"The kind of case" perhaps referred to its publicity. At eighty-five, Belli was particularly adept at knowing what would draw the media, and how to handle them when they arrived. He had enjoyed a long legal career built on many high-profile cases, not the least of which was his defense of Jack Ruby, who shot Kennedy's assassin Lee Harvey Oswald. Belli was better known, however, for his work in civil cases, which years ago had earned him the nickname "The King of Torts."

Antonio knew that Belli now carried few, if any, cases of his own, acting more as mentor to his assistants. This was a sizable one, and a hearing was scheduled for the next day. Wouldn't it be great if she could handle it? She decided to call Belli at his home.

"Hi!" she sang. "This is Shelley from work."

Months later, she would laugh as she recounted his response.

"Work!" Belli growled in his gravelly voice. She assumed she had caught him in a foul mood over the trouble with his partners. "Does anybody do any work around there?"

"I told him about it," Antonio remembered, "and he goes, 'well, which one of those *expletives* can I get to appear at that detention hearing tomorrow?' "

"I don't know, Mr. Belli," she countered, "but I'd be willing to."

"Can you do that?" he bellowed.

"Yeah."

"Okay. That would be great."

Shelley Antonio now held Serena Moore's fate in her hands.

Melvin Belli's firm would take their case—free! Sharri and Michael were ecstatic. In a long conversation that same day,

Sharri told Antonio the details of Serena's arrest and history of lying. Serena's most immediate need, Sharri said, was psychiatric help. She was still being held in suicide watch at juvenile hall. Alone in that cell, her every move recorded by a camera, Serena was fast deteriorating. The first three days, she had even refused to eat.

Antonio agreed. They must do something—quickly.

At the detention hearing on January 6, Antonio informed the court that a psychologist had been hired to evaluate Serena's mental state. Findings would be presented the following Monday to a court referee, who would then rule on whether or not Serena could be placed in a hospital until her trial.

"We believe that every day she is in a juvenile facility is hazardous to her emotional and mental health," Antonio stated. "We'd like to have her placed in a hospital where she can get some help."

Monday's hearing, January 11, was the first in a series of ill-fated attempts to release Serena into psychiatric care. Although Dr. Paul Berg, a psychologist from nearby Oakland who would later testify at the trial, had examined Serena and recommended treatment, Acting Juvenile Court Referee Bob Shuken denied Antonio's request. The county could not be burdened, he ruled, with paying for counseling and medication and the "extraordinary" costs of guarding Serena day and night since she was such a high "flight risk."

"I'm not sure she will be better served in a psychiatric facility," Shuken rationalized. The defense attorney's "best interests would be to expedite and resolve the allegations, then seek treatment." He would reconsider, Shuken added, if placement could be found that isolated the minor from others and protected her from hurting herself, without cost to Alameda County. Perhaps the parents could pay.

Antonio found it a near-impossible task. As she tried to meet the court's demands, Serena remained locked in juvenile hall, receiving only the help of one crisis counselor who was responsible for all girls at the facility. Then, over a week later, Antonio thought she'd found adequate placement. A 108-bed private psychiatric hospital in Walnut Creek, about a half hour's drive away, would accept Serena at no cost to the county, since the Moores' medical insurance with Massachusetts Mutual would pay the bill. There remained only one problem—the required twenty-four-hour guard.

"The district attorney has told me," Antonio stated to reporter Bob Salladay, "that he has never seen a court allow someone to be transferred who is a flight risk and who is charged with murder." However, she added, she hoped "to convince the judge that we don't need a guard."

Surely, reasoned the Moores, this was enough. Since Mallory's death, Serena had gone off the deep end, attempting suicide and requiring placement in a psychiatric hospital twice in one month. Even Dr. Berg had said she was severely disturbed. What more could the county want? But on Wednesday, January 20, Juvenile Court Referee Paul Seeman held fast to Shuken's demands. The Walnut Creek facility was not secure enough to hold the minor. Protecting Serena from herself and others, Seeman admitted, and providing her with adequate psychiatric help was "a delicate balance," but the concerns of the county won out.

Next hearing—Monday, January 25. At that time the case would either be settled with a plea or scheduled for trial. Antonio, however, requested that the date be postponed until February 5. This would be the first of numerous such requests by the defense. February rolled into March with yet another continuance.

With each hearing, press coverage on the case increased. Afraid of being hounded at home, the Moores moved out of their rented condo in Fremont into an old two-bedroom house about fifteen minutes north. Their new phone number was unlisted. Soon, they began hearing rumors that Lorimar Productions had sent a scout to check out their story in hopes of making a movie. Sharri and Michael agreed they "wouldn't give Lorimar the time of day." They could just imagine the resulting sensationalism! Their instinctive reaction to all media was "to go underground." Their privacy had been violated; they would talk to no one. When nationally known journalist Connie Chung approached them for her new "Eye to Eye" show, however, the Moores changed their minds, albeit with reservations, feeling that the publicity for Belli was a way to pay back the attorney for taking Serena's case *pro bono*. They also sensed that Chung would treat their story with sensitivity.

*   *   *

In juvenile hall, a depressed Serena languidly watched her fifteenth birthday on February 12 come and go, just one more day of incarceration. She was *so lonely,* she wailed to her parents, who could only visit for one hour Monday, Wednesday, and Saturday afternoons. Unless the girls' unit was filled, Serena could not have a roommate because of the charges against her. Most nights, she cried herself to sleep. She longed for freedom and still desperately missed her little sister. "I just want to die," she told her mother.

To friends, however, Serena presented herself through letters as cheerful and strong—a typical denial of her tumultuous emotions. She would turn a blind eye to her grim situation, occupying herself with thoughts of boyfriends. Before her birthday, she wrote to her best friend, Mary Corren:

> *Hey everything is cool here right now! I can understand how you could be shocked. Im just glad your still my friend! That sure proves the point that friends are forever. Thanks for being here for me Mary I really appreciate it! Does everyone know I didn't do it! Well if not tell them. Well can you do me a huge favor? Could you call Troy and ask him what is up between me and him? I told you before that he won't except my phone calls and he won't write me back could you ask him why!? Oh, and also make shur to let him know I didn't do it! Well I gotta go.*
>
> *Love ya always, your sister! Serena*

She would hear months later why Troy was not responding to her calls and letters. Shortly after her arrest, he had married. A baby was on the way.

Serena's next hearing took place on March 15. She and her defense had agreed to reject a plea bargain. "We're not prepared to have her admit to it," Antonio told reporters. "She didn't do it." Trial was scheduled to begin April 19.

At that hearing, Shelley Antonio did not come alone. Belli, her coach on the case, was at her side as he would be throughout the trial. Since her hiring in December, the bond between the two of them had grown. Over the coming months, their relationship would appear to observant trial watchers to be many-faceted. Antonio seemed to have placed Belli on a pedestal. He was her mentor and perhaps somewhat of a father figure. At the same time, she, as other employees in his firm, looked out for him, protected him with the sort of loving care that a child would give a revered aging parent.

Lacking Belli's years of experience, Antonio would rely on him to navigate her through the rough waters of trying Serena's case.

Eighty-five, with thick white hair and a lined, jowly face, Belli propelled himself beside Antonio in a slow but erect shuffle. His hands were empty. Even in an undertone, his voice bounced off walls like the throaty growl of an old dog. He was now back in the courtroom, he told a journalist, after "a leave of absence" due to trouble with his hearing. Before Serena's trial was over, he would wear new hearing aids that sometimes seemed more trouble than they were worth.

Aged though he was, Belli still basked in a certain charisma. During the trial, he would seem an enigma, a mixture of aggression, petulance, and humor as he waffled between flashes of brilliance and curious non sequiturs. On one point he was consistent—he always attracted a crowd.

The final key player in the "Diary Girl" trial also made his debut at the March 15 hearing. Deputy District Attorney Matt Golde, the son of Stanley Golde, a well-known judge in Alameda County, had taken the case over from his colleague John Poppas when it became clear that the scheduled opening day for trial, April 19, would fall during Poppas's vacation. In his mid-thirties and with ten years' experience, Golde was attractive in an open-eyed, boyish kind of way, with light brown hair, gray eyes and a trim physique. As it turned out, Antonio asked for further continuances, and trial did not begin until May 24. By that time, Golde was knee-deep in working on the case, and remained as prosecuting attorney.

Golde's "doing a trial" was unusual in itself. The "Diary Girl" case would be the first juvenile trial he had prosecuted since his first few years on the job at the Alameda County Juvenile East Branch. Typically, his responsibilities were in charging youths—reviewing reports of in-custody and some out-of-custody minors to decide whether or not to file charges. Rarely would a juvenile case present enough serious or complex issues that would require his taking on its prosecution. Not that he hadn't dealt with minors charged with murder before, but those juveniles usually were remanded to be tried as adults, then falling outside his jurisdiction.

From the start, Golde believed unequivocally in Serena's guilt. He also believed, based on Serena's multiple past accusations against Michael, that she had been molested and that the Moore home was dysfunctional.

As they began piecing together their case, Golde and his investigator, John Samuelson, were faced with immediate barriers. As expected, not all friends and extended family of the Moores were eager to speak with them. "I think," Golde later noted, "they thought we would do whatever we had to do to win at the expense of the truth and paint Serena as a monster. Or maybe they were embarrassed by it. For whatever reason, there was a tremendous amount of reluctance on the part of family members."

The Moores' friend Mia Black was willing to talk to Golde, yet in the final analysis, Golde would not call her as a witness, maintaining that her information was "not very directed" and "unhelpful." In trying to discover the truth about what happened the night of August 17, 1992, and why, Golde had to find the answer for specific questions. How did Sharri and Serena Moore relate to one another? What kind of relationship did Michael and Serena have? How about the grandmother in Carson City, Tessie Dornellas? How would Mallory react when Serena came back from visiting Carson City?

Friends were only on the outside looking in, Golde felt. To get a clear picture of the family, he had to speak with the relatives to whom Serena had turned—primarily, her grandmother in Carson City, and perhaps her Aunt Roxanne, who also lived in that area. Serena evidently had visited her grandmother often, even living there for a few months in 1991. It seemed to Golde that the defendant considered her grandmother's home a "safe haven," that he would hear most of the truth from Serena's Grandma Tessie and Aunt Roxanne.

A point Sharri and Michael Moore would most vehemently dispute.

PART II

🦉

Turbulent Years:
The Family's Story

February 1986–December 1992

*It started with a commitment, a desire—
however ill founded it may have been—to
help this girl, who already had problems.
Sharri needed a husband and Serena needed
a father. Unfortunately, I thought I could pull
Serena out of her problems a lot sooner than
was possible.*

—MICHAEL MOORE

Ten

IN THE WINTER of 1986, California was taken, literally, by storm. By March, rain was falling in torrents, wreaking havoc throughout the state as hillsides gave way amidst the downpour, their foundations first weakening, crumbling, and finally collapsing under the unsupportable weight of saturation.

In the year-round resort area of Lake Tahoe, straddling the border of northern California and Nevada, the driving rain meant particular trouble. It pounded the snow-packed ski slopes, causing the dreaded, frozen versions of sliding mud—avalanches. During those terrifying weeks of storm, the citizens of Lake Tahoe would grow skittish, cocking their heads anxiously at so much as a hint of a distant roar.

Looking back, Sharri Moore might say it was an omen.

When the phone rang one evening in early February—three weeks before the storms—the last voice Sharri expected to hear was that of her sister. Roxanne called maybe once a year. The sisters had never been close, their enmity perhaps, thought Sharri, a by-product of the casual and often unpredictable atmosphere in which they had been raised.

Roxanne posed an unexpected request, one that could be rather fun in light of the volatile years Sharri was struggling to put behind her. She wanted to set her sister up on a blind date.

"He's been so grouchy lately," Roxanne complained, talking about the owner of the house in which she and another woman rented bedrooms. The living arrangement was purely a business deal, not uncommon in the San Francisco Bay Area, where mortgages could consume half a month's pay. "He walks around the house like he's lost—he's been that way ever since he broke up with his girlfriend months ago."

Sharri demurred. How old was he? Did he like children? Even if it was only a blind date, she had eight-year-old Serena to consider.

His first marriage, a childless one, was over in 1982, Roxanne told her. He was thirty-three, loved children, and was a real gentleman. "Just have a drink with him, show him a good time," she urged. "And hopefully he'll come back in a better mood."

Sharri mulled it over. That Saturday would be perfect; Serena would be visiting overnight with her grandmother, as she did every other weekend. Men weren't too high on Serena's list these days, ever since she'd lost her stepfather when he and Sharri divorced. Kevin was the first real father Serena had ever had. Serena had been born out of wedlock when Sharri was only twenty and her biological father had been out of their lives for years. Serena had loved Kevin in that all-forgiving, self-effacing way that children often do when faced with an abusive parent. She had also hated his violence whenever he beat Sharri, knocking her across the room, pulling her hair, gouging at her face, throwing her against a wall. Now, with that relationship nine months behind them, Serena was confused about her own emotions, resenting her mother for the divorce some days, only to scream in fear of sleeping alone at night, afraid that her stepfather would return to force his drunken way into their now-peaceful home, as he so often had done whenever they tried to escape his abusiveness.

Sharri pulled herself back to the present. This wasn't marriage her sister was proposing for her. It was only a date. "Okay," she said. "Tell him to give me a call."

Michael arrived around noon Saturday. Feeling a bit awkward, Sharri introduced herself and her daughter. Pursing her full mouth, Serena looked him up and down. He wasn't a real big man, but he looked tall enough next to her mother, who was only five-foot-four. She liked his neat little mustache that probably tickled when he kissed.

After Serena had gone to her grandmother's for the night, Sharri learned, as she and Michael shared a fat-laden Monte Cristo sandwich and smoked cigarettes at a casino restaurant, that he had been raised on the San Francisco Peninsula, had played varsity football on the Redwood City Sequoia High School team and now worked at Raychem. He'd been through one childless marriage and another recent serious relationship. In the latter, he'd balked at a commitment, and by the time he was ready to settle down and gain an instant family, he'd lost his girlfriend and her young daughter to another man. It sounded like his mother and father, who still lived in Redwood City, were wondering when he would find the right woman. Although William and Sarah Moore were in their early fifties, both were retired. William had worked as a district manager at a ball bearing factory for many years; Sarah had driven a bus for the handicapped. They had spent their money wisely and managed to make a few sound investments. Michael also had two brothers, one in the East Bay and one living in Hawaii. He said the family was "close."

Michael stayed with Sharri Saturday night.

Sunday morning after Serena returned, Michael took them both out to breakfast. Serena was impressed. She and her mom couldn't afford to eat out, and had little food in the house, for that matter. Even with her mom working a lot, they never seemed to have much money.

That evening, the threesome's quiet day skidded abruptly to a halt when Sharri tried to put Serena to bed.

"Please, Mom, let me sleep with you! I'm scared," she whined.

Sharri was firm. "No, Serena, you know you can't do that." She drew the covers over her daughter. "I'm not going to bed now anyway. Michael and I are still talking."

She turned on Serena's small television set. "Here. This will keep you company." She smoothed back her daughter's thick brown hair, then bent to kiss her forehead. "We'll be right outside. No one can hurt you."

In the living room, as they sat in front of Sharri's small wood-heating stove, she apologized to Michael. Serena had been hard to handle ever since she was very small, she explained. But she couldn't be blamed for her fear at night. Sharri often faced it herself, so distant were her memories of falling to sleep secured in a peaceful night's rest. Only recently had she begun to feel safe once again, but not until she'd finally had enough of Kevin, had borrowed an empty twenty-two pistol from her mother, and pointed it at him through a window when he banged, cursing, on her door in the wee morning hours. Bug-eyed, he had vanished into the night, a despicable stereotype of a coward who begat violence but couldn't face the threat of it down himself.

Serena was not mollified for long after being tucked into bed. Soon she was up again, crying, begging to sleep in her mother's room. Sharri longed to give in for the sake of some quiet, but remained adamant. Shortly after leaving Kevin, she'd allowed Serena to sleep with her for comfort, but now felt it was time to break the habit, particularly after hearing from a child psychologist that allowing a child Serena's age to sleep with an adult was not healthy.

Michael stayed out of the altercation for a while, then offered his help. Intermittently, for almost three hours, he talked quietly with Serena, trying to reason with her each time she emerged, crying and protesting, from her room. "I'll tell you what," he said. "I'll sit on the couch all night if you want and guard the door. No one will come in."

Sharri was amazed at Michael's patience; he seemed so concerned with Serena's well-being. Nevertheless, when she waved good-bye to him the next day, she had no illusions about any future with Michael Moore.

I'll never see him *again,* she thought.

Sharri was pleasantly surprised. Michael called soon after arriving home, and continued calling. Their conversations grew longer and longer as the days passed, with only the threat of a whopping telephone bill urging them to hang up each night. As they talked, the vast differences in their personalities became more clear. Sharri's mouth often ran a blue streak in the hopeless quest of keeping up with thoughts that bombarded her brain. She had the irritating habit of interrupting others mid-sentence. All the same, Michael admired her glib tongue. His own words were slow in coming, well gauged before utterance. While Sharri was "out there," blatantly honest and direct, he was reserved to the point of seeming standoffish.

Michael was also a "fix-it" person, literally and figuratively. He couldn't understand Sharri's frosty relationship with Roxanne. "I'd like you to come down here," he told her on one of their calls. "I want to see you again, and you need to patch things up with your sister."

Sharri tried to tell him there was nothing to patch up; she

and Roxanne just didn't get along. Sharri had always been intimidated by her older sister, due in part to ancient—and perhaps exaggerated—memories of Roxanne's once trying to strangle her when they fought as children. But their enmity began long before that. At two and a half, according to what Sharri had heard, a jealous Roxanne had fallen into convulsions when their mother left for the hospital to birth Sharri.

Michael remained nonplussed by such volatile behavior among siblings. His quiet family life had been worlds apart from the raucous, emotions-on-the-sleeve Irish upbringing in Tessie's household. He and his two younger brothers, Ben and Andrew, got along just fine. Ben lived in Benicia, about a half hour's drive away, and the two of them liked to watch football games and do "brother stuff" together. Michael hadn't seen his youngest brother, Andrew, however, since he had moved to Hawaii two years before.

Frustrated, Michael cornered Roxanne. "Why do you dislike your sister so much?" he asked.

"Because she was born," came the reply.

The relationship between Sharri and her mother seemed just as tumultuous, running hot and cold and often dipping below freezing when it came to Serena. Twice in the past, Serena had lived with her grandmother when Sharri became overwhelmed with balancing long employment hours and single motherhood. Those temporary circumstances had fomented Tessie's initial dim view of Sharri's parenting into chronic accusations of negligence and abandonment. Perhaps Tessie's predisposition to judge her daughter was due to insecurities about her own mothering in earlier years, just as human nature breeds the strongest reactions to those failures in others that are seen within oneself. Sharri's own memories of feeling loved and nurtured were checkered, particularly as a teenager.

Even as Sharri was pleased that Tessie now lavished so much love on her granddaughter, she also felt that Tessie managed to add to Serena's confusion by constantly "badmouthing" Sharri. Uncomfortable with her mother's behavior, Sharri was nevertheless acutely aware of Serena's fondness for Tessie, and so tolerated it. As for Tessie, she would argue that she had always "been there" for her granddaughter, regardless of whether Sharri was or not. Over the years the mother/daughter relationship had worked its way into an intricate choreography, a *pas de deux* now leaping, now bowing as the two women danced warily around each other.

Despite the enmity with her sister, in February Sharri visited Michael in Newark while Serena stayed with Grandma Tessie. Soon, the couple was seeing each other every other weekend, either in Tahoe or Newark. Sharri was getting used to sharing Michael's room in his four-bedroom home. Painted brown and gold, with wood siding and a shingle roof, the house was a typical California tract, but it sure beat her small rented duplex. Michael, of course, occupied the master bedroom suite in the house's back corner. Roxanne and Kelly each rented a bedroom and shared a bath. The fourth bedroom was empty. Perfect for Serena.

As soon as Serena finished second grade, mother and daughter moved to Newark, with Michael and Sharri planning an August wedding. For the new family, life was exciting. Serena and her new stepfather-to-be were getting along fairly well, and Sharri and Michael were helplessly romantic.

Tessie, however, seemed to resent Serena's moving away from her. Sharri and Michael sensed that her initial favorable response to their relationship was turning sour. It was as if Tessie felt that Serena needed her more than a father, that Serena already had two parents—and Michael wasn't one of them.

"Don't worry," Michael told Sharri. "Your mom will get over this. She's just used to having Serena nearby and she misses her. Serena can visit her a lot and everybody will end up happy. You'll see."

He couldn't have been more wrong.

Eleven

SHARRI FELT THE blood drain from her face as she stared at the director of Allen's Ranch, a day-care facility in Hayward. Outside the administration office, she could hear the sounds of children playing.

You understand, of course, the director was saying, they had to report this allegation. An employee from Alameda County Child Protective Services would be visiting the Moore home to check out Serena's story.

"It's not true!" Sharri blurted. "Not true at all!"

It wasn't even an *exaggeration*, for God's sake. Sharri knew Serena had trouble with lying, but she'd never done anything like this before. To this point, her stories had been told mostly to gain acceptance or attention. If a friend had been to Florida, so had Serena. If some little girl's mother just bought her a new dress, Serena's mother had bought her two. If a friend's uncle owned horses, Serena's uncle owned an entire ranch. Other times she seemed to lie for no reason. Serena, Sharri knew, would lie about what she ate for breakfast.

This particular claim on a summer's day in 1986, told a few weeks after Sharri and Serena had moved to Newark, was different.

The director's face remained impassive. Sharri opened her mouth to deny the accusation again, then closed it as she felt her throat tighten. She was not going to cry in front of this woman.

She drove home with an unusually contrite Serena and sobbed to Michael. "They'll take my baby!" How could Serena do this? Didn't she understand she could be taken away from them?

Serena could have gotten that bruise on her leg anywhere, from bumping into her dresser or even playing at the Ranch. But at sharing time that day, Sharri wailed to Michael, Serena

69

had pointed to it and told the group that her mother "beat her with an electrical cord."

Michael worked to calm her down. He did not confront Serena, preferring to let Sharri handle it. His relationship with his stepdaughter-to-be was too new—they were still cautiously circling each other. At the outset, Serena had liked Michael well enough, but as each day passed, she seemed less willing to trust him. It was as if the more attached she became, the more fearful she was of losing him. "I don't *want* to love you," she had blurted to him more than once. She had good reason to be afraid, Michael told himself, considering that her first stepfather had beaten her mother and then disappeared from her life, and her real father had hardly seen her since she was a baby.

"Don't worry," Michael told Sharri. "It'll be all right. Someone from Child Protective Services will come over here, check us out, and see that it's a lie. That'll be the end of it."

The CPS employee questioned Sharri and Serena separately, Serena soon admitting with a shrug of her shoulders that her statement wasn't true. Another girl had told their group that her parents had beaten her, she explained. Serena felt left out. She didn't have anything to share that day, so she just made up something.

After her first visit, the social worker concluded that Serena had not been abused and closed the case.

"Serena," Sharri later fumed, "if you wanted something to share, why didn't you tell the group that you're going to be a bridesmaid in your mom's wedding? Isn't that special enough?"

Serena glanced sideways at her mother, mouth trembling. "I told them that *yesterday*."

Sharri and Michael were married on August 10. Serena wore light blue in the Victorian-style wedding, carrying a lacy matching fan in her white-gloved hands. Roxanne was to be maid of honor, but ended up spending that day in the hospital because of a drug overdose ingested during an apparent suicide attempt. On the morning of her wedding, Sharri visited Roxanne at the hospital. Sharri's cousin Cindy took Roxanne's place as maid of honor. Fortunately, she fit perfectly into Roxanne's violet dress.

After a honeymoon in Las Vegas and Mexico, the Moores settled down to family life. During their honeymoon, Serena stayed with Grandma Tessie. Roxanne and Kelly moved out of the house that same week. Roxanne would not visit again for six years, until tragedy brought her to her sister's door.

For the first few months, things ran smoothly. Sharri went to work as an office manager for a ceiling and paving company. It was there that she met Mia Black, who worked in a nearby office.

Serena started third grade at Maloney School in Newark. Gradually, she began to move out of her I-don't-want-to-sleep-alone phase. Sharri, too, had to overcome her midnight demons. With Michael working a 3:00 P.M. to 11:00 P.M. shift, she would often find herself in a sweat as she lay in bed, dreading the sound of his key in the lock. Too many nights during her marriage to Kevin she'd been awakened by his drunken pounding on her front door. She told herself she was safe now, but to no avail. Michael had an idea that eventually worked. He installed a phone by their bed and began calling home when he left his shift. Assured she would be awakened by a ringing phone rather than someone on the porch, Sharri was able to go to bed in peace.

After about six months, Serena began to resent Michael's parental role.

At Tessie's insistence, Serena was visiting Tahoe every other weekend. The Moores first drove the eight-hour round-trip to take her on Fridays and again to pick her up on Sundays, then began asking that Tessie meet them, although they still drove over halfway. Sharri was tired of the long drives and, further, disapproved of the apparent freedom that Serena was given in Tahoe. Tessie was lax with Serena, Sharri felt, and seemed unwilling to enforce the rules under which the child lived at home. Sharri argued about it with her mother. Serena was becoming more and more difficult to handle, she said. Admittedly, times had been tough for her, and her unruliness could be attributed to a difficult younger childhood. Sharri was well aware that she had been neglectful of Serena in the past. But now, working together, Sharri and Michael wanted to "rein her in" before it was too late. Sharri pointed to Serena's increasing resentment toward Michael, particularly prevalent after her visits to Tahoe, as proof that she was being allowed too much liberty at her grandmother's. Serena spurred on the fight. "I want to live with Grandma" became her standard wailing protest in altercations with her parents over rules. What resulted was a vicious circle of escalating arguments between Sharri and her mother, with Sharri accusing Tessie's boyfriend, Kirk Dornellas, of drinking too much while Serena was around and Tessie countering that Sharri was and always had been an unfit mother.

In time, Sharri cut Serena's Tahoe visits to once a month. And, she threatened, certain things needed to happen in order for Serena to be allowed to continue visiting. Tessie had to respect her and Michael's authority. And she must stop letting Serena sleep with her, an unhealthy indulgence, said Sharri, that was not helping Serena sleep in her own bed at home.

By the time Serena turned nine on February 12, 1987, Sharri and her mother were waging a continuous battle over the child's welfare, each unable to compromise with the other's conflicting viewpoint. Sharri finally declared a stop to Serena's visits to Tahoe, saying that Tessie must visit her in Newark.

All-out war lay just over the horizon.

Serena was causing problems of her own. Her lying grew worse. Many times Sharri would hear from Serena's friends, "I heard about Serena going here or having that" when none of her claims was true. She also was beginning to steal, as if urged on by some inner impulse. At first it was makeup off her mother's dresser. It spread to money lying around the house, then to other children's money and possessions.

The Moores grounded Serena, made her return stolen items and write letters of apology. Nothing seemed to help. Frustrated, they sent her for counseling at Second Chance, a non-profit agency in Newark. Serena attended private weekly sessions with a therapist at Second Chance for a few months, but told her mother in no uncertain terms that she "didn't like the woman." With Serena's cooperation lackadaisical at best, the sessions were, in Sharri's words, "going nowhere," and Serena was allowed to stop going. Shortly thereafter, the Moores tried another therapist provided through their insurance with Kaiser Foundation Health Plan. Again, Serena wouldn't cooperate, arguing that she didn't need counseling.

After three visits, the therapist informed the Moores that under the circumstances he was unable to help. Future attempts for counseling included Serena's seeing two other therapists one time each and a six-week group course at Kaiser. The Moores would not seek more intense therapy for Serena until after Mallory's death.

Mia Black was full of advice about what to do with Serena. Sharri and Michael were letting her get away with too much, she said; the child was out of control. Mia spoke often with Sharri about the situation, advising her to discipline Serena and "get her more help." Mia cared for Serena, even though it seemed to her that Sharri and Michael didn't believe that. Serena just had no respect.

Sharri cherished Mia's friendship, but was put off by the constant criticisms. She didn't need a friend to remind her that Serena had problems. Nor did she want an armchair referee telling her what shots to call.

In March, daily contact with Mia was broken when Sharri lost her job because of the paving company's going out of business. She and Mia visited each other's homes occasionally. A month later, Sharri entered Fremont Beauty College, sponsored by a local Regional Occupational Program that paid for her tuition. With the sixteen-hundred-hour course behind her, she would be qualified to work as a manicurist, makeup artist, hairstylist, and aesthetician. She was excited about the prospects of a new career. But when she had to quit only halfway through the program later that year, she would tell herself it didn't matter.

The reason for her cancellation would excite her more.

Summer rolled around again and with it, Serena's second "attention-getting whopper," as her mother termed the story.

Serena and a friend were playing in the backyard. Sharri was in the house, checking on them occasionally. Then suddenly, they disappeared. Sharri first looked for them on her own, driving around the park across from their house, checking at the homes of neighborhood girls. Nothing. She began to panic. She phoned Newark police, whose office building jutted into the air on the other side of the park. Darkness fell. The girls were still missing.

Around 10:00 P.M. an employee of Bob's Giant Burgers in

Newark called the police. We have two girls here, he reported breathlessly. They're scared and their clothes are ripped and they said they'd been kidnapped and attacked by "a man in a multicolored pickup truck." Yes, the girls said they could describe the man. Please hurry.

Policemen soon arrived at the burger joint and separated the girls for questioning. Serena repeated details of the kidnap, then began to relent. Finally, she admitted that she had made up the story. She and her friend had just run off to play, see. They didn't mean to cause trouble or nothin', but it got later and later and they just didn't think about it. Then they got scared they'd get in super trouble and decided they'd better figure out a way to get out of it.

The police lectured her sternly, but did not charge her for making a false report. At the time, it seemed, that was enough. After all, she was only a nine-year-old kid with an overactive imagination. Hindsight, however, has a way of sharpening one's vision. In this and worse incidents to come, Serena was never called up short, made legally to face the consequences of her lies.

The court summons was dated October 23, 1987, from petitioner Tessie Dornellas to respondent Sharri Moore.

Whereas the respondent had "denied Petitioner any and all contact with the minor child despite a long and close relationship between the Petitioner and the minor child" and whereas "Petitioner has a vested right to visitation with the minor child, Serena, due to the frequent and continuing contact that has occurred between the Petitioner and the minor child for the past nine years including periods where the minor child was in the sole physical custody of the Petitioner," therefore the Petitioner prayed "judgment against Respondent as follows: That Petitioner be awarded visitation rights with the minor child .. one weekend per month; one week during Christmas vacation; Easter week; one month during the summer and that Respondent be ordered to pay costs of suit herein incurred."

Sharri was furious. "Why," she fumed to Michael, "can't she just butt out of our lives?"

She'd be the first to admit that her mother and Kirk had helped her numerous times when she was struggling to make ends meet in Tahoe. Yes, mom *had* watched Serena many times. Serena had even lived at Mom's when Sharri's work hours left her little time to care for her own daughter. Before, during, and after Sharri's disastrous relationship with Kevin, Mom had been a source of help. Sharri regretted the times she'd had to rely on her mother and carried more than her share of guilt over the inconsistent nurturing she'd given Serena during those years. But now things were different. Gone was the party-it-up way of living, the casino, nickel-in-the-slot mentality. She'd settled down, found a man with whom to make a stable home for Serena.

She did not, therefore, choose to place Serena back into what she deemed a volatile atmosphere, even for a weekend visit. And volatile it was, Sharri charged, due mostly to what she termed as Kirk's "active" alcoholism.

"I have taught my daughter that [Kirk's] behavior is in fact unacceptable," Sharri wrote in her responding court declaration. "Petitioner refuses to restrict her boyfriend's drinking and repeatedly told my daughter 'that's just the way men are.' I am strongly opposed to any visitation by Serena at her grandmother's home or in the company of her friends at Lake Tahoe. I believe that her lifestyle is not compatible with the values I desire my child to be raised around."

In addition, Sharri alleged, petitioner constantly defied her wishes to keep Serena away from her Aunt Roxanne, who "has had extensive mental problems" and has "made threatening remarks to Serena, including a threat to lock her in a closet."

Tessie wasn't going to take the latest round on the chin. Her Irish blood boiled. In her answer to the court, she labeled Sharri's declaration "full of twisted half-truths and outright lies." Sharri had made false statements about not only her, but also about Kirk and her sister, Roxanne. Yes, she admitted, Roxanne has had extensive mental problems, but those problems were in the past. Tessie then threw in a thinly veiled threat.

"I believe that the Respondent is trying to discredit my daughter," she stated, "because Roxanne lived with the Respondent, her husband and my granddaughter and has intimate details of their family life that I am sure the Respondent and her husband would not like known. Since the actions of the Respondent and her husband are not the issue in this case at all I have refrained and will continue to refrain for the present, from making known any of these very damaging facts.''

Sharri read the final statement with indignation, marveling at how far Tessie would go in her own discrediting. What ''damaging facts'' could Roxanne possibly know of her relationship with Michael? During the few months before the wedding, she would argue, any problems in the house had been caused by Roxanne. Further, her sister had moved out while she and Michael had been on their honeymoon, and hadn't been back since.

Such backstabbing was not new to the family. For years, Sharri had watched, or been involved in, fights between various factions. She was tired of the bickering, the ''she-said-this'' or ''he-did-that'' whispered conversations. This visitation rights case was the ultimate. Why should a family drag its dirty laundry into court?

In November, Sharri petitioned that the case be moved to Alameda County, where she and Michael now lived. Her mother had brought the suit: *she* should be the one having to travel to hearings. A month later, Sharri and Michael drove the familiar northeastern route to Tahoe, this time to attend the change of venue hearing. Thank God the weather wasn't bad, Sharri griped. At least they didn't face the hassle of putting on snow chains to get through Donner Pass.

Change of venue was granted. Until the case was settled, the court ordered, Serena would be allowed visitation with her grandmother one weekend a month. Tessie was to pay transportation costs. In addition, Tessie was ordered not to ''allow alcohol to be consumed in her home during the visitation of the minor'' and should ''make no disparaging remarks concerning respondent and her husband to the minor.''

Sharri felt somewhat vindicated.

Little did she know that the visitation rights would drag on for months. And, as it would turn out, the case would have far greater consequences than whether or not Serena could visit her grandmother, greater than Sharri or any family member could imagine. Lingering resentments from the flurry of accusations and counteraccusations would surface over five years later, once again in court.

But the stakes would be much higher.

*   *   *

During their stay in Tahoe for the change of venue hearing, Sharri noticed some tenderness in her breasts while showering. At the time, she didn't think much about it. She had been trying to get pregnant for over a year and nothing had worked. She and Michael had gone through the thermometer routine, hitting the sack on schedule whenever her temperature peaked. Romantic, it was not. In August, they'd seen a doctor at Kaiser Hospital, who recommended that Michael produce a sperm sample for a motility test. That hadn't gone over well. As much as Michael wanted the pregnancy, he wasn't about to close himself in a doctor's cubicle, jar in one hand and a *Penthouse* in the other.

Stepping out of the shower that day in Tahoe, Sharri pushed any suspicions of pregnancy out of her mind. Not until a week later, after her period was late, did Sharri take a home pregnancy test. The stick turned pink.

She and Michael were thrilled. Before long, Michael was puttering around in the fourth bedroom, changing it into a nursery. He bought a used bassinet, crib, and changing table and spray painted them white, trimming them with primary colors. New carpeting went into the bedroom, as well as wallpaper designed with flying doves. Serena proudly helped arrange Muppet Babies pictures and decals on the walls. They all chose sheets, stuffed animals, and a blanket. Thirty-five years old, Michael grinned, and finally he was going to have a child of his own!

For the baby's health, Sharri quit smoking.

Serena hoped and prayed the baby would be a girl. She was going to hold her, feed her, help raise her. She told all her friends about it, and no, this wasn't a lie. This was very real.

She was going to have a baby sister.

Twelve

THE PREGNANCY WAS awful. Sharri had cramps in the early stages, severe enough to send her to the emergency room on one occasion. When those ceased, the nausea began. Throughout the nine months, she vomited almost daily, sometimes two and three times. In March 1988, she was hospitalized due to dehydration, spending three days hooked to an IV tube. Michael, with help from his parents, managed to balance work and taking care of ten-year-old Serena.

Sharri had to discontinue her beauty school classes.

During the following months, the grandparent's visitation suit dragged on. Even Serena's biological father became involved, signing a statement on Tessie's behalf that he believed her visits with Serena were a "very good influence."

Interesting, seethed Sharri, that Tessie had dragged him into this, considering that he hadn't seen Serena in almost six years.

After change of venue was granted, Tessie countered by requesting to delay the case until the summer of 1988. By then, Sharrie would be in her seventh month of pregnancy. "She's doing it on purpose," she complained to Michael. "She knows I'm sick and she's taking advantage of it, waiting until I'm at my worst."

In the beginning of May, Tessie wrote Sharri, telling her daughter how hurt she was over the issue and "worrying" about Serena's welfare. Although Sharri had taken to ignoring her mother's letters, she was so angered by what she considered to be an "emotional, self-righteous tone" that she sat down to pen a lengthy reply, which expressed compassion for her mother while reasserting Sharri's right to raise her daughter as she saw fit.

Serena was well aware of the controversy that surrounded her visits to Tahoe. She loved going there and missed the more frequent contact she'd had with Grandma. Even though she had settled into her new family and had made friends in Newark, Tahoe still seemed like home. Besides, Grandma let her get away with things. She got to watch movies there that Mom wouldn't let her see. She had more freedom to run with friends. Then there was the sleeping thing. She'd always slept with Grandma, since she was a little girl. She'd share Grandma's bed while Kirk took the couch. Now, Mom was making a big deal of that. She said it wasn't "healthy." Mom had even gotten the courts to order that they couldn't sleep together anymore. Grandma got around that, though. She had pushed together twin beds, saying that way, they weren't really "together."

Throughout the battle with Tessie, Serena remained stubborn and headstrong, and she continued to have trouble with lying. Socially at school, she was not faring well, due mostly to her telling stories to classmates. Nevertheless, her parents were grateful that at home she was fairly stable. She was taking roller-skating lessons and was working particularly hard in her new dance classes at the Fremont Recreational Center, performing well in various talent shows.

When her sister was born, Serena began to brag, she would teach her how to dance.

Thirteen

"ARE YOU ALL right?"

It was August 1, 1988, 10:53 A.M.

"I'm *sick*," Sharri breathed. Her face was chalk white. She had reacted to the anesthesia and begun to vomit, choking until nurses suctioned out her mouth.

Michael stepped around the sterile field to Sharri's head, careful to avoid the sight of her uterus being cut open. He'd been pacing nearby in a small waiting room, wondering why the hell no one had called him into surgery, not knowing that the doctors and nurses had been too busy tending to his wife to remember him. Sharri's insistence that Michael be brought in had nearly sent her into a panic, and a nurse had hastened to find him.

Michael was well aware that Serena's birth had not been easy. Labor hadn't gone well for Sharri, and an emergency C-section had been performed when a fetal monitor indicated the baby was in distress. Serena's difficult birth could be a factor, Michael had been told, in her behavioral problems, although no doctor could say that with certainty.

A sound caused his head to snap up involuntarily. His blue mask hid a sudden grin. "He's got a lot of hair!" he blurted.

"Is it a boy?"

Michael hesitated. He'd used the male pronoun automatically, a Freudian slip, perhaps. "I don't know yet."

"It's a girl!" the doctor cried.

Sharri rolled anxiety-filled eyes up to her husband's face. "Is that okay?"

Michael's focus was riveted on his baby daughter. "Sure," he soothed, suddenly wonder-struck. "You bet it's okay."

Sharri underwent another procedure while still on the table. After such a difficult pregnancy, she and Michael had discussed the matter thoroughly before deciding not to tax Sharri's body any further. The doctor cauterized her tubes.

Serena couldn't wait to hold her little sister. She was giggling, jumping with excitement.

"Sit down now," Michael told her. "Sit down and be still. Then you can hold her."

Obediently, Serena plopped down in a chair near her mother's hospital bed. Michael carefully handed her the small bundle. A small mark on the baby's foot immediately commanded Serena's attention. "Look," she wailed, "they *hurt* her!"

Michael calmed her, promising it was only a needle stick where a nurse had taken blood.

That day, Serena was the first to give Mallory a bottle. This initial act of mothering was of vital importance to Serena, and in later years, would become an important memory to which she would cling.

As Serena nuzzled her new sister, her parents watched, thrilled with her reaction. Michael's parents, Sarah and William, were also crowded into the small room, both of them longing to hold their latest grandchild, but not until Serena was willing to give them a turn.

It was at this small family gathering that the baby's name was first announced—Mallory Kirsten Moore. Mallory, in honor of Sharri's Irish blood and Kirsten, after one of her half-Danish cousins.

A month after Mallory's birth, ten-year-old Serena entered fifth grade at Graham Elementary School in Newark. Graham was a new school for Serena, her attendance the result of an interdistrict transfer that Sharri had requested because of Serena's social problems at Maloney the previous year. Sharri, determined to shield her daughter from further upheaval and consciously trying to make amends for her lack of attentiveness to Serena in the past, had promised her a "fresh start" and moved her to Graham.

When Serena wasn't at school, she often helped with the baby, insisting on holding, feeding, bathing, and dressing her. Typically, the Moore's fluffy gray cat, Madison, was in their midst. He had taken a special liking to the baby.

Beyond her relationship with Mallory, however, Serena was having what her mother would term "little problems." She wasn't ditching class, nor was she a troublemaker to her teachers. And her grades were fairly good. But her lies were escalating, causing trouble between her and friends.

In addition, puberty had set in early. Serena had begun menstruating at age nine, and was already wearing a bra. With her hormonal induction into a new stage of life came a sudden precocity. Boys began turning her head—and she began turning theirs.

On the home front, Serena's life seemed to take on two dimensions—patience and delight with Mallory, and increasing rebelliousness against her parents. Arguments often erupted at home over her behavior. In fits and starts, she would vascillate from abiding by the rules to being what her mother termed "a creep." Sharri believed that her acting-out problems often stemmed from some inner pain—losing the attention of a certain boy, perhaps, or hearing teases from classmates. Repressing her hurt, Serena would fall into an "I'm-fine" routine until, invariably, she blew.

Mia Black would visit the Moores once in a while and shake her head over Serena's antics. "My daughter would never act like that," she said on several occasions, referring to eighteen-year-old Terri. Sharri, although hurt by the remarks, understood. She couldn't blame Mia for not taking to Serena; her daughter's better qualities weren't always displayed.

That year, Serena met a new friend—one of the few who would show her unwavering support years later, when she most needed it. Mary Corren was in Serena's class. A throwback to her Mexican grandmother, Mary, with her dark skin, full lips, and large hazel eyes, was far different in appearance from her light-skinned sister, Esther. At fourteen, Esther was a troubled teenager, a runaway who would not return to her mother's house for another two years. When she did come back, Esther would become another of Serena's closest friends, taking on almost a mentor role as she acted as confidante and advisor to the young girl with problems so like her own.

Mary lived on Civic Terrace in Newark, close to Serena's house on Plummer Ave. Serena would cut across the park, then walk the few blocks to Mary's, passing the city library and the police station along the way.

Serena and Mary became fast buddies. They had a lot in common—hanging out at the mall, the same taste in boys and in music. That year, New Kids on the Block were hot stuff, and the two girls would turn the group's songs up loud on the radio. These common interests would cement their friendship, even while most other girls in their class would avoid Serena because of her lies.

In fifth grade, Mary thought Serena's stories no more than little white lies—"like she was gonna get this or go here or there." Mary learned early in their relationship to overlook them. "When you become Serena's friend, you learn to accept the lies," she later explained. "You know when they're lies and you know when they're not. I could tell by the way she told them. When something was off the wall, you'd know it wasn't true. Then, after a while, it became hard to distinguish the lies from the truth. But I'd ask her and she'd think about the answer. If she had to think about it, you'd know it was a lie.''

Mary and Serena would have their share of fights over the years, but surprisingly, not about the lies. Just as their similar taste in boys brought them together, so would it later cause dissension between them. It seemed that every time Serena broke up with a boyfriend, Mary would grab him next, sometimes even *before* Serena was through with him. But the girls' arguments always ended in a renewal of their friendship.

When Mallory was less than two months old, the visitation rights case, now dragged out for over a year, would finally be laid to rest. While Sharri was still pregnant, the Moores' attorney discovered a pertinent case, *White v. Jacobs,* in which the granting of visitation rights to grandparents had been reversed upon appeal.

Two weeks later, the Moores' lawyer wrote Tessie's attorney, asking for a dismissal of the case. Tessie refused. On March 10, the Moores received a letter from their attorney, informing them that the case was not being dismissed because Tessie ''would push as far as possible for a visit'' regardless of the decision of the court in *White v. Jacobs.* Tessie's position, according to the letter, was that if a parent consented to visits, a lawsuit could be brought, and Serena's biological father had executed a declaration to that effect. The waters were therefore considerably muddied. In order to continue fighting, Sharri might have to seek additional orders against Serena's father as well as her grandmother, who might join together in battle. The Moores' attorney suggested that they dismiss.

Sharri was tired. Tired of all the arguments, tired of the fighting. A second legal battle she did not need. She now had a new baby to contend with and didn't relish the thought of traipsing back and forth to court. She gave up. Reluctantly, Michael and she agreed instead to meet Tessie at Family Court Services in Hayward, a county organization that provided mediation services regarding custody and visitation issues. On Monday, September 19, while Michael held Mallory in a waiting room, Sharri met with her mother and worked out an agreement. Serena was to be allowed one visit every other month, at Tessie's expense, plus three days during Christmas vacation and two weeks in the summer. Sharri's requirements included "no drinking" around Serena, that she "sleep by herself" and that she "not be left with anyone other than her grandmother."

Little did Sharri know, as she signed the necessary papers, that, one and a half years later, Serena's bimonthly visits would be unnecessary.

At that point she'd be *living* with Grandma.

Christmas 1988 was expected to be a happy occasion for the Moores—their second together as a family and their first with Mallory. Instead, on Christmas day, they had what Sharri would call "a real scare."

Lifting Mallory out of her crib that morning, Sharri noticed that the baby's hands and feet were a dark blue. Mallory seemed unusually lethargic as well. In a fearful burst of activity, Sharri and Michael rushed Mallory to Kaiser Hospital, the health maintenance organization that provided their insurance. There, they were referred to a pediatric clinic across the street. A doctor at the clinic listened to Mallory's heart, but did not perform an EKG. He took her blood pressure. She remained blue throughout the examination.

Had she recently been given any penicillin? he asked. Sharri replied that she had. This could be a reaction, the doctor noted. Or maybe she's just cold.

No, Sharri said. Feel her. She's not cold. Besides, Mallory had been wearing booties. Her feet were warm enough when Sharri had taken the booties off that morning to dress her.

Well, the doctor replied, he couldn't find anything wrong. Not to worry.

Sharri was not happy with his approach. "He didn't do *anything*," she said to Michael. It was a complaint she would voice many times in the coming months. It seemed to her that whenever Mallory had a blue spell, the doctors treated it "as no big thing."

Three weeks later, on January 17, the symptoms recurred. In total, between January 1989 and that summer, Mallory had three more "blue spells." On each of those occasions, Sharri would call Kaiser and talk to a doctor, who assured her she was not to worry and that there was no point in bringing the baby in. When Sharri returned to work, this time as a sales-person for advertisement space in a small paper called *Potpourri*, Mallory's day-care provider, Chris Pauling, also became well acquainted with the unusual symptoms. She came to understand why, in winter, Mallory wore so many layers of clothing when she was brought to day-care. Just in case "being cold" *was* the culprit, Sharri went overboard in protecting her against any chills.

Then on a warm summer day on July 26, Mallory had a particularly nasty episode while her mother was at work. Chris called Sharri at the *Potpourri* office and said she'd better come at once—Mallory's hands, feet, and mouth were very blue, and she seemed to be short of breath. According to medical records, the Kaiser physician listed the symptoms as an "acrocyanotic spell," meaning, simply, blue hands and feet. But no cause could be found. "Reassure" parents, the doctor noted.

In the fall of 1989, Serena started sixth grade, her last year at Graham Elementary. Sixth grade would bring Serena the joys, disappointments, and pastimes typical for a precocious eleven-year-old—hanging out with friends, sleepovers, heart-rending "breakups" with boys, passing notes in class. As Serena rode the roller coaster of adolescence, her emotional state would become as unpredictable and surprising as a sudden drop of the tracks in a darkened tunnel.

She was considered by her small group of friends as charming and fun-loving, always on the move, cooking up things to do. When she wasn't hysterical over breaking up with some boy, that is. For other students, she remained the target of jokes and vicious backbiting, again either because of her grandiose lies or her ample figure.

As she wound up in more and more trouble at home and at school, Serena began keeping a diary, writing of her trials and tribulations. Sharri, increasingly distraught over her erratic behavior, took to snooping in her room, scanning through her school notebook for letters passed to friends in class and reading her diary. Most of her entries were true. Some were fantasy. Others were downright shocking. While in the sixth grade, for example, Serena would write that a boy at school raped her and she was pregnant, and that another boy was going to kill him over the incident. Sharri would doubt that one's validity. She knew Serena's periods were occurring normally at the time and had no indication that her daughter was anything but a virgin. Not wanting Serena to know she had seen the entry, Sharri posed oblique questions. Had anyone hurt Serena? Had she been attacked? Serena eyed her mother warily, said "no," then asked if Sharri was reading her diary. Sharri would admit that she had.

Serena's stealing—again often for attention—also worsened. Michael and Sharri had borrowed money to open a pet store, Sharri often juggling her job at *Potpourri* with running the shop. It wasn't long before Serena grabbed an opportunity to sneak twenty-dollar bills out of a bank deposit, which she passed out to kids at school the following day in a less-than-subtle effort to buy their friendship.

Michael and Serena were arguing more and more frequently over her antics, Michael increasingly trying to enforce his authority as stepfather, and Serena responding with sullenness and resentment. "I don't have to listen to you!" she would scream. "You're not my *real* father!" Sometimes, he slapped her for her insolence.

Sharri found herself caught between them. She wanted Michael to assert himself, but her motherly instinct to "rescue" Serena would prompt her to intervene whenever she felt his rules were too strict. Then she and Michael would argue.

Serena's one source of happiness was Mallory.

Deprived as a young child of consistent nurturing, Serena heaped love and devotion upon her little sister. It was as if she were reliving her early childhood vicariously through Mallory, so focused was she on caregiving. She wanted to spend every moment at home with the baby, even begging Sharri to wake Mallory up from naps so she could hold her. Serena helped feed, bathe, and dress the baby, and they played together for hours at a time.

"I never loved anyone like I loved Mallory," Serena would later declare.

Mallory reciprocated those feelings. When learning to walk, she would toddle after her sister, expecting to be a part of whatever activity Serena was involved in. Serena would do her homework, balancing the baby on her lap while Madison rubbed across her legs. She would practice her dance steps, often with Mallory in her arms, then, as her little sister grew, pulling her up onto the coffee table so they could sway to music in each other's arms. "Unchained Melody" became their favorite dancing song.

Mallory's undying devotion took on particular significance in light of Serena's low self-esteem. No matter the difficulties she faced in getting along with her parents or schoolmates, Serena knew that Mallory would always be there, always love her. More importantly, the little girl *needed* her. As a self-appointed surrogate mother, Serena felt a new, exciting purpose in her life. She boasted about Mallory as a new parent would brag about her own progeny. She'd take pictures of the two of them to school, showing them to other students. Friends that visited the Moore home, boys and girls alike, all came to know and love Mallory.

"When all this stuff came out [about Serena's arrest]," Mary Corren recalled later, "everybody that knew Serena before was just shocked. Even one of her old boyfriends who had moved away called me from Washington. Nobody could believe it, nobody. Because everybody knew how close she was to her sister. Every boyfriend she ever had knew her sister very well, she'd brag about Mal so much."

In fact, the two girls were so close, Mary noted, that Mallory couldn't bear to be apart from her big sister. On school days, Serena began leaving the house before Mallory awoke in order to avoid the little girl's screams over her departure.

In her role as big sister and protector, Serena displayed a fierce concern over Mallory's health. The mystifying "blue spells" were particularly disconcerting to her, as well as her parents. As 1989 drew to a close and 1990 ushered itself in with all the fanfare of a new decade, the spells continued off and on. After four trips to the hospital because of the symptoms, Sharri and Michael stopped taking her. The doctors continued to reassure them it was nothing to worry about, and the spells lasted no longer than an hour. Mallory would seem tired afterward, but would be back to her own bubbly self the following day.

Then she and Serena could play.

Serena and Mary would have a hard time remembering all the boys they "went through" during the first years of their friendship. Seems like every boy Serena broke up with, Mary started to like.

"There was Mike," remembered Mary. "He was before and after Randy. Then there was Danny and Doug and Shane."

While Mary and a few other girls remained friends with Serena, her lies continued to alienate the rest of her classmates until, by the middle of sixth grade, Serena could no longer face their taunting unacceptance. She asked her mother to place her in a different school. Sharri, all too aware of Serena's falling grades and social improprieties at Graham Elementary, once more tried to fix things by allowing the move. If the first school transfer between fourth and fifth grade made its mark, this second move a year and a half later clearly established a pattern. Instead of learning how to work through unpleasant issues, Serena would learn to run. Unfortunately, with no change in her own behavior, her problems would follow.

On a short-term basis, however, the move to Musick School was beneficial. Serena's grades once again improved as she was surrounded with new classmates. By the time they realized that most of her claimed life experiences were merely tall tales, sixth grade was drawing to a close.

Fourteen

"WHEN SERENA WAS in seventh grade," Sharri would remember, "it all went to hell."

Serena's life was becoming increasingly complicated. She excelled in extracurricular activities such as dancing and later, cheerleading. She continued to forge an even tighter bond between herself and her now two-year-old sister. But her relationship with her parents, her grades, and her socializing at school all took a major dive. Worse, reports of her home life took a new twist. She began telling friends that Michael was abusing her.

Even though Serena and Mary couldn't see each other during the school day, they were often at each other's houses in the afternoon and evening. That's when Serena would fill Mary in on the latest. She would visit Mary, saying, "Michael just hit me, so I left." Then one day her stories changed. "Michael's molesting me," she said.

Mary told her to stop lying.

As the weeks went by, Serena insisted it was true. "I'm trying to believe you," Mary told her one day, "but it's kind of hard because of all the lies you've told in the past."

Mary could not believe Serena's stories because she felt she knew the Moore family so well. They simply weren't that kind of family. She'd been at Serena's house almost every day and had never seen any signs of abuse.

Even more unimpressed by the rumors was Mary's sister, Esther, who had returned home at sixteen to straighten out her life. Serena had begun going to Esther with her problems, viewing her as one of the few people she trusted. Esther saw in Serena a young girl threatening to become all too like herself. Serena's low self-esteem was driving her toward the same self-destructive behavior—lying, fighting with parents. Next, Esther knew, would come the running away, the troubles with police, maybe drugs. She wanted to spare Serena the same fate.

Esther was one person Serena couldn't lie to.

"She knew that if she told me the stories she told everyone else," Esther remembered, "I would listen to her and then say, okay, what's *really* going on. She knew I wouldn't put up with her stories. And she knew no matter what she said to me that eventually she would have to tell the truth."

Esther knew about conniving, about having another person corroborate stories. She'd pulled the same stunts herself at Serena's age. Esther felt she understood Serena so well that she knew when Serena was lying and when she was telling half-truths. When she was lying, Serena tended to act nervous, talking very fast and fidgeting with her hands.

So it was of particular significance, Esther believed, that in seventh grade, Serena never told *her* any stories of sexual abuse, even while continually seeking her advice on a myriad of problems at home and at school.

At home, Serena began continually to disrespect her parents, fighting with them over rules, furiously yelling curses at them when she didn't get her way. Her ambivalence toward Michael grew, ultimately manifesting itself in anger and resentment over his dogged determination to parent her. He's not my *real* father, Serena would yell, and he had no right telling her what to do. Someday, her real father would return and bestow upon her all the love he had heretofore denied. In her more rational moments, Serena admitted to herself that Michael lavished more attention on her than her biological father ever would. But that only exacerbated a deeper problem. She had never overcome the fear of losing another father figure in her life. Sure, Michael had hung around for a few years, and it was obvious he and her mother loved each other. All the same, she couldn't be sure of the future. He could be gone tomorrow. Meanwhile, he was making her life miserable with his regulations about friends, homework, and school.

And she hated him for it.

In November, the Moores received a surprising invitation to spend Thanksgiving in central California with Sharri's maternal grandmother. Tessie's sister, Laura Stannard—called ''Aunt Laura'' by both Sharri and Serena—lived nearby, and would also attend the holiday dinner with her husband, Phil. Neither Tessie nor Roxanne would be present. Somewhat tenuously, Sharri and Michael accepted. They would stay with Sharri's grandmother for two days.

Aunt Laura had heard about Serena's claims of sexual abuse, and believed them. As far as she was concerned, the claims were indicative of what she had suspected all along. Laura would say she had witnessed the ''hell'' that Serena had lived through while Sharri was single, and she had heard through Tessie how traumatic the girl's life had been when Sharri was married to Kevin. Later, both Laura and Tessie had heard plenty of stories from Roxanne about the Moore household after Roxanne moved out of Michael's home. Sharri, Aunt Laura would declare, had married Michael for security and in so doing had ''chosen her lot.'' Since then, Laura had heard talk of the heightening difficulties with Serena. To Aunt Laura's way of thinking, she, Tessie, and Roxanne were the ''other side of the family'' who wanted little to do with Sharri and Michael, not wanting to "be dragged down to their level," but who desperately wanted to help Serena.

That two-day visit would be the only time Laura Stannard saw Mallory. Having spent over twenty years running a day-care facility, Laura believed in her perceptions regarding child development. After just one day with Mallory, Laura decided the two-year-old was being abused. The signs she would point to after Mallory's death were: 1. that Mallory was a "discipline problem," 2. what Laura termed "delayed speech," 3. that Mallory "pulled at her bottom," and 4. the close interaction between Mallory and Michael.

Six months after that visit, following another major altercation with Serena, Laura would feel prompted to write Sharri, saying that she believed Serena was being abused and admonishing Sharri to open her eyes to the truth. Sharri was furious at the letter and at Laura's allegations years later that Mallory had been abused as well. Mallory had been only two years old that Thanksgiving, Sharri would argue, and many two-year-olds could be called "discipline problems." Besides, how could Aunt Laura have been able to draw such a conclusion after seeing Mallory for only one day? And so what if Mallory pulled at her bottom—she was still in diapers or training pants and maybe had simply been wet. As for the interaction between Michael and Mallory, Sharri would allege that Laura and her husband had allowed their own daughter to sleep in their bed beyond the child's sixth birthday, which Sharri couldn't find particularly appropriate.

Sharri believed that her family just couldn't accept the fact that she had pulled her life together when she married Michael. She dashed off a scathing letter in reply to Laura, reminding her aunt about the time when Roxanne, then eighteen, had accused Laura's husband, Phil, of trying to rape her. (Laura later denied that her husband had been accused of any such thing.) Everyone in the family had risen to Phil's defense, Sharri wrote, knowing well that he would not have tried to harm his niece. (Serena's propensity for storytelling and her histrionic personality, Sharri felt, were very similar to that of her Aunt Roxanne's.) Remember how it felt for your husband to be unjustly accused, Sharri added, and remember how you believed him. That was no different than what she, Sharri, was doing now.

As Serena ricocheted through the first half of seventh grade, Mallory began to experience new difficulties with her health. Sharri's worry about her blue spells, which were growing more infrequent, was replaced with concern over trouble with her breathing. In January of 1991, the reason became clear. Her pediatrician at Kaiser diagnosed asthma. Liquid Alupent and Albuterol were prescribed.

The asthma was mild. Overall, as medical records indicate, Mallory was "active and alert." During a full checkup, the doctor had noted on July 31 of 1990, one day before Mallory's second birthday, that she displayed the "usual negative two-year-old behavior." Her speech was developing normally, then at "three-word phrases," spoken "clearly." There was no mention of signs of abuse.

Naturally inquisitive and outgoing, Mallory wanted to be in the middle of all the action. The two-year-old seemed to be on an endless quest to explore and experience the world. She would chatter gaily at anything and everything, squealing when she was delighted and wailing loudly when she didn't get her way. True to feminine form, she appeared to have entwined Daddy around her little finger.

Mallory was also close to Grandma and Grandpa Moore, usually staying at their house across the Bay whenever Sharri and Michael left town overnight or for the weekend. Serena typically chose to stay with a friend. During those visits, Delores Braden, one of Sarah Moore's friends, would bring her granddaughter over, and the two girls would play. Delores perhaps best summed up Mallory's personality.

"She was a pistol."

Asthma flare-ups, however, would put a temporary damper on Mallory's fun. Too little to express any discomfort, she would appear winded and tired. Initially, Sharri or Grandma Moore could hear wheezing, but over the months, that common signal of an attack stopped. Instead, they learned to watch Mallory's stomach. When her abdominal muscles were straining in an effort to help her breathe, it was time to reach for medication.

Around January of 1991, a third issue with Mallory's

health arose—another that would never fully be understood. Her "clear" speech had begun to garble, to the point that her baby-sitter, other children at day-care, and even her own parents sometimes could not understand what she was saying. Sharri spoke about it with Chris, Mallory's day-care provider, who promised to continue to note Mallory's interaction with the other children for any signs of further problems. Sharri knew she could rely on Chris; she was the best baby-sitter that Sharri had ever seen. Besides the speech problems, Chris kept watch for Mallory's blue spells and asthma.

Sharri had switched her employment from advertising sales at *Potpourri* to part-time work as Assistant Animal Services Officer for the city of Fremont. Working three to four days a week on various shifts, she dealt with adoption of animals, complaints about neighbors' pets, renting out wildlife traps, plus handling impounded animals' feeding, care, and kennel cleaning. Her experience from the pet shop, which had gone out of business after only a year, served her well in her new capacity.

The hardest part about the job was not the work itself, but the constant interruptions she received from phone calls about Serena's behavior at school. Threats from other girls to "beat Serena up" were increasing, and her grandiose lies to new schoolmates had driven most of them away. Her grades plummeted.

By midyear of seventh grade, once again social problems were making school unbearable for Serena. And, as usual, her attitude at home suffered as a result. Sharri applied for and was granted another transfer, this time to a different district. Serena began attending Centerville Junior High in the neighboring city of Fremont. The transfer was tenuous. Serena would be allowed to attend Centerville only as long as she kept herself out of trouble and her grades up, Sharri was forewarned. Serena did develop a new social life, but became so wrapped up in her new friends that she soon was failing nearly every subject.

Up to this point, Sharri and Michael had been unaware of Serena's descriptions of sexual molestation at home. That was about to change. One evening, Sharri found a note Serena had written to a girlfriend at school. Thank God, breathed

Sharri after reading it, Serena had not passed it. According to the note, on the previous night, Michael had forced Serena into oral copulation, then had hit her, giving her a black eye. Sharri angrily confronted Serena.

"*Why* did you write this? You know very well it never happened. You weren't even *here* last night, for God's sake! You spent the night at your friend Martha's house. And you sure as hell don't have any black eye!"

In time, Serena let spill the reason for her letter. The week before, she said, a girl at school had talked to Serena about turning in her own father for molestation. Just as she had done at Allen's Ranch, Serena had tried to top another girl's experience with one of her own. If a friend had been sexually assaulted, then *she* had been at once sexually *and* physically abused.

Perhaps another, as yet unconscious, reason for such a statement was Serena's growing hatred toward Michael. Her parents, upset with her lack of cooperation at her new school, established disciplinary consequences for her at home, mostly involving grounding her. Serena's rebellious "you're-not-my-real-father" retorts escalated in both frequency and volume until at times the Moores' very walls would shake under the din of arguments and slammed doors.

"Serena," Sharri would plead, "don't *do* this! If you can't stop acting this way for us, think of your little sister. This is upsetting her terribly!"

The reminder would calm Serena at times. But even Mallory would come to bear the brunt of Serena's anger, eliciting a temperamental yell to "get out of my room!" when the little girl bothered Serena's things. Nevertheless, Mallory remained unflinchingly loyal to Serena, even siding with her sister against their parents when Serena was in trouble.

By the spring of 1991, Sharri and Michael were at their wits' end. Sharri was constantly getting calls about Serena at work; Michael couldn't seem to enjoy a moment's peace in his own home. He adored his "baby girl" Mallory and resented that Serena could single-handedly wreak such havoc in his family.

Then in early April, Centerville Junior High expelled Serena because of her failing grades.

The Moores gathered for a family conference. What are

we going to do with you now? Sharri challenged Serena.
How many schools, how many "fresh starts" were they supposed to give her? Properly chastised, Serena thought of an
answer, but was afraid of hurting her mom's feelings. She
couldn't bring herself to say the words, so she wrote a note,
as if from a third party. "Your daughter would like to move
up with her grandmother," it read.

Time for another "fresh start," this time in Carson City,
Nevada—a town close to Lake Tahoe—where Tessie and
Kirk Dornellas, now her husband, lived. It seemed the only
solution. Tessie, apparently having wanted custody of Serena
all along, agreed to take her. In the midst of her own unhappi-
ness, Sharri realized the depth of her daughter's pain. As
much as Serena loved her grandmother, she would not lightly
choose to move away from the little sister she adored.

Sharri clung to one positive point—Tessie had promised
to send Serena to counseling. Providing therapy for Serena
had been a real problem for the Moores. Private counselors
were unaffordable; those obtained through county mental
health or their insurance plan hadn't seemed to do much
good. Of course, the question remained as to whether or not
Serena would cooperate with a counselor.

How ironic, mused Sharri. After all the disagreements with
Tessie over how to raise Serena, once again, she needed her
mother's help. Why was it that things were going so badly
with Serena *now*—now that she had finally gotten her own
life straightened out? She would never, ever believe Serena's
claims of molestation. After those horrendous years of trying
to parent Serena alone, and badly failing, she was glad to
have found a man she knew to be a good husband.

Sharri began wondering—was "now" too late?

Fifteen

WHAT WERE ALL those cars doing in front of their house?

Sharri pulled to a stop and eyed two men on her front lawn. She could tell they were Newark plainclothes detectives. Even from her car, she saw the bulk of their guns. She slid a look toward Mallory in her car seat. Mallory didn't seem concerned. She was far more excited about seeing the big doctor, the one who had checked her ears. Sharri had just taken her for a hearing test at Kaiser, the culmination of her worrying to the pediatrician about Mallory's garbled speech. Test results were normal.

But this wasn't.

Sharri hopped out of the car, extricated Mallory from her seat, and began striding up the walkway. A detective stopped her. You don't want to go in there, he said.

She impulsively tightened her grip on Mallory. "Why?! What's happening?"

Michael was being arrested for "repeated counts of molesting Serena," she was informed. The two detectives inside had search warrants for "child pornography, including pictures of Michael and Serena having sex." They didn't think she'd want to wait around and see her husband brought out in handcuffs. Might scare the little one.

Serena.

Sharri gulped in air until she thought she would hyperventilate. Shaking, in a fog, she turned away on weak legs, wondering what to do. The detective nodded his approval. Go on, he seemed to say. Her mind numb, she headed slowly across the street toward the park, clutching Mallory to her chest.

What had Serena done now?

On April 30, 1991, Carson City Police Officer Schoenfeldt interviewed Serena at Tessie's house.

96

She said that Michael had started touching her on the breasts and inserting his fingers in her vagina when she was eight years old. Allegedly he would come home from work and slip into her bedroom, where he would keep her in bed for three hours. She accused Sharri of being blind to the events which were happening right under her nose. In fact, she had even snapped a photo of Michael and Serena "snuggling" on the bed. This despite repeated warnings from Aunt Arlene and Tessie.

In Serena's tale Michael molested her in California and once in Nevada. He picked her up at Tessie's and drove her to a place "where there's a bunch of trees and no one could see and he made me do it then and there . . ."

Serena went on to say that she avoided confronting her mother because she feared Michael's reaction. In fact she was only coming forward now to protect Mallory, whom she accused Michael of hitting.

When pressed by Officer Schoenfeldt, Serena reluctantly agreed to testify against her stepfather. The entire interview only lasted twenty-five minutes.

Sharri flung the police report to the floor. It was sick. Sick, sick, *sick*. And not an ounce of truth in it, not an *ounce*. She could see that Serena had gotten most of the stuff from her grandmother's corresponding hand-printed statement to Carson City police. In it, Tessie said Sharri had told her that Michael would come home from work at 3:00 A.M. and lie in Serena's bed until five. That the one time she visited the Moore home she witnessed Serena's staying in Michael's room for "an hour or so" while Serena got "in bed with Michael and they played." She mentioned a photo in which Michael was "asleep on top of my granddaughter." That the California CPS had been contacted in June 1986 regarding physical and emotional abuse and "did nothing about it."

Hands trembling in anger, Sharri reached for a cigarette, lit it, and took a deep drag. The story about the picture was particularly ridiculous. It had been taken before she and Michael were married, she would later argue, while Roxanne still lived in the house. In fact, Roxanne had been the one to take the picture as Michael curled up on top of the covers next to a dozing Serena and feigned sleep. Sharri had thought it so cute, she'd sent her mother a copy. Now, thanks to her mother's version of the incident, those detectives had come into her home and taken every family photo album they owned. Sharri laughed, smoke puffing out the sides of her mouth. She hoped they enjoyed all their pictures of birthday parties, outings, and dance shows. Real pornographic stuff.

Wait a minute.

Sharri bent over and snatched up the report, flipping through its pages until she found what she wanted. There it was. She turned the page. And here was something else. Her mind had been so overloaded in her first reading, she'd almost missed it.

Pushing back her disgust, she sat down to read the report again, carefully this time. Michael had been in jail a day already. At instructions from police, she hadn't even bailed him out. If you bring him back into the house, Newark Detective Roy Brazil had told her, they would take Mallory away. Sharri had left him in jail. Better her husband than her little girl. Michael had agreed.

Tomorrow, Sharri had heard, the D.A.'s forty-eight hours would be up. He'd have to file charges, if he was going to at all.

She still had time to save Michael.

Sixteen

AFTER MICHAEL'S ARREST, Detective Brazil questioned him at length regarding Serena's allegations. Despite the detective's attempts to elicit an admission to the charges, Michael remained adamant that Serena's report was another in a series of fantastic lies and that he had never molested her in any way. Tessie Dornellas's statement he waved off as wild exaggerations.

Brazil took notes and later wrote a paraphrased report, but did not tape the interview.

A check on Michael's background came up "clean." At

age thirty-eight, he had never been arrested or accused of molestation in the past.

Sharri met with the detective also, carefully going over each of the details in Serena's report and pointing out discrepancies. From a family photo album she showed Brazil the picture of Michael feigning sleep next to Serena as the one her mother claimed that depicted him "asleep on top of [her] granddaughter." Good Friday, the day Serena claimed was the last time Michael forced her into intercourse, was the day that a small fire had erupted in their kitchen. Serena had gone to the hospital, then the whole family had stayed together at Woodfin Suites. "It's documented," Sharri told Brazil. "Check with the fire department, the hospital and the motel; they'll tell you." As for the "bunch of trees" on the way to the racetrack in Reno, where Michael supposedly stopped with Serena, it didn't exist. "Check it out," challenged Sharri. Most important, she said, as to Serena's fear that she was pregnant from Michael, it was impossible. And that could certainly be checked too.

Serena was a virgin.

After talking to Detective Brazil, Sharri longed to call Serena, but didn't dare. Michael's attorney, hired on retainer for $750, had warned that she could be accused of pressuring her daughter into changing her story if they spoke. It was all for the best, Sharri knew. What would she say to Serena anyway? She still loved her daughter fiercely, realized now more than ever that she was emotionally disturbed. At the same time, Sharri felt so angry, so betrayed, that she didn't trust her emotions during a conversation. She may say something she'd regret.

Serena called Sharri instead. She was crying. "Do you still love me?"

Sharri hesitated. "Yes, but I can't talk to you now. Our attorney told me not to." She couldn't stand to hear her daughter cry. Hanging up, Sharri felt a wrench inside as the line disconnected.

After Detective Brazil investigated the details that Sharri contended as proof that Serena's report was false, the sexual abuse case against Michael skidded to a halt. Apparently, there were enough discrepancies in Serena's story to convince authorities to drop the case without forcing her to undergo a gynecological examination. Had such an exam been conducted, Serena would have been found to be a virgin.

Sharri and her father-in-law, William Moore, drove to Pleasanton to pick up Michael after he had spent two nights in the Santa Rita County jail. Their reunion was strained. Michael was glad to be released, but the stigma of his humiliation still surrounded him like a lingering stench. As for Michael's father and mother, they were appalled at Serena's treatment of their son, and would find it difficult to forgive her.

Serena eventually admitted to her grandmother that she had lied, but never recanted her story to the police. This fact, however, would be greatly twisted a few years later during her first trial.

After about two weeks, Sharri wrote Serena a letter, warning her that she would not be able to come back and live with them if she continued to tell such stories. How can we be a family, Sharri asked, if you continue to act like this? Months later, when Serena was once again living in Newark, she showed the letter to her friend Esther.

"Serena talked to me about the letter because she was upset," Esther would recall. "Basically, Sharri had told her that if she kept lying and doing things like this, she wouldn't have a family in the sense that they wouldn't trust her. They wouldn't know what to believe and what not to believe." Esther tried to soothe Serena's feelings, explaining that her own mother had told her the same things when she'd insisted on lying and deceiving her family a few years back. "You got to understand," said Esther, "that your mother loves you and she doesn't want you to destroy your life. That's why she wrote these things."

Why, Esther pressed, do you want to push your mother away?

Serena insisted that she *didn't*.

"Then why do you do these things?"

Serena looked at the floor. "Because I'm afraid of being close to her."

Sharri did not see her daughter again until the last weekend in July. Serena wanted to visit home to be with Mallory on her third birthday on August 1. Little did Serena know she was coming home for good. Things had fallen apart at Tessie's.

"My mother had said for years how great it would be if Serena lived with her," Sharri later remarked. "But in just the first few weeks after she went up there, she was acting horribly, running off, cutting school. Her counseling wasn't doing a bit of good. Mom couldn't handle it. Once she ran off with a carnival worker and was found drinking with him in his apartment. The second time she ran off with a girlfriend. Right after that she made up the report about Michael. She started smoking, not doing schoolwork, had many social problems with kids. Some safe haven at Grandma's."

When, according to Sharri, Tessie said that Kirk "would divorce her" if her granddaughter didn't move out, Sharri knew she had to bring Serena home.

Michael said no. No way was Serena coming back into their house. Sharri was still employed as Assistant Animal Services Officer for the city of Fremont, working three to four days a week on various eight-hour shifts. What was Michael supposed to do when he got home around 4:00 P.M. and Sharri was working until 9:00 P.M.? Stay alone with Serena? Make himself vulnerable to more sexual abuse charges? Not on your life.

Sharri, wrenched between her daughter and her husband, tearfully offered Michael divorce. "If you want out," she said, "I'll understand. I *know* she's done awful things to you. Most men would have been gone long ago. But still, I can't abandon my daughter. Please don't ask me to choose you over her."

Michael said he'd think about it until the following day. It was a long night for both of them.

By the next morning, Michael had his answer. Serena, he'd decided, *may* tear their family apart. If he left, *he* would be tearing it apart for sure. "We'll try again with Serena," he told Sharri. "But you work it out—*I will never be alone with her.*"

Michael wouldn't set foot in Nevada to pick up Serena. Sharri and Mallory made the drive together.

When told she was to move back home, Serena cried and refused to comply. Sharri did not want her to know that she was in effect being kicked out of her grandmother's house. She didn't tell Serena they had no choice, but simply said she and Michael felt it best that Serena return to Newark. Besides, Mallory missed her so.

Mother and daughter ended up in the office of Serena's therapist, Valerie Wood, Sharri asking for help in calming her hysterical daughter. When Serena started to run out the door, Sharri blocked her path. Serena retaliated by holding a lit cigarette near her mother's face, threatening to burn her if she didn't get the hell out of the way. The police were called. They gave Serena an ultimatum—either she would go to a psychiatric hospital or they would handcuff her and take her to juvenile hall.

Serena spent ten days in the adolescent unit at Truckee Meadows Hospital in nearby Truckee, California. She was supposed to stay at least a month, but Sharri and Tessie, in rare agreement, pulled her out early against medical advice, believing she was being subjected to poor facilities and treatment. Sharri had again "rescued" her daughter.

By the time Serena returned to Newark, Mallory's third birthday party had long since passed.

Sharri and Michael worked out a schedule. If she was working, he would pick up Mallory from the baby-sitter and visit the park or his parents until Sharri came home. Serena stayed home alone. Sharri wondered how long they could manage such an inconvenient routine. She worried that keeping her job might become impossible.

Their schedule only lasted a week.

When Japanese friends flew into town, the Moores made dinner reservations at a Japanese restaurant. Mia Black came over to baby-sit. Mia was fond of Mallory and had on numerous occasions taken the little girl to her house for visits. As her love for Mallory had grown, so had her criticism of Serena. Unlike the Moores' other friends, Mia found Serena's treatment of Mallory "abusive." This opinion would later carry significant weight in the case against Serena, and ultimately destroy Mia's friendship with the family. In hindsight, given Mia's judgment against Serena, one might ask why, on this night in August 1991, she allowed Serena to take Mallory across the street to play in the park.

Before she and Mallory left, Serena snatched the keys to Michael's blue Ford Ranger, sitting in the driveway. While Serena had lived in Carson City, her Aunt Roxanne's current boyfriend had allowed her to practice driving a pickup truck, and Serena now felt confident that after a few minutes she could "get the hang of it" again. Once outside, instead of going to the park, Serena buckled her sister into the truck and drove to Mary's house. There, Mallory played for a while as the two older girls talked. Mary did not sense anything untoward, or notice that Serena had arrived in her stepfather's truck.

Serena had figured on going home afterward, but as she pulled away from Mary's house, she had an idea. She had wanted to go back to Carson City, and knew that if she couldn't live with Grandma, she could stay with the family of a friend in the area. Impulsively, she headed for the freeway. She drove north, then turned east toward Sacramento and swung onto Interstate 80. It was a familiar route. She *and* her sister were headed for Carson City. At first she was a tad uneasy driving so fast on the freeway, but after a while she relaxed and drove with one hand.

Problem was, she hadn't thought very far ahead. Mallory was in shorts and a tee shirt and was bound to get cold in the mountains when it turned dark in a couple of hours. And there wasn't one penny in the truck. How she was going to pay the dollar fee at the Carquinez Toll Bridge? She wasn't sure how long the gas would last, either. But, damn it all, she wanted to live in Carson City. Some of her happiest times had been spent with her grandma. Now, Mallory could be there too.

Serena ran the toll booth.

Darkness was falling. Serena turned on the lights and continued on course. About that time, Michael was calling home from the restaurant to check on the girls. Mia was panicking; Serena and Mallory were nowhere to be found. The Moores cut their dinner short and rushed home.

"The truck's gone!" Michael groaned as he and Sharri pulled up to the house. Like dual arrows, pangs of anger and fear hit him in the chest. Mia was sitting on the front porch, waiting for them. She hadn't even noticed the Ranger was missing.

Sharri called the police and filed the truck's license plates as a stolen vehicle. Michael drove around town looking for the truck, then returned home to call a number of shipping and cab companies, asking them to inform their drivers to look out for the Ranger. Mia, meanwhile, went home. Then all the Moores could do was wait, smoking one cigarette after another and checking the clock with jittery eyes.

Serena would pay this time, Sharri promised Michael. With all her lies, never once had she been charged for *anything*. It was bad enough to endanger herself, endanger her mother, or even Michael. But Mallory was something else again. Sharri knew Serena loved Mallory more than anyone else in the world. She wouldn't intentionally try to harm her sister, but her own impulsiveness made her actions a threat just the same.

Face it, Sharri told herself, Serena was too emotionally unstable for them to help. Things had gone way too far. The "system" would have to come into play—the police, county mental health, the courts—*somebody* had to help this kid.

Midnight. No news. One o'clock. Still nothing. Two o'clock. The phone rang.

It was a highway patrolman calling from Truckee, not far from Tahoe. The girls were safe. He'd spotted Serena, Mallory in her arms, on the side of a highway, trying to flag down cars after the Ranger ran out of gas.

"I was in total shock," Sharri later remembered. "There were my two girls, cold, in the middle of the night, waving to any car that went by. They could have flagged down a *serial killer,* for heaven's sake!"

Serena told the police she stole the truck because she and her little sister were being molested.

A sheriff took the girls to Grandma Tessie's house, about an hour's drive away. Sharri and Michael drove the remainder of that night to Carson City, stopping to replace their car battery, which, true to Murphy's Law, gave out around 4:00 A.M. They took Mallory's car seat.

"Mommy, Mommy," Mallory cried when she saw her exhausted parents the next morning. "Nana took me for a ride in the truck!"

Michael changed the car's front right tire, which he believed to be unsafe, buckled Mallory into her car seat, and headed for home. He did not care to linger in Nevada since that state's participation in the investigation of Serena's sexual abuse charges had yet to be formally dropped.

By that time, Serena was missing again, having run from her grandmother's house in the early morning. The sheriff called a short time later, informing Sharri that he had her daughter in custody. Sharri told him she would not pick up Serena. She'd had enough; no rescuing this time. "She's got to have consequences for this," Sharri insisted. "I want her *charged*."

The sheriff's department refused, saying Serena had only been "out for a joyride." Sharri still would not take her daughter. Serena spent the night at the Carson City juvenile hall. The following day brought another round of arguments, Sharri standing firm against their insistence that she take Serena home. In effect, they told her, she was abandoning her daughter. Fine, she countered, if that's what it took to get her some help.

The sheriff called Newark police for assistance. In a compromise move, Detective Brazil agreed to meet Serena at the Oakland airport if Sharri would buy her a plane ticket. Sharri balked. "Are you going to arrest Michael again?" she asked.

No, Brazil told her. He did not believe Serena's latest molestation story. Further, he planned to take along another detective and a female police officer when he met Serena. He wasn't going to drive her *anywhere* alone.

True to his word, Brazil, a second detective, and a female officer in uniform met Serena at the airport and eventually took her to a foster home in Union City. There, she'd have a chance to calm down and get back into counseling. Within two weeks the plan fell apart. Numerous times, Serena ran off to see her current boyfriend, Nick. Sharri would pick her up and take her back to the foster home. Then, Serena stole some items from another girl and argued violently with the foster mother, who declared she'd had enough. Serena was sent, in the middle of the night, to Kairos group home in Oakland.

That was too much for Sharri's rescue instincts.

"I freaked," she later recounted, "when I was told that. Serena arrived at night with a paper bag full of her things, standing around, not knowing what to do, wondering why she was being moved so much. It hurt me to think of her like that. My heart broke. She'd caused terrible consequences, but she never meant to.''

Nothing else had worked. The Moores were a family; they had to keep trying. Sharri drove over immediately to rescue her daughter.

Serena came home.

Seventeen

A FEW WEEKS later, Serena started eighth grade at Newark Junior High. Within a month, her old problems arose. This time there was another way out. The Moores had just bought a tract home on Lucia Street in the neighboring city of Fremont, which placed Serena within a new district. In the few weeks' interim before moving, Sharri pulled Serena out of school and taught her at home. Sharri was pleased with the results; the one-on-one seemed exactly what Serena needed. She didn't have to worry about peer relationships or other kids wanting to beat her up, and there were no opportunities to lie to friends.

On November 15, the Moores moved into their new home. Serena began attending Thornton Junior High. She made new friends and settled into a fairly stable routine. She began dance classes again through the Fremont Recreation Department, where she proved talented enough to join the high school girls in the advanced division.

In January, Sharri was laid off from her job as Assistant Animal Services Officer and decided not to seek further employment. She began volunteering at Tiny Tots preschool, where Mallory attended three mornings a week. After working various jobs, Sharri loved "just being a mom." While Serena was in school, she spent the days taking Mallory to the library and the park, teaching her letters and numbers. Mallory quickly learned to recognize simple words like "dog" and "cat" and could count to ten in English and Spanish.

Mallory was three years old now, an exceptionally beautiful child with long dark hair, green eyes, and a pixie face. She had grown to be open, inquisitive, and vivacious, a ball of energy. She was going to be a ballerina when she grew up, and dreamed of turning four, when she could begin dance lessons like her big sister. Meanwhile, she and Serena had perfected their dancing together, Mallory stepping daintily across the long wooden coffee table in the family room.

Mallory loved the new house on Lucia. She had a super room with a big girl's bed and a blue railing down one side so she couldn't roll off at night. Her pillowcase and blanket had "pretty hearts" and "so many flowers!" A brown teddy bear, Minnie Mouse, baby dolls, movies, and books crammed her bed and walls, and helped keep her safe at night. She often had bad dreams about alligators and black holes swallowing her. When that happened, she would shriek for her daddy. Michael would come in with a rubber mallet hammer and pretend to pound nails into the wood so the alligators couldn't squeeze through.

Her dad still called her "Daddy's baby, Daddy's little girl." Mallory loved playing with him, especially when he'd get down on the floor to walk her zoo animals or build a castle with blocks. Sometimes, Madison would knock the castle over. She liked being Daddy's little girl, but started to protest at the "B" word.

"I'm not a baby anymore," she pouted one day.

"I know. But you'll always be my baby."

Okay, she decided, a serious look on her face. He could still call her his baby girl—for a while.

Big sister "Nana" was also a special person in Mallory's life. So special, in fact, that sometimes Mallory sided with her against Michael when the two of them argued. The arguments between Serena and her parents were increasing in number and intensity, Mallory witnessing these occurrences with growing indignation. One particular fight left a residual effect for months, and would become the focus of attention during Serena's trial.

As was typical, the altercation began over Serena's talking back to her mother after being told she was grounded. Angrily, she slouched on her bed with Mallory, filling her little sister's ears with complaints over how badly she was being treated. Michael heard the conversation and put a stop to it.

"Mallory," he said, poking his head into Serena's room, "you come on out now. Serena, you shouldn't be talking to your sister that way. She doesn't need to hear it."

Serena answered with a few choice words. At the sound of her daughter's retort, Sharri came to join the argument, then turned to leave. Something inside Serena snapped. Running out of her bedroom and down the hall, she rammed her mother broadside, sending her careening to the far end of the family room. Michael quickly stepped between mother and daughter. Serena flailed her arms at him, wild in her anger. Michael pushed her to the floor in an effort to control her. She kept swinging. In a sudden burst of frustration and anger, he aimed a short punch into her stomach. Serena's eyes bugged in surprise, then she lay still, Michael still leaning over her, wary of her next move. A moment later, she rolled to her side, choking theatrically.

"Oohh," she wailed, "I'm going to call the police. I'm gonna tell them you hit me!"

"Oh, no, you're not!" Sharri shot back as she marched over to a phone hanging on the wall and unplugged it. "You started this, and we're going to handle it by ourselves."

Although still angry, Michael was awash with regret. He had slapped Serena two or three times before, but had been careful not to close his fist, no matter how much she had cursed him, slammed doors, "trashed" the house, or thrown things. Now as his stepdaughter lay on the floor, sobbing, he left the room. Sharri helped Serena to her feet, then talked to her until she calmed down.

It didn't take Serena long to admit that she had started the fight. Michael shouldn't have hit her, she accused, but then, she had attacked her mother and tried to hit him, too.

Mallory wasn't so quick to forgive. "Don't you *ever* hit Nana again!" she commanded her father with all the force of an indignant three-year-old. "Don't you do it again!"

"I'm *sorry*," Michael assured her, "and I'll never do it again."

"You promise?"

"Promise."

Mallory nodded, satisfied. But she couldn't forget the incident. "Don't you ever hit Nana again," she declared more than once to Michael over the next few months. In time, he'd had enough of her guilt trip.

"Didn't I promise you I would never do it again?" he replied with exasperation one day as they stretched out on the floor. "Have you ever seen me hit her since then?"

Carefully placing one block on top of another, Mallory answered quietly. "No."

"Then why are you still hassling me about this?"

Mallory's mouth pursed as she turned her eyes on him. She did not mention the subject again.

During a medical checkup in December, Mallory's garbled enunciation had improved enough for her doctor to note, "clear speech now." Her asthma would render her breathless while playing, but not to the extent that her activity had to be consistently limited. Other issues with her health worried Sharri, who nervously took her to the doctor at every bump and sniffle. Usually a constant ball of motion, Mallory would tire at times for no apparent reason. She also had many colds and bruised easily. Linking the symptoms together, Sharri asked the doctor if Mallory had leukemia, and was assured that Mallory did not display signs of the disease.

Then why, Sharri countered, is she sick all the time?

Mallory's asthma took a short but frightening turn for the worse that spring. One night, Sharri allowed Mallory to stay with her on the couch while she watched a movie. Before long, Mallory fell asleep, tucked under her heart blanket. Sharri watched TV late into the night. Then, when time came to move Mallory to bed, she pulled back her blanket, "just for a mother check." Mallory was quiet, with no wheezing, but her stomach was pulling in and out, straining to help her lungs suck in air. Something was wrong.

Sharri woke Michael. They called Kaiser, but, after hearing that Mallory was not wheezing, a doctor told them that the symptoms did not warrant bringing her in to the emergency room. Sharri continued watching Mallory, then called again. Something was *wrong*. A short time later, not believing the doctor, they took Mallory to Kaiser's emergency room at 1:00 A.M. Serena elected to stay home alone and sleep. Sharri had been right; their daughter was having serious trouble. Mallory was given one, two, then finally three treatments on a breathing machine until her air passages were opened and her oxygen intake brought up to normal. The doctor prescribed a small machine called a nebulizer to be taken home and used regularly. After a time, she told the Moores, you can use it whenever you feel it's needed. She also put Mallory on the steroid prednisone for five days.

Shaken, Sharri and Michael drove home after 4:00 A.M. The nebulizer and other medications would settle Mallory's asthma, and she did not have another such attack. She would occasionally need to be put on the breathing apparatus, her straining abdomen becoming the indicator for treatment. Sharri, who had begun smoking again after Mallory's birth, vowed to quit once more, as did Michael. The cigarettes could be exacerbating their daughter's asthma.

"What," Sharri asked Michael as they pulled into their driveway, "would have happened if I hadn't checked on her?"

Despite Serena's mellow start into eighth grade, by the spring of 1992 her behavior was once again an erratically swinging pendulum. Two events then occurred that caused her to spin out of control.

The first was Troy Cole's entrance into her life. Serena met him through a friend and was instantly attracted. He was different from her other boyfriends, older and more streetwise. A seventeen-year-old boyfriend was a big notch in her belt, support for Serena's perception of herself, at fourteen, as grown-up and mature.

Mary and other friends warned Serena that Troy "only wants you for sex." Her parents also disapproved, but that didn't stop her. She began sneaking off from school to meet him. Before long, he was pressuring her for intercourse. In April, Serena began asking her mother questions—what was sex like, did it hurt the first time, etc. Sharri encouraged her to wait, but could see that her words were falling on deaf ears.

Of equal concern to Michael and Sharri were the tales they heard from Serena's friends of how Troy was treating her. They claimed he was abusive, shoving her, ordering her around "like some private slave." Sharri worried, then blamed herself. Serena was probably allowing it because she had watched her mother endure rough treatment from her first stepfather. Sharri talked to Serena, begging her to learn from her mother's mistakes.

In May, Serena lost her virginity to Troy. She told her mother about it the next day, admitting it was "not a pleasant experience." Sharri knew Serena had gotten herself into a situation that she would not be able to handle.

Once she became Troy's sex partner, Serena began running away more frequently, often slipping through Troy's bedroom window to spend the night with him. Sharri and Michael were frustrated that his parents didn't seem to know or care what was going on in their own house. "She's only fourteen, for God's sake!" Michael would storm. Sometimes, Serena didn't literally "run." She drove off in her mother's car instead.

The atmosphere in the Moore home was chaotic. Serena seemed bent on having her own way, with no thought to responsibilities or her family. Once again, the only argument that could cause her to rethink her actions involved Mallory.

"*Please,*" Sharri would say, "even if you're mad at us, no matter what you want to do, think of your sister."

Hardest for Michael was seeing his own little girl upset. Michael had made a commitment to help raise Serena; at times that commitment had kept him going when his emotions told him the hell with it. But watching Mallory suffer was something else. He longed for quiet in the home as they had enjoyed when Serena lived in Carson City. Now, the house contained nothing but arguments. As close as they were, Serena was taking some of her anger out on Mallory. Sometimes Serena would order her out of the bedroom or boss her around and be rewarded with offended screams. Mallory was never quiet about her emotions.

A few such incidents occurred when Sharri began taking Serena to an orthodontist to be fitted for braces. The appointments were always in the afternoons, during Mallory's nap time. Dragged along, Mallory would be tired and grouchy and act "like a brat," as Serena would say. After some unpleasant episodes in the dentist's waiting room, Sharri vowed to find Mallory a sitter rather than take her again.

A bright side for Serena that spring was her excitement about using her dance skills to cheerlead for football. Michael and Sharri knew the cheerleading uniforms and practice camps would be expensive, but felt Serena's self-esteem needed a boost. In May, Serena attended cheerleading workshops after school every day for two weeks. She was serious enough about going that she did not run away during that time. Then came the tryouts—a series of team routines performed in a gym full of parents and siblings. The lucky girls elected to squads enjoyed a victorious moment as they heard their names called over the loudspeakers and ran to meet their new team on the floor. The losers were left sitting, humiliated, alone on a bench.

The second important event in Serena's life that spring was her failure to make the cheerleading team. She was crushed. She cried and cried, then fell into what Sharri termed her "I'm-fine routine." She could not admit her emotional distress. Her anger and disappointment were reflected instead through her behavior.

Fortunately, she performed well in her dance revue at the end of May. She and her dance class were thrilled at the loud whistles and applause they received. Next year, Serena told Mallory, the revue would be even more exciting. Every year the show included one song, "Sisters," during which sisters who were enrolled in the dance school would perform together. Next year, Mallory would be on stage with her!

A few weeks after the revue, school let out for the summer. June and July were filled with uncertainty, with Serena cooperative one day and rebellious the next. She ran away often, usually to Troy's. One time she disappeared for three days with Sharri's car. Although the Moores turned in the license plate number to police, they knew that finding their daughter would be their responsibility. Running away was not a legal offense; the police wouldn't spend much time tracking down juveniles. Sharri checked Troy's house each day during that stint, but he and Serena had become adept at sneaking in and out at odd times and were never there when she drove by. On the third day, with the help of Mia Black, who drove by Troy's house on her way to work, Sharri finally caught up with them and brought Serena home.

*   *   *

The Moores looked forward to August, which promised to be the best month of that summer. Hopefully, the events they had planned would calm Serena and allow family ties to strengthen. They could all use a break in arguments.

On August first, Mallory celebrated her fourth birthday with a party, attended by her little friends as well as Serena's. Mia Black was there, too. Mallory's eyes sparkled at the presents, the cake and candles. *And,* she squealed, jumping up and down, this day meant something else. She could have dance lessons! Mom would take her down soon to sign her up for classes.

But first—another dream would come true. She, Mommy, Daddy, and Nana were going to Disneyland!

It was the trip of their lifetime.

"For those few days," Sharri would later reminisce, "we were so happy. Serena seemed so excited to share this with her sister, to show her all the sights and sounds she could."

At Wild Bear Country, Mallory was enthralled by a machine that "made a penny all flat." Daddy pressed a penny in the machine for her, and she clutched it gleefully in her palm, opening her fingers now and then to gaze wonderingly at its funny oval shape.

Night time brought the fireworks. Wide-eyed, Mallory watched the sprays of color against the darkened sky. Daddy held her up so she could see better. "Look at that one!" she breathed. "Looook how preeetty!"

The Moores spent two wonderful days in the park. When it was time to pack up, Mallory's flattened penny was placed, and temporarily forgotten, in the side pocket of a suitcase. Tragically, the coin's significance would soon turn from vacation memento into a poignant, bittersweet reminder to Sharri, Michael, and big sister Nana of a life forever lost.

Eighteen

I walked into Mallory's room to say good-night to her. She was reading the Sesame Street book and she was all, "Nana, Nana, I want to sleep with you." And I said, "No, because Mommy says no." And then she laid down and I asked her for square lips, because we had this little thing that she would poke her lips out and I would kiss her and we called it square lips. And I asked her for that and I kissed her and she laid down and I left the room. I told her I loved her, and she said, "I love you too."

—SERENA'S TESTIMONY OF LAST SEEING MALLORY ALIVE.

AUGUST 18, 1992, 7:30 A.M. Sharri was still in bed. She'd heard Michael leave for work around six, then had drifted back to sleep. The previous day she'd had an earache severe enough to prompt her to pay the doctor a visit. He couldn't find anything wrong. Her ear had pained her throughout the day and into the night, allowing her to sleep only intermittently until the early morning hours. Now, she was trying to catch some extra rest before the girls woke up. Mal, Sharri thought sleepily, would soon be pestering her to get out of bed so they could register for dance classes at the Recreation Department as promised.

Serena was already awake. She hopped out of bed, pulled on a pair of shorts and a shirt. The day promised to be a hot one. She stopped to listen. It was awfully quiet. Usually by that time, Mallory was bursting open Serena's bedroom door to yank her hair and wake her up.

Stepping outside her bedroom, she closed the door again, then walked down the hall past an empty bedroom and bath until she came to Mallory's open door. She looked in. Mallory was still. Serena padded across the floor.

"Maaallloory," she sang. "Time to get uupp." Mallory didn't move. Serena sang out a second time. "Maaalllory." She hesitated, then nudged her sister. Nudged her again, a little harder. Her little body rocked, then lay still.

Serena felt fear prickling her skin. She leaned over to look at Mallory's face. Oh, God! It looked all blue, and there was some wet stuff on her face. And something smelled. Serena ran out of the room. "Mom, Mom!" she cried, dashing through her parents' open bedroom door. "Something's wrong with Mallory! I can't wake her up!"

With a mother's instant alertness, Sharri sprang out of bed, fearing some problem with Mallory's asthma or another "blue spell." She saw the panic in Serena's eyes. "Everything's going to be okay," she declared, then pushed her daughter aside to hurry down the hall.

Sharri would never forget the smell as long as she lived. It hit her as soon as she rushed into Mallory's room. Serena followed behind and leaned against the wall. Sharri shook Mallory, then shook her again, voice rising as she called out her daughter's name again and again. Mallory wouldn't move. Mallory wouldn't wake up.

Mallory was dead.

In her heart, Sharri knew it. Her child had been dead for hours. But she could not *believe*. "Oh, God," she sobbed. "God, no, *no*!"

Serena, watching in horror, slid to the floor, her back against the wall. She waved her arms crazily, as if to push the truth away, her cries echoing those of her mother.

Sharri leaned as far as she could over the bed railing and smoothed Mallory's hair, wiping the bloody foam from her face. For a moment, she was lost in a whirlwind of shock and grief. Then, instinctively, she wheeled around and headed for the kitchen, hoping against hope that someone, *anyone,* could help. Serena, panic-stricken, followed. Grabbing the phone, Sharri dialed 911.

"Fremont Fire and Emergency."

Sharri fought to speak coherently, her voice quivering. "I think my four-year-old's dead. We found her in bed this morning and she's stiff and cold. . . ."

Serena fell to the floor, wailing. "No, no, no!" It was not true, it *was not true*! She could not be in this world without her little sister. Suddenly, she had to get out of the house. Scrambling to her feet, she ran outside, not caring where she was going. Heading south on Cabrillo Street, she sobbed and moaned to herself as she saw two police cars approaching. "Please, somebody come and kill me," she gulped to herself. "Somebody come and hit me, *please*!"

Responding to the 911 call were Crime Scene Investigator Paul Dejoy and Officer Joseph Geibig, followed in a second car by Officer Robert Sischka. Spying the distraught Serena, Sischka rolled to a halt for a "welfare check" of the teenager. After talking with her briefly, he gently guided her into his car, not yet realizing that the dead sister she was crying about was the subject of the 911 call he was investigating.

Sharri's mind reeled as she slammed down the phone. She was aware of Serena's screaming, heard her rush outside, but her head was not yet clear enough to fear for her older daughter. She stumbled back to Mallory.

Tearfully, she crooned to her little girl as she bent over to wrap her in a quilt, pick her up, and lift her over the bed railing. Hugging Mallory close, she walked numbly to the front door, open from Serena's panicked escape. She sat weakly on the entry rug, crying and rocking her baby as she waited for the paramedics. "Why, *why*?" She looked upward, as though seeking an answer from heaven. She could hardly bear to see Mallory's face, it looked so terrible—splotchy and blue-white.

As she waited, Sharri crushed Mallory to her chest, willing her own life to flow into her little girl's veins.

Seven forty-one A.M. Fire Captain Mike Sanchez and his paramedic, Russell Peterson, found Sharri in the doorway when they arrived. Sharri looked pleadingly at the uniformed men, then quickly lifted Mallory toward Sanchez. In a daze, she watched him look at her child, heard him comment softly.

"Oh, God. She's been gone a long time."

Then she felt Sanchez leading her away, backing her by a grip on both elbows out of the hall and into the family room. Peterson, after lugging in his equipment, had taken Mallory in his arms and was laying her down once again on the hallway floor for an examination.

Sanchez closed the family room door behind them, then nudged Sharri toward the kitchen. She leaned against the counter, waiting for she knew not what, crying uncontrollably. In a few minutes, Peterson returned, saying that his examination was finished and apologizing that "there was nothing they could do." As difficult as it may be, he would need to complete some paperwork. Sanchez left the room.

As Sharri wailed, young, dark-haired Peterson watched her, feeling ill at ease, his compassion for her frozen into nonaction by his sense of sheer helplessness. He had not the slightest idea of how to control a grief-stricken woman. Seeing him through a haze of tears, Sharri felt a sudden rush of anger. She wanted help, she wanted comfort, and he *was just standing there.* Furiously, she smacked him on the chest with the palms of her hands, pushing him backward. "Can't you *do* something?" she screamed. "*Help* me! Give me a *hug*!"

Startled, Peterson grasped her awkwardly by the arms for a moment, then, with an excuse, rushed from the room.

In the hallway, police officers Dejoy and Geibig had arrived and were examining Mallory's body. Sanchez briefed them both, noting that he found no petechial hemorrhages on the little girl, which could have suggested some form of suffocation. Dejoy inspected Mallory and concurred that no petechiae were present. He did see a small amount of brown-tinged fluid that had seeped from her mouth.

Hearing Sharri's cry, the two officers went to her aid, leading her to the family room couch and offering her some water. Mallory was left lying in the hallway, just beyond the front door.

"Please find my other daughter," Sharri pleaded. "She ran out of the house and I don't know if she's all right."

Sischka recognized Serena from her numerous past escapades of running away. Then he realized her connection with the 911 call. She could not stop crying.

"Is there somewhere I can take you?"

"Just take me to a friend's house," she begged. "I can't stand to go back home right now."

Sischka drove Serena the few blocks to Troy's house. Troy answered the doorbell, half-asleep, and made an attempt to comfort her when she collapsed into his arms. Sischka watched them hug for a few minutes, Serena hiccupping against Troy's chest until, exhausted, she finally grew quiet. "It's time to go back now," he encouraged Serena. "Your mother needs you."

Placidly, weighted by grief, she obeyed.

Five to ten minutes after Dejoy and Geibig entered the Moores' house, Sischka drove up with Serena. In dread, she traversed the sidewalk leading to her house. She could see her sister lying in the hallway just beyond the front door. Oh, God! She would have to step over Mal's body to get inside. Numbly, gathering her courage, she jumped over Mallory, ran to her hysterical mother, and held her, feeling a surge of protectiveness. Mom *needed* her. She had to be strong.

Sischka and Dejoy began to inspect the house, including Mallory's room and bed, looking for anything that might suggest foul play, but saw nothing unusual. A small spot of fluid was noticed on Mallory's pillow.

Sharri clung to Serena, then let go long enough to beg the paramedics to move Mallory from the floor back to her bed. She couldn't bear to think of Michael having to step over her body as poor Serena had done. We can't move her, she was told again and again. Sharri insisted. Finally, one of the policemen said it was all right and carried Mallory to her room.

Gently, Sischka and his partner began posing questions. "She had asthma and some funny kind of seizures," was all Sharri could think of, remembering the blue spells. "She'd been on a machine before, and medication, and sometimes she'd wake up a little breathless. But she seemed *fine* last night."

The sound of footsteps in and out, in and out were filtering through the family room door. Dazedly, Sharri and Serena answered questions. What time had Mallory eaten last night? What time did she go to bed? Who found her? What time did that person get up? Sharri tried to focus on their questions, her mind screaming all the while at the thought of strange people examining, handling her baby.

"You've got to call your husband," Sischka told her.

Sharri was horrified. "I *can't*. How can I tell him his little girl is *dead*?"

Instead, she called security at Raychem, asking them to find Michael and have him call home. When the phone rings, she told Sischka, you answer it. You tell him. I *can't*.

Michael was leaning over a machine in the extrusion lab, programming equipment for a morning test run, when the security officer delivered his message. Call home. Michael was immediately apprehensive. "Home" knew where he was, had his beeper number. Why hadn't Sharri called herself?

A man answered the phone at his house, identifying himself as a police officer. Your daughter seems to have had some kind of seizure, the officer was saying.

Michael felt the world drop from beneath his feet. He heard himself ask the question. "Which daughter?"

The little one, he was told.

From the tone of the officer's voice, Michael knew. He closed his eyes. "Is she dead?"

"Yes, I'm afraid so."

For a moment, Michael could not move. Silently, he hung up, trying to gather his wits, willing himself to wake up from the nightmare. In a daze, he found himself walking to the office of his plant manager, Guy Fletcher, and relaying the news like some automaton. Afraid that Michael was too shocked to drive, Guy drove him home in his car, followed by Bill, another employee who would take the supervisor back to work.

The ten-mile trip seemed interminable to Michael. The news was so unexpected, so final. There was nothing he could do. His baby girl had died while he was sleeping. It was too much to absorb. He remembered leaning into Mallory's room just two hours ago to make sure she was all right. How many, many times he'd checked her in the early mornings, then tiptoed in to adjust her covers. But this morning she'd been lying there, *dead,* and he hadn't even gone inside her room! What if he could have done something? What if he could have saved her?

As Guy pulled the car to a stop, the sight of uniformed men in the hallway of his house filled Michael with dread. He stepped across the threshold, asked an officer where his wife was. Hurrying to Sharri and Serena, he grasped them in a three-way hug. They stood, holding each other and crying, until Michael stepped back. "Where is she?"

Sharri, too choked to speak, pointed to Mallory's room.

She was laying on her bed. Michael crossed the room silently, gazed at his baby, touched her, kissed her. Her beautiful little face was blue and splotched. Unreal, like some grotesque wax doll. Michael squatted on the balls of his feet, gripping the blue bed railing. A sound escaped from his throat then, one he had never before heard—a wailing moan, an expression so primal, so laden with pain that it was frightening. In his peripheral vision, he saw a police officer look in. He rocked on his heels, back and forth, back and forth, crying, unable to stop his own groans. Vaguely, he was aware of the policeman checking him once more. He did not know how long he rocked there, or what finally prompted him to leave.

Michael called his mother. Sharri left a message on Tessie's answering machine. Serena's friend Mary was on her way, running across Newark and the freeway separating it from Fremont, soap still in her hair. She had been in the shower when the phone rang. Another of Serena's friends, Tina, would soon arrive, as would Mia and Terri Black.

Then questions. So many questions. It seemed as though Michael answered the same ones over and over again. He had to be strong, be the man of the family. The scene was surreal—the uniformed men, his hysterical wife. It wasn't enough that Mallory was gone, but in the midst of his grief he had to talk about recent events of her *life* as she lay in her bed, *dead*.

At 9:30 A.M. Frank Gentle and J.D. Lawson, from the county coroner's office, arrived. Sischka and Dejoy briefed them, then together all four inspected Mallory's body and the house once again. None of them noticed anything suspicious. Once their inspection was done, it was time to take the body. Sischka would sign their receipt as witness to the removal.

Gentle returned to the family in their living room. Singling out Michael, Gentle informed him that, because of the unknown cause of death, the county coroner would review the case and most likely call for an autopsy. Sharri, unable to bear the thought of her daughter's body being cut, had told Geibig and Dejoy earlier that she did not want one performed. Hearing Gentle's explanation, however, Michael replied that he understood.

"Why don't you go in the other room now," Gentle suggested, indicating toward the kitchen, "so you won't have to see her being carried out."

They all complied. Even so, Michael caught a glimpse that would haunt him forever—the outline of his baby girl zipped up in a body bag, lying cold, lifeless, and alone.

With the worst possible timing, Sarah and William Moore arrived just as Mallory was being wheeled down the sidewalk. From inside, Sharri could hear her screaming. "Please let me see her, let me see her!"

When Gentle and Lawson wouldn't oblige, she collapsed, sobbing, on the gurney. William firmly but gently led her away.

Within a few moments, the house was still. All the uniforms—the paramedics, policemen, firemen, and coroner's investigators—were gone, leaving a chill hanging in the hot August air.

Mallory was gone, too.

Michael, Sharri, Serena, Sarah, and William gazed numbly at the friends who gathered around them, minds scrabbling to grasp the finality of the morning's events. Surely, any moment now, Mallory would prance in, giggling, and the ice in their hearts would melt away in the sudden sunlight. The stage for her entrance was set. Her playthings still lay scattered on the family room floor. A Disney video was in the VCR. Her toys, her baby dolls, her stuffed animals, the hearts and flowers blanket cluttered her bedroom.

In three horrific, heart-wrenching hours, the Moores' lives had been changed forever.

Nineteen

THE DAYS THAT followed were smudged with pain, a blur of consoling friends, funeral arrangements and agony-filled nights. The Moore home was crowded with people. Tessie and Kirk headed for Newark within an hour of receiving their phone message. Roxanne also came. Sharri hadn't seen her sister since the day of her wedding, six years earlier. Michael's mother spent that night with the Moores as well. In the four days before the funeral, Serena was rarely home. She could not stand being in the house and often took refuge with her friends. Even the morning of Mallory's death, she had gone out to a store, then to the mall with Mary and a few other girls, trying to push away her pain.

Grief dulls the mind, paralyzes the muscles. Amidst the chaos, Michael and Sharri could barely cope with their loss; the grim decisions of death were beyond their comprehension. Michael's brother Ben came to their rescue, offering logistical help with choosing a casket, securing a funeral home, and making other arrangements. He also loaned them money until funds from Mallory's life insurance, provided by Raychem, came through. When the insurance proved to be a few hundred dollars short, he waived the balance, saying it was a gift. Ben stayed with the Moores that week until the funeral.

"He was my strength," Michael later remembered.

Both Michael and Sharri began smoking again.

Desperate to know why their daughter had died, the Moores agreed to an autopsy. Dr. Paul Herrmann conducted the autopsy the morning of August 19 in the presence of Fremont Police Detective Greg Whiteley, whom Dr. Herrmann had summoned when external inspection of Mallory's body yielded "suspicious" findings.

With the coroner's indication that the death might be from unnatural causes, Fremont police found themselves in a situation that was embarrassing, at best. The morning of Mallory's death, inspection of the scene had been perfunctory. Sischka's report of the investigation noted:

> *Dejoy, Geibig and I discussed the nature of the incident and the scene and, after going over what we had with the Coroner's Investigators, determined that there was no evidentiary value to a diagram or photographs of the scene. This was passed along to Sgt. Eads, who concurred.*

Now, things looked very different.

That afternoon, Whiteley called the Moores, asking that they report to the police station for further questioning. Michael's father, William, answered the phone. Michael, Ben, and Sarah Moore were at the mortuary, he told the detective, and Sharri was sleeping after having been heavily sedated. They would have to call him back.

Upon waking, Sharri was incredulous at the phone call. "How can they want to talk to us *now!*" she protested. "We've told them everything we know. Can't we at least have the *funeral* first?"

Sharri returned the call at five-thirty that afternoon, complaining to investigative liaison officer Susan Bankston, who relayed the message to Whiteley. Within forty minutes, Whiteley was phoning the Moores again. Instead of informing them about Dr. Herrmann's suspicions, he explained to Michael "the necessity of follow-up interviews as a matter of procedure." Reluctantly, Michael acquiesced, saying he would speak to Whiteley the following morning.

August 20, 7:30 A.M. Michael broke into tears as he told Whiteley over the phone that he and Sharri must "attend to funeral business" before they could come to the police station. And could they please release his little girl's body from the morgue? Whiteley checked with Dr. Herrmann at eleven-thirty. As they discussed the case, Dr. Herrmann noted that there were still "signs that suggest" that Mallory's death was unnatural. He had completed all the microscopic exams, and that was about all he could do. His disposition on the death was "still open."

At 12:25 P.M., Sharri, Michael, and Serena arrived at the police station, along with Ben and Roxanne. Each family member was interviewed and taped separately. Michael spoke so low during his interview session that many of his words were later unintelligible.

Serena was questioned in the presence of her Aunt Roxanne. Discussing signs that could indicate a cause for Mallory's death, Serena noted Mallory's asthma, a bump on the head sustained earlier the evening she died, a swollen bug bite on the hand, nightmares, the blue spells, that she "maybe just stopped breathing," and even foot blisters from walking through Disneyland. Asked if she had a "parting shot" that she thought the police "ought to look at," Serena replied, "No. Probably look into maybe suffocation at night. Suffocation, but, you know, can't breathe, so they just stop breathing."

Although months later, Serena would shrug that it was no more than a parroted statement gleaned from snippets of her parents' conversations as they searched for an answer, at the time the police took the remark very seriously since it seemed to agree with Dr. Herrmann's suspicion of asphyxia. On the transcript of Serena's interview, a large star was drawn next to the remark.

Sharri's recounting of events was interspersed with sobs as she berated herself over her child's death.

"Keep in mind," Whiteley told her, "you can't beat yourself up over this. I know it's difficult not to do."

"She wanted to sleep with Serena that night," Sharri cried. "That would have been worse because it was probably something nobody could do and then she would have died in the bed with Serena. That would have been worse."

Whiteley tried to calm her. "I'm sure you would have been there, right? You're just, from what you told us you're very conscientious about the child's health, her needs and what have you. Probably much more common sense of what goes on with your child than a lot of people are, probably the vast majority of people."

"I inspected every part of her body all the time," Sharri wailed. "I was ridiculous."

"So, you can't hold yourself responsible. It could be very well that you missed nothing."

Sharri wiped her face with a tissue. "Maybe I should have

yelled and screamed and made them take tests, made them do more, but they said she was *fine.*"

Well, Whiteley replied, you can rarely tell doctors to do anything.

"But what if there was something *wrong* with her? They wouldn't, like with her heart or something and they didn't— how will I ever *forgive* myself?"

In the preliminary investigation, Whiteley assured her, "They [the coroner] weren't able to find anything."

"But if there's something wrong with her heart; it would've showed."

"Yeah. As a rule the doctors are very good."

"What could have possibly—I need to know this, okay, and I can handle this, okay? What possibly could make someone die that would not show up? What did they check for? What did they test for? I need to know!"

"After the preliminary," Whiteley explained evenly, "what they do is check the blood for anything that could be in the bloodstream."

Sharri searched for an answer, waving her hands in the air. "She couldn't have gotten ahold of any poison; there was *nothing* within her reach. . . ."

Whiteley did not tell her the coroner's suspicions.

After interviewing the Moores, Whiteley and Detective John Anderson drove to Lucia Street to search Mallory's bedroom again. It's just routine, Sharri and Michael were told, we're looking for anything that might indicate cause of death. Unable to handle watching the detectives paw through her daughter's room, Sharri waited in the motor home that her grandmother had driven up from central California. Looking out the window, she saw Whiteley and Anderson pull duffel bags from the trunk of their unmarked car when they arrived. Upon leaving, the detectives threw the bags back into the car. As far as Sharri knew, they were empty. Neither she nor Michael were given a list of seized items.

Whiteley's report on the inspection noted, "The purpose of this was to photograph the room where Mallory had been located and seize the bedsheets. We arrived there at approx. 1715 hrs., doing so as stealthily as possible at the family's insistence."

"*Wrong!*" Sharri later declared. "They screwed up the morning of Mallory's death. Then they screwed up again when they came to our house two days later because they *still* didn't notice Mallory's bedsheet even then. That report was a cover-up for it."

Sharri told a different version of how the police obtained the bedsheet. The next day, she said, she was frantically searching Mallory's room for a glittery Barbie headband. It had been Mallory's favorite, and Sharri wanted her to wear it in her casket. Sarah Moore, in an effort to channel her nervous energy, was gathering up Mallory's sheets to wash. On the floor, Sharri noticed a *101 Dalmations* dress, worn the day before Mallory died and stained with chocolate from her last ice-cream cone. In tears, Sharri hugged it to her chest. "Don't wash this," she told Sarah. "I want to keep it just the way it is."

Then as Sarah Moore began to strip Mallory's bed, Sharri noticed "the spot"—a large dried area of fluid on the bottom bedsheet. Again, she stopped her mother-in-law. She called the police department and told them she would bag the sheet and leave it on the side of the house for them to pick up.

Maybe, she hoped to Michael, the spot would give the police a clue.

The *101 Dalmations* dress she placed under her pillow, where it would remain.

Mallory's casket was pink, as was the decor in the viewing room at Chapel of the Roses Funeral Home. With a clear view of Fremont's shrub-dotted foothills, the chapel's peach-colored stucco building was bordered on its west side with tall rosebushes in all tints—white, yellow, pink, peach, and red. The chapel's name, however, came from its owners, the Rose family, and not its multiplicity of flowers. Seeing its stained glass, beautiful lobby, and wood paneling, Sharri thought the funeral home lovely, the right choice for her little girl.

Friday, one day before the funeral, Mallory's casket was open for viewing. Sensitive to friends and family members who could not bear an open casket at the funeral, Sharri and Michael planned for it to be closed then, but had agreed to give others a chance to say their final good-byes. True to promises they had made to themselves, they stood stoically at the door of the chapel, greeting each person who came to honor their child. For Sharri, whose emotions flowed like a stream skittering over rocks, it was an act of sheer will. Michael's grief ran deeper, a hidden river far beneath a barren desert. To gaze into that river, he knew, to hang over its edge, was to fall in and drown.

Serena did not have a choice in handling her grief—it handled her. One moment she was hysterical, the next, oddly detached. Other times her behavior was wild and inappropriate as she giggled with friends bent on cheering her spirits.

One of the worst moments for Serena occurred that Friday. Walking down the chapel's center aisle in dreaded first approach of her sister's casket, she stumbled, her knees caving in. "She was my little girl!" Serena wailed as Michael helped her battle her way forward to place a favorite stuffed animal by Mallory's lifeless form. "I'll be your little girl now," she whispered to Michael as they gazed into the satin-lined casket.

Of Sharri's memories from the day, Serena's farewell to her sister would remain one of the most vivid. Other images swirled hazily—the thick smell of Mallory's pancake makeup; a yellow rose offered by the roughened hand of a weeping man, a stranger; the awkward, whispered condolences of friends who could not begin to understand the depth of their pain.

And her own fingers, wet, after running them gently over her daughter's body.

"She's leaking!" Sharri gasped, voice cracking as she gazed in horror at her hand.

A chapel attendant was quickly by her side. I'm sorry, she tried to explain, but an autopsy on one so small—sometimes the embalming fluid seeps through the stitches. . . .

As Sharri, Michael, and Serena turned to leave Chapel of the Roses that afternoon, with final, lingering gazes of Mallory seared into their minds, Sharri froze. Irrational though it was, she could not leave her little girl lying in the room alone. "Please stay with her," she blurted to the college-age attendant. "Please stay until we're gone."

Dutifully, the young woman took up her post. Looking over his shoulder, Michael glimpsed her standing, straight-

backed and solemn, beside the small pink casket as he and
Sharri stepped through the doorway.

Saturday, August 22. Mallory's funeral was held in the
Chapel of the Roses. A despondent but determined Serena
managed to read a poem in her sister's honor. Pastor Doug
presented the eulogy. "Unchained Melody" and "Music Box
Dance" were played. Afterward, the Moores' white limousine
led a long procession over San Francisco Bay, across the
Peninsula, and into hills rolling lazily above the ocean. There,
in the Moores' family plot at Skylawn Cemetery, Mallory
was buried atop a windswept knoll that overlooked the ever-
surging waters of the mighty Pacific. In about five weeks'
time, a specially ordered poured bronze marker would be
placed on her grave. The marker, with raised pictures of ballerina slippers and an angel with its arm around a small child,
was inscribed with the words of hope that Pastor Doug had
proclaimed at her funeral.

SHE DANCES WITH THE ANGELS.

Twenty

THE DAY AFTER Mallory's funeral, Mia Black contacted Detective Whiteley. Devastated over Mallory's death, she
"wanted to provide whatever information she could." She
had seen Mallory the day before her death, Mia told him,
and knew the little girl's health was fine at the time. She
"didn't want to hurt anybody, but wanted to help" the police
find the truth. Whiteley scheduled a meeting with her on
August 24. In paraphrasing that interview, he noted:

*Black last saw Mallory on the 17th, and says that "Serena
concerns me." According to Black, there is a "lot of jealousy" of Mallory by Serena. She describes her perception of
Serena as having to be the center of attention, and would
"push" Mallory out of the way to try and get it. Black has*

not seen any recent physical aggression by Serena, but says about 2 yrs. ago she saw Serena shake and spank Mallory at a store. She described Serena's envy as "unreal."

Black has an obvious fondness for Mallory. She describes her as a good girl who would be influenced by Serena. She describes an incident where Serena had been picked up by the police, resulting in Mallory saying, "I hate police." Black also described Serena's actions the day of the funeral. She says Serena read a poem but did not cry, smirked and giggled during the funeral, and did a cheerleading dance for the family at home afterwards. Black believes that if Serena had anything to do with the death she would confide in no one, and block it out.

With Mia Black's statement, suspicions about the cause of Mallory's death heightened. As investigations continued, Officer Sischka was confronted regarding an error he had made in his original report. It seemed that Sergeant Eads, whom Sischka had stated "concurred" that there was no evidentiary value to diagraming or photographing Mallory's room, did not care to accept the rap for the less than thorough investigation of a case that was beginning to look like a homicide. Sischka wrote a supplemental report on August 25 to "clarify/correct" the point.

This [reported concurrence] was based not on a direct conversation between myself and Sgt. Eads but on my conversation with Dejoy regarding this matter and his discussion with Sgt. Eads. The statement was, therefore, an interpretation of Dejoy's remarks; and does not reflect Eads' actual statements and/or opinion regarding the incident. Sgt. Eads, therefore, was not party to the decision to not photograph and/or diagram the scene once the matter had been determined to be an unattended death of undetermined cause(s).

Sischka was also questioned regarding his stopping to help Serena while on the way to Mallory's "code blue." The officer defended his actions in the supplemental report and, perhaps in response to Mia Black's finger-pointing at Serena, further detailed his conversation with the teenager. He stated that he saw nothing unusual in the girl's behavior.

* * *

Months later, after Serena's first trial, Sischka would be amazed that her attorney hadn't called him to testify on her behalf. "When the case came up," he remembered, "the D.A. called and asked me some questions. I guess he didn't like my professional, seventeen-years-on-the-force opinion. He got mad and never called me again. I don't believe Serena Moore did a damn thing."

Sischka's beliefs notwithstanding, Detective Whiteley's view of Serena Moore would grow more bleak. On August 27, he spoke with Terri Black, Mia's daughter, who said that Serena had been acting "suspiciously" on the night of Mallory's death.

Unaware of suspicions against Serena, the Moores struggled to "take it one day at a time" as Serena's grief and guilt over Mallory's death began to drive her over the edge of despair. She couldn't live with her "if onlys." If only she'd let Mallory sleep with her that night, if only she hadn't been so quick to say no, she could have saved her sister. The thought was too much for her to bear. She began running away, staying out for days at a time. When she was home, she could not stand the sorrow of her parents.

"Stop *crying!*" she screamed at her mother. "All you want is attention!"

Out with friends at a skating rink, Serena met Larry Wellington, a black boy who temporarily replaced Troy as her boyfriend. Two weeks after Mallory's funeral, Serena ran away to stay overnight with Larry. Sharri, hearing where she was, called the police. Officer Sischka located Serena and transported her to the police station. Sharri and Michael then drove to the station to pick her up.

They immediately noticed "hickeys" on Serena's neck and argued with her about them, Sharri saying that they made her look "like a slut." Home less then ten minutes, Serena flew out of control when Sharri wouldn't allow her to speak by phone to Larry and ran out the door. Sharri followed in her car, trying to persuade Serena to get inside and return home. Furious, Serena picked up a rock as if to throw it at her mother's car, then bent the radio antenna with her hands. Sharri drove home alone. Serena eventually ended up at Mary's house.

"Look," she told Mary, pulling aside the collar of her jacket, "look at these. Michael gave them to me." Mary didn't believe it, but didn't want to confront her. Esther had no such compunctions.

"Where were you really?" she pressed.

Serena wouldn't answer.

Esther called Sharri, who phoned the police again. Serena spent the night at Mary's, then was picked up by Officer Sischka the following morning. At her wits' end, Sharri asked the police to take Serena to Malibar, a juvenile halfway house in Castro Valley. She and Michael just couldn't handle her anymore.

Serena reacted angrily to being "dumped" at Malibar, and retaliated by showing social workers the marks on her neck and bruises on her leg. "My stepfather did this to me," she claimed. Once more, Fremont police were called, Officer Lamb responding. Lamb photographed Serena's bruises, then asked her what happened. She said that Michael punched her and kicked her after Sharri argued with her over a hickey on her neck.

Officer Lamb asked Serena why she hadn't told the story to Officer Sischka that morning.

Serena said, "He didn't ask me why I ran away. He just told me that running away wasn't the answer to my problems and it wouldn't solve anything."

While Officer Lamb was taking Serena's statement, Sharri called Malibar, asking that her daughter be transported to a psychiatric facility in Oakland. Lamb balked, saying that Serena was "displaying normal behavior," that she was "considered a victim" because of her allegations and was "now under the protective custody of the county." She would be placed in a foster home.

Sharri fell apart. Serena already had those marks when Officer Sischka picked her up at Larry's, she cried. Sharri told Lamb how difficult Serena had been since Mallory's death. She had already lost one child and now she was about to lose another. She just couldn't take it anymore. "It makes me wish that I never had children," she sobbed.

During his ensuing investigation, Lamb first spoke with Larry and his mother, who confirmed that Serena had been at their house overnight. All three of them had been at a park together, Larry's mother said, where "Serena talked about the recent death of her sister," saying that Mallory had "died of seizures" and "had asthma and leukemia." Mrs. Wellington continued, "Serena said she felt that her sister's death was her fault because her sister had asked her to sleep in Serena's room the night before her death. Serena said she told Mallory to sleep in her own room. Serena said she felt that she could have saved Mallory if she would have allowed Mallory to sleep in her room. Serena said that she had found Mallory dead."

Lamb also spoke with Mary Corren. Serena had told Mary, too, that Michael had beaten her, but Mary knew better. According to Lamb's report, Mary did "not believe that Michael or Sharri had abused Serena. She said she has been over to the [Moore] house many times and her parents are not that way to Serena. She believes that Serena is making this up to keep herself from getting into trouble again."

It was clear that Serena was lying. Wherever she may have been when she sustained those bruises, it couldn't have been at her own house. Lamb concluded his report.

From speaking to all involved parties, I believe that Serena has made a false police report and I recommend that this report be unfounded.

Serena was placed in an Oakland foster home while Lamb conducted his investigation. While living there, Serena once again ran off, this time trying to find her way back home, only to flag down a police officer in the middle of the night when she became lost. Sharri, meanwhile, was pestering social workers daily to release her from the foster home and into a psychiatric facility provided by Kaiser Foundation Health Plan. After Lamb's report was filed, Serena noted in her diary on September 13 that "they found out I made a false report against Michael so the court might press charges against me and I might be facing a sentence in juvenile hall." Serena added she was "kinda scared" about the prospect. (No such charges were filed.)

Serena was removed from the foster home and twice in the next four weeks was placed in a psychiatric facility. She then was denied further insurance payment even though, according to Sharri's calculations, they had thirty days' coverage left. (The Kaiser plan allowed six weeks of inpatient psychiatric care per year.) One of the two hospital admissions followed a botched suicide attempt carried out on the front lawn of a friend's house. Serena tore a soda can in half, then aimed its jagged edges at her wrists. Sharri, having just driven over to pick up Serena, watched, heart in her throat, as four of her friends wrenched the crude weapon out of her hands.

After further inpatient coverage was denied, the Moores hired a private psychologist for $130 per hour, whom Serena was supposed to visit once a week. But keeping those appointments soon became all but impossible since Serena was running away from home so often.

Furious at Kaiser, both because of what they felt to be inadequate care of Mallory and the denied psychiatric treatment for Serena, the Moores set about changing insurance plans through Michael's employment at Raychem. They eventually signed on with Massachusetts Mutual, but by then, Serena had been arrested.

In the meantime, Michael and Sharri felt they had not the strength to go on. As if Mallory's death wasn't enough, now they were constantly worrying about their other daughter. Heaped on top of it all was their own guilt. They still did not know *why* Mallory died, and constantly asked themselves what they might have done to save her. Michael had looked in on Mallory that morning, but had not entered her room to check her. Perhaps Sharri's guilt as a mother was the worst of all. She had been awake with an earache, just on the other side of the wall, while her child had struggled for breath and died.

On the other side of the wall.

Visiting Mallory's grave on Sundays became a ritual, the forty-five-minute drives to and from Skylawn Cemetery often spent within the silence of their own anguish. Not once did Serena accompany them, always finding an excuse. Sharri and Michael knew she could not face the harsh reality of seeing it. The grave drew them in the inexplicable way that memories beckon those who remember. They believed that Mallory was in heaven, tenderly cared for by angels and God Himself. At the same time, the tombstone and grassy mound, shielding the precious body that they had nurtured, were a testament to her earthly presence. No longer able to tuck their little girl in bed with a teddy bear, they placed stuffed animals on her grave. They couldn't smooth back her hair, and so trimmed the grass. Offering her a drink became watering carefully planted flowers; watching her run was replaced with gazing at a grave site pinwheel as it spun in the breeze.

And, day after day, they asked themselves *why*.

Shortly after Mallory's funeral, a chance occurrence gave the Moores a tangible remembrance to cling to. Sharri was packing for a desperate getaway weekend in Reno when her finger closed on something hard and thin in the side pocket of her suitcase. Drawing out the item, she gasped in recognition. It was Mallory's flattened penny.

At that moment, the tragedy of their loss pounded Sharri's body like storm-driven waves on a foamy seashore. She clutched the penny tightly and held it to her heart, willing the happy memories it represented to drown out her sorrow. What she wouldn't give to be back in Disneyland with Mallory, wide-eyed and chattering! Her fingers squeezed tighter. The penny was special. It was as if Mallory was reaching out from the past, offering her parents a profound and inspirational gift.

Sharri and Michael entrusted their find to a jeweler, who cut the penny into serrated-edged halves, each with a hole for a chain; plated them in gold and inscribed letters on the undersides. Hearing the reason behind their request for the necklaces, he charged them nothing. MALL filled Michael's half; ORY graced Sharri's. Hung on gold chains, the penny halves could lie against their hearts. Michael, fearful of catching the necklace on equipment at work, took to wearing his only at home. Sharri fastened hers around her neck and never took it off.

For weeks, Sharri had been calling Detective Whiteley, frantically asking if he had heard from the coroner's office. Whiteley, in fact, had not heard, and had been phoning Dr. Herrmann requesting his conclusions. During at least two of these phone calls, Whiteley had discussed background details regarding the Moore household, including the fact that Michael had been arrested in the past for allegedly molesting Serena. Despite Dr. Herrmann's immediate "suspicions," Whiteley was not told of his final ruling until September 22—over a month after the autopsy. On that day, Investigator Frank Gentle told Whiteley that the cause was "traumatic asphyxia, mechanism undetermined." Mallory's death was "considered unnatural, but the pathologist could not prove homicide at that time."

There remained one other important item regarding the case on Mallory Moore. Although Dr. Herrmann's report did not draw conclusions about what he determined to be "healed scars" in, and "dilation" of, the anus, the pathologist was now sure of his opinion on the matter.

Mallory Moore had been sodomized in the past—and again, just before her death.

On October 6, one day after Serena's suicide attempt, Detective Whiteley requested a second interview with the Moores. He finally had the coroner's report, he told them, and could explain the findings. Sharri and Michael readily agreed, hoping at last they would hear an answer to their "why's."

They didn't. Whiteley told them the cause of death, but was vague. Mallory was suffocated, he interpreted, but they didn't know by what. He was also vague about the anal dilation and one small healed tear.

I inquired of the Moores about the anal adhesion that the autopsy had discovered. They responded by saying that Mallory would complain of stomach aches and have trouble with bowel movements.

Sharri and Michael attributed the small tear to one particular bowel movement during which Mallory had bled. It seemed to them that Whiteley accepted their explanation since he did not pursue the matter further.

Whiteley turned again to cause of death, as described in his report.

[I] advised the Moores that we would continue trying to find out the cause of her death. They were told that as hard as it

*may be, there were questions regarding Serena. They under-
stood the position and agreed to let [me] speak with her
previous therapist in Truckee. Her name is Valerie Wood and
she works at Carson Professional Group. Sharri said she
would have Wood call me. It was quite obvious that until the
Moores were convinced that all potential medical reasons for
Mallory's death were eliminated, the Serena angle would be
one they would not readily entertain.*

Sharri had brought Mallory's medical records to the interview and explained to Whiteley she had discovered that Dr.
Herrmann did not have them when he wrote his report.
Surely, the complete records would be helpful in determining
cause of death. Whiteley later sent copies of Mallory's full
medical history to Dr. Herrmann. Because of the pathologist's
conclusions regarding the "anal adhesions," he also sent oral,
vaginal, and rectal swabs that Dr. Herrmann had taken from
Mallory to the Alameda County Crime Lab for examination.

Result in all three areas—"no evidence of semen was
found."

Her emotional battery spent, Serena sputtered to a halt in
December. During that month, she was home enough to attend weekly youth group meetings at church, but still sneaked
out to meet Troy whenever she could. He gave her a ring—
"pre-engagement," he called it—and she lunged at the
chance for excitement like a drowning child grabbing for
a rope.

As, one by one, children around the world opened pictur-
esque doors on their Advent calendars, the Moores also
counted the days until Christmas. But without Mallory, they
dreaded its impending approach. Christmas would be spent
in Carson City. Tessie had invited the Moores, and they had
readily accepted, both parties once again pushing aside tally
sheets of past betrayals in their time of shared sorrow. Roxanne would be there too, along with Tim, her new boyfriend.

The Moores usually spent Christmas with Michael's parents, but this year, they longed for a break from reality. Sarah
and William Moore's holiday would be spent traditionally,
each person opening gifts one at a time, a formal meal served
like clockwork. Tessie's celebration would be laid-back,

opened-ended, with potluck meals and raucous laughter as Bailey's Irish Cream flowed. They would eat, dance, and play silly games in their driven determination to have a merry, merry time, to fling themselves through the bitter holiday.

Despite their best efforts the pain remained right under the surface. Late Christmas Eve after the others had gone to bed, Sharri and Michael sat glumly in the living room. Michael closed his eyes in a vain struggle to push away thoughts of Mallory. Across the room, Sharri saw the pain on his face. "Michael?" He opened his eyes, suspended for an instant in grief. "I was going to fill Serena's stocking. Then we can go to bed." He nodded slightly.

She padded into their bedroom, feeling warm and comforted in the new pink ruffled nightgown she'd just received from him. It felt like a protective "I-wrap-my-arms-around-you" gift, as if he had offered her a big teddy bear. Much like the long sweatshirt nightgown he'd given Serena two weeks ago as an early present meant to cheer her while she struggled with her own loss. And it had cheered her, if only temporarily. Serena had reached for it, thrilled, and had run to her bedroom to emerge, skipping, a few moments later, sporting the nightgown along with pigtails and cute freckles painted across her nose.

Tomorrow, Christmas day, a few more surprises lay in store for Serena. Sharri pulled a hidden stash of treats from her suitcase and retraced her steps to the living room. Into Serena's stocking went the small gifts—candies, tapes, a key chain, nail polish, pink lipstick.

And a $1.99 diary, its cover designed in green stripes and petite roses.

PART III

The Trial

May 1993–June 1993

This is a who-dun-it that you go to the movies for.

—MELVIN BELLI

Twenty-one

THAT MONDAY, THE trial in *The Matter of Serena M.* was about to unfold in what would become three weeks of tabloid-style accusations and surprising prosecutorial theorizing. The face-off between flyweight, thirty-five-year-old Deputy District Attorney Matt Golde and the heavyweight defense firm of Melvin Belli promised the media a battle of David and Goliath proportions. Golde was already gathering his rocks.

In anticipation, reporters and cameras from local television stations cluttered the halls of the Alameda County courthouse. CBS news was also present, poised to film for Connie Chung's "Eye to Eye" weekly magazine show. While cameras would not be permitted in the courtroom, CBS would be allowed to audiotape proceedings for the show.

The case would have unique twists from the start. According to California law, Serena, being a juvenile, would be tried before a judge rather than a jury. Shelley Antonio and Melvin Belli did not agree with the rationale. As the law seemed to theorize, juries may interfere with the state's compelling interests to set the rules of the juvenile justice system in that the state viewed itself as a second parent for delinquent minors. Therefore, a judge must be free to determine both punishment and placement for children. In practice, however, many juveniles sixteen or older who were charged with homicide circumvented the law. Remanded to be tried as adults, they automatically invoked rights to a jury.

What the defense faced in this case, Antonio believed, was a mountain of adult rules and procedures without equal balance of protection through a jury. Nor were she and Belli pleased that the judge—Sandra Margulies—wasn't from within the juvenile system, having been chosen from the adult trial calendar. Antonio and Belli could have used their one challenge to try to remove her from the case, but had been afraid to take the chance. Belli knew there were two judges he definitely did not want, and neither of them had been assigned. Challenge this unknown, he reasoned, and they might end up with someone worse. Margulies was a woman; perhaps she would prove more compassionate. On the downside, she was a former prosecutor, and her husband worked with the D.A.'s office.

By lunch recess the first day, Belli would dislike her.

Serena's trial would take place in Department 39 on the third floor of the redbrick Alameda County Hall of Justice. Entrance through the courtroom's large wooden door led first into a small foyer, which in time would provide the Moores an inner sanctum from the media. Standing in the foyer, one could peek through a window of the door that led into the courtroom and view proceedings, although voices would be unintelligible.

Four rows of black-cushioned chairs ran the length of the courtroom from the door to the far wall. The first row was separated by a brown wooden railing from a long table at which both counsels and the defendant would sit. The prosecution would sit at the left end, with defense attorneys and the defendant on the right, allowing easiest access for the defendant's entrances and exits through a far right door. Outside that door, Serena, transported from juvenile hall in full wrist-to-waist and ankle shackles, would stand impatiently as a bailiff unlocked them before escorting her inside.

Judge Sandra Margulies's black leather swivel chair was positioned behind a wall of wood paneling, raised just enough to afford her a sweeping view of the room. To her right, below, was the witness stand, an unassuming wooden chair behind more wood paneling and a microphone. A large round skylight directly over the inner circle of counsel table, judge's seat, and witness stand lent a degree of openness to the otherwise stuffy room.

When facing the witness stand, on one's left, straight ahead of the courtroom door, was the jury box. During Serena's trial, it would at first seem conspicuously empty, then, with time, grow all but invisible.

* * *

Camera crews fought for best position as Michael Moore, clad in casual slacks; a teal shirt and tie, and gray sweater, strode down the tiled hallway toward Margulies's courtroom. A small diamond earring was in his left ear. Sharri skittered behind, head bent, chin nearly touching the ivory lace on the V-neck of her flowered dress. Sunglasses and long hair hid her face. She hadn't been prepared for the volume of press, and was particularly upset at being pursued from the first floor of the courthouse up to the third. Hang in there, she told herself, it wouldn't last long. The trial should be over in a few days, a mere matter of putting forth the medical evidence. Then, finally, after a six-month nightmare, Serena could come home.

The Moores would never have guessed the fate that awaited them, although clues were present. First, the autopsy report. By this time, they were aware of Dr. Herrmann's opinion that Mallory had been sodomized. Antonio had been the first to tell them what the pathologist meant by a "dilated anus"; Detective Whiteley had never been specific. Sharri and Michael thought those findings unbelievable and pointed to the pathologist's statement, "no sign of fresh trauma." Anal dilation was supposed to indicate that Mallory had been abused just before her death, yet there was no "fresh trauma"?

A second clue lay in Golde's pretrial interview with Connie Chung. He had indicated obliquely that he would attack the family, and Chung had asked the Moores about it. Without knowing the particulars, Sharri and Michael had declined to comment, although Michael guessed it had something to do with Dr. Herrmann's opinion and Serena's past accusations of abuse against him. All that stuff was on record, he reminded Sharri; it wouldn't be surprising for "someone with a D.A. mentality" to link it all together.

Superseding in importance any inkling of Golde's intentions was the Moores' recently gained knowledge about the cause of Mallory's death. After so many months, for them the "why" question had finally been answered. The defense team's expert medical witness, Dr. Martha Warnock, had told them that Mallory had died from a sudden asthma attack. Asthma! Their relief at finally understanding "why" had been mixed with guilt and remorse. They had *known* Mallory suffered from asthma. If only they had watched her more closely; if only they had understood the illness better. The "if onlys" were endless.

Hustling away from the cameras and into the courtroom, the Moores claimed seats near the far end of the second row. The first row, they were told by a bailiff, was off-limits to all, being so close to the counsel table. Pastor Doug and his wife, Sheila, were there, as were Mary Corren, her sister, Esther, and Esther's boyfriend, Greg. Other friends surrounded them, giving reassuring hugs and pats. Lana Bridges, an ex-neighbor from Lucia Street, sat behind Michael. Lauren Fielding, one of Sharri's childhood friends from Tahoe, had come down to lend her support. Michael's parents sat behind Sharri, next to Lana. Sarah Moore had butterflies in her stomach at the thought of having to testify. She, Mary Corren, Pastor Doug, and Marietta Wilson, who had helped Sharri dodge cameras after Serena's hearing the past January, would soon be barred from the courtroom, pending their potential testimonies. This "witness exclusion" resulted from a typical prosecutorial motion designed to preclude one person's testimony from being swayed or colored by another's.

As family and friends clustered on the right, reporters grouped in seats nearer the door. Among them were Bob Salladay from the *Argus*, Sandra Gonzales from the *San Jose Mercury,* and Catherine Bowman from the *Chronicle.* Joan Lynch, a free-lance artist, was already opening her sketch pad and choosing from a large array of colored pencils. She sat on the second row's far left chair, from which she best could see the faces of the attorneys and defendant in a side-angled view.

Judge Margulies, an attractive woman with short black hair and smooth fair skin looking to be about forty, would soon announce that, because the defendant was a minor, she was not to be named in any form of media, either written or televised. Neither could Joan Lynch or any other artist draw her features in detail. Lynch would have to be satisfied in producing a vague outline of the "Diary Girl."

At ten o'clock, Serena, clad in a purple dress, was led into the courtroom. Sharri's eyes traveled up and down her daughter's figure. It was the first time in many months she'd seen Serena in anything but the baggy juvenile hall sweatshirt and pants. Because of a starchy diet and lack of exercise, Serena had gained weight in juvenile hall, growing from a size nine to fourteen. Her larger frame was now far more apparent in street clothes. Sharri had been forced to borrow numerous outfits from friends for Serena's court appearances.

In the six months since Serena's arrest, the Moores had never missed a scheduled visit with her. Sharri went on Monday and Wednesday afternoons while Michael worked. Saturdays, Michael could go. Most of the time, Sharri went with him, not willing to miss any possible moments with her daughter. The occasions when Michael went alone had been productive in building a foundation for a renewed stepfather/stepdaughter relationship.

Now, Serena took a chair between her attorneys, Belli on her left and Antonio on her right. Soon, she and Antonio would switch seats so that Antonio could be next to Belli in order to accommodate his difficulty with hearing.

As soon as Serena was seated, Court Officer Kathy Sturgeon introduced to Judge Margulies the two defense attorneys and Matt Golde. Antonio, her thick, long hair flowing down the back of a black suit, seemed nervous. Belli, also in black with a white shirt and plain white tie, sprawled easily in his chair. "Good morning, Your Honor," he boomed. Golde, clad in a light gray suit, perched forward in his chair, resting his elbows on the table as if ready to spring into action.

Margulies greeted them all and asked if they were ready to proceed, showing not the least sign of recognition or impression at the name Melvin Belli. She and the defense team then proceeded to get off on the wrong foot almost immediately.

First Antonio moved that *in limine* motions—made to exclude pieces of evidence questionable in their admissibility—be heard before another judge. "The reason for requesting a separate judge hear these matters," she stumbled, "is that the sensitive nature of the matters that we're asking to exclude would obviously be heard by you and you would be the trier of the fact, you would hear this evidence."

Antonio could state no legal authority on the matter. Golde had not yet seen the *in limine* motions to which she referred, so could not respond. They were faxed Friday, Antonio noted, when he was not in the office. Her statement only worsened the situation.

"You didn't serve him until Friday knowing the trial was on Monday?" Margulies asked.

Golde had agreed that would be okay, Antonio explained, since she and Belli had asked for a continuance and he hadn't been able to accommodate. In addition, the defense was not waiving any right to challenge the judge's hearing the case, pending her ruling on the *in limine* motions.

Margulies seemed taken aback. Defense had been informed of their case's assignment to Department 39, she reminded them. They'd had their chance to challenge. If the attorneys had wanted to exercise their one allowed challenge, they should have done so prior to the trial. Now, it was too late. In quick succession, she ruled that, absent any offered authority or precedent for excusing herself from *in limine* motions, she would preside over such arguments; secondly, because of "untimeliness," the motion to challenge her from the case also was denied.

Antonio then tried to exclude testimony, considered prejudicial, of Serena's behavior at Mallory's funeral and statements she made to an orthodontist while being fitted for braces. Motions again denied. The "probative value," or relative necessity, of the evidence, stated Margulies, "outweighs the prejudicial effect."

Two other important requests were touched on. Defense wanted the diary excluded, based upon the grounds that it was obtained without a search warrant. And Matt Golde argued against allowing a psychologist hired for the defendant to testify as to the actual truth of Serena's written confession. Rulings on these motions, Margulies declared, would be postponed until counsels were prepared to submit such evidence during their cases-in-chief—direct questioning of their own witnesses.

Unfortunately for Serena, the prosecution would triumph in both issues.

Belli was incensed at the rulings. He and Antonio hadn't known "how horrible" Margulies would be until they saw her in action. Now, just two hours into the trial, he was convinced they should have gotten rid of her.

Shuffling down the hallway at lunch break, he muttered a bleak prognostication to Antonio. "She's gonna screw us."

Antonio may have been disgruntled at Golde's refusal for one more continuance, but Serena, smiling at her parents as she was escorted out of the courtroom for the break, was thrilled. Finally, she'd be breaking out of that "juvey" hell-hole. The days since Christmas had been interminable. Housed in a cramped, dingy room in the county's under-funded juvenile hall, she'd counted in-house schooling as her biggest daily diversion. The remainder of time was spent mostly in her cell or occasionally watching television in a group lounge. The smallest infraction of stringent rules bought her extra room time. She blamed the facility's starchy food and lack of opportunity to exercise for her extra thirty pounds. Even more disgusting than her fatness was the long hair under her arms. Precautions for safety in juvenile hall abounded; the girls were not even allowed electric razors to shave.

In time, Serena had managed to fall into the inmate way of life even though a certain part of her could not quite grasp the dismal reality of her situation. Many nights she cried in bed alone, missing her parents, missing freedom, and, most of all, mourning Mallory. But during the day, and particularly during her parents' visits, she exuded an air of strength and acceptance of her fate. More of her "I'm-fine routine."

At certain hours, she could write letters; otherwise, items as simple as pencils were not allowed in the juveniles' possession. This, again, for reasons of safety. She wrote often to Mary Corren, working hard to sound upbeat and positive, and cherished the letters she received in return. Between the girls, boyfriends remained the favorite topic. Thoughts of boys and plans for the future helped Serena from "going crazy."

Margulies ran a rather languid courtroom. Mornings and afternoons could contain recesses as long as half an hour. Lunch breaks were typically from noon to two.

At lunch the first day of trial, Joan Lynch was busy taping various large sketches to the wall for filming by local television stations. She hoped the "Eye to Eye" producer, Judy Schaeffer, would use her drawings for Connie Chung's show.

CBS crew members were making pests of themselves, lowering their long-stemmed microphone over the heads of local reporters as they clustered to gab about the case. Another CBS journalist unabashedly thrust a microphone into a pay phone area while one of the reporters phoned his office to recount the morning's proceedings. The reporter let loose a few choice four-letter words and the journalist backed off.

After lunch, CBS hustled to catch Sharri and Michael's return to the third floor. As before, Michael walked purposefully down the hall, head up, seemingly unintimidated by the cameras. But try as they might, cameramen could not film one glimpse of Sharri's face.

No one would have guessed, watching Michael, that within a few hours he would be cowering under his gray sweater.

Twenty-two

IN 49 B.C., Julius Caesar and his army crossed the Rubicon, a small river flowing into northern Italy. This illegal entrance into the country was seen as Caesar's irrevocable decision to institute civil war for, once across the waters, there was no turning back.

While planning his case, Matt Golde had made a tactical decision regarding his war of prosecution. In *The Matter of Serena M.* his opening statement would be his Rubicon.

At Margulies's invitation to proceed, Golde pushed back his chair and rose behind the counsel table. He had a difficult fight ahead of him. He believed wholeheartedly that Serena Moore was guilty of murdering her little sister, and would not be waylaid from doing whatever was necessary to prosecute her to the fullest extent. Sometimes in his job, he would say, you had to be willing to "get people pissed at you."

His nervousness was apparent as he launched into the basic facts of the case—Mallory's death, the diary, Serena's arrest—but seemed to subside as he warmed to his topic. Then he turned to the pathologist's findings, which he called "extremely disturbing," and crossed his point of no return.

"What Dr. Herrmann found," he stated, "was that, number one, there's a homicide and Mallory Moore was a victim of traumatic asphyxia, in other words, she was smothered. But, what's more disturbing is what he found was a dilated anus. And from that, in his expertise, Dr. Herrmann concluded that Mallory Moore had been sexually molested at or near the time of death. And when I say 'at or near the time of death,' I mean, you know, within minutes.

"But that isn't all. Inside the anus, Dr. Herrmann found tears from stretching—long, old, healed wounds demonstrating a long-standing history of sexual abuse. It is quite clear that Mallory Moore, who died at four years old, had been a victim of sexual molestation. That is what the physical evidence shows. So with this information the police again talked to the family and essentially the investigation stopped."

Golde's voice dropped. "Serena Moore is a very troubled girl. She had reported that her stepfather, Michael Moore, had sexually molested her and suspected that he had molested Mallory as well.

"There is also evidence that on occasion Serena Moore tried to get her younger sister, Mallory, away from Michael by taking the family truck and driving to Tahoe, which is where her grandmother lived, with Mallory in the truck. When asked why she did that, Serena said to get Mallory away from Michael.

"In considering all the facts it's important to look into the family because this is an extremely dysfunctional family. Serena is a victim of serious emotional, physical, and sexual abuse, as was Mallory. And I ask when you listen to the facts that you consider the abuse of all kinds to understand why Serena would do this and why she would write about it. It's imperative that you consider the great degree of dysfunction in this house. That will explain why this minor is so damaged, why she killed Mallory, and why she confessed to her crime."

Serena sat motionless beside Antonio at the defense table as Golde resumed his seat. Somebody had hurt Mallory? *Nobody* had told her that, not her parents, not the cops, not even her attorney! She was sick to her stomach. Her hands began to fidget, an outward sign of her feeling upset.

Sharri turned to stare, openmouthed, at Michael. His eyes were closed, mouth wincing in humiliation and anger.

Passage of time in a courtroom is an elusive thing. Sometimes testimony drags on and on, while much-anticipated or key events can streak past, trailing their emotions behind as attorneys turn, poker-faced, to the next item. The Moores had little time to recover from Golde's scathing statements. He was already calling his first witness—Dr. Herrmann—for what would be the most difficult testimony they would hear.

The pathologist stepped to the witness stand and settled himself with a certain fluidity of motion. Standing about five feet eleven, Herrmann had close-cropped, curly gray hair, a Vandyke beard, and glasses. His face portrayed a stonelike quality that could only be characterized as humorless. Although he had testified in many trials, he had an air of impatience about it all, as if he were late for a more important appointment. Leaning forward in his seat, he rested his hands on the wooden podium before him, ignoring the pitcher of water and glass supplied for witnesses. Waiting for Golde to begin, he silently drummed his fingers.

Dr. Herrmann would be one of four expert witnesses to testify in *The Matter of Serena M.*—he, alone, for the prosecution and three for the defense. The first item of business in an expert witness's testimony is the procedure of *voir dire*—literally, truth-telling, in which both attorneys clarify the person's background, education, and experience in order to prove his or her expertise in a particular field. The attorney who has called the witness establishes the expert as someone highly impressive, whose statements are to be heeded, while the opposing attorney pokes holes in those seemingly impenetrable credentials in order to undermine opinions of the witness.

Before his *voir dire* of Dr. Herrmann, Golde began spreading out color autopsy photos for review before defense counsel while Antonio watched in silence, seemingly unthinking about the fact that they were in full view of her young client, seated next to her. Serena glanced down to find herself faced with multiple gruesome glimpses of Mallory cut open on the doctor's slab. A shock ran through her body. Her head went down instantly, both hands waving in an odd pantomime of panic. Sharri saw her shoulders heave.

"*God*," Sharri exclaimed to Michael, "he's *showing* them to her!" They were furious that Antonio had not insisted upon shielding the photos from Serena.

At Serena's reaction, Antonio scooped up the photos and turned to help her client. "Your Honor," she requested, "can we take a quick break and can I talk to the defendant?"

Margulies, distracted with turning on the witness's microphone for Dr. Herrmann, glanced up.

"Oh, I'm sorry. All right. Let's take a five-minute recess."

Serena, accompanied by Antonio and a bailiff, fled the room.

Sharri and Michael chose to wade through the press for a quick, anxious smoke on the balcony. Hurrying back through the courtroom door a few moments later, they were slowed to an ill-timed halt behind Belli's shuffling gait. A reporter saw his chance and thrust a microphone in Michael's face.

"Mr. Moore, are these charges true?"

"No."

"Did you abuse your daughters?"

"Of course not."

Belli turned, mouth flopping open in an unvoiced objection to the illicit interview.

"It didn't happen," pressed the reporter.

"Didn't happen."

Michael escaped through the courtroom door.

When court reconvened, with a calmed but pale Serena in attendance, Dr. Herrmann completed *voir dire*. Then, under the Deputy D.A.'s direct questioning, he discussed Mallory's autopsy, explaining in particular the "petechial hemorrhages" on Mallory's face

These hemorrhages, Dr. Herrmann stated, were breaks within small capillaries, causing patchy red areas to form on the skin. The kind of petechiae in this case were associated with the type of asphyxia that would inhibit blood flow from the head back into the chest. "The most common situation causing the hemorrhages in the face is strangulation," he continued in a clipped, confident tone. "Blood continues to get through the heart through the deeper lying arteries, but can't get back up. The little blood vessels, particularly on the eyelids, break and one sees petechial hemorrhages. Also, a form of asphyxia that causes this to happen is when a person is compressed, that is if the chest is compressed. And the classic example of that is a cave-in accident when people are working in a ditch and the dirt or sand or something caves in and compresses the person. Now his chest is compressed. The pressure is so high on the chest that blood continues to be pumped out by the heart but it can't get back in the chest. And if the head is protruding above the sand, it's the head to which the blood continues to be pumped, and it can't get out. So again, we have petechial hemorrhages. This also occurs if someone squeezes someone's chest for a period of time or is lying on top of a person compressing the chest and that will cause the petechiae such as we see in this case."

Margulies's head was bent as she took notes.

"What caused the petechial hemorrhages in this case?" Golde asked.

"I think that these petechiae were caused by traumatic asphyxia, and by that I mean something has compressed this little girl's chest. The exact mechanism for it I am unable to determine." There were no signs of strangulation, he added; neck organs were normal and no ligatures were visible.

"You mentioned a compressing of the chest. Did you check for that possibility?"

Yes, and he had found no telltale marks on the body. "But," he noted, "that possibility can certainly exist without leaving any evidence for it except for the petechial hemorrhages."

Michael frowned. A person could kill someone by compressing the chest *without* leaving traces of damage?

"Is it your testimony that in this case it's compression of the chest that is responsible for the petechial hemorrhages?"

"I believe that is the mechanism that occurred here," Herrmann replied, drumming his fingers. "There are other things that could possibly produce this as well. If someone were to place a pillow or something of that sort over the face and then, I think, if there were a great deal of struggling on the part of the victim, then that could increase the pressure on the chest perhaps high enough to produce these petechial hemorrhages. But I think that's a less likely mechanism than compression of the chest. Of course, there's also a possibility that several things could be happening at the same time to produce asphyxia."

Golde picked up the autopsy photos. Sharri cringed. As if Dr. Herrmann's testimony wasn't bad enough, she found his manner detached and cold; every opinion seemed as unwavering as it was insensitive. His voice sounded "hissy" to her, like that of Gollum in *The Hobbit*. Thoughts of his handling her daughter like some piece of meat rolled over her nauseatingly.

Golde was proceeding through the alphabet, holding up one picture at a time for identification.

At the defense table, Serena bowed her head and began to cry. Sharri felt herself go numb.

"I have three additional photographs," Golde noted. "Showing you 1R. Can you describe what's shown there?"

Dr. Herrmann studied the glossy. To spectators, this would be the worst; to him, it seemed merely another speciman. "This is a picture of the genitalia and her anus after I had removed them from her body. The skin surface is still intact."

At that moment, Golde turned and looked at Sharri. Later, he would not remember his action, or why he did so. Perhaps it was merely to check on how the family was holding up. Whatever the reason, for Sharri, his glance was the final blow. He was purposely trying to nail her, she thought.

"I can't *take* this," she gasped, jumping out of her chair. She was sobbing before she reached the courtroom door. In the hallway, she scooted awkwardly along the wall toward a woman's rest room, shielding her face from cameras vying for an unexpected emotion-filled shot. Lauren Fielding, her friend from Tahoe, followed.

Determined to hear the testimony, Michael remained transfixed in his seat, staring at Dr. Herrmann as if stabbing him with daggers. Michael's presence alone was intended to be a challenge. As Dr. Herrmann continued his matter-of-fact explanations, Michael saw the pathologist's confidence as giving way to haughtiness, his exactness to cold calculation.

Dr. Herrmann proceeded. "When I first looked at it simply from the outside the anus appeared to be dilated by about three-eighths of an inch. When I started to remove the anus from the body I reexamined it and felt that it was slightly larger than that, approximately a half inch in diameter, not including the tears.''

"Can you say when in relation to death it was dilated?''

"Well, I think evidence is that it was dilated at or around the time of death. It's possible that it could have been dilated slightly before the time of death, maybe up to a half hour or so. I think if it had been dilated much before that, it probably would have constricted again and not been dilated. But, you know, possibly it could have been dilated a slightly longer time than that.''

"How does the body dilate or undilate itself and how does death affect that process?''

"The anus is held closed by muscle which rings the anal opening so it's not dilated. It dilates, of course, when one has a bowel movement to allow the passage of stool and it can be dilated from the outside when something is placed inside of it or pushed inside of it.'' Normally, he continued, the anus undilates in a short period of time, but after death the muscle loses its viability. "It's possible that it may actually dilate, or it may actually constrict slightly after death. As the body goes in postmortem rigidity, sometimes that muscle also is subject to rigidity and it might actually contract. But, very often, if the anus is dilated at or around the time of death, it's simply going to stay that way.''

Expressions on the faces of spectators were grim. Reporters were furiously taking notes. As if the case were not already sensational enough, Dr. Herrmann and Golde's accusations of sexual abuse were about to send it into the ozone.

Mallory Moore also had tears in the anus, Dr. Herrmann went on—star-shaped lacerations extending forward, backward, and to each side. They had healed in the form of scar tissue. These tears were "caused by something having been placed into the anus from the outside, and whatever was placed in there was so large that it dilated the anus to the point that the skin around the anus tore.'' The tears could have been caused by one incident or many. Because they were completely healed, the doctor concluded they could be anywhere from one year—maybe even longer—to one month old. Constipation could not have caused them.

Considering the possibility of sexual assault, Dr. Herrmann noted, he had looked for the presence of semen in the anus, vagina, and mouth, but found none. He also had examined the dried, slightly blood-tinged fluid on the right side of Mallory's face for the presence of semen, and had found none. There were no signs of lubricant in the anus, and the vaginal area was normal.

"Now, you indicated that upon removal, you determined that the diameter of the anal opening was about a half inch, is that correct?"

It was critical for Golde to bolster the issue of sexual abuse in the Moore family, for those accusations were the foundation upon which his motive for the crime rested. Not that he was obligated to prove motive; that was one burden the prosecution did not bear. No one could crawl into the mind of the defendant and know "beyond reasonable doubt" the twisted reasoning he or she employed in committing a crime. Nonetheless, Golde apparently had determined that offering a motive was important. Excepting Mia Black's claim that Serena was jealous of Mallory (and she would not be testifying), other friends and family members had insisted that the two girls loved each other dearly, which begged for an answer to the question—*why?* Golde intended to provide one.

"Yes, that's correct."

"And is that something that could have been caused by a penis?"

Michael's face felt hot. Flexing his jaw, he continued to stare at the pathologist.

"Well, I don't believe that it would be the result of a penis at or around the time of death. I think if a penis had been in there at the time this little girl died, that that opening would be larger than that. I can't, however, rule out the possibility that there could have been dilatation of the anus by a penis at a time somewhat earlier than that so that the anus could have been dilated even more, say a half hour or so before death, and then during the interval while the child's still alive, the anus began to recontract."

"How about a finger?"

Yes, that was possible.

Golde changed the subject. Reviewing photos of food in Mallory Moore's stomach, what could the pathologist say regarding time of death based upon stomach content?

Herrmann was vague in his answer, but just as firm regarding the reasons for his vagueness. Ordinarily, he wouldn't expect as much food to be present as he had found in Mallory Moore. But certain factors, such as severe emotional distress, could slow down the stomach considerably.

Golde was through with direct questioning. By the time Antonio began cross-examination, Sharri had regained her composure enough to sidle into the courtroom foyer. Peering through the small window, she checked on Michael and saw Lana Bridges sitting forward in her seat behind him, hands soothingly on his shoulders.

Sharri could not bring herself to reenter the courtroom as long as Dr. Herrmann was on the stand.

Michael expected easier treatment by his daughter's attorneys, but soon felt he was mistaken. If sexual abuse could lay a foundation for Golde's purported motive, it would also become an underlying part of Antonio's defense.

Belli's and Antonio's decision to "use" the sexual abuse accusations was the culmination of their own journey as they prepared their case. Initially, Antonio had not believed the stories of sexual abuse. Serena had told Antonio her past reports of Michael's molestation were untrue. In addition, the defense's expert pathologist, Dr. Martha Warnock, thought Mallory's anal dilation was "within normal limits" and could not detect from slides the "abrasions" that Dr. Herrmann had found. Antonio, working closely with Michael and Sharri in gathering documents and witnesses for the trial, thought the issue "unsavory" and had been happy to believe that no abuse had occurred. Then, the attorney had received what she termed a "wake-up call." Dr. Herrmann showed her tissue slides of Mallory's anus, and argued that *he* was right— molestation had occurred.

Antonio found the opinionated doctor "very convincing." With that evidence in mind, she began to think that perhaps Serena's earlier stories of molestation had not been fabricated and that Mallory could have been abused as well. Ultimately, Antonio believed Dr. Herrmann over her own medical expert and client, rationalizing that Serena had an interest in denying the abuse, despite the fact that whatever tarnish Serena may have felt as a result of abuse should pale in comparison to the stain of being charged with homicide. At any rate, as a "last-minute twist," the defense, in Antonio's words, "decided to go ahead and go along that this was a dysfunctional family.'' Also, she reasoned, dysfunction could shed light on why Serena would write a fake confession. The judge may view the diary entry as a cry of desperation from a ''nutty'' girl trapped in a troubled family.

There was another reason for ''using'' the sexual abuse. Antonio's defense rested on Dr. Warnock's conclusion that Mallory Moore died of a sudden asthma attack, and traumatic situations—such as molestation—could trigger such an episode. This was the final ingredient in the defense's tactics, never mind that Antonio was mixing the opposing opinions of two medical experts, Doctors Warnock and Herrmann, to create the formula. Dr. Warnock had concluded death by asthma; Dr. Herrmann insisted on the molestation.

Let's go ahead, Belli and Antonio agreed, and let Golde make his sexual abuse case. They wouldn't challenge him on it.

Antonio stood and took a deep breath. ''Dr. Herrmann, you stated that the petechial hemorrhages could have been caused by compression to the chest. Could it also have been caused by pressure to the back?''

Yes, Herrmann agreed, as long as it restricted blood flow.

''So this could—the petechial hemorrhages and asphyxiation could have been caused by someone lying on the child, on Mallory at the time of death compressing her back or her chest?''

Yes again.

''So couldn't it—isn't it true it could have been caused, the asphyxiation could have been caused by an adult lying on Mallory's back or stomach?''

''Yes.''

''Now, the tears to the anus that you saw, does that indicate a repeated and regular violation by an adult penis?''

''Oh, I have no idea whether an adult penis caused this in the first place. As to whether they were repeated, I can't say that either.''

Antonio pursued her course. ''Isn't it possible that the penis in the anus stretched the anal opening and caused the healed tears that you found?''

''Well, a penis could be a responsible object to cause these, yes.''

"Doctor, you've seen evidence of child abuse in other autopsies that you performed, haven't you?"

"Yes."

"And is this something typical of sodomy, evidence of sodomy that you have seen in other autopsies?"

"Well, actually, sodomy with resultant death of a child of this age is in our experience very rare, that is in the coroner's office. But, sure, this would be an expected result from sodomy at some time previous to the death in this case because there's healing of these lacerations."

"And it's your opinion that at or near the time of death something in the anus caused the dilation. Isn't it true that it could have been a male organ?"

Herrmann wouldn't budge. "At or around the time of death, I think that's not at all suggested. The amount of dilatation here is, I think, too small relative to the size of an adult penis."

Michael's jaw began to hurt. He realized he was gritting his teeth.

"And you're basing that on the size of the dilation at the time of death?"

"Yes."

"And you have no opinion as to the size of the male organ that could have been in there?"

"No."

"So it could have been a small penis that caused a smaller dilation, isn't that true?"

Herrmann inclined his head slightly. "Well, I think it would have to be a very small penis and I think we're talking about something about the size of one's finger, but I suppose that could be a penis that size."

"And isn't it true, though, the penetration could have been—could have occurred up to a half hour prior to the death by a male penis?"

"I think it's a possibility that a penis could have been in her anus perhaps an hour before, and that would allow time for the anus then to begin to retract. And that at the time of death, if she were killed following that by, say, a half hour, perhaps the anus would have been dilated by a half inch. I suppose that's a possibility."

Antonio seemed satisfied. She veered to another subject,

then returned, asking if Sharri Moore could have cleaned sperm away from Mallory's face when she wiped it. I suppose, answered Herrmann, but he had taken swabs inside Mallory's mouth and had not found any evidence of sperm.

Margulies interrupted for a much-needed recess.

Michael rose dazedly, pulling off his gray sweater. He passed Sharri in the foyer, unspeaking, pushed through the door and made for the outside balcony. He just wanted to hide, to wrap himself in a blanket and he left alone. How absurd, he protested inwardly, that those old accusations were coming back to haunt him again now. It was the ultimate slap in the face for all he'd endured over the years with Serena. At once beset by the hallway cameras, he flung his sweater up to hide his face—the stance a far cry from his confident entrance just a few hours before. Sharri, hands shaking as she shielded herself from the media, scurried after him.

Out on the balcony, Michael recounted to Sharri the gist of Herrmann's testimony. "Let me get this straight," he breathed, staring at the concrete beneath his feet, a cigarette dangling unsmoked between his fingers. "You have an earache and you can't sleep. I get up in the night out of a sound sleep, go sodomize my own daughter, come back to bed, and fall back asleep like nothing ever happened. A half hour later, Serena gets up, and, like her diary says, goes into Mallory's room, takes Mallory to her room, smothers her, then takes Mallory back to her own room and puts her in bed." He raised his chin, eyes meeting Sharri's. "And you don't hear *anything.*"

"Oh, yes," she hissed, "they think I heard something, all right. I'm *protecting* you, don't you *get* it? And I'm protecting Serena." She dissolved into tears.

Too wrapped up in the implications against himself, Michael could not find the energy to share his wife's pain. He turned away.

As they huddled on the balcony, inside the press had regrouped and surrounded Belli, throwing out questions about the alleged abuse. Serena's family was a "tortured household," Belli told reporters, likening its environment to a home in Charles Dickens's dark tale *Bleak House*. "You've got to look at it through the eyes of a child who was being pestered and beleaguered by her mother.''

Forcing himself to view the matter objectively that evening, Michael tried to understand the defense's tactics. It made a certain amount of sense, he told Sharri, if Antonio and Belli were bringing into question *who* killed Mallory as a means of deflecting suspicion away from Serena. Sharri, on the other hand, could not forgive the Belli firm. The Moores found themselves facing a traumatic catch-22—whether to deny the despicable allegations or keep quiet and hope that it would help Serena. Viewed that way, the choice left little room for discussion; they had to save their daughter. Upset as he was at the revival of sexual abuse allegations, Michael at the same time knew it wasn't Serena's fault. He had grown closer than he'd ever been to Serena in the past six months. After all the family had been through, he could not desert her now. Besides, he told himself, sometime during the trial Antonio would "make everything all right" with the truth.

Later that evening, while Sharri was curled up on the couch with the Moores' cats, Misty and Madison, Serena called from juvenile hall, her voice quivering. "What happened to Mallory's bottom?" she cried. "Shelley said Michael did it," Serena told her mother; he was molesting Mallory. "I have to know what happened to her!"

After assuring her daughter that nothing had happened— Dr. Herrmann was *wrong*—Sharri angrily dialed Antonio's home. "Don't *tell* Serena those things," she pleaded with the attorney, "no matter what you may believe or what you have to prove. You're *upsetting* her; she's got enough to face right now."

Antonio denied she had said anything of the sort and was not happy with what she deemed an interfering circle of communication. Serena was obviously being influenced by her mother, the attorney felt, particularly regarding the sexual allegations. The next day, Antonio told the Moores they were not to visit or call Serena during the remainder of the trial. The Moores complied, but as the trial progressed and the allegations of sexual abuse grew, they would become increasingly angry at Antonio's action.

Had the Moores pushed the issue, they would have found

that Antonio could not force juvenile hall to block visits or phone calls between a parent and child. But they did not. Once again, their inherent trust in the Belli firm and the "System" overcame their niggling intuitions of doubt.

Twenty-three

ANDREW WONG, DDS, appeared ill at ease as he took the stand Tuesday morning. The Moores, shaken and exhausted after a poor night's sleep, thought the Deputy D.A.'s tactics in calling the young orthodontist far-reaching at best.

While in his waiting room, Dr. Wong testified, Serena and Mallory had been fighting over a toy. In the course of the argument, Serena angrily shook her sister and later commented to the doctor, "I'm going to kill her." On subsequent visits, she repeated the words.

Antonio, upset that the court had overruled her motion to disallow Dr. Wong's testimony, objected often to Golde's questions. Belli made a few of his own.

"I assume," posed the judge, "that one counsel is going to be making the objections, is that correct?"

"I am getting my hearing aid this afternoon," Belli replied. "I will participate with Her Honor's permission."

Margulies remained firm—only one counsel for the defense should speak, and apparently that was Antonio.

In cross-examination by Antonio, Wong, looking relieved, agreed that Serena's statements and "angry" behavior had been made in the context of Mallory's "acting rambunctious and running around the office causing disruption." During redirect, Golde sought to undermine Antonio's "context" for behavior. What type of toy could a fourteen-year-old and a three-year-old possibly fight over?

Golde was breaking a cardinal rule in courtroom tactics—never ask a question unless you know the answer.

"We have this 'Where's Waldo' stick," explained the doctor. "You have to find Waldo inside a stick filled with fluid which is mixed in with other specks of color."

Golde's expression went blank. "At the risk of demonstrating my ignorance," he plunged ahead, "is this a toy designed for fourteen-year-olds?"

"It's a toy that's enjoyed by any age," Wong answered.

"Oh, okay. I have no other questions."

After the previous day's grisly testimony, the short exchange offered a moment of refreshing comic relief. Golde had good-naturedly conceded his "ignorance," but to Sharri and Michael, an underlying point was better taken. The Deputy D.A. was a quintessential yuppie, thirty-five and unmarried, with a boyish face and light brown hair hanging below his collar. What could he possibly know about raising a child, loving a child, *grieving* over the loss of a child? It was *that* ignorance, the Moores felt, not his lack of knowledge about some toy, that was important, for it allowed him to fling his caustic accusations against them without one hint of empathy for their pain.

Golde next called Michael Sanchez and Russell Peterson, from the Fremont Fire Department, to testify about their responses to the 911 call regarding Mallory on August 18, 1992. In describing events, Sanchez characterized Serena as "detached" when she entered the house that morning, and Michael's demeanor as "detached" with an "angry look" on his face. "That's when I kind of made up my mind that maybe we should probably be picking up and getting out of here because the situation didn't look like it was going to be real friendly."

In her second row seat, Sharri snorted. If anybody hadn't been friendly, it had been her. She was the one who'd smacked the kid Peterson in the chest. And she highly resented Sanchez's subsequent statements that *he* had "suggested" moving Mallory from the hall to her bed.

"*I* asked them to do that!" she protested to Pastor Doug during a recess. "I *begged* them because I didn't want Michael having to step over Mal's body like Serena did!"

Doug had not heard Sanchez's testimony, having been barred from the courtroom because he was a potential witness. (Sharri and Michael, as parents of the defendant, had been exempted from the witness exclusion ruling.) Doug had promised to support Serena with his daily presence during the trial, and so remained holed up, away from reporters, in the small witness waiting room tucked behind the courtroom foyer. He was troubled by what he had heard of the proceedings. Regular visits with Serena in juvenile hall had only strengthened his belief that she could not have committed this crime. Further, the accusations of sexual abuse did not fit with his perception of the Moore household. He had counseled with Serena on many occasions, both before and after her arrest. Assured of the confidentiality required of a pastor, she had entrusted him with intimate glimpses into her life. Yet never once had she mentioned being molested.

Shelley Antonio would soon release Doug from her witness list, saying that he wasn't needed. He was glad, then, to sit with the Moores inside the courtroom and hear testimony for himself. But his failure to take the stand would have repercussions. He, and Fremont Police Officer John Morillas, also not called to the stand, could have explained why the Moores, if they in truth thought their daughter innocent, would turn over her diary to police—an issue that Sharri would only be allowed to touch on during her testimony.

Sharri, under subpoena, fearfully took the stand Tuesday morning and did not finish her testimony until Wednesday afternoon. Under Golde's careful questioning, she spoke of Serena's disappointment about the absence of her biological father and the "stormy" relationship between Serena and Michael that occasionally resulted in physical confrontations. Her answers were deliberate, her emotions controlled—until she recounted the events surrounding Mallory's death.

On the afternoon of August 17, she had gone to the doctor with an earache, leaving Mallory with Serena. The doctor could not discover the cause of her symptoms. After she returned home, Michael arrived from work. He and Mallory sat on the back patio, playing "zoo" with Lego toys and little animals. Dinner was on a make-your-own basis that night. Mallory chose Cup O' Noodles and, later, ate an apple. The family watched an old Elvis Presley movie, which Serena found "stupid." She retreated to her room. After the movie ended, sometime between ten and ten-thirty, Sharri told Mallory it was time for bed. Mallory asked to sleep with her sister; both mom and dad said no, she was becoming too used to sleeping with Serena. Big girls slept in their own rooms. As Michael went to bed, Sharri tucked Mallory in her bed with the blue railing.

Mallory had taken asthma medication two nights before. The doctor had prescribed it to be given whenever Mallory was having a difficult time breathing—noticeable only by her "abdomen retracting in and out."

She didn't cough or wheeze or say "it hurts"? Golde asked.

No, answered Sharri, never any noise; the attacks would come without warning. Maybe it was her fault, she added, a sudden catch in her voice, that she hadn't known more about Mallory's symptoms.

Guilt settled warmly on her shoulders like an old, familiar blanket. She broke into tears.

Golde would not let the matter rest. "So the doctor just gave you this medicine and said, when it happens give it to her?"

"When she has—"

"Excuse me. She didn't tell you how to look for things and you didn't ask?"

"Well," Sharri's chin quivered, "I knew. I mean, I *knew*."

Antonio objected. "Argumentative."

The judge sustained. "Mrs. Moore," Margulies asked, "do you want to take a recess at this moment?"

Sharri shook her head. "I am all right. As long as I am not bothering anybody else. I'll be okay."

Golde switched the subject back to the night of August 17. With Michael, Mallory, and Serena all in bed, Sharri began to watch another movie at 11:00 P.M. Her ear was painful; she knew she would not yet be able to sleep. After about twenty minutes, Serena came out of her room to get a drink of water, passing her sister's open bedroom door. Mallory's whining, she told Sharri, you should check on her. Sharri couldn't hear Mallory's complaints, but did hear her turning the pages of a large picture book. I'll wait and see, Sharri responded, she probably just wants to get out of bed. Serena went back into her room and closed the door.

At midnight, Sharri gave up on the movie. Before entering

the master bedroom, she checked on Mallory. The little girl was asleep under her covers, the picture book lying next to her on the pillow. Afraid that its edge might hurt Mallory's face, Sharri picked up the book and placed it on top of the dresser.

"Did you say anything to her?" Golde asked.

"She was asleep."

"Was she breathing?"

"Yes."

"Are you sure?"

"Yes."

"How do you know?"

Sharri raked a glance across his face. He hadn't a clue, she thought. "Because this is something that all mothers do. You *stand* there and you watch them and you want to see your kid *breathe* before you leave the room. It's just a mom thing."

She kissed Mallory's cheek. It was warm.

Once in bed, Sharri dozed fitfully, her sleep inhibited by the earache. She watched the clock turn one, two-thirty, three. She heard no noise then, until between five and six, when Michael arose and showered.

Sharri faltered. She had begun to regain her composure, but now, faced with the recounting of finding Mallory, she began to sob. At the defense table, Serena was crying.

"Let's take our time here," Margulies said gently.

"As I stepped into the doorway," Sharri said, hiccupping, "I saw her laying on her side. She had one leg on top of the covers, kind of bent at the knee, and I looked at the side of her face and it didn't look right. It—oh." Sharri's hand flew to her lips. "I go, oh, God. I mean, umm—there was like some foam bubbles."

"You're pointing to your lip," Golde noted.

"Coming out of the side of her mouth. The side was, that was lying on the bed, the cheek that was lying on the bed."

Margulies leaned forward. "You are pointing to your right side."

"Yes, ma'am. Her right cheek. And there was a big purple blotch on the top of her ankle. And, and I just knew. I touched her leg and it was *ice-cold*."

The judge allowed Sharri a moment.

Golde pursued another avenue. Hadn't Sharri gotten rid of Serena's mattress by August 20, when police visited her home and asked to see it?

No, she replied. Serena's grandmother was visiting then, and she slept in Serena's bed all that week. Serena got a new mattress a month or two later, when they moved from Lucia Street to their rented condo. Serena had slept with Mallory too many times on that bed, explained Sharri, and couldn't bear the memories.

But, Golde wondered, didn't you tell police on August 20 that the mattress was already gone?

Sharri's anger at what she felt were deliberate misstatements dried her tears. She turned to the judge. "I think perhaps Mr. Golde has his dates incorrect, but that was after we had already moved. After Serena had been arrested, the detectives came *that* night and asked for Serena's mattress. Yes, it was gone then."

Despite her stirred-up sorrow, that late-afternoon interchange nipped at Sharri all evening, like a worrisome puppy. Matt Golde didn't seem to miss much, she commented to Michael; he certainly wasn't dense enough to mix facts in evidence. He knew *perfectly well* the police hadn't asked about Serena's bed until she was arrested, *four months* after Mallory's death, Sharri fumed. He was just trying to make it sound like they were covering up for Serena by getting rid of that mattress as soon as Mallory died.

First Monday with Golde's opening statement and Dr. Herrmann's testimony, now *this* horrible day. Sharri wondered aloud how she could face another.

Belli, dressed nattily in another dark suit with white shirt and tie, emerged distractedly from the elevator beside Antonio Wednesday morning, right hand fumbling with something behind his ear. It would be the first day in court with his new hearing aids, and they seemed to be bothering him already. He shuffled down the hall, mumbling "goodmornings" to reporters, still fiddling.

Two minutes into court's first session, a piercing screech emitted from the defense table.

"Excuse me," Margulies interrupted Sharri, back on the stand. "What am I hearing?"

"Mr. Belli's hearing aid," Antonio replied.

"Oh, okay."

"They're whistling a bit."

Belli's fingers furiously twiddled the earpiece. The screech stopped abruptly. "There!"

"Are you hearing me better today?" Margulies queried.

Belli's lips spread slowly into a smile. "A little bit. But I don't know, Judge. It's just awful—I was going to say getting old; I was going to say getting hard of hearing. One, I don't mind."

Margulies volleyed. "Which one?"

Belli waved a hand in the air. "I'm not ready to answer that yet."

The defense lost a key ruling that morning with the court's denying a motion to exclude Serena's diary from being entered into evidence. Antonio argued her point based on Fourth Amendment grounds against illegal search and seizure and Fifth Amendment rights against self-incrimination. The judge disagreed. Regarding the former, she stated, the Moores had voluntarily turned the diary over to police. And Fifth Amendment issues were not "relevant at all to the situation."

For the record, Belli threw in numerous other grounds for exclusion—lack of foundation, prejudicial, and hearsay—then quipped that he was through, unless Her Honor could "think of something."

"No," Margulies replied, "I think you've covered it all."

Further objections notwithstanding, the motion remained denied; Serena's diary would be placed into evidence. Margulies's ruling was not unexpected. Without the diary, the prosecution would have had no case, since it was Golde's only piece of hard evidence against the defendant.

At least, Sharri thought, the argument had afforded her a few moment's relief from Golde's haranguing questions.

Golde read the diary entry aloud. He asked Sharri about its being given to police, allowing her to explain briefly that she and Michael had first called their pastor. Then he turned to the issue of Serena's sexual abuse. Sharri immediately was on guard, but optimistic that under Antonio's cross-examination, she would be given the chance to explain away the Deputy D.A's allegations. Neither she nor Michael yet realized the extent to which *both* counsels had decided to "use" the alleged abuse and dysfunction within their family.

Golde focused on a particular incident. Was she not aware that Serena had driven her sister away in the family truck, later telling police she wanted to "get Mallory away from Michael"?

"Yes," admitted Sharri, "I'm aware. I know exactly why she went, and I corroborated it with the other person that made the plan with her for her to go."

Antonio objected, calling the answer nonresponsive. Margulies sustained. The reference as to why Serena drove toward her grandmother's was stricken from the record.

Golde quizzed Sharri about Serena's note to a girlfriend, claiming that Michael was molesting her, and reports of the same to her grandmother Tessie. And hadn't Sharri told her mother that Michael would go into Serena's room around 3:00 A.M., spending several hours there before going to work?

"I absolutely did not tell my mother that," Sharri said vehemently. "I do not know where she got that, and I told her at the time, 'Why are you saying that? I absolutely never said that to you!'"

"Well, did you admit to your mother that he did it and that you thought it was good because the stepfather and the daughter were getting close?"

Sharri grimaced. Here it was again, another public courtroom argument with her mother. Tessie had visited the Moores once, before filing her grandparent's visitation suit, and it had been a disaster. "Absolutely not. I told her that what he did was stop in and talk to her for a few minutes in the morning and sit on the edge of the bed and visit with the door open, with me up. And I assured her, I said, nothing weird is going on. He's not in there all hours of the night. It was during the conversation when I confronted her and told her, you know, I never said that to you, and I corrected her. I would not think that was normal. I would not have said, oh, it's good for them. He was not doing that."

"Are you aware that your mother says that you admitted that it was happening?"

"I don't care *what* my mother says, sir! That is not true." Sharri glared at Golde, willing herself not to look away.

Sandra Gonzales, from the *San Jose Mercury,* noted

Sharri's hostility. Her article the following day would twice mention Sharri's "angrily defending" her husband.

What about when your mother visited the Bay Area, Golde continued, didn't she witness Serena's and Michael's staying in his bedroom together?

"Serena went in and sat on the edge of the bed and talked to him. Everybody was up. There was nothing inappropriate." Sharri forced her voice to remain calm. "My mother is quite obsessive about Serena and wanted her with her every second of every visit. She has related before that she felt she was the other parent, and I think there was a little bit of jealousy of Michael there with her. She really expressed that that morning. 'While I'm here, Serena should be here with me, not visiting someone else.' Those were her exact words."

Golde changed the subject to a cursory coverage of Sharri's work history during her marriage to Michael, then turned her over to the defense. Antonio rose quickly. Inwardly, Sharri let out a sigh of relief.

"You never believed that Serena was molested by Michael, because she had this history of making up stories?"

"Exactly."

"And that's also why you didn't believe the diary entry either, isn't that correct?"

"Exactly. The police have proof in their files of many false reports and claims about this and that and that and something else. It goes way back."

Golde objected. "There's no foundation for that."

Margulies sustained and struck the last two sentences from the record.

"So when you read the diary entry," Antonio tried again, "you didn't believe it, because you knew she had written other fantasies in her diary and had told other tall tales?"

"Same objection, Your Honor—there's no foundation, and speculation."

Margulies glanced at the ceiling, as if looking for an answer. "Well, it's sustained. The ultimate opinion of the witness is irrelevant."

"Your Honor, I think it goes to Serena's—Serena's state of mind as it was observed as her—based on observations by her own mother," Antonio argued.

Margulies pressed her lips together. "Sustained."

A hurriedly whispered conference between Belli and Antonio ensued.

"Sharri," Antonio continued, "didn't Serena tell lots of tall tales?"

"Yes."

"Same objection, Your Honor," Golde intoned. "I think there's no foundation for that question and answer."

Another upward glimpse. "Overruled. I think the foundation got laid in your direct examination, Mr. Golde, and there was a lot of testimony in direct examination where this exact testimony came out, so you actually opened it up."

"Okay."

"And Miss Antonio, I take back sustaining the objection to your question about whether Ms. Moore believed or didn't believe what was in the diary, because that was also opened up in Mr. Golde's direct examination, and it came out in direct exam. So I'm reversing my ruling on that. Go ahead."

Antonio blinked. "So let me ask you again that question—"

"Maybe I can just short-circuit this," Margulies interrupted, turning to Sharri. "You indicated previously that you never believed that Serena was molested by Michael or the diary entry because?"

"Because she had made up so many stories, just as big, for so long that—it was kind of a given. When she's real upset or she's under stress, she just makes up stories."

Margulies made a note. "All right," she indicated, still writing. "Go ahead."

Antonio leaned over to whisper again with Belli, then straightened. "Have you read Serena's diary?"

Sharri hesitated. Besides the Confession Diary, there were the other journals that she had turned over to police the night of Serena's arrest. "The one that was brought into evidence?"

"No. Any of her diaries."

"Yes."

"And in those diaries, in those entries in the diary, isn't it true that there are stories and fantasies?"

"Yes."

"That are not accurate?"

"Yes. Things I know not to be true."

Golde objected. The answer was stricken.

Antonio, looking frustrated, turned to Mallory's medical history, asking Sharri about the night she took Mallory to the hospital.

"Well, I let her fall asleep on the couch watching TV, and I looked at her and her abdomen was pumping in and out real hard. I just started watching her at that point, and she would wake up a little bit like she was a little uncomfortable, but she'd fall back asleep. And it went on, and I called the hospital twice, and they said, 'Do you hear any wheezing?' And I said, 'No, but her stomach is going in and out. I know something is wrong.' So finally we just took her anyway."

No wheezing noises or general signs of an asthma attack? prompted Antonio.

"No noise at all."

"So it was just the stomach pumping in and out rapidly."

"Yes."

"Did anyone ever tell you that that was a sign of her having an asthma attack?"

"No."

"And when you took her to the hospital, did the doctor then confirm, yeah, that's what was happening?"

"Oh, yes."

Antonio inquired about Mallory's "blue spells," then led Sharri at length over her earlier testimony, focusing on particular events such as the position of Mallory's body and the argument between Serena and Mallory in Dr. Wong's office. Sharri felt her energy draining away with each tick of the large clock on the courtroom's side wall. Fortunately, midday recess was imminent. When Judge Margulies finally interrupted for the break, she closed her eyes in surging relief.

It would not last long. By that afternoon, when she resumed her testimony, Sharri would be tingling with nervous energy. Her heightened fear would be due to another grim surprise during lunch recess—the unexpected appearance of two of the last people she wanted to see.

Twenty-four

Are you down here to spread more lies about my son?

—SARAH MOORE TO TESSIE DORNELLAS

MICHAEL HAD SCHEDULED a meeting with Antonio during Wednesday's lunch break, planning to protest the accusations uttered both inside and outside of court. The meeting was not to be. As he, Sharri, and Marietta Wilson were wolfing down hot dogs from a sidewalk vendor near the courthouse steps, he spied Sharri's sister, Roxanne.

"Oh, God."

"Hi!" Roxanne cried merrily, running over to give Sharri a hug.

Despite Roxanne's display of affection, Sharri's bite stuck in her throat. If Roxanne were there, her mother couldn't be far behind. She would not believe they were attending the trial only to support Serena. Something's up, she whispered to Marietta, and it couldn't be good.

In the third floor hallway, the bees were already buzzing. Expecting to speak with Antonio after their hurried lunch, Sharri and Michael instead found themselves eyeing the attorney from a distance as she, Golde, and Sharri's mother, Tessie, engaged in deep discussion. The Moores were too distracted to hear Roxanne's comment to Marietta, but heard about it later from their friend.

"She pointed out Sharri's flowered dress and hairband," Marietta told them, "and goes, 'Who does she think she is, Alice in Wonderland?' "

Out of earshot, the attorneys and Tessie continued their conversation. Since Tessie was in town only for the day, Antonio was explaining to Golde, she had to take the stand that afternoon. Which counsel should call her to testify? Although Golde may have appeared nonchalant, silently he was

172

thrilled. In the past weeks, he'd tried to persuade Tessie to testify, but she was adamantly against it, saying she didn't want to speak about the "abuse she witnessed" in front of Michael and Sharri. He had not subpoenaed her.

Antonio suggested that she interrupt Golde's case, putting Tessie on the stand as a defense witness. Golde agreed. The revised lineup, then, would include the completion of Sharri's testimony, scheduled prosecution witness Delores Braden, followed by Tessie Dornellas. Once in court, however, Antonio punted at the last moment, informing the judge and a surprised Golde that the prosecution was calling Tessie. After a hurried conference, Golde acquiesced, thinking it "no big deal," even though he viewed the move as a tactical ploy. The Belli firm obviously didn't want to appear to the family that *they* were trying to prove Michael molested Serena, he believed. They wanted to lay that responsibility on him, when in fact *they* had brought Tessie to the trial. All the same, he was far from disappointed with the situation.

For her part, Sharri was livid—both with the "little game" in which her mother was the central figure, and at Roxanne, who was, in Sharri's words, "Running around patting a satchel over her shoulder claiming, 'I have *all* the evidence right here!' " Exactly what evidence would remain unknown; neither Antonio nor Golde put her on the stand. Sharri was equally unhappy with the bold manner in which Roxanne introduced herself—"Hi, I'm the defendant's aunt"—to members of the media. With their own natural aversion to the cameras, the Moores viewed Roxanne as using Serena's plight for her own "cheap shot" at a television appearance. That was unforgivable.

"People call Delores Braden."

As the heavyset woman was sworn in, Sharri cast an apprehensive glance at Michael. Before the trial, she had warned certain family members and friends not to speak with the prosecution. "You can't trust him," she had insisted to Michael's mother and her friend, Delores. That was proving to be more true than Sharri could have guessed. Neither her mother-in-law nor Delores had heeded her words, assuring themselves that any bits of truth related to Mr. Golde could only encourage him to believe in Serena's innocence. Sharri and Michael had thought them incredibly naive. "That's not his job," Sharri had argued. "His job is to find things to use *against* Serena."

In her *in limine* motion, Antonio had argued against Delores's testimony and had lost. As a result, the witness's answers to Golde's questions would be peppered with frequent objections from the defense team.

After asking about the times Delores had brought her grandchild to play with Mallory at Sarah Moore's house, Golde steered the conversation to Mallory's funeral. According to Delores, Serena appeared anything but sorrowful there, talking excitedly about riding in a limousine to Mallory's grave and worrying about her appearance in a new dress. She read a poem at the funeral without emotion. Later that day, as mourners assembled in the Moore home, Serena and a friend "went out in the backyard and proceeded to practice their pom-pomming." Sharri then announced that the girls would perform a dance cheer for everyone, and turned on a tape. Sarah Moore, added Delores, "couldn't stand it, and left."

"God," Sharri exhaled to herself. Delores made the events of that horrendous day sound so cold, as if she and Michael didn't care that Mallory had just been lowered into her grave. Had *Delores* ever lost a daughter? Could she or the Deputy D.A. even remotely imagine the grief a parent endured at the burial of their little girl? Serena had *needed* a distraction, as had all their friends. In the Irish tradition of boisterous wakes, she had allowed Serena to perform, hoping to cheer others and herself. Most of their friends had enjoyed Serena's dance, even if Sarah Moore had not.

As Golde stated he had no further questions, Sharri leaned toward Michael to comment, then pulled back, a commotion at the counsel table distracting her attention. Antonio and Belli were whispering animatedly.

"Just," Belli waved his hand at his assistant, "I just must—"

"Let me make it," Antonio cut him off and turned toward the judge. "A—"

Margulies paused. "You want to maintain your objection to—"

"I want to maintain my objection all the way through this

testimony,'' Antonio retorted. "I want to move to strike it. Prejudice, irrelevant, and immaterial. And we're not trying Serena's behavior at the funeral. And many people grieve in many different ways.''

Belli was on his feet. "I'm going to move for a mistrial, Your Honor!''

"Mr. Belli,'' the judge frowned, "please have Miss Antonio make the objection. I can deal with one attorney—''

"I'm still a member of this bar, Your Honor!''

"Mr. Belli—''

"Although I can't hear very well.''

"Mr. Belli—''

"I'm going to move for a mistrial,'' he bellowed, "and I do move for a mistrial! I can't properly hear this case.''

Serena hid her face in her hands while reporters scribbled furiously. Joan Lynch was frantically sketching Belli's outraged stance. Sharri laughed to herself, grabbing at Belli's craziness as a welcome respite from her anger. Michael reacted differently. He felt a new fear twisting in his spine. Belli was whacking out, for heaven's sake, right in the midst of Serena's trial. As a matter of fact, as far as Michael was concerned, neither member of the defense team seemed to be doing a very good job.

Golde managed to keep a poker face as Margulies denied the motion.

A calmer Belli fiddled with his hearing aids as Tessie Dornellas took the stand. Sharri, a disdainful expression on her face, was anything but calm. Settled back in his seat, both elbows on either chair rest, Michael appeared at ease, but inwardly was "all ajitter." Faced with the worst, his demeanor rarely changed. It was his protection, his wall against hostile forces.

Golde soon touched on Serena's report to the Carson City police and other claims of molestation. Yes, Tessie responded, Serena had told her of those things too, but not in detail. Michael had been arrested, but "then [Serena's report] didn't wash, or whatever."

Tessie avoided looking at Sharri or Michael as she told of a weekend visit she'd made to the Moore home a few years back. On the morning of her departure, she testified, she waited "two hours" to see her granddaughter while Serena remained in the master bedroom with Michael, under the auspices of "waking him up." (This testimony doubled the accusation in Tessie's written statement to Carson City police, in which she'd charged that Michael and Serena were in the bedroom "an hour or so.") What's more, Tessie had witnessed Michael kissing Serena "on the mouth" and had felt "uncomfortable" about it.

Tessie's testimony fell to Michael's expectations, in light of what he considered her "sick, perverted inclination" to say that he was doing awful things to her granddaughter. Tessie, he felt, through her jealousy, wanted to believe that he was anything but good for Serena.

For Sharri, it was the grandparent's visitation suit revisited, replete with similar, wild exaggerations. She was having a terrible time keeping quiet. She wanted to jump up and scream, "Liar!" *No way* Serena stayed with Michael for two hours in a bedroom. The very thought was absurd—three adult women in the house, with Michael and Serena rolling around in bed just down the hall. If that were the case, why didn't Tessie put a stop to it herself? How could she justify that she knew something inappropriate was going on, but did nothing about it? And the kiss on the lips was just as ridiculous. It was common in Michael's family—his father bussed him on the lips to this day, and Michael was forty years old!

Under cross-examination, Antonio referred to Serena's Carson City report. Did Tessie know why charges against Michael were dropped?

"Well, Serena's mother did not believe her. She was very distraught over that. She felt her mother might question it, and she was very upset because she wanted her mother's love so. She denied it to get her mother's love."

Tessie's claim flew in the face of her earlier indication that Serena's report "did not wash."

"Do you know if Mrs. Moore ever threatened Serena?"

Grandma nodded her head. "She told Serena if she ever made up another story about Michael, that she would no longer have a family."

Antonio paused as the accusation hung in the air. *No longer have a family.* It would become one of the Deputy D.A.'s most acrid quotes against Sharri—the mother who allowed her child to be molested, then threatened her if she told.

Michael felt hatred seeping from his pores against Antonio, Golde, and, most of all, Tessie. How could all this be allowed? It was all the judge and media were hearing. Where were the policemen who could testify that Serena's reports weren't true? Tessie and the attorneys all knew damn well that Detective Brazil himself had closed that sexual abuse report, but no one was *saying* it! How could these people so defame a man's character and get away with it?

The Moores later pieced together what they believed was the reason for Tessie's appearance that afternoon. Apparently, Antonio and Tessie had discussed removing Serena from their home after her acquittal, agreeing that she should live in Carson City. In light of Tessie's past history of fighting over Serena, Sharri could well imagine her jumping at the chance to gain custody of her granddaughter. (Months later, Sharri's Aunt Laura would make two statements that tended to back up the Moores' contention—that Antonio had called Laura after Sharri and Michael reacted against the sexual abuse allegations in court and that Tessie was "trying to get custody" of Serena.)

Serena evidently had been informed of the plan, but, separated through Antonio's request from her parents during the trial, was unable to tell them. She confided instead to Mary, in a letter written after the second week of court proceedings.

> *. . . I have to tell you something thats not so good. Im probably gonna go live with my grandma again in Carson City. Don't go and tell my mom because she's not supposed to know just yet. . . .*

Matt Golde's case-in-chief was nearly over. He planned to finish up on Thursday; the testimony of his last two witnesses, Sarah Moore and Fremont Police Officer Charles Uhler, would be short. Allowing plenty of time for the defense's case, he estimated the trial could well be wrapped up by the end of the following week.

That was not to be. Antonio arrived Thursday morning accompanied by a new partner. With Belli sick and unable to attend court, Vince O'Brien from the firm had taken his place for the day. Alerted of Belli's illness, Margulies called counsel to side bar to discuss an alternate schedule. Belli was planning to make the defense's opening statement, Antonio told the judge, so they needed to postpone proceedings until he was better. Golde said okay. Margulies suggested that, once Golde completed his case, they recess until the following Tuesday, Monday being Memorial Day. All sides concurred.

With court called to order, Serena agreed on record to waive proceedings accordingly.

Given the go-ahead to call his next witness, Golde left the courtroom briefly to call Sarah Moore to the stand.

As she settled herself uncomfortably in the witness chair, Sarah Moore trembled. Thank goodness her husband, William, was there to support her. The whole experience had been so horrible—losing a beloved granddaughter, watching her son be publicly humiliated and scorned. Sometimes she just wanted to cry and cry and hide from the entire world. Sarah felt the trial was so unfair, that any person in his right mind should know Serena was innocent. Still, a part of her was deeply angry at Serena, had continued to be ever since the girl's statement to police caused her son's arrest. If Serena hadn't done those terrible things, Sarah reminded herself, the girl might not be in such a mess today.

But a subpoena from the prosecution! She was being forced to testify for Matt Golde, who was being so brutal to Michael and Sharri. Sarah didn't know if her nerves could bear it; she just wanted it to be over. The only good news was that, when she stepped down from the stand, she could join her husband in the courtroom instead of waiting in the tiny witness area or out in the hall with the cameras.

"Good-morning, Ms. Moore," Golde greeted her deferentially.

"Good-morning."

Sarah Moore's testimony was important to Golde on two issues—to indicate that Mallory's asthma, as she had witnessed, was only mild, and to establish that Serena could "sneak out of the house without making any noise."

Serena had said that she could sneak out her bedroom window or down the hall and through the garage door in order to meet her boyfriend at night, Sarah testified. Once her parents were asleep, Serena had remarked, they didn't hear anything. Sarah faltered in trying to remember when that conversation took place, and apologized. Golde told her it was okay.

Relieved that he was being so understanding, Sarah was hit unawares by the next question and responded automatically.

"Did Serena ever say anything to you about participating in anal sex?"

"Yes, she did."

"Objection!" Antonio cut in. "Prejudicial, irrelevant."

Serena ducked her head in embarrassment, then threw a quick glance over her shoulder at her parents. Sharri caught her eye and shook her head in disgust. Even if her mother-in-law had been trusting enough to tell that to Matt Golde, he had no business bringing it up in court, she railed to herself. What purpose did it serve other than just to make Serena look bad? It didn't have anything to do with proving whether or not she committed this crime.

Michael, as usual, did not outwardly react. He didn't like the fact that his mom had been so open with Golde, but forgave her, knowing that, at the time, she hadn't understood the potential consequences.

"Side bar," Margulies curtly responded.

Huddled with Antonio and the judge, Golde offered his argument for pursuing the matter, but Margulies was not convinced. Back on record, she sustained the objection.

"Well," he responded, "I don't have any other questions."

To a certain degree, Margulies's ruling was a moot point. Sarah Moore had already answered the question, casting one more sexual taint on the Moore family household.

Fremont Police Officer Charles Uhler was the prosecution's icing on the cake. Golde had strategically built his case, starting with proof of a homicide with Dr. Herrmann, then leading into testimonies that supported Serena's committing the crime and his theory of motive. Lastly, he'd leave 'em with a zinger—Serena's declared relief when her deed was done.

Uhler, a crime scene investigator with red-blond hair and a matching mustache and eyebrows, had been assigned to patrol the morning of December 27, 1992, when he received a call asking him to respond to the police department and transport a prisoner to juvenile hall. That prisoner was the defendant, Serena Moore, he told the court. Once he had placed Serena in his patrol car, he did not try to speak with or question her. However, she volunteered a remark.

Antonio cut in with objections, arguing that the information was hearsay and prejudicial. Margulies hesitated. She would hear the testimony, she decided, then make her ruling on the prejudicial aspect.

"She said," Uhler stated in a matter-of-fact tone, "that her sister would be better off dead."

"Did she say anything else in that context?" Golde pressed.

"When she said that, I turned over my shoulder and I said 'What?' And she said, 'Well, what I meant was, my sister would be better off dead, because this is a crummy world and a crummy place to grow up.' "

"I just wanted to make it understood," Antonio complained, "that my objections are running through this whole—"

"Just one second, please." Margulies, head bent as she took notes, did not look up. She continued her writing, asking court clerk Nancy Cardoza to read back the last answer. Then, after hearing passionate arguments on either side, she ruled that Uhler's testimony would remain on record.

In cross, Antonio worked to place Serena's words in context. Serena, Uhler explained, had just been informed that she was under arrest for violation of 187 of the Penal Code—homicide—in the death of her little sister. This occurred immediately *after* her interview with Detectives Davila and Anderson. Serena had been very upset. "She had been talking about how angry she was with the two detectives," Uhler added, "and she did not like them."

Amidst Golde's objections, Antonio unsuccessfully tried to show what happened in the interview room to anger Serena but Uhler, not present during the interview, was not allowed to testify about it. Such testimony was considered "hearsay"—not allowable because the statements had been made outside his hearing.

Antonio tried another tack. "Isn't it true she never said she killed her little sister, did she?"

"I never heard her say that."

"She never said she was happy that she was dead, that Mallory was dead, did she?"

"Not in so many words. I think that's open to interpretation."

"Well, *exactly,* detective," Antonio snapped. "Didn't she just—"

"Argumentative," Golde protested.

"—say that she was better off—"

"All right, sustained."

Antonio abruptly closed her mouth. She could do nothing else to discredit Uhler's testimony.

With the dire implication of Serena's angry words hanging over the courtroom, Golde rested his case.

DEAR DIARY MURDER TRIAL CREATES MEDIA SENSATION, read the headline for Salladay's weekend article. FAMED ATTORNEY, DRAMATIC CRIME IS RICH FODDER FOR PRESS.

Michael slammed down the paper in disgust. At the sudden noise, Misty and Madison, catnapping on the couch, raised their heads curiously. Sexual abuse and Belli's quips, fumed Michael. They were "rich fodder" for the press, all right. And he could just imagine the kind of sensationalistic movie that Lorimar Television would produce. One thing was certain, he and Sharri agreed, no way would they cooperate with that production company—not for all the money in the world.

Twenty-five

BELLI WAS BACK in court Tuesday morning, chipper as usual with reporters and responding positively to questions about his health. Getting used to his hearing aids was still a problem, but he remained good-natured enough about it.

Cameras had dwindled to nothing by this second week of trial. The CBS and local crews would not return until the verdict. Sharri and Michael, scurrying off the elevators in anticipation of another onslaught, were surprised and grateful when none occurred. Clad in a flowing summer dress and sandals, Sharri removed her sunglasses and placed them in her purse as she trailed Michael down the hall. They stopped to greet numerous friends. One of Serena's buddies, Tina Craig, a frail-looking, pretty blonde, was there with the reluctant permission of her teachers and parents. She expected to testify for the defense, and would await her turn sitting in the witness room or dallying on a bench in the hallway. Marietta Wilson, also waiting to testify, would keep her company.

Memorial Day weekend had seemed endless as the Moores waited for Serena's trial to resume. Sunday afternoon, they had made the drive over to Skylawn to "see Mal." They'd tended the grass, brought her new flowers and a brightly colored pinwheel. It had been a particularly tough visit. Standing above her marker, gazing over the green rolling hills to the twinkling ocean beyond, Sharri had been hit with the realization that their little girl, forever gone, forever young and beautiful in their memories, had been as tainted as they through the trial. Sharri cried harder than usual that day. Michael, so staunch and emotionless in public, had knelt down to run a finger over Mallory's gravestone and erupted into wrenching sobs.

At least this week, Sharri told herself as she and Michael took their seats in the courtroom, it would be *their* turn. Despite the past week's numerous indications of what was to come, she and Michael had convinced themselves that, regarding the sexual allegations, Antonio and Belli would "make everything all right."

The morning did not begin well for Shelley Antonio. She was about to be lectured by an irritated Judge Margulies.

In preparation for Margulies's ruling on Antonio's *in limine* motion about Dr. Berg's testimony, Antonio was supposed to have faxed the judge her offer of proof—the argument, including case citings, for reasons why Dr. Berg should be allowed to testify as the defense desired. Tuesday morning, Antonio told Margulies she had sent the fax the previous Thursday.

I never received it, replied the judge. What's more, Margulies continued, last Friday she had asked a court clerk to phone Antonio's office twice, asking for another fax. By 6:00 P.M., none had been received. Now, Tuesday morning, she had just received the offer of proof, as had Golde. Neither had had adequate time to review it. As a result, the testimony of Dr. Berg, who was already present and waiting to testify, would have to be postponed until the following day. Antonio could give her opening argument, Margulies said, then call other witnesses in the meantime. Although her face was impassive, Margulies's tone implied that Antonio, given the extra long weekend, had been allowed more than enough time for this bit of housekeeping.

Antonio, clad again in black, her cheeks rosy with blush and perhaps from embarrassment, remained quiet throughout the lecture. Over the weekend, she and Belli had decided that she would present the opening argument. When Margulies finished lecturing and told her to "go ahead," she rose behind the counsel table and plunged in.

"Your Honor, the defense will disabuse this court of any notion that a murder occurred here. There's really no crime. Mallory Moore died of natural causes. In fact, she died of asthma, a condition which she suffered almost all her life. . . ."

Defense would call expert witness Dr. Martha Warnock, Antonio told the court, who would testify that, according to Mallory Moore's autopsy slides, the little girl died of asthma. Further, "psychiatrist" Dr. Paul Berg would explain the "mental condition" of the defendant. (Berg was, in fact, a psychologist; Antonio later realized her mistake and set the record straight.) "He will explain what types of behaviors Serena exhibited that have been offered in evidence, her inappropriate behavior at a funeral, her detachment from emotion. He will explain that this is all the result of a very troubled childhood that Serena had. He will explain the abandonment that she experienced from her original biological father, the unstable home life, the emotional abandonment of her mother, and finally the loss of Mallory, the only connection that she really had. He will explain that Serena's psychological condition is one which presents a very theatrical girl, very overly dramatic, a tendency to do whatever it takes to get attention, to be flamboyant, to tell tall tales and to do anything to get away from the sadness that she felt at the loss of her sister. . . ."

A series of phone tag calls that Sharri had placed soon after Serena's arrest had led her to Dr. Warnock. She'd passed the name on to Antonio. Warnock's agreement to take the case had been a blessing on many counts. In addition to her having supervised over three thousand autopsies, her specialty was in pulmonary medicine—medicine pertaining to the lungs. Moreover, she had agreed to help for free. It was not her policy to accept money for such things, she had informed the Moores.

Dr. Berg was a different story. To meet his charge of $125 per hour as he interviewed and tested Serena, the Moores racked up payments of nearly $1800. Even Grandma Tessie had chipped in, sending monthly payments of $50 to total $300. For testifying, Dr. Berg demanded an additional $1000 per half day (apparently $250 per hour, as his bills later showed, although he would testify that he was "charging $125 in this case"). The Belli firm offered to split the testifying fees with Sharri and Michael.

Antonio concluded, "The defense will offer testimony from her friends and her family that she loved Mallory. That the relationship between Mallory and Serena was unique. It was special. That Serena looked to Mallory to give Mallory the mother that she did not have. That this type of sisterly love went so deep and that Mallory was her anchor in this world that she would not have, therefore, ended that life."

Preparing to sit down, Antonio stopped to exchange whispers with a beckoning Belli. She nodded. "Your Honor, I have one more addition to this. That we will also offer testimony that, that the asthma could have been triggered by an emotional, traumatic event and if that emotional trauma can be triggered, can be explained by the anal dilation, then that points away from our client and to some other perpetrator."

Michael pressed his lips together and closed his eyes. Here we go again, he thought.

Sharri let out a sharp hiss of breath. Antonio had told them time and time again that she didn't believe the sexual abuse, until she'd stopped talking to them altogether. She had done her best to avoid them the past week. Now they were hearing the truth, Sharri realized; Antonio *did* believe the stories, and she *had* told Serena that she thought Michael hurt Mallory. It just wasn't *fair*. How much did God expect her to take? Sharri felt so tired. Tired of the accusations, the media, the trial, tired of being forced apart from Serena. And tired of living without Mallory.

They were killing her by the inches. She wished she could just die and get it over with.

Preceding the expert witnesses were two family friends— Mary Corren and Ruby Jacobs from Carson City, who knew Serena through acquaintance with Grandma Tessie. The Moores had counted on Mary's testimony to help clear their names. She had been in their home many times and did not believe a word about the abuse. But Antonio did not question her about the matter.

Antonio called Mary to the stand to back her claim that Serena and Mallory loved each other dearly. And, she planned to introduce testimony of Serena's propensity to lie. The latter point was of utmost importance to Antonio. She had to prove not only that Serena was a "nutty girl in a troubled household," but that she told incredible tales. Only then could the diary confession be discredited.

Once again, Antonio's intentions were thwarted by Golde's sustained objections as she tried to elicit information about the lies. The testimony was "hearsay." Or it was "speculation." Or there was "no foundation." Despite Margulies's restrained prompting, Antonio did not phrase the question in a way acceptable to the judge. Finally, she gave up.

Ruby Jacobs's testimony was offered to counteract that of Delores Braden. Serena *was* sad at the funeral, Ruby told the court, and she was obviously grieving a week later, during a visit to her relatives in Tahoe.

At ten-forty, Margulies called a ten-minute recess.

After Antonio's initial confident statement to the press that Serena would not testify, she and Belli came to disagree on the matter. On the pro side for considering the defendant's testimony, Antonio later implied, was the need for Serena's own disputation against the diary entry's being a true confession and the need to display her grief over Mallory's death. On the con side was the fact that, once on the stand, Serena would be subject to Golde's cross-examination, which was likely to be relentless.

The question for the defense team became one of deciding the lesser of two evils. Was it better to allow the diary entry to loom as truth before the court, unchallenged by Serena's own words, or was it more important to allow her testimony, knowing that it might be disassembled by the prosecution? In her daily conferrings with Belli, Antonio began to argue against Serena's testifying. Belli dug in his heels.

Recounting their conversation months later, Antonio said she pointed out to Belli that Serena had lied too many times. The prosecution had all kinds of evidence to that effect; Golde would tear her apart on cross.

"She's smart," Belli rejoined, "she can handle it."

Well, countered Antonio, she's "just gonna look like a liar."

To which Belli replied, "That's okay, because that's what they say anyway."

Belli played on Serena's unreliability in the media as well as in the courtroom. In the hallway during a recess, he made a point of telling reporters that "you can't be sure [Serena is] telling the truth at any time." Point unspoken—the diary entry, therefore, should not be believed.

During the ten-minute break, Belli and Antonio conferred about Serena's testimony. She was supposed to testify next, but Belli was having second thoughts about the lineup. Better to call the experts first. Their statements would lay a more firm foundation for testimony by the defendant.

Back in session, Antonio informed Margulies of the last-minute pivot. With neither expert witness in attendance, court would have to recess until the next day. Dr. Warnock would be available the following morning, followed by Dr. Berg in the afternoon.

"Your Honor," Golde spoke up, "there's one additional request I would like to make on the record." Despite "numerous requests," he had received no discovery about either of these two experts. Given the fact that the rest of the day was free, he wanted the documents as soon as possible for review before tomorrow. Otherwise, more delays would follow.

On the heels of Margulies's own problems in obtaining documents from the defense, Golde's complaint could not have been more ill timed for Antonio. The judge took a hard line. Golde would have all expert witness reports "ahead of time" or she would be forced to recess court while he perused them, in which case the expert witnesses would be called back at a later date, whether it was convenient or not.

Antonio responded that Dr. Berg had not made a report, so she couldn't turn over to Golde what she didn't have.

Margulies pursed her mouth. "So what you report to the court is that Dr. Berg examined the minor in this matter, took no notes and no report, and is testifying primarily from memory?"

Antonio wasn't sure about the notes. Golde then asked to see any documents Dr. Berg had been given as aids in making his diagnosis.

"So ordered, so ordered," declared Margulies. The same applied to any documents give to Dr. Warnock.

Dr. Martha Warnock was a bright, well-educated and successful woman who carried herself with the air of a servile mouse. Sharp-featured, with glasses, gray hair, and thin lips pressed primly together, she looked more like a grandmotherly hausfrau than a pulmonary pathologist.

Warnock's qualifications, as brought out in direct *voir dire* under Antonio, were impeccable. A graduate of Harvard Medical School, she had been chief resident and then professor at the University of Chicago's Department of Pathology, later specializing in pulmonary diseases, including asthma. She had later served as director of Autopsy Services at the University of California San Francisco for eleven years, and currently held the title of professor emeritus at the school. Out of the three thousand autopsies she had overseen during her career, she had diagnosed ten deaths due to asthma.

Arms resting on the table, Golde leaned forward, carefully studying the doctor as she answered Antonio's *voir dire* questions. Pushing beyond her almost timid demeanor, his impression of Dr. Warnock was that she was primarily an academician. He guessed that she previously had testified in few, if any, criminal trials. That turned out to be true; she had testified in one noncriminal case some eight years before.

In his *voir dire* cross, Golde managed further to temper the weight of Warnock's experience. She had supervised three thousand autopsies but personally had conducted only around two hundred. Golde suggested that she spent far more time teaching than performing autopsies.

That was true, Warnock admitted, then added, "And in no cases excepted, it's very important to have the history in order to make a diagnosis at autopsy. It's almost impossible to make a diagnosis at autopsy based solely on the autopsy findings."

Golde paused. "By 'history' you mean what?"

"I mean the patient's complete medical history."

An indication of Warnock's thoroughness, the point certainly was not one that Golde wanted to make. Dr. Herrmann had *not* seen Mallory Moore's complete records before coming to his conclusion as to cause of death. Face impassive, Golde switched to another topic.

Under Antonio's direct exam, Warnock explained that she had reviewed the deceased's medical records, noting Mallory's diagnosis of the treatment for asthma, including one five-day prescription for prednisone after a midnight attack. And she had read the autopsy report, which stated that "the lungs remained inflated when the chest was opened, and they remained inflated after being removed from the chest." Not clear about some of Dr. Herrmann's notations, she had asked Ms. Antonio, who had checked with the pathologist. Antonio had reported back from Dr. Herrmann that "the lungs filled the pleural spaces and did not collapse when removed from the body." Those were very important pieces of information in patients who died of "obstructive airways disease" such as asthma.

Normally, when the chest is opened, Warnock explained, lungs tend to collapse to varying degrees. But in asthma, because of the narrowing of the passages, air is trapped, causing the lungs to remain inflated. Lungs that "filled the pleural spaces" referred to such inflated, or "hyperinflated," lungs. Congestion or "mucus plugs" in the lungs' bronchial tubes, or bronchi, were apt to be found after a prolonged asthmatic attack that ended in death. Sometimes, on rare occasions, a rapid attack could lead to "sudden death." The lungs of someone who had died from a "sudden death" asthmatic attack would have only a small amount of mucus plugging. In Mallory's case, Dr. Warnock discovered mucus plugs in three bronchi.

(The issue of mucus plugging would not be fully explored with Dr. Herrmann. While performing the autopsy, he had jotted in his notes that "the large bronchi show little mucus but at least one shows plugging." Later, in his written report, he stated that "the bronchi show a very small amount of thin, clear mucus" and said nothing about the plugging he had found.)

Dr. Warnock continued her explanation of sudden death asthma attacks. These deaths could occur in patients with histories of severe attacks, she noted, or could happen in the first severe episode. Wheezing or coughing would be minimal to none; consciousness most likely was lost a few moments before the heart stopped beating. She cited a 1992 article entitled "Pediatric Asthma Deaths in Victoria; the Mild Are at Risk" that attributed the deaths of numerous patients under age twenty to such attacks. Two other articles were also placed into evidence—"Deaths as a Result of Asthma in Wayne County Medical Examiner Cases" and "Sudden Asphyxia Asthma: A Distinct Entity." According to these publications, Warnock testified, "Attacks that are sudden and cause respiratory failure within a few hours or a few minutes are cases that seem to be just mainly bronchospasm; that is, contraction of the muscle." These attacks could be caused by "heavy doses of allergens or pollen" or "perhaps an emotional problem."

Antonio jumped at the last statement. "So you agree that an emotionally traumatic event could trigger an asthma attack."

"Yes."

The faces of court spectators indicated the complexity of Warnock's testimony. The Moores' entourage was frowning slightly, pitched forward in their seats, at times shaking their heads somewhat confusedly. Margulies, Golde, and reporters were busily taking notes, chins bobbing up and down as they glanced between the witness and the papers before them. Serena glanced about distractedly as a student in a thoroughly boring class. Seated at her right, Belli looked for all the world a learned mentor, now keeping watch over apprentice

Antonio's every move, now steepling his fingers and leaning back in his chair to gaze at the ceiling.

In a lengthy review, Dr. Warnock showed a series of slides depicting asthmatic deaths, attempting to explain in layman's terms their comparison to slides of lung tissue from Mallory Moore. In a sudden asthmatic death, she testified, she would expect to find the following in the lungs: 1. some degree, however slight, of mucus plugging, 2. "sloughing off" or breaking away of epithelium cells in the airways—typical in asthmatic attacks, 3. thickening of the bronchi's basement, or underlying, membrane, 4. tissue inflammation and swelling of the mucus membranes and 5. "degranulation of eosinophils"—the breaking down into toxic granules of cells in the blood called eosinophils. In Mallory Moore, she had found evidence of all five features.

In short, Dr. Warnock stated, she "had concluded that Mallory died of an asthmatic attack based on her history of asthma, her noncollapsing lungs [at autopsy] and all of the slide features taken together." Ergo, she disagreed with Dr. Herrmann's conclusion as to cause of death.

As the slides clicked by in the darkened courtroom, Sharri cast her eyes down, a pained expression on her face. Half-listening to the doctor's quiet drone, she thought back to countless times after Mal's death when she had shaken her fist at the heavens and cried, *"Why?"* How relieved they had been to finally hear an answer, and how horrified. The knowing only added more guilt. They had *known* about Mallory's asthma. She could have, should have, done something to prevent Mal's death.

Michael was remembering the drive from Dr. Herrmann's office in Oakland across the Bay Bridge and into San Francisco to see Dr. Warnock. He and Sharri had told Antonio they would do all they could to transport documents and other items in order to save money on delivery services. But they'd never expected having to carry an envelope full of Mallory's pulmonary slides and tissue cuttings from one doctor to the next. Hit with the grotesque reality of that brown manila envelope, Michael had hesitated first to touch it. Then, realizing that it held the only piece of Mallory he had left, he had clutched it to his chest.

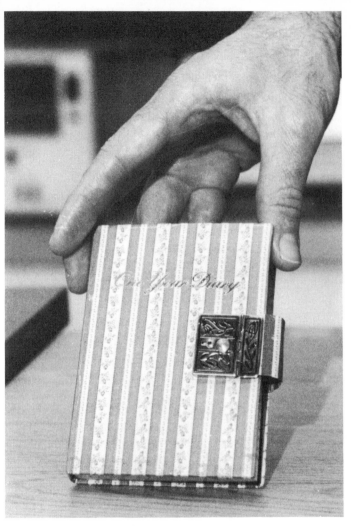

Serena's diary is displayed by Fremont police captain Michael Lanam during the December 30 press conference.

Photo by Brad Mangin/The Argus, Fremont

Eleven-year-old Serena, clad in a dance costume, poses with her baby sister, Mallory.

Photo by the Moore family

Sharri and Mallory at Disneyland in August 1992. This was the last photograph taken of Mallory before her death, one week later.

Photo by the Moore family

Attorney Melvin Belli and his associate Shelley Antonio confer
with Sharri after a court hearing. Sharri attempts to hide her face
from the suddenly ever-present cameras.

*Photo by Victoria Sheridan/*The Argus, *Fremont*

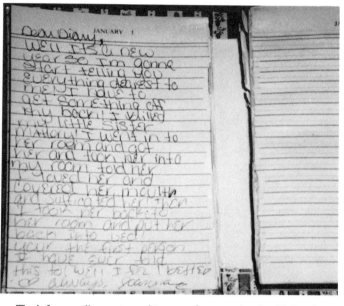

The infamous diary entry, written over four months after Mallory's death, that resulted in Serena's arrest. *Photo by the author*

Serena's actual diary entry describing Mallory's death, written shortly after it occurred.   *Photo by the author*

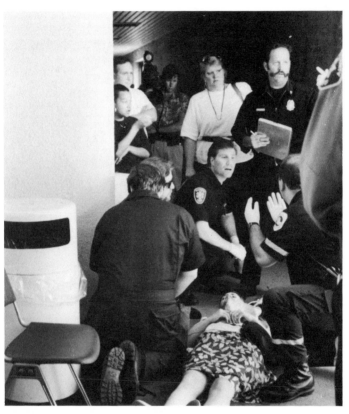

Sharri is surrounded by family and paramedics after she collapsed from grief and exhaustion following Serena's first verdict.

*Photo by Laura A. Oda/*The Argus, *Fremont*

Deputy district attorney Matt Golde, who prosecuted the case against Serena M. *Photo by the author*

Doug Horngrad was the defense attorney hired by the Moores after Serena's conviction.

Photo by the author

Michael flashes the victory sign as he takes Sharri and Serena for a spin in his old convertible shortly after Serena's release.

Photo by the author

Warnock's slide presentation was over. As the courtroom lights were flicked back on, Sharri glanced at Michael. He was immersed in studying his lap.

During a break in the middle of Warnock's testimony, Judge Margulies received a Federal Express package from Tessie Dornellas. She did not open it. Reading direct correspondence from a witness in the case would not be appropriate; any admissible evidence to the trier of fact had to follow the proper channels—elicitation in court and in the presence of counsel.

In side bar, Margulies gave the envelope to Golde and Antonio, who opened it and read its contents. Tessie's letter was a brief, somewhat "scattered" plea, as Golde would later recall, to "help Serena." Someone needed to "look into all of this," according to Tessie, because "the whole truth was not coming out."

Once court was in session, Margulies acknowledged for the record that she had received the envelope and noted that a bailiff would make photocopies of the letter for the defense and prosecution. "But I will not look at it," she declared. "It's not evidence in this case."

Michael rolled his eyes in disgust. He didn't need to see that letter to know what was in it—more horrible things about him. It was just like Tessie to do something that unethical and underhanded, he thought.

"Why doesn't she just mind her own business?" Sharri hissed at him under her breath.

He shrugged and shook his head.

In the afternoon session, the complex medical testimony continued, Antonio leading Dr. Warnock through Herrmann's autopsy findings. Regarding the petechial hemorrhages, Dr. Warnock stated, they could be found on a person who had died of asphyxia from asthma. The hemorrhages were "very nonspecific," she said, and didn't in her opinion necessarily point to asphyxia. Nevertheless, in asphyxia by asthma, the petechiae occurred when blood was trapped in the head, expanded lungs not allowing it to return to the chest. These were even more likely to occur on a child's skin, which was "less firm" than that of an adult.

Dr. Herrmann's finding of "marked cerebral edema," or brain-swelling owing to fluid, also could occur during an asthmatic attack. Congestion of the lungs, liver, and kidneys again were "nonspecific"—consistent with asphyxia, not necessarily "traumatic asphyxia." As for Dr. Herrmann's findings of the anus, Dr. Warnock "did not want to render an opinion" since that lay outside her specialty.

Dr. Warnock's conclusion regarding cause of death was based on the "totality" of her findings, the patient's medical history, and an absence of signs of trauma to the body. Mallory Moore had died from "asthmatic asphyxia."

Antonio concluded her direct, obviously pleased. Despite Dr. Warnock's meekness, her testimony had raised a significant amount of reasonable doubt as to cause of death.

Within an hour, a quick-thinking Golde would tear the testimony apart.

His performance was impressive, considering that he had no idea of the territory into which he was about to stumble. After hearing that Dr. Warnock had not discussed the case with Dr. Herrmann, he asked "Why not?" She had asked to speak with Dr. Herrmann about some questions, Warnock said, but Ms. Antonio preferred to call Dr. Herrmann herself and relay any information.

Golde saw Judge Margulies shoot a glance at defense counsel.

"Did you explain to Ms. Antonio that talking to the coroner would have been helpful to you?"

"I think that's what she understood."

Antonio objected and was overruled.

Through Golde's careful queries, Dr. Warnock admitted that she was "at somewhat of a disadvantage" in not personally having viewed the autopsy. Therefore, Dr. Herrmann's explanation as to his statement "the lungs filled the pleural cavity" was a most important piece of information. That was because, Warnock told the court, lungs that failed to collapse after removal from the body could only signal airway obstruction, not traumatic asphyxia. She had specifically requested that Antonio ask Dr. Herrmann if "the lungs filled the pleural cavity" meant that they had not collapsed when removed. She also had asked Ms. Antonio to inquire whether the "lungs met at the midline" of the chest, another indication that they were "hyperinflated." In reporting back to her, Dr. Warnock testified,

Antonio had said that Dr. Herrmann's answer was "I don't know."

I don't know.

Golde was stunned. The answer did not match Dr. Herrmann's testimony during Antonio's cross-exam, when the judge had asked why he believed that the evidence of asthma in Mallory Moore's lungs did not point to cause of death from the disease. In his long response, Herrmann had explained, "The problem with someone with asthma is that they can breathe in but they can't breathe out. The obstruction of the airway is to the flow of air out of the lungs. So that when someone has it bad enough to cause their death, their lungs are very hyperinflated with air. Frequently the lungs are inflated to the point that they almost meet or may even meet in the middle of the chest, which is abnormal. . . ."

"So her lungs were not hyperinflated?" Margulies had quizzed.

"No. They were not hyperinflated."

Now, hearing Dr. Warnock's testimony, Golde sensed that Margulies remembered Dr. Herrmann's statement as well as he did. Antonio's flurry of nervous objections only seemed to heighten the judge's resolve to hear out the matter.

Golde asked his key question. Was it accurate to say, then, that without that "most important question" being answered by Dr. Herrmann, Dr. Warnock could not "reasonably opine that Mallory Moore died of asthmatic asphyxia"?

"Yes, essentially that's the case."

Taking copious notes, Margulies asked that the question and answer be read back, then rephrased the question and asked it again. Well, Warnock hedged, there were still other pieces of evidence, as she had mentioned, but this was key.

Had the doctor read the transcription of Herrmann's testimony in court? Golde wondered.

No, she had not.

There it was. Golde knew he had her, or more correctly, had the defense team. As he saw it, Antonio had placed herself between doctors and then proceeded to misstate Herrmann's answer to Warnock's question. With those actions, Golde felt, Antonio had hanged her own expert witness and left the doctor to twist in the wind.

Golde covered other points, undermining Warnock's cause of death item by item, leading her to reiterate that her conclusion was based on the "totality" of evidence. But this, again, only led back to the "pleural spaces" issue—in her words one of the most important subjects in that picture of "totality."

As Dr. Warnock prepared to step down late in the afternoon, Margulies covered the matter one more time, her question posed carefully and precisely. "*If* you had received information that the lungs were *not* hyperinflated, would that have had an impact as to the cause of death in this matter?"

Warnock blinked behind her thick glasses. "I don't think I would have taken the case in that case," she said softly.

Golde could not have hoped for a better answer. Leaving the courtroom, he barely managed to contain his jubilance over tearing a star witness apart. He couldn't wait to tell his girlfriend, Julie Gaines, of his victory.

Little could he have known that the issue with Dr. Warnock would later become dual-pronged. If it helped him win the battle at hand, it eventually would help cost him the war.

Twenty-six

THE MOORES RECEIVED great news Wednesday evening from the defense's second expert witness, Dr. Robert Lawrence, a pathologist from Delta Pathology Associates Medical Group in Stockton, California, about an hour east of the Bay Area. Initially satisfied with one expert witness, Antonio apparently had changed her mind midway through the first week of the trial and set about searching for another opinion to back up that of Dr. Warnock.

Despite the grim details, the Moores had been quick to help. With firm resolve not to fall apart emotionally, Sharri rode with Michael to Dr. Warnock's office, picked up the brown manila folder containing Mallory's slides and tissue samples, then headed back across the Bay Bridge and farther east to deliver it to Dr. Lawrence in Stockton.

Wednesday evening, June 2, just one week later, Dr. Lawrence was phoning the Moores to tell them his report was

ready. His findings were what they had believed all along—
Mallory's death was natural. Further, like Dr. Warnock, he
believed the death was caused by asthma, *and* he saw no
sign of sodomy from either the scars Dr. Herrmann found or
the anal dilation. Sharri and Michael were ecstatic. Eager to
read the report, they asked Dr. Lawrence to fax it to Michael's office, also mentioning that Antonio would probably
need an immediate copy for Golde's discovery. As soon as
Sharri hung up, Michael climbed into their Ranger for a trip
down Interstate 880 and across the Dumbarton Bridge to pick
up the fax at his office. While there, he decided to fax the
report to Shelley Antonio so that it would be waiting at her
office before court the next morning. Just in case, he also
made an additional copy to hand-deliver to defense counsel
the following day.

Michael thought the report even better than Dr. Lawrence
had explained, particularly in dealing with the molestation
issue. Warnock may not have been willing to testify about
it, but Dr. Lawrence was more than ready.

Once again, the Moores' hopes soared that the unpleasant
matter finally could be laid to rest.

Thursday morning, the Moores triumphantly handed a copy
of Dr. Lawrence's report to Belli. Sharri then caught Antonio
in the hallway regarding another matter. When were Tina
Craig and Marietta Wilson going to testify? They'd been
hanging around the courtroom all week without any word.
Tina was missing classes, Sharri reminded Antonio, and it
was near the end of the school year. Tina had already asked
for a subpoena so she could be formally excused from classes,
but hadn't received one yet. Marietta wanted a subpoena, too,
as notification that she still was needed.

Antonio promised to get subpoenas for both of them. As
to when they would testify, she could only say it would
be soon.

While waiting for court to begin, Sharri and Michael introduced themselves to psychologist Dr. Berg, who was middle-
aged, balding, and somewhat pudgy. The encounter was far
from positive. The psychologist began the conversation by
warning Sharri that in his testimony he would "have to say

bad things about her" regarding the kind of mother she had been when Serena was young.

"It wasn't that bad, it's not that I *beat* her or anything," Sharri countered testily.

His reply was like a slap in the face. "Your mother says you did."

Sharri had no idea her mother had spoken to Dr. Berg. "Well, I didn't!" she retorted, "and why wasn't *I* asked about it? I don't want you saying things that aren't *true!*"

"Do you want your daughter to go to CYA?"

CYA—California Youth Authority—the dreaded juvenile prison. Berg's rhetorical question sent ice running through Sharri's veins. So that was it, she thought. She and Michael were to continue "playing the sacrificial lambs" while Belli's office, the psychologist, and Tessie were "plotting" a defense at their expense. No wonder her mother had helped pay Dr. Berg! she railed to her husband.

As soon as the courtroom was unlocked, the Moores hurried in to claim their seats. Sharri in her anxiety felt overheated and sweaty.

Before the psychologist took the stand, Judge Margulies listened to Golde's and Antonio's arguments regarding whether Dr. Berg should be allowed to testify as to the truth of Serena's diary confession—a decision that she had postponed pending the doctor's appearance in court. After hearing lengthy orations, particularly from Antonio, Margulies handed down a ruling that was to have long-term repercussions. Dr. Berg could "testify to the factors, characteristics or features of psychological conditions and/or disorders that may affect the reliability of a confession in a typical case or generally speaking," but he could not "discuss the evidence in this case, other than his examination, testing, and diagnosis of the minor, or give his opinion regarding the overall reliability of the diary entry." In other words, he could not tell the court that he believed the diary to be untrue.

Under *voir dire,* Berg told the court that he had received his B.A., master's, and doctorate in psychology from Michigan State University. His current practice often led him to "see juveniles" who had either committed crimes or who displayed the tendency toward such behavior. Antonio quizzed him at length about articles he'd written, other cases in which he had testified, and the like.

Golde's brief *voir dire* focused on one particular issue. "Would you agree that you are not infallible in determining whether or not somebody is or is not a truth teller?" he posed.

"I would agree with that in a hot minute."

"Would you also agree that some people lie to you and you can't tell?"

Antonio objected, arguing that the question was outside of *voir dire.* Margulies overruled.

"Have you ever been fooled, in other words?" Golde prompted.

Berg smiled. "I have been fooled both in my practice and at home."

Margulies's lips curved slightly. "By your children?"

"Yes."

Golde had made his point.

Dr. Berg had visited Serena three times in juvenile hall to administer a battery of psychological tests, and had reviewed various records made available by defense counsel, including documents from Alta Bates and Truckee hospitals. His diagnosis was threefold—that Serena suffered from a conduct disorder, a bipolar or "manic-depressive" disorder and a general personality disorder termed "N.O.S." or "not otherwise specified." Bipolar tendencies, he testified, would be displayed in extreme mood vacillations. Serena's symptoms included grandiosity, self-importance and "flight of ideas," meaning that her thoughts tripped over one another in rapid succession, causing excessive talkativeness and distractability. She was a "terrible exaggerator" with opinions and final answers "on everything." She indulged in fantasizing and was not aware of the social consequences of many of her actions.

Within the personality disorder, there were two aspects—histrionic and borderline personality. "Histrionic" described someone who was overly theatrical, dramatic, bent on remaining the center of attention. Borderline personalities lacked a sense of identity, suffered from very low self-esteem, and typically were apprehensive about being abandoned. Serena's actions did not lie completely in one aspect or the other, leading to the N.O.S. diagnosis.

Dr. Berg indicated that Serena's history, including a mother who could not adequately care for her when she was young, a biological father who had abandoned her, and possible sexual abuse from her first stepfather and Michael Moore, had caused the personality disorder. As for the possible sexual abuse, Serena had told "many different versions." Dr. Berg himself had no "independent verification" as to whether it had occurred or not.

"Did you determine how the birth of her sister, Mallory, entered into her psychological condition?" Antonio asked.

"Yes. I think she was an extremely important figure in Serena's life." Mallory represented stability in Sharri and Michael's relationship and, far more important, allowed Serena to become a sort of surrogate mother, taking care of Mallory in a way in which Serena herself had not been cared for. Mallory's death was, therefore, "even greater than the normal tragic situation of losing a sibling" because the little girl had such "extraordinary meaning for Serena."

As Antonio tried to delve into the issue of Serena's lying, she could not elicit the information she needed around Golde's constant objections, posing the same questions in various ways to no avail. When Margulies encouraged her to rephrase a query, the ensuing question would prompt another objection—"beyond the scope of the witness's expertise." After conferring with Belli, Antonio requested a "clear record" of what the judge was sustaining. Was Margulies saying that Dr. Berg could not "assess Serena's repertorial capacity to report events in her life accurately"?

"The record speaks for what I've done," was Margulies's clipped reply. Antonio could "get at that information other ways," but Dr. Berg could not speak as to Serena's truthfulness.

More whispered conferences between Belli and Antonio, who nodded her head, then stated that she understood the court's position, but wanted to "put questions in the record," with individual rulings. Antonio was playing an age-old defense game—asking questions that she knew would draw sustained objections as a means of laying a foundation for a potential appeal. Margulies acquiesced.

Did Dr. Berg have an opinion as to whether Serena's diary entry was "reliable and credible"? Antonio wondered.

Objection.

Sustained.

What psychological factors within Serena would lead her to take credit for something she did not do?

Objection.

Sustained.

Would someone with Serena's disorders take responsibility for killing someone "whether that wouldn't be true"?

Objection.

Sustained.

Question after question went by, tension in the courtroom heightening with each one. Margulies finally broke the rhythm, suggesting a phrasing that she would allow. Antonio said okay, then proceeded to ask the question in the same way. Again, Golde objected.

Eventually, Antonio was able to phrase the question without objection.

General characteristics lending to unreliability of a confession, the psychologist noted in his answer, included impulsivity, uncontrollable periods of emotions, and low self-esteem that would lead to "thinking in guilt terms." A confession could, under such circumstances, "become a vehicle . . . to get attention, to cause harm to yourself, to let fantasy life creep into reality." Children often felt guilty for things not under their control, such as the divorce of their parents.

"How would Serena react to strong emotions?" Antonio asked.

She would react through denial of her feelings, Dr. Berg replied, either becoming "very unemotional, having no response at all, which is self-protective, or the opposite, which is to become very active and sort of top the emotion."

Antonio moved on to inquire if Serena's behavior was consistent with that of sexual abuse victims. Yes, Berg stated, in that the minor had low self-esteem and a sense of guilt.

"Would you say that Serena's a borderline not-guilty-by-reason-of-insanity?"

Golde immediately objected. Margulies sustained and, on that note, called a ten-minute recess.

*   *   *

While Michael was in the men's room, Sharri stopped Belli in the hallway, asking if he'd read Dr. Lawrence's report. Yes, he had, Belli replied, and it was a great one. Well, what about the findings on the anal scars and dilation, Sharri pressed. Antonio was going to cover that in detail, *wasn't she?*

Belli shrugged that he wasn't sure they would use that part.

"Not use it!" Sharri's face contorted into a mixture of surprise and scorn. "You'd *better* use it!" Swiveling on her heel, she stomped away to find her husband.

In cross-examination, Golde steered Dr. Berg in a direction that fell under one of the defense's pretrial *in limine* motions. Antonio had requested that the court exclude evidence of Serena's "prior acts of misconduct," including threats against people other than Mallory. Golde had countered that he was not planning to introduce any such information. Okay, Margulies said, but if he changed his mind, Golde first should alert the court. She would hear what the evidence was about at that time and then rule on its admissibility.

Now, over a week into the trial, the territory of "prior acts of misconduct" loomed before Golde. He was requesting that various pieces of a report from Truckee Hospital, where Serena had been sent after living with her grandmother, be marked for identification as People's Exhibit #101-F. He did not, however, alert the court. Neither did Antonio remind Margulies of the judge's pending ruling. With the *in limine* motion not invoked by defense counsel, Golde proceeded to introduce the information he sought.

Serena had become verbally abusive toward her mother in a therapist's office and had threatened to burn her with a cigarette, Dr. Berg testified. In addition, according to an interview at Truckee Hospital with Tessie Dornellas, Serena's mother had neglected her when she was small, placing her in a "urine-soaked bed," failing to provide food, not bathing her, and exposing her to other "horrific behaviors." Serena's violent act with the cigarette toward her mother had occurred years later when she had been told that she would have to leave her grandmother's home and return to that of her mother.

Sharri's face burned with humiliation and anger. Part of

her felt "a ton of guilt." She was all too aware of the fact that she *had* been selfish and uncaring in her younger mothering days. But she would insist that she had *never* abused her child. They had been poor and often had little food to eat. She had grown thin along with Serena. The urine-soaked bed thing was puzzling. Where could her mother have come up with that one? Sharri did remember a time, before breaking up with Serena's biological father, when she would leave baby Serena in his care while she worked graveyard shift at a restaurant. One night, Tessie had told Sharri how upset she was over watching Serena's father place the baby on a wet sheet he had neglected to change, and Sharri had bawled him out for it.

By the time Berg stepped down, the comprehensive effect of his testimony had allowed Golde to paint a picture of a young girl turned overly aggressive and violent because of the extreme dysfunctionality of her home. That portrait cast Serena in a light conducive to committing the act of homicide and supported the motive for murder that the Deputy D.A. would state in his closing remarks.

It would also destroy whatever hope the Moores had for regaining their reputations.

Golde would later decry the "wet sheet incident" as indicative of the onerous neglect that Serena had faced, in time slipping in an "s" until Dr. Berg's "placing her in a urine-soaked bed" became "being left in urine-soaked bed*s*," plural—a heinous testament to the continued neglect of a helpless baby.

As the accusations against them grew, the Moores found Antonio more and more remote. She would barely speak with them in the hallway or on the phone at night, and when they did talk, the conversation typically would end in argument. The Moores wanted Antonio to clear their names and were furious that she seemed to want to "smear" their reputations as much as Golde did. They also wanted to visit Serena. Antonio's response, Sharri would later claim, was "I'm the lawyer; I know what I'm talking about."

The Moores' right to control their own lives was becoming a bigger and bigger issue. Mallory's death had been out of their control, as had Serena's behavior, her arrest, and charge of killing her sister. Now they couldn't control the events that were unfolding in the courtroom, in front of the eyes of the harassing media and ogling spectators. Case in point, Dr. Lawrence's report. The defense's own expert witness believed the molestation never happened, they exclaimed to each other, and Belli wasn't even sure he'd use it?

◆

Twenty-seven

WHEREAS THE NUMBER of media representatives had dwindled to a handful of local newspaper reporters in the last few days and up through that morning, suddenly after lunch the courthouse hallway was dotted by television cameras and crews in anticipation of Serena's testifying. A defendant's taking the stand was a high note in any trial; in this proceeding, it promised to be a sensation. The young girl would finally tell her own story about the abuse she'd suffered.

Present also that afternoon was Belli's recently hired full-time "media relations coordinator," Janice Joson, an attractive young woman with short dark hair. Part of Joson's responsibilities lay in ferreting out opportunities for publicity for Mr. Belli. He loved the limelight, was comfortable in it, and the media loved him, enjoying his wry humor played out in a seemingly endless spiel of stories and quips. Upon her hiring, Joson had found herself assigned the mighty task of procuring for Belli one radio interview per workday. She had risen to her boss's challenge, sending out countless queries to radio stations across the country in hopes of filling her quota. Although many responded, she still found that part of her job "difficult."

On the heels of Dr. Berg's testimony, Sharri found it unconscionable that the defense was about to place her daughter as an open target before a sword-wielding Golde. "*Don't* put her on the stand!" Sharri pleaded with Antonio when she learned during lunch break that Serena was to testify. "I don't want her *hurt!*"

Now, upon seeing the cameras and recognizing Joson, Sharri guessed that Belli or some representative had tipped the media that Serena would be on the stand. Accompanying the Moores was Serena's young friend Tina Craig, who was still waiting to testify.

As television crews caught sight of Sharri and Michael stepping off the elevator, cameras whirred on and swung in their direction. Instinctively, Sharri ducked and whisked Tina in a frantic race toward the courtroom. Besieged by reporters, they reached the door only to find it locked and themselves trapped. While Michael turned his back to the cameras, Sharri and Tina hid their faces under a dress that Sharri had brought to be given to Serena to wear the following day in court. Sharri was incensed that Tina, a juvenile, might appear on television.

"She's just a kid; do you *mind!*" she yelled.

The threesome huddled for what seemed a long time until a bailiff unlocked the courtroom door.

Clad in a pink shirt and black skirt, her hair in a ponytail to accent her youth, Serena trembled as she walked toward the witness stand. Her steps seemed to echo in the courtroom, the sound of someone's muffled cough the only audio emanating from the anticipation-filled spectators. Suspense was further heightened as the media and hangers-on realized that Belli was leaning forward at the defense table and fiddling with his hearing aid as if preparing to conduct the questioning.

"Go on, honey," Belli nudged as she faltered. "Be seated up there please."

Judge Margulies instructed Serena as she did all witnesses, her usual clipped, recitative tone slowed to ensure comprehension and carrying a hint of compassion not heard before. "Mr. Belli will start by asking you questions. When he's done asking you questions, then Mr. Golde will have questions for you. Please just answer the question that's asked of you. If you don't understand the question, let me know and we'll repeat it for you. Be sure and keep your voice up; talk right into the microphone."

Sketch artists and reporters were reminded not to display

any likeness of the minor or print her name. "Mr. Belli, are you doing the questioning or Miss Antonio?"

"This time I'm coming out of retirement, and I'm going to do it, Your Honor." The attorney's gravelly boom box of a voice brought a smile to a few new faces.

Softly, then, in a gentle cadence as if talking to a small child, he warned Serena that he would be asking her "a lot of questions" and wondered if she was ready. Saying yes, she could not know she would be on the stand that day—Thursday—as well as all of Friday and half of Monday.

Belli quickly established an aura of sentimentality around Serena. Yes, she told the court in a voice at times barely audible, she loved and missed her sister and yes, she believed Mallory was "looking over [her] right now." Golde objected, citing irrelevance, in order to break the mood. He was overruled. Under Belli's prodding, Serena told the court how she played with her sister, slept with her, said prayers with her, and often woke up in the morning to her impatient hair-yanking, a sign that Mallory was ready for action.

When the audience seemed fully captivated, Belli changed the subject.

"Now let me go into this very briefly, and then we'll depart from it. Did you go out with a number of boys while you were very young?"

"Yes."

"And did you have any relations, sexual relations, to be more explicit, with them?"

"Yes."

"Did your mother and dad talk to you any about this?"

"Not really. I told my mom one time when I did, actually the first time I had sex, and she just, like, said, well, why didn't you talk to me before you did it? And then my dad just looked at me and didn't really say anything much."

Her response, on the surface benign, held the implications of an important point—that her first sexual encounter, occurring with a boyfriend, was a year after she told Carson City police that Michael was forcing her into sex. It was not a point, however, that either the defense or prosecution apparently wanted raised, and both would glide over it.

Serena admitted she smoked cigarettes, but did not deeply "get into the dope field," as Belli phrased it. She did drink, going at it particularly hard after Mallory died because "there were things going on in [her] life that [she] didn't understand."

In vague questions, Belli tried six times to ask why she engaged in activities, such as drinking, that she knew to be wrong. Margulies finally helped him out, prompting him to mutter, "Thanks, Judge." Serena replied that she knew when she was doing "wrong things" and at Belli's urging gave a few examples, such as "snooping around and getting into my parents' stuff."

Was her household a happy one? "Sometimes it was and sometimes it wasn't," she said. "It would, sometimes we would all just get along and it would be fantastic, it would be great. And then other times there would be a lot of conflict, a lot of anger, a lot of tension and then at those times we wouldn't get along. But that wasn't, that wasn't really that often that it would have a lot of conflict."

Belli wondered if she had helped cause the anger and tension. Yes, Serena admitted, she "had a big attitude problem" and "would disrespect [her] mother and father" when she didn't get what she wanted. She did not compete with her sister for attention, however. They played together all the time, building forts and sharing secrets. Mallory would tell her that when they grew up they would live in the same house and drive the same car.

The questioning turned to Mallory's asthma, Golde objecting constantly to Serena's being asked to explain the length and breadth of her sister's illness. The majority of his objections were sustained. Belli abruptly changed the subject to Serena's "attitude problem." After a short discussion, he switched course again, inquiring about Serena's school years and what kind of student she had been. Serena indicated that she had been out of the mainstream, many students not liking her because she wouldn't "give them a chance to know the real me," owing mostly to her making up stories. She did not show them that she could be trusted, never really gave them the chance.

What was the true Serena? Belli wondered.

"Well, people can count on me when they really want to come to me and tell me something that, like, just, you know, something that's really bothering them, they can always come to me and tell me, they can always cry to me and I will understand. They can tell me a lot of problems and I will understand them because I most likely had those problems myself.''

In school, she sometimes played the truant because she was bored or not getting along well with others. At times she tried hard in school, only to "fall back again."

So far, Serena, "the liar," was coming across as believable and sincere. She was sitting fairly still, a difficulty for her, although she couldn't resist throwing an occasional smile or grimace at onlookers, actions which, to the undiscerning eye might seem inappropriate or even flippant. Belli did not appear concerned; Dr. Berg's testimony of her manic-depressive disorder should have shed the proper light on that kind of behavior.

It was time to discuss the events surrounding Mallory's death. Serena grew somber as she spoke about the night of August 17, her testimony closely matching that of her mother's. Usually in the mornings, she told the court, she would hear "little footsteps running around the house," but the morning of August 18, she heard nothing. . . .

Serena paused as her voice choked and her eyes filled with tears that spilled down both cheeks before she wiped them away. At the sight, her mother's chin began to quiver. Mushmouthed, Sharri tried to hold her lips firm.

The courtroom was strangely silent as Serena grappled with her emotions.

"I didn't hear the rustle in her bed or anything," she managed, her head bent down. Inwardly, she was reliving the moment. "And so I got up and looked in her bedroom. I saw her and she wasn't moving. She was being real still. She wasn't awake. And I went in there and I tried to wake her up and she wasn't waking up at all."

The recounting bore a startling resemblance to the entry in Serena's journal written shortly after Mallory's funeral—*I woke up, went in there and something was wrong. She wouldn't move or breathe or anything*. Sharri had reminded Antonio of that diary as the case was being prepared, but once the trial began, with its immediate accusations of child molestation, all thoughts of Diary #1 were driven from the

Moores' minds. Caught up in Serena's grief, they did not think of it now.

"All right," Belli soothed, "take your time, honey." He asked if she wanted to "take a minute" but Serena said it was okay, she could do it.

She told the dramatic tale of running for her mother, hearing her call 911, then dashing out the door into the street and falling on her knees until an officer came by.

Her testimony for the day was almost complete; the large clock on the courtroom's right wall was nearing four-thirty—Judge Margulies's quitting time. Serena's last statements that Thursday, told in a voice once more under control, were of her reentering the house and "trying to calm down her mother" because the situation was "real hectic."

Antonio gave Serena a hug before the teenager was led out of the courtroom side door to be handcuffed, shackled, and transported back to juvenile hall. Despite her qualms, Antonio seemed pleased with the testimony. Serena's emotions were "right there," at once stark and poignant, a good mix for a prosecution-minded judge. To Antonio, Serena's crying was more believable than her mother's. Sharri, the attorney believed, was disassociated enough from her own emotions to make her tears seem insincere. Antonio was sorry that Serena had to go through today's ordeal, but felt the personal recounting helped their case.

The attorney would later concede—in definite understatement—that the honesty pouring from the stand that afternoon "kind of got destroyed in cross."

Michael, finding his built-up anger prompting him into more aggressive action, phoned Antonio that evening, only to hear her answering machine. He left a message, saying that he wanted to testify to clear his own name, and that if she and Belli wouldn't listen to what he had to say, "there were others who would."

Gearing up for a fight, Michael and Sharri then photocopied Dr. Lawrence's report and placed one copy each in a dozen manila envelopes, addressing them to various newspaper reporters covering the case; Connie Chung's "Eye to Eye" producer, Judy Schaeffer; and all four network TV stations, including the Fox channel. They would keep quiet no longer. The media would hear Dr. Lawrence's findings, one way or another.

Next morning, they planned to take the envelopes to court. They'd leave the stack in their Ranger for easy retrieval whenever they decided it was time to hand them out. And they'd make sure Belli saw them do it.

The Moores' friend Marietta Wilson and Serena's chum Tina Craig were conspicuously absent from court that day. Tina had given up hope of obtaining a subpoena from Antonio and had returned to school at the insistence of her parents. Marietta had asked Antonio for a subpoena also, and when she didn't receive one, had assumed she was no longer needed. Without her own car, she had found getting to court day after day a major hassle. She and her boyfriend, Ted, had moved onto a houseboat a few months before in an all-out effort to save expenses after both of them had lost their jobs. Ted was now working, but Marietta was still unemployed. They were down to one car and, of course, Ted needed it for transportation to work.

As soon as Serena entered the courtroom Friday morning, Sharri felt all her hopes drain away. Something was very wrong, Serena's demeanor told her. Where Serena had been nervous but controlled, today she seemed shaken, confused, fearful. She slumped at the counsel table next to Antonio and immediately began picking at her clothes, then turned to cracking her knuckles and twisting her ponytail. She barely gave her parents a glance. The dark yellow dress she was wearing fit fairly well, considering that Sharri had hurriedly borrowed it from a friend Wednesday night.

Sharri's scrutiny of Serena continued as the judge entered and court was called to order. That sizing up, the glances between mother and daughter each morning had become the extent of their communication. Sharri ached to hold her daughter now, sensing that she needed extra support at that moment, but not knowing why.

Belli and Antonio both greeted Serena effusively, shoring her up for what would likely be another full day of testifying.

Golde seemed particularly chipper as he took his seat, his hair spilling over the collar of a gray suit. Among his files he carried an ever-present pad of paper and pen, ready to take notes during the remainder of Belli's direct exam.

As Serena took her seat on the stand, Belli played with his hearing aid. Occasionally the previous day, he had asked her to repeat a sentence, sometimes more than once. Serena swiveled in her chair.

Without preamble, Belli took Serena back to the morning of August 18, 1992—once again to show her pain and shock at the death of her sister. A number of the prosecution's witnesses had introduced the idea that Serena had not seemed to care, either that day or during the funeral. Belli's job was to place any inappropriate actions in the context of her inability to cope with tragedy and also to counteract those testimonies by proving that upon other occasions she *had* displayed her sorrow.

In telling the court about reentering the house after running into the street, Serena remembered, "I ran over to Mom and hugged her and she was like—now, I felt so much love for my mother at that moment because I knew she needed me and I was there for her."

Belli did not elaborate this nurturing aspect of Serena's personality, concentrating instead on her inability to handle the situation, which caused her to go "in shock." She had rushed out of the house later that day, she admitted, and had even gone to the mall with her friends in an attempt to "get away from the pain." In "staying away from the sadness" she "went out and did things just to make it look like there's a regular day, nothing has changed because I didn't want to be around that."

When the attorney asked for a further description of her feelings, Serena struggled for an explanation. "I was afraid that if I broke down, if I went home, I was afraid that if I went home that I would—it would—well, it's kind of hard to describe the way I was feeling. I was—I was kind of afraid if I went home and started crying and started letting out my feelings and everything started coming, I wouldn't be able to stop because I knew if I went back there and faced all the pain and stuff and faced it I would go crazy. I would just break down, and I would probably not be able to stop crying."

Belli was on a roll. In rebuttal to Delores Braden's testimony, he asked Serena to explain her "pom-pomming" after Mallory's funeral.

"The adults were trying to get drunk," she said with an embarrassed laugh and a tilt of her head. "Sometime after that they were like trying, they were cracking really weak jokes trying to make each other laugh or trying to build their spirits just a little bit. And me and my friend were observing all this, also feeling very sad. And so we consulted each other and I also consulted my mother about it and asked her if this was appropriate. We were going to show a dance that we had learned at cheerleading camp to show them, maybe try to help them lift their spirits a little bit. And I consulted with my mother. My mother said, yes, that would be a really nice thing to do. Go ahead with it. And so the whole family piled into the living room and we came out and did one dance and then everybody said that was very nice. We said thank you and we walked back into my room, changed clothes, and came back out and sat down and started talking with everybody. That's all that happened."

Later that evening, Serena noted, her mother "really needed me and I was there."

For the next few months, Serena had run away a lot because she couldn't stand to be in the house. She was particularly bothered by her mother's continuous questions if she "knew anything" about Mallory's death. Do you know anything at all about that night? Mom would ask. Can you tell me why? "Then she would cry to me," Serena continued, playing with the buttons on her blouse, "and she would say, 'Why, why, I don't understand why!' And I couldn't answer those questions and I would ask her, 'Please, can you please stop asking me those questions?' And she said, 'Well, you need to talk about it; we need to talk about it.' " During Christmas at Grandma Tessie's, her mom had cried and asked those questions again. Serena had consoled her, saying they would know a cause of death soon.

Belli had led Serena up to the moment of writing the confession. Did she remember writing the diary entry? he queried.

Serena replied that she did not "remember specifically doing it." She bit her lip and glanced sideways as she made the statement, as if she were bored.

Did she remember what she wrote?

The only way she knew what she wrote, Serena said, was "because people have been telling me."

Golde was watching her intently. She was lying about not remembering, and he knew it.

When pressed why she would write such a statement, Serena explained that she felt very guilty because she had not let Mallory sleep with her that night, that she wanted to answer her mother's questions and that she wanted her mom to realize that she, too, was feeling "really bad." At the time, she had remembered a conversation with her mother in which Mom had admitted reading her diary "only when I took off and she did not know where I was." So Serena wrote the diary entry, then "got up and walked out of the house." She did not see her mother again until she was in the "camera room," the suicide watch cell with a TV monitor at juvenile hall.

Belli tried to elicit from Serena what she had told her mother about the diary entry during their "camera room" visit. Golde's immediate "hearsay" objection was sustained.

When Belli wondered again why she wrote the entry, Serena grew exasperated. Hadn't she already answered that? It had been a split-second decision, she said, writing words that she thought only her mother would see. She knew her mom would get in the diary. She was "a very determined person."

The Moores watched in near-disbelief as their daughter fidgeted and threw them oddly amused glances as her testimony continued. The distress on her face must be due to her replies, they thought. Why was she so adamant in saying, "I don't know, I don't remember" when she so clearly was upset in giving those answers? Michael was convinced she had been coached.

Serena went on to say that she told Fremont police she hadn't written anything about her sister's death because at the time of that interview, she didn't remember having done so. Then when they showed her the diary, she lied, saying she had never seen it before. "It was the first thing that came to my mind," she explained, "because I was in such a habit of lying to people."

Her comment launched a brief discussion of her lying—a "hard habit to break." This habit, Belli prompted, she had it when she wrote the diary entry? Serena couldn't understand the question. Over Golde's objections, Belli managed to elicit her reasons for writing the entry one more time. She wanted her mother to stop asking her questions because she felt upset, insisted Serena, that was all.

"All right." Belli settled back in his chair, glancing at Golde. "You may cross-examine."

Margulies called a recess.

Twenty-eight

GOLDE'S GIRLFRIEND, JULIE, took a seat in front of the Moores as court reconvened. Anxious to watch Golde in action, she had followed his advice to attend on the day he cross-examined the defendant.

After talking to Matt Golde, Sharri whispered to Michael, the girl probably thought they were scum.

Pastor Doug and his wife, Sheila, were also in court, taking a seat on the third row behind the Moores. Although Doug's church responsibilities precluded him from viewing the entire trial, he had managed to attend every day, at least for a few hours. He had promised Serena during his last visit to juvenile hall that he would be present throughout her entire testimony. Doug was grateful that he had been able to support Serena in lieu of her parents. She had particularly needed his encouragement after hearing from Antonio that Michael had "hurt Mallory's bottom," as Serena put it. According to Serena, Shelley Antonio had told her that Michael had been in the act of abusing Mallory, had leaned on her too hard and killed her. What's more, Serena had recounted to Doug, Shelley Antonio suggested that Michael had abused *her* as well, and that she had "blacked out" all memory of the abuse. As close as she had become to Antonio, and blocked as she was from seeing her parents, Serena was beginning to believe it. She was very confused.

Doug was shocked at Antonio's opinions and even more

surprised that she would foist them upon her teenage client. He assumed these opinions were behind Antonio's reason for not allowing the Moores to visit Serena; she most likely would have told her parents what Antonio had said. As a pastor and counselor, Doug could not divulge his conversations with Serena; her secret was safe with him. But knowledge of it, and Serena's growing unrest over the matter, made him miserable.

Golde's cross of the defendant was to be long, nit-picking, and arduous. Serena was already nervously swiveling in the witness chair as he rose behind the counsel table. He began with a dig at her alleged lack of memory, establishing that she remembered other incidents in her life back to the age of one. Then, step by step, he led her through events from age seven to the present, starting with her mother's relationship with her first stepfather, who was physically abusive, and continuing on to life in the Moore household. Under his conversational-style questioning, Serena began to relax.

She had found marijuana in the home when she was about nine, she told the court, and had been "extremely mad" about it. About that time, she began to dislike her stepfather, Michael, whom she had liked before. She had been, and remained, close to her grandmother in Carson City.

In discussing Serena's school experiences, Golde "painted his picture," as he termed it, of a child who was continually disruptive, acting out until, numerous times, she had to change schools for a "fresh start." After running out of alternatives, her parents had sent her to live with her grandmother in Carson City when she was thirteen, but she had soon returned because "it didn't work out."

She'd had many, many boyfriends, as many as a dozen in one four-month period when she was twelve. But she didn't kiss any of them. Then in the summer after eighth grade, when she was fourteen, she had sex for the first time, with her boyfriend Troy.

It was Serena's second indication of the first time she had sex—over a year after her interview with Carson City police, during which she talked of Michael's forcing her into intercourse. In his opening argument, Golde had couched his references to sexual abuse very carefully, saying that the defendant "had reported" being "molested" by Michael. Serena could not deny having made the reports.

Golde needed to downplay Serena's tendency to lie in order to uphold her diary entry as a true confession. In covering Serena's relationship with Troy, he managed to do that to an extent by undermining Dr. Berg's testimony that Serena was a wild "exaggerator." For example, Dr. Berg had mentioned Serena's accounts of being engaged twice and having sex with Troy numerous times in one day, calling these accounts "exaggerations." But Serena had been engaged to Troy, had she not? Troy had given her a ring. She also *had* engaged in sex with Troy many times a day on occasion, and had been "engaged" to a previous boyfriend. Those weren't exaggerations either.

Golde steered Serena toward discussing her first years with Michael Moore. Serena conceded that when her mother and Michael argued, she would grow afraid, thinking it would escalate into hitting, as it had with her former stepdad. She would run to her room and cry. She never saw Michael hit her mother, though. After a while, she began hating Michael because he was trying to act like a father, disciplining her and spanking her "when [she] deserved it." Sometimes when she was really mad, she would "haul off and punch him" to provoke him. Then he would slap her to get her attention. Once or twice Michael may have gone "a bit too far" in his responses, but for the most part, Serena said, "I pretty much deserved what I got."

Hadn't one of those occasions included Michael's punching her hard in the stomach?

Not with his full force, Serena responded, but still it hurt.

"Weren't the police called on that occasion?"

Serena thought a moment. "Not right after that. Right after he did that, umm—oh, but I do want to say one thing."

"Go ahead."

Serena explained that she had attacked her mother, and Michael "was responding to his wife getting hurt by this child." She ran to the phone threatening to call the police, but her mom "ripped it out of the wall." After that, the argument settled and "everything turned out." Serena calmed herself down.

Golde continued with no objections from the defense.

Hadn't Serena eventually told the police about the incident? Yes, she said slowly, although she "overdid" it, adding a "bunch of stuff that really wasn't true." And when the police investigated, asking her parents about it, Golde prompted, hadn't her mother told them that Michael had never hit her?

Yes.

Had that lie bothered Serena?

Well, she hadn't really talked to her mom anymore about it. She apologized for "being rude" and "just wanted to gain a fresh start." They were okay awhile after that.

Sharri was furious. "He's mixing up stories again," she whispered to no one in particular. And, she later insisted, he'd managed to confuse Serena, who had never spoken to the police about that incident. Serena *had* told the police a lie months later, when she accused Michael of giving her the bruises she got while staying overnight with her boyfriend Larry. That's when Sharri had told the police that "nothing happened" at home between Serena and Michael. Officer Lamb had investigated that incident, declared Serena's report "unfounded," and dropped the case. The two events had been months apart, one when Mallory was alive, the other after she had died. Officer Lamb's police report was in Serena's fat file, Sharri would declare; she and Michael had seen it. If Serena had spoken to the police about the stomach-punching, where was that report? It was *nowhere,* she would fume, because it didn't *exist.*

Sharri realized her story could not be told now. She was done testifying and even if put back on the stand, she could only answer questions the attorneys wanted to ask. She and Michael weren't supposed to talk to the press. And they couldn't even talk to Serena to find out why she had been so easily led into agreeing that the police had been called. She'd told so many lies over the years, Sharri offered later, she probably was mixed up herself about what report she did or did not make.

At any rate, the Deputy D.A. had succeeded in making Sharri Moore out to be a liar, a heinous term to her way of thinking. She had worked *very hard* to be honest on the stand, she exclaimed, and hated the continued implications, the name-calling. Everybody in the courtroom except for her friends and family members were looking at her in derision.

She couldn't stand much more. She wanted to *wring Matt Golde's scrawny little hairy neck!*

Golde moved on. "Isn't it true that your mom and stepdad had a lot of verbal arguments?"

Yeah, Serena said, but mainly they "encircled" around her and her bratty behavior.

Next came a thorough investigation into Serena's "attempt to kill her mother" with a cigarette. No, Serena insisted, she had only threatened to "hurt" her mother. And what about her stepfather? Golde pulled out a document provided by Dr. Berg, labeled by the court as 10E. Did that refresh the defendant's memory that she had had "aggressive fantasies toward shooting Michael with a gun?"

Neither Antonio nor Belli raised an objection to Golde's question, asking only to see 10E before it was shown to Serena. Belli looked it over, said "thank you," and passed it back to Golde. A few questions later, after Serena denied telling anybody that she wanted to shoot her stepfather, Belli did object, stating there "was no foundation laid." It was also "incompetent, irrelevant, immaterial, and hearsay." Margulies overruled, saying that the foundation had been laid by Dr. Berg's testimony.

Golde continued to hammer Serena into remembering about wanting to shoot Michael. In frustration she finally retorted, "I do not *ever* remember saying that to *anybody* at all at *any* time in my *whole* life!"

Margulies came to her rescue, instructing Golde to move on.

Well, had Serena "yelled vulgarities" in the psychologist's office when she had threatened her mother with a cigarette?

Belli's booming voice drowned out Serena's answer. "Objection as incompetent, irrelevant, and immaterial!"

Overruled.

Yes, she had, said Serena, but she couldn't remember exactly what. And yes to Golde's question about breaking the antenna to her mother's car. That was after they had been fighting about her boyfriend Larry. He had put hickeys on her neck and her mother had called her a slut.

Golde's portrait of Serena and her parents was growing darker by the moment. By the time he turned to a new line of questioning, he had clearly established that she was unpredictable and violence-prone. The implication hung in the air—if she had threatened to "kill" her mother and had "fantasies" of shooting her stepfather, who was to say she wouldn't murder her little sister?

Court recessed for lunch.

Golde was back at it that afternoon, honing in on the diary entry and Serena's interview with police. The ensuing discussion, Golde later remarked, proved so damaging for the defense that he believed the case "turned" on Serena's testimony. By the time his cross-examination was complete on Monday, Golde would be almost certain he had won.

Relentlessly, he asked about her writing the diary entry; again and again she stubbornly denied any memory of it— "Like I said before, I don't remember." Golde then covered her statements to police in detail. She had first denied writing any such entry, then, having been shown the diary, had denied it was hers. *Then* she'd said, well, maybe the diary was hers, but that handwriting certainly wasn't. She had lied continuously to the police, had she not?

Serena "couldn't recall" much of the conversation.

When asked for handwriting exemplars, she had deliberately tried to change her penmanship, wasn't that true?

That Serena hotly denied, saying she "had changed her handwriting many times over the years."

Belli objected loudly and often; the questions were argumentative, the witness had "no obligation" to answer. Margulies's responses were just as repetitive. "Overruled."

Throughout her testimony about the diary and her arrest, Serena shot nervous glances at her parents, picked at her clothes and swung right and left in her chair. Sharri and Michael were astounded by her answers. Where were these answers coming from? they wondered.

Before court recessed Friday afternoon, Serena's discomfort grew, and her parents' anger increased. Just as she'd hedged regarding her memories of writing the diary and her arrest, she began hedging when Golde asked her questions about sexual abuse. Sharri believed Antonio was behind that, as well.

Golde, attempting to prove his theory of Serena's motive for the crime, asked her about taking her sister in the truck as a means of "getting Mallory away from Michael." To Michael, it was a chance for Serena to tell the world that it had been merely an impulsive joyride and had nothing to do with "getting away" from abuse. Instead, she faltered in her answers, which prompted Golde to read aloud her statement to police after being picked up. Serena "couldn't recall" the discussion.

"*Why* did you take Mallory in the car?" Golde pressed.

"Because I wanted to leave. And I felt, like I said before, that there was a lot of things, that there were a lot of things going on that right now I don't think were happening. That I didn't really know."

"Such as?"

She hesitated. "I don't know."

"So there was something that you thought was happening but now you think really wasn't happening, right?"

"Something like that. It's, it's kind of hard to—back then I thought something—I didn't know what was going on, but now I really don't know if it was."

"Are you talking about sexual molestation?"

"No." Serena's eyes darted around the room. "Well, not, no. Not altogether."

"Is it hard for you to talk about this in front of your mom and stepdad?"

Serena twisted her mouth. "Not really."

"What was it that you thought was going on?"

"I didn't know." Her voice was quiet.

"What was it that you now think really wasn't going on?"

"I don't know. I wish I could remember, but I can't."

"Was it abusive?"

"Like I said, I really can't remember. If I could remember, I'd tell you, but I can't."

"Are you afraid that your mom might get upset at you if you said something bad about Michael here?"

"Not really."

"She's done it in the past though, hasn't she?"

"Yes."

"Is that influencing your testimony right here?"

"No, not really."

"Maybe a little bit, though?"

"Maybe the tiniest bit, but not all that much."

It was all the conceding that Golde needed to further his certainty that Serena Moore had been abused and that her mother had and would continue to silence any proof of it. If Serena had admitted that it was "the tiniest bit" hard telling the truth in front of her parents, then as far as Golde was concerned, it was *extremely* hard. After all, according to her own grandmother's testimony, when she'd tried to tell the truth in the past, Sharri had turned against her, warning that she "would no longer have a family."

Michael felt sick as Serena continued to flounder at the questions, even going so far as to say that she thought "a stepfather" may have molested her, while purposely not clarifying which stepfather she was talking about. Midway through the afternoon, he'd had enough.

"I'm tired of this," he muttered loudly enough for those around him to hear, including Golde's girlfriend. "I'm not taking this shit anymore." He stood up, pushed his way past people's knees and retreated to the witness room, a temporary shelter from the accusations in the courtroom and the constant cameras roaming the hall.

Golde's questions pounded on until Serena's face took on a pained expression. She began listing awkwardly to one side as if she were uncomfortable. Judge Margulies asked if she was all right.

Yes, Serena replied, but her side hurt "real bad."

Margulies called a recess, during which she met with counsel at side bar to work out the upcoming week's schedule. When Golde told the judge that his cross would take another forty-five minutes, Margulies decided Serena had endured about all she could take, and stopped for the day.

Back on record, Margulies summarized her discussion with counsel during side bar, noting that the minor's testimony would conclude sometime Monday morning, followed by one or two "short" witnesses. Monday afternoon would be filled with yet another defense witness—meaning Dr. Lawrence— whose testimony was anticipated to spill over until Tuesday morning. Golde's rebuttal would begin Tuesday afternoon.

Both counsels concurred.

As soon as court adjourned, Pastor Doug made a beeline for Serena's probation officer, requesting special visitation that evening because Serena so obviously needed counseling.

He was in luck. The P.O. said he could see Serena right then, before she was transported back to juvenile hall. Led by a bailiff, Doug wound his way through a neighboring court-room and into a small holding area that included a window covered with chicken wire, through which he could talk to Serena via telephone.

She was eager to see him. When he tried to reassure her, she cut him off, saying she just didn't know what to do. What if Michael *did* kill Mallory, Serena asked Pastor Doug, as she claimed Antonio had said?

"Look, Serena," Doug enjoined, "that's *their* opinion. They're putting this in your mind. Remember the truth, re-member it as *you* remember it, not what they're trying to get you to remember."

They were allowed only a few more minutes. Doug left their encounter not entirely sure she had heard his admonishment.

Twenty-nine

DR. LAWRENCE'S REPORT must have presented Antonio with a major dilemma. His finding of asthma was what she wanted to hear, but his opinion that the molestation never happened didn't fit with her certainty that it had. After that "wake-up call" from Dr. Herrmann, she apparently couldn't shake the belief. Dr. Lawrence had been a coroner in San Joaquin County for twenty years, had studied forensic pathology ex-tensively in six carefully chosen locations nationwide, had been at the Mayo Clinic for three years, and had even studied under Dr. Herrmann, a man whose opinion Lawrence held in high regard. Yet he couldn't have disagreed more with Dr. Herrmann's conclusions.

According to his two-page report:

> . . . *At the time of death the child was undergoing an asthma attack. This is evidenced by the prominent eosinophilia*

around major bronchi and the presence of mucus plugs. There is also evidence of long-standing asthma in the form of thickening of the bronchial basement membranes.

The autopsy findings of SIDS deaths and suffocation or asphyxial deaths can be identical . . . and include such things as petechial hemorrhages and congestion of the lungs and other organs. However, in the case of asthma, there will be additional findings in the bronchi as described above, said findings being absent in SIDS and suffocation.

The petechial hemorrhages described about the face in this case are not usual in cases of SIDS or asthma, but can occur. It is my opinion that, without additional circumstantial evidence of assault, the medical findings are insufficient to allow a conclusion that there is a reasonable medical certainty that death was due to traumatic asphyxia.

Traumatic asphyxia infers pressure on the body sufficient to preclude adequate respiratory activity, such as overlying of the body with an adult's body or massive pressing of the child's face down into the bedding. In either of these mechanisms, with an apparently robust and healthy four-year-old, I would expect to find evidence of the mechanical forces applied, such as tooth cuts or at least contusions about the lips and perhaps bruising about the held areas of the body.

The most common cause of facial petechial hemorrhages in my experience is sudden death due to arteriosclerotic heart disease. Here the patient is undergoing hypoxia [lack of oxygen] from heart failure . . . as the person grunts and gasps for air. I can envision the same sort of hypoxia and respiratory activity in a child dying from obstructive airway disease.

The other subject that I must address is that of possible trauma to the anus. Dr. Herrmann describes a "relaxed and dilated" anus during the external examination and later describes what seemed to be several radiating healed laceration injuries. Then, after the anogenital block was excised and dissected, he states that the old healed lacerations were no longer definite. In the microscopic examination of the anus he describes possible fibrosis. I did not find significant fibrosis. The only fibrosis seen is around nerves and, in my opinion, represents normal anatomy rather than scarring of an old healed injury.

As to the anal dilatation itself, I believe that this is often a postmortem phenomenon. I have seen several cases in children and adults in which the anus is relaxed and dilated in the absence of any anal trauma whatsoever. The medical findings do not establish a reasonable medical certainty of either fresh or old anal sexual abuse.

I respect greatly Dr. Herrmann's skill, knowledge and ability, and feel that, as usual, he has done a thorough and competent postmortem examination. I merely question his interpretation of some of his findings, and believe that he has perhaps arrived at conclusions that the medical data do not prove.

Lawrence's reference to the petechiae being normal, and the eosinophils and mucus plugging as indicators of an asthma attack were strikingly similar to the conclusions reached by Dr. Warnock. This was of compelling significance since the two physicians had never spoken. Conclusions regarding the anus were identical also, even though Dr. Warnock had declined to offer her opinion about it in court.

The weekend did little to settle Sharri's or Michael's nerves. They did not venture from their house, feeling too exhausted and overwhelmed to make the effort. Madison and Misty prowled continually under their feet, as if sensing their anxiety. Sharri was hardly eating, existing for the most part on coffee. Since Mallory's death, she had lost twenty-seven pounds, going from a size nine dress to size three, which had been her normal size before her pregnancy with Mallory. She'd wanted to take off the extra weight ever since Mallory was born, but could think of a lot better ways to do it. Of those twenty-seven pounds, she'd lost seven during the trial. By week's end, she would lose three more. Her nervousness had grown so acute that the thought of food made her nauseous.

She was on the edge, and she knew it.

Monday's temperature would reach into the eighties. Sharri donned a light-colored long summer dress and sandals. Her legs were bare. Michael pulled on a pair of brown slacks and a short-sleeved shirt. His Mallory penny lay underneath.

An hour later, stepping anxiously out of the courthouse elevator, he and Sharri discovered one consolation. The TV cameras had disappeared.

*   *   *

The two-day break hadn't helped Serena either. Life in juvenile hall was grim enough without the dread of more testifying. As in the previous week, she appeared on the stand Monday morning in an apprehensive, even manic state, swiveling in her seat and throwing strange smiles and other facial expressions at spectators. To those who did not understand her emotional repression, she would seem as though she failed to realize the seriousness of her situation. Or didn't give a damn.

Sketch artist Joan Lynch, drawing only the defendant's outlined form, seemed frustrated that she could not better depict the girl's attitude.

Golde launched immediately again into the sexual abuse, as if Friday's court session had never recessed. Under his questioning, Serena admitted she had told numerous friends and relatives that she had been abused. Golde did not ask whether these statements had been true. Regarding her mother's alleged threats to her after Michael had been arrested, Serena said that on the phone her mother indicated she could not speak with her, as advised by the police. Nevertheless— it was not clear whether Serena was referring to the phone conversation or her mother's subsequent letter—her mother had warned her that she "would not be able to come back [home] and live." It wasn't, Serena noted, "like 'you're not going to have a family or you're never going to see me again.'"

Golde pulled out another report, marked 10F, a conversation between Serena and a doctor at Truckee Meadows Mental Health Clinic. Had she not told the doctor that "her mother did not believe [the sexual abuse charges] and told her she would not speak to her or let her see her sister?" Serena couldn't remember saying that, but allowed as though she probably had.

People's Exhibit #14 was the long Carson City police statement. Golde covered it in detail, asking Serena if she had made the various accusations contained in the transcript, with particular emphasis on the discussion with the police officer regarding her fear at having to testify in court against her stepfather. Again, Serena couldn't deny having made the statements. She was not asked if the allegations themselves were true.

Defense counsel was silent until Golde abruptly changed subjects, asking if Serena remembered telling her grandmother Sarah Moore that she had engaged in anal sex. Belli objected, iterating he wasn't sure where the prosecution "was going with that." Margulies sustained.

"And to Officer Uhler," Golde continued smoothly, "you said that Mallory was better off dead than alive and it's a lousy place for a kid to grow up?"

"I didn't say it like that, no."

"You didn't say that?"

"No, no," Belli declared suddenly, "she didn't say that. She said she didn't say it like that."

Serena glanced at him amusedly, then shook her head. "Didn't say it like that."

"Excuse me, Mr. Belli," Margulies interrupted, "if you have an objection, make the objection."

"Object, Your Honor. That wasn't what the reply was."

Serena tried again to explain the now infamous phrase. "All I could say is that my sister is better off in heaven than down here. Because, what I mean by that is that when I am getting accused of something I didn't do, I was mad at the world and so I was trying to express that everybody is better off in heaven than this world."

"You didn't say it's a lousy world to be a kid now?"

"No." Serena's voice was firm.

His cross finally over, Golde sat down.

Belli remained seated for redirect and began with the grim mistake of addressing Serena as Mallory. Then he stated—not questioned—that she had been willing to take a lie detector test.

"Objection, irrelevant," Golde called.

"Sustained," Margulies replied. "Answer stricken."

The defense attorney asked to be heard on the matter. Margulies shot him down, reminding him that information about lie detector tests, whether actually given or simply offered, were not relevant. "That's real well-known, Mr. Belli."

Belli seemed in a particularly cantankerous mood. "Not well-known," he argued. "I remember writing an article in 4 Villa—"

"*Mr.* Belli, the objection is sustained. Ask your next question, please."

He requested allowance to "make a record on that" and Margulies told him to go ahead. He wanted to show that Serena had been willing to take a lie detector test as offered by Uhler, Belli informed the court. Authority on the matter was "4 Villanova on law review." He had written the article, but couldn't remember the pagination. . . .

"Is it your position, Mr. Belli," Margulies countered, "that lie detector tests are admissible as evidence in the State of California?"

"May I finish, Your Honor?"

"Is that your position?"

"Yes, Your Honor, for one sole purpose." Mouth pursed, Margulies waved him on. The tests could be used to show consciousness of innocence, Belli insisted. The officer had asked whether Serena wanted to take a lie detector test and she had said yes.

Margulies's feet were in cement; the sustainment remained.

Belli turned to the diary entry. Serena told him again that the confession she had written was not the truth. Now, wondered the attorney, did she want to take a lie detector test at this time?

"Objection!"

Belli ignored Golde. "As to whether you killed your sister or not under any circumstances?"

"Objection! Irrelevant!"

"Sustained."

"Would you take one now?"

"Objection, irrelevant!"

"Sustained."

"I am trying to make a record on this, Your Honor," Belli rejoined.

Margulies kept her voice calm. "That's fine. You can ask the question and I'll make my rulings."

"Thank you, Judge."

"But the objection is sustained."

Belli would not back down, posing three more questions on the matter before an irritated Margulies asked one of her own on a different subject to throw him off course. What followed was information that would not be embellished until months later, after the trial. Serena stated that she had written other lies in her diary. Belli asked for an example, which she willingly gave—that one boyfriend had gotten her pregnant and a second wanted to kill him for it. Belli then moved on, hopping from one issue to another until he circled back to the lie detector test, eliciting another objection from Golde, once again sustained. Again and again, he quizzed Serena as to why she wrote the diary entry.

"Didn't I already [answer] that—?" she finally retorted in frustration.

Margulies looked up from her notes. "I am sorry?"

"Like *five times.*"

"Well," Margulies hesitated, "there's no objection so go ahead and answer the question."

"Objection. Asked and answered." Matt Golde to the rescue.

Serena emitted a sigh of relief. "Thank you."

"Sustained."

On to another series of subjects, Golde objecting regularly as to their relevancy. Margulies consistently sustained. By the time Serena was allowed to step down, sometime after 11:00 A.M., she seemed almost reticent, as if she couldn't quite believe the ordeal was over.

"Do you want to stay up there some more?" Belli teased.

"No, no. That's okay. I'm just fine sitting right there." She hurried to the counsel table and flopped thankfully into her chair.

"The defense calls Mrs. Moore."

Sharri cocked her head in surprise, then rose, smoothing her dress as she made her way to the stand. What was this for? She wished she had been warned.

Antonio resumed the questioning, asking Sharri about her sleeplessness the night of Mallory's death, the position in which Mallory lay when found dead, and "other lies" in Serena's diary. Without success, Antonio tried to introduce additional testimony as to Serena's tendency to lie, over Golde's continuous objections. Numerous answers to the queries were stricken from the record. Sharri did manage to mention Serena's lying to police when she ran off with her friend at age nine, and the report of pregnancy in her diary.

Golde's cross was brief. Serena had lied to police at age nine in order to keep out of trouble, wasn't that correct? It was important for the prosecution to establish the difference between the lie at age nine and the diary entry, which was not written as a response to Serena's "being in trouble."

Sharri agreed that was the case.

Golde had nothing more.

Antonio was about to enter into some trouble of her own. When Margulies instructed her to call the next defense witness, the attorney checked the witness room, expecting to find Tina Craig and Marietta Wilson. She apparently hadn't realized they had not been at court since Thursday. Margulies, Golde, reporters, and spectators waited in the silent courtroom as Antonio reentered and hurried over to Sharri, seated again next to Michael, for a whispered conference. "Where are they?"

Angry and upset over this "latest example of Antonio's sloppiness," Sharri vindictively reminded her that both witnesses had requested subpoenas and that Tina had been forced to return to school when unable to produce one to satisfy her parents and teachers. Without comment, Antonio turned on her heel and approached the bench, failing in an attempt to hide her fluster.

"Your Honor, the two witnesses that were—did not come today that I had asked to come and I thought that Mr. Golde's cross would be a little bit longer."

Margulies did not seem pleased. Antonio had been unprepared one too many times, previously with discovery materials, now with witnesses. "I thought our discussion was that we would have these two witnesses available this morning."

"Yes. I asked, I wanted them to come today and apparently that didn't happen."

Well, were they going to show up at all?

Antonio replied that she would try to locate one of the defendant's friends, who was now back in school, according to Sharri Moore. She wasn't sure why the other witness had not shown up.

"When did you talk to them?"

"I talked to them on Friday."

"What time did you tell them to be here?"

"For the morning session."

"Did you give them a time?"

"I said we were starting at nine-thirty."

"Did you subpoena them?"

"No, I didn't. They were voluntarily to come."

Margulies suggested a recess to give Antonio time to locate her witnesses. If unable to do so, she could then call her next expert witness, as discussed last Friday.

That would be Dr. Lawrence, Antonio volunteered.

Golde spoke up, complaining that he still hadn't received any discovery for Lawrence.

Antonio responded quickly, "I talked to Mr. Golde this morning and he said all I have to do is give him the report."

Margulies would not be placated. "Why didn't you give him the report sooner since we have been talking about this since last week?"

Antonio had only received Dr. Lawrence's report on Friday, she answered. Then she simply had forgotten to give it to the prosecution.

"She's *lying* again," Sharri muttered to Michael. They'd personally handed that report to Belli on Thursday morning, plus Michael had faxed a copy to their offices Wednesday night.

Margulies exhaled audibly. Antonio would call Dr. Lawrence, she declared, and his testimony would probably go into tomorrow morning. If Golde needed extra time to prepare for cross, she would simply order the witness back. She had discussed this matter with counsel last week, and thought it clear that the report was to be turned over in advance.

Antonio apologized. She had "just forgotten."

Without further discussion, Margulies ordered prosecution and defense counsel back for a side bar conference at 11:30 A.M. to report on the status of witnesses.

Her vindictiveness quickly abating, Sharri knew the repercussions of Marietta's not testifying could be far greater on Serena than Shelley Antonio. She checked her watch. Ten fifty-five. She had thirty-five minutes to race down Interstate 880, cross the San Mateo Bridge, take 101 to Redwood City, where the boat on which Marietta and Ted lived was docked, and then make the return trip to court. Since there was no phone on the boat, Sharri could not call ahead.

She practically ran to Michael's Ranger, hastily paying the attendant at the parking garage exit, then heading onto Winton for a quick entrance onto 880. The round-trip would take about an hour; she could only hope that, once informed by Antonio in side bar that a witness was on her way, the judge would agree to wait. Eventually pulling to a jerky halt at the Redwood City Marina parking lot, Sharri ran down its old wooden docks and hopped onto Marietta's boat. She was in bed, asleep.

"Come *on,*" Sharri cried without preamble as she woke her friend, "you're on the stand next."

Marietta blinked her eyes, then hopped out of bed, instantly alert. "You're kidding!"

"No, I'm not. You should've seen Shelley's face when she went to get you and you weren't there! She told the judge she talked to you on Friday and told you to be there."

Marietta's mouth dropped open. "How could she do that? I don't even have a phone!"

"I know, never mind," Sharri said abstractedly. "Just get dressed and let's *go!*"

Back in court, Antonio asked Marietta questions about Mallory's and Serena's relationship, wanting to strengthen Mary Corren's testimony that they had been very close. Marietta told the court that Serena often acted more like a "second mother" to her little sister, and also that Serena had a "reputation for telling stories." Antonio pressed her for examples but once again was unable to pursue the subject, Margulies agreeing with Golde's objections that the information was hearsay.

Antonio then elicited information as to the position of Mallory's body, telling Judge Margulies that she was using the testimony to "impeach"—prove untrue—Sharri Moore's statements. Marietta told the court that as she understood from Sharri, Mallory had been found "on her back with her right shoulder slightly raised, her head back, her knees bent and angled outward."

Marietta's statement, Sharri would later insist, "wasn't right"—her friend had misunderstood her explanation regarding the position of Mallory's body. Again, she was livid, not at Marietta, but at Antonio's "impeachment." What was the point of it? If Antonio was making her out to be a liar, how could the judge believe *anything* she had said, like the fact that she'd heard nothing the night Mallory died?

In his short cross-examination, Golde capitalized on Marietta's account of the loving sisters. Did Serena protect and take care of Mallory? Marietta agreed that she had. The answer provided another layer in the foundation for Golde's alleged motive, which he would forcefully argue in his closing statements.

Court recessed for lunch. Dr. Lawrence—defense counsel's potential ace in the hole and Michael's final chance for vindication—would take the stand at 2:00 P.M.

◈

Thirty

NOT SURPRISINGLY, SINCE she agreed with his report, at first sight Sharri found Dr. Lawrence much more likable than Dr. Herrmann. Dr. Lawrence looked to be in his mid-fifties, about six feet tall and fairly slim, with a measure of warmth and compassion she thought missing in Dr. Herrmann. A tan sport coat blended with his light brown hair, creating a bland, washed-out look. Glasses and a receding hairline lent a sense of distinction.

Dr. Lawrence seated himself in the witness chair as if he belonged. He seemed calm, yet confident—just another day at the office. Antonio, appearing anxious for his testimony, launched aggressively into *voir dire* without so much as a greeting.

Board certified in anatomic and clinical pathology, Dr. Lawrence had been practicing in Stockton for twenty years, where, among other duties, he performed autopsies for the San Joaquin County coroner's office. A strategically planned series of courses in numerous medical examiners' offices across the country had enabled him to become board certified in the subspecialty of forensic pathology. His criteria for choosing the various locations included national reputation as well as specific strengths in each one. The Los Angeles Medical Examiner's Office was chosen for its sheer volume and variety of cases. Dallas was an all-inclusive site, including trace evidence examination equipment, etc. New York City provided toxicology training; Detroit afforded him experience with gunshot trauma. And he had spent extra time in San Francisco to learn about "death involving sexual situations."

There was little damage Golde could do in his *voir dire* cross except to strengthen the point that Dr. Herrmann had been involved in Dr. Lawrence's forensic pathology training.

At the outset, Dr. Lawrence's answers in direct questioning were as brief and to the point as Dr. Herrmann's had been lengthy and lecturing. To Antonio's first seven queries regarding his review of Mallory Moore's case, he responded a mere "yes."

Using photographs taken of Dr. Herrmann's original slides, Dr. Lawrence then pointed to conditions in Mallory's lungs he believed indicated asthma, much as Dr. Warnock had done a week before. The case, he conceded, was difficult in determining cause of death, but absent any other information regarding an assault, he would have certified the death as due to asthma.

Golde was not pleased with the way Antonio was eliciting information from Dr. Lawrence. "I would ask the court to admonish at this point that Miss Antonio refrain from asking leading questions," he complained. "Every single question she's asking is leading."

"Miss Antonio," Margulies responded tonelessly, "please do not ask leading questions."

As the defense attorney posed more specific queries about the condition of Mallory's lungs, Dr. Lawrence's answers lengthened. Were there any signs of trauma to the body? she asked. It was a subject she had not pursued with Dr. Herrmann.

No, Dr. Lawrence said, there were no bruises, fingernail marks, cuts of the lips, or other such signs. Neither did signs exist of smothering by a pillow or by covering the nose and mouth with a hand. "It's just inconceivable to me that you can do that with a struggling child long enough to cause death without leaving bruises," he remarked, "especially on mucosal surfaces of the lips, but also about the face and nose and perhaps around the neck or at the angles of the jaw where the bony ridges are present. You would leave some bruising."

"What about the inside of the mouth? You would expect to find something to show abrasions from the teeth?"

"There would be tooth cuts and bruises about the lips."

"Did Dr. Herrmann note any of that in his report?"

"No."

Much to the Moores' relief—and surprise—Antonio allowed Dr. Lawrence to announce his conclusions regarding the anal dilation and scarring, explaining carefully in a long discussion how and why he disagreed with Dr. Herrmann's findings.

"So you would not conclude from that finding that there was sexual abuse at the time of death?" Antonio said.

Golde voiced an irritated objection. "Would you caution Miss Antonio to stop asking leading questions, especially at these issues," he petitioned.

Margulies pushed back her chair and called counsel to side bar, where a short discussion ensued. Back on record, Margulies helped Antonio rephrase her questions.

Reading from Dr. Herrmann's autopsy report, Dr. Lawrence noted the coroner's notation of star-shaped lacerations extending outward from the circumference of the anus. "What this means to me is that he saw either some scarring or some irregularity in the region of the anus that looked like they could be old, healed cuts. Now, if I saw this I would be alarmed that there was some history of perhaps sexual abuse and it needs to be looked at further. He then says, 'When the anorectum is opened, evidence of tearing of the junction is not so apparent . . . no evidence of erosion or contusion or laceration of a fresh nature is seen.'

"So what this means to you now is that he was concerned about the possibility of old, healed cuts, but he then opened it up and looked at it carefully and said that those apparent cuts now were difficult to see. So he again seems to be backing off from that."

Lawrence noted there was a "small area that could be a scar from an old injury, a very small scar in the anus," and that was it. The injury could have been caused by anything from sexual abuse to "straining at stool with constipation" or even, perhaps, by passing a foreign object such as a chicken bone.

In concluding her direct, Antonio returned to the subject of traumatic asphyxia. According to the diary confession, Serena had put a hand over Mallory's mouth and suffocated her. Antonio wanted to make the point that the confession did not correlate with the autopsy findings—an important avenue that she had not pursued with Dr. Herrmann. Would covering someone's mouth be enough to suffocate that person? she wondered.

"It can be if it's done correctly. Technically, that would not be traumatic asphyxia. Traumatic asphyxia means that the person has so much pressure against their body that they're unable to have respiratory movement and therefore suffocate."

"So," Antonio hesitated, "so if you cover the nose—if you just cover the mouth you wouldn't even have suffocation?"

"That's correct, you would not. If you cover both the nose and the mouth completely for several minutes, then you would have death due to suffocation, smothering."

"Okay. Would you have traumatic asphyxia?"

Not really, Dr. Lawrence replied, but they were "splitting hairs."

Antonio nodded. "Thank you. That's all." She resumed her seat and patted an unusually quiet Serena on the arm.

Golde's cross was aggressive, his questions clipped, almost argumentative. Exuding an air of impatience, he asked if Dr. Lawrence had spoken with Dr. Herrmann about the case, then interrupted the witness's answer to demand "why not?"

There was no time to check with the attorney if that would be appropriate or not before testifying, Dr. Lawrence said. Most of his communication had been with the Moore family.

Golde grilled the doctor about the information he had used to reach his findings. Had he thought Mallory Moore a severe asthmatic? Had he seen medical reports, police reports, etc.? Had he talked to Martha Warnock?

Again, Lawrence replied that there had been little time, and that, by looking over past medical records, he felt he may have been overly influenced in reaching his own conclusions.

Well, countered Golde, was the witness saying he purposely did not want other information? Hadn't he said earlier that such information would be useful?

Antonio seemed as wound up as Golde, bombarding the judge with one objection after another, most of which were overruled. She fell into such a rhythm that she threw one out after Margulies posed a query of her own. The question was "asked and answered, irrelevant, incompetent, and immaterial."

"You're objecting to the *court's* question?" Margulies inquired evenly.

Antonio back-pedaled, then, within the next ten minutes, offered another series of multiple objections, earning herself another trip to side bar for a second conference with Margulies.

Belli sat quietly throughout much of the testimony, fingers steepled, gazing at the ceiling. Occasionally, he leaned over to whisper in Antonio's ear.

With nit-picking precision, the Deputy D.A. kept at it, leading Dr. Lawrence finally to admit that someone could have attacked Mallory Moore, but, absent any further indication of such an attack, he could not agree with the cause of death being traumatic asphyxia. He also conceded that he was at a disadvantage in not viewing the autopsy himself.

The clock was nearing 4:30 P.M. Golde gave no sign that his energy was abating. With a final triad of objections from Antonio, Margulies called it a day, announcing that everyone return at nine-thirty Tuesday morning.

Dr. Lawrence was dismayed. He was the only doctor scheduled to cover at Lodi Memorial Hospital in the morning, he told the judge. Perhaps they could wait until the afternoon session?

Margulies's tone remained neutral, but her message was unmistakable. She'd had enough of the Belli firm's scheduling mishaps. She'd been over this with counsel, she declared, had made it very clear that their witness should be prepared to return to court Tuesday morning.

Dr. Lawrence replied that, as he understood it, if testimony spilled over into Tuesday, it would not occur until the afternoon.

"Could it go over to tomorrow afternoon, Your Honor?" Belli broke in.

"No. We are going to go into tomorrow morning."

"Are they life-saving measures or what is it that you can be there?" Belli directed to Lawrence. Then in confused syntax, he attempted to persuade the judge and reassure his witness in the same sentence. "Your Honor, if it's a life-saving situation I am sure Your Honor would accommodate you."

"*Excuse me,* Mr. Belli." Margulies turned back toward Dr. Lawrence. "There are other pathologists. I know you could find other doctors to cover. And I made this very clear to counsel." She did not fault Dr. Lawrence, as he had been given erroneous information; nevertheless, she could not fill his request to wait until afternoon session. "Okay," she pronounced, "we'll see everyone tomorrow at nine-thirty, please."

Abruptly, she rose and left the courtroom before Belli could argue further.

Tuesday morning.

TV cameras were still nowhere to be seen, making it easier for the Moores to roam the hallway during recess. The usual gaggle of reporters was present, Bob Salladay's articles still appearing regularly on the front page of the *Argus* in a blow-by-blow account of proceedings. Reporters and observers were beginning to feel antsy as the trial drew to a close. With a verdict expected in a few days, general consensus among the media was for acquittal. Matt Golde had done a good job on prosecution, they agreed, but the medical testimony had produced enough reasonable doubt to go around. They were far less certain about the defendant's actual guilt or innocence. That, some felt, may never be known.

Based on the plethora of testimony, reporters' coverage had included continuous references to sexual abuse in the Moore household, ranging from Dr. Herrmann's conclusion of sodomy to Serena's past statements to police. Golde, repeatedly questioned as to what he intended to do about the accusations, particularly the alleged sodomy, was playing his cards close to his chest. Whenever a reporter pressed him on the subject, Golde declined to say who he thought was responsible, although his belief as to the culprit was clear enough in court.

Michael and Sharri had clipped every article they'd found regarding the trial, sick as they thought all of them were, placing them in a quickly fattening file. They also taped every segment on the evening news, switching back and forth between channels. In the midst of the allegations, their only salvation at this point was the knowledge that the trial would soon be over and Serena would be back home again. With the verdict drawing near, however, they were beset by increasing apprehension. Even with Serena home and their nightmare behind them, the future was nebulous at best. Serena undoubtedly would need long-term, intensive psychiatric treatment, which they could ill afford. Even more frightening, without the current distraction, however horrible it was, they would be left finally to grieve for Mallory, which was sure to send them on yet another emotional roller coaster.

For Michael, life without Mallory lacked fulfillment and any sense of anticipation.

Caught in a state of flux, the Moores chose their usual seats on the right side of the courtroom Tuesday morning, vascillating between resignation that their reputations would never be vindicated in court and hope that their story still could emerge. They had abandoned their decision to hand copies of Dr. Lawrence's report to members of the media since he had testified on the issue of the anal dilation and scarring. They still did not know if Michael would be allowed to speak for himself on the stand.

Dr. Lawrence was back Tuesday morning as ordered, having scrambled to find a replacement at Lodi Memorial. At 9:38 A.M., Serena was led in, wearing slacks and a summery shirt with multicolored stripes. Her hair was in a ponytail. She shot a sad smile at her parents without parting her lips, then slouched unceremoniously in her chair, accepting greetings from Belli and Antonio silently.

Sharri knew the signs. Things were coming down to the wire, and Serena was scared.

Margulies called the session to order. Golde was already standing behind the counsel table, looking as if raring to go. He kicked off his remaining cross of Dr. Lawrence abruptly, delving into the now-familiar medical matters of petechial hemorrhages, eosinophils, and mucus-plugged bronchi. Regarding the first, Dr. Lawrence noted, he did not fully agree with Dr. Herrmann that all the reddish spots on Mallory's face were indeed petechial hemorrhages. Even if they were, he still believed unequivocally that there was insufficient evidence to "make a positive determination that death was due to traumatic asphyxia."

Some time later, he remained as firm on his opinion about the anal scar, saying that it "could be from a minor tear of the mucosa such as during straining with a constipated stool." As for the dilation, he'd seen it "many times in adults and children" after death; therefore, the sight "did not upset" him.

Antonio objected five times and was overruled on the first four. On the fifth, Margulies ignored her and turned to ask Dr. Lawrence a question.

Golde couldn't seem to get very far, and concluded his cross in less than a half hour. He'd managed to score a few points, but overall, his questions lacked results that came anywhere near his serendipitous discovery during Dr. Warnock's testimony.

Antonio began her redirect falteringly, posing questions often compound and confusing. From the topic of eosinophils she jumped to a query regarding the lungs' filling of the pleural spaces. Did that mean the lungs filled the chest cavity? Golde objected to the question, was sustained, then asked Margulies again "to admonish Miss Antonio not to lead in these areas."

"Well," Margulies responded matter-of-factly, "I've tried admonishing. Why don't you just object if you feel the question is leading, Mr. Golde. And if it's leading, I'll sustain the objection."

Five minutes into redirect, Antonio tried to mitigate the point that the original coroner, Dr. Herrmann, was at an advantage in assessing cause of death. "Is there anything in the—anything that you would have gained—let me rephrase this. On cross-examination you stated that an expert evaluating the evidence without being present at the autopsy is disadvantaged. What would you have liked to have seen to be fully certain of your findings? If you had been present at the autopsy?"

The witness frowned. "I don't understand your question."

Antonio nodded. "Let me withdraw the question." She leaned down to whisper with Belli, then straightened. "That's all. Thank you."

Golde had one more question about collapsing of the lungs, then said he was through as well.

Dr. Lawrence started to rise, only to hear that the judge had questions of her own. After the brouhaha with Dr. Warnock over lung inflation, Margulies apparently needed to be absolutely clear on Dr. Lawrence's findings in that area. Had he been able to determine if the lungs had been fully inflated, or "hyperinflated," when the chest was opened?

Lawrence had no way of knowing, other than Dr. Herrmann's description that the lungs were "that way"—in other words, that the lungs "filled the chest cavity."

What did that mean? Margulies quizzed.

"It means they weren't collapsed away from it, so that they were equal in size to the cavity in which they lay." They were fully inflated, but not described as hyperinflated, in which case they would have been bulging out across the midline, almost covering the heart.

"Did you receive any information as to whether or not the lungs collapsed upon their removal from the chest cavity?"

Dr. Lawrence cocked his head slightly. "Only secondhand, through Miss Antonio. She told me that the lungs did not collapse on removal, but I don't recall reading that in the report."

Margulies paused to write in her notes. "And just for clarification for my purposes, *if* you received information that the lungs collapsed upon removal, what does that indicate to you regarding the cause of death?"

He gave a slight shrug. "Normally in an asthma death, I would expect them to remain quite inflated and overly resilient and a bit rubbery and so forth."

Again, the judge wondered, *if* he had received information that the lungs collapsed upon removal from the chest cavity, would that change his opinion as to cause of death?

Dr. Lawrence did not think so. He would expect the lungs to be just as overly inflated and "resilient" after death by traumatic asphyxia. Therefore, the lungs collapsing after removal would detract from both the possibility of a death by asthma and a death by traumatic asphyxia.

Margulies told him of Dr. Warnock's statement that, if the lungs had collapsed, it would be essentially inconsistent with an asthma death.

Dr. Lawrence agreed, reiterating that it would also be inconsistent with a traumatic asphyxia death.

Finally, the judge wanted to clarify why the doctor felt there was lack of evidence to conclude death by traumatic asphyxia.

It was two things, he noted—lack of evidence of trauma to the body, plus insufficient patterning of petechial hemorrhages.

At 10:20 A.M., Dr. Lawrence was allowed to step down. Margulies asked Antonio if she had other witnesses to call.

"I do." She hesitated, then conferred with Belli. "Can we take a short break at this point so we can kind of regroup and figure out?" They had "maybe one or two" more witnesses, and would perhaps recall Serena to the stand.

Sure, Margulies replied, and called a fifteen-minute break.

Serena was not happy about retaking the stand. Antonio tried to appease her during the break, promising it would be short.

Antonio and Belli felt they had no choice but to recall the defendant. To them, Golde's modus operandi had seemed to veer midway through the proceedings. First, he had tried to establish jealousy between Serena and Mallory; now he was acknowledging the sisters' closeness, presumably in some twisted attempt to prove that Serena could have killed Mallory out of a sense of protectiveness. Antonio thought the motive "out there"—far beyond the scope of reality or reason. All the same, she had to rebut it in court.

As Serena plunked into the witness chair, Margulies wondered aloud which defense counsel would be asking the questions. A whispered conversation between Belli and Antonio ensued.

"I guess I'll do the questioning," Antonio replied.

"All right. Go ahead."

Antonio stood up and crossed her arms. "Serena, were you protective of Mallory?"

"Yes."

What had she done in the past to protect her sister?

Well, she would take Mallory in her room if her parents were fighting.

And would she take her away from a problem?

Yes, Serena said, if it was "a very big problem" like somebody in the house trying to kill her family, she would probably pack up a bunch of clothes, leave the house, and come back when everything was safe.

"Would you kill her to protect her?"

Serena made a face, as if the question were ridiculous. "Of course not. When you want to protect somebody you don't want to harm them."

Antonio had no further questions. Golde declined to cross. With an animated expression of relief, Serena jumped out of the witness chair.

The defense had one more witness. Combining acquiescence to Michael Moore's demand to testify with their own need for further information about events on the night of Mallory's death, Antonio and Belli had agreed to call him to the stand. They had not, however, informed him about it.

"I want to call Michael Moore," Antonio declared.

Throwing a baffled look at Sharri, Michael pulled himself to his feet. Suddenly, he felt awkward. He hitched up his pants, slid past empty chairs to his right and self-consciously walked behind and around the counsel table toward the stand. He wished he'd had some warning. His communications skills weren't the greatest; he needed time to think through his answers.

As he positioned himself behind the witness microphone, he felt a surge of energy. After almost three weeks, this was what he had been waiting for. He glanced at Sharri. She nodded her head in encouragement, looking half-frightened half-triumphant.

Serena was sitting very still, watching him.

What followed in direct questioning was a discussion of what time Michael had gone to bed the night of August 17, 1992, and what time he had arisen the next morning. Michael acknowledged that he had looked into Mallory's room twice that morning, had thought she looked "comfortable," and therefore had not entered to "adjust her bedding," as he sometimes did. In the past, he added, he'd done the same with Serena, but had been forced to stop after "all of the garbage that had gone on." At the oblique reference to molestation, Antonio steered him back on course. Why hadn't he entered Mallory's room the second time he checked?

Because she still looked comfortable, Michael said, and he didn't want to take the chance of waking her up. "There were times that she would wake up but not that often," he explained. "I felt at the time, as I do now, I feel a little guilty in the sense that I used it as an excuse not to go in and check on her." He gazed at a silent Antonio. "Is that clear?"

In one of her rare moments of sounding more like a parent than a judge, Margulies answered. "I understand."

Michael gave her an appreciative glance. "Thank you."

"What did you use as an excuse not to check on her?" Antonio pressed.

Margulies intervened. "I understood his answer."

Michael raised his eyebrows at Margulies inquisitively. "Would you like me to—?"

"No. I understand your answer."

Michael was grateful. The judge had kept such a poker face throughout the trial, had seemed to him so distant and aloof. Her understanding of his comment and the months of pain it represented were some of the kindest words he'd heard in court.

In response to Antonio's continued questions, no, Michael could not remember getting up in the night, and yes, he remembered Sharri had been in "quite a bit of pain" from her earache. He was beginning to wonder if he would get his chance to talk about the molestation. Antonio's two final questions provided Michael the moment he had desired, but for him it was not enough.

"Did you molest Serena?"

"No."

"Did you molest Mallory?"

"Of course not." He sounded disgusted.

"Thank you." Antonio abruptly sat down.

"Mr. Golde, cross-exam?" Margulies offered.

Watching Golde rise, Michael grew warm under a rush of adrenaline.

"Do you recall an incident where you removed the door from Serena's room?" Golde wondered.

"Yes," Michael, remembering it well, sensed where Golde was heading. After his arrest two years ago, Michael had mentioned the incident to Sergeant Brazil, only to refuse to speak of it further when the officer had "grabbed at it like some smoking gun," as Michael would phrase it.

"Did you tell the police that the reason you did that was that you caught Serena masturbating?"

Sharri nearly came out of her chair. Her sharp intake of breath was audible. She didn't know who made her more angry, Golde for asking the question, or Antonio for throwing Michael to the prosecution after what she thought an insipid direct.

"No."

Antonio objected, invoking hearsay, and was overruled.

"You didn't tell the police that?" Golde challenged.

"No. If I did, it was a mistake on their part in the interpretation. I was very confused and overwhelmed by the whole experience of being dragged out of my home on a child's accusations—"

"And that caused you—"

"—and I'll tell you why I took the door off the room if you would like to hear."

Margulies held up a hand. "Okay."

With an effort, Michael calmed himself. "I'm sorry."

"Mr. Moore," the judge cautioned, "just wait for the question and answer the question that's asked of you."

Michael apologized again.

"I am sure if Miss Antonio wants further information, she'll come back on direct."

Yeah right, thought Michael. Either "Miss Antonio" wouldn't want further information, or if she did, she wouldn't know how to go about getting it. Aloud he said, "I understand. I do apologize."

Reading from a police report, Golde asked whether Michael had told police that, when Serena was eight or nine years old, he had walked into her room and found her masturbating with her fingers inside her vagina. Michael started to interrupt. "Hold on. Let me finish," Golde warned. Another apology from Michael. After that, continued Golde, you removed her bedroom door to "take away her privacy and prevent her from masturbating." Had Michael made those statements to the Newark Police Department?

Michael was livid. "Is this a transcript, Mr. Golde?"

"Sir," Margulies broke in, "if you can answer the question, please, rather than asking Mr. Golde, please. Just answer the question as best you can, please."

His deference to the court momentarily lost, Michael dug in his heels. "Why?"

"So the question is," Margulies prompted, "did you make that statement to the police?"

"No."

Had he caught Serena masturbating?

Yes.

And was the bedroom door open at that time?

"The bedroom door was removed."

For a split second, Golde wavered. "Are you saying the bedroom door was removed *before* you caught her masturbating?"

"Yes, Mr. Golde." As he had tried to tell the police, who had "lit upon it," causing him to stop trying for further clarification. "The point that I was trying to make at the time—may I continue on that?" Golde nodded. "Was to show that even though she was doing something sexual, I was *not* involved and I told her to stop."

"Why did you tell her to stop?"

"Prejudicial; calls for hearsay," Antonio objected.

"Overruled."

"It's also compound," Antonio added.

Michael pushed ahead. "I walked by and if you—"

"Overruled."

Michael, confused, looked to Margulies. "More?"

"I asked you a question," Golde pressed.

"I am sorry." Michael swiveled back toward Golde.

"Is there any further explanation?"

"About the door or why I told her to stop?"

"Why did you tell her to stop?"

"I didn't tell her to stop. I called out her name."

"And is that what you told the officers—that you just walked by, observed this activity and just said 'Serena'?"

"Something to that effect."

"Did you ever tell your mother, Sarah Moore, that you removed the door because you caught Serena masturbating?"

Michael was disgusted. Even if it were true, why would he ever tell his mother such a thing? *"No."*

Golde let the subject drop. He'd managed to place the

information into the court record with barely an objection, and that was enough. Despite Michael's insistence of innocence, the implication of his so much as glimpsing the scene left sordid insinuations hanging in the air.

In a long, often testy discussion, subsequent topics covered by the prosecution continued to "paint the picture" of an ignominious man and stepfather. In the past, Michael had occasionally indulged in speed and marijuana with Sharri partaking in a smoke of pot "once in a great while." As for Golde's suggestion that the Moores' relationship was "stormy" and that Serena "regularly complained" about arguments between him and Sharri, Michael disagreed, noting with cynicism that his stepdaughter had never complained about that "as regularly as she is today." Yes, he had punched Serena once in the stomach, after which Mallory had chastised him long and loud until he promised never to hit her sister again. And yes, at one time, he had possession of an X-rated movie, which he placed in the trunk of his car so Serena would not discover and watch it.

The anger steaming from Michael was palpable. He was caught in the "System's" game, he thought, and the prosecutor held all the dice.

As for Tessie Dornellas's testimony, he had lain *by* Serena on her bed, fully clothed, and feigned sleep so Sharri could snap a picture. He had also kissed Serena on the lips at times; he had a habit of kissing both his children that way. The exact kissing incident reported by Tessie he did not remember. "I said it was a good-bye kiss. Okay? *She* made the issue of it. I don't recall it, to be truthful. That's—how innocent I perceived the situation." He had also been in the bedroom with Serena on one occasion when Tessie was visiting, but Tessie had been wrong in saying two hours passed before either emerged.

Antonio voiced no objections. In a short redirect she asked Michael again about checking Mallory the morning of her death. He had leaned into Mallory's doorway to check on her, he explained, and had seen her clearly without completely entering the room.

The attorney looked toward Margulies. "That's all."

Defense rested.

Thirty-one

COURT BROKE FOR a half hour recess after Michael's testimony. The Moores spent it in a fog of anger, automatically stepping into rest rooms, then outside for a smoke. Michael was so irate he could barely talk. Sharri said enough for both of them. To her, the three "despicable" attorneys, Belli, Antonio, and Golde, had now fallen to the bottom of the barrel. The defense team had put Michael on the stand like some pesky puppy that barked too much, then had thrown him a tiny little bone, as if that was enough to shut him up. *Then* they'd handed him over to Golde, who proceeded to heap another bunch of crap on him.

This was going too far; they had to do something. The trial would be over in a few days and Serena would be home. The attorneys would walk away from it and go on to other cases. Meanwhile, Michael's reputation was *shot* and there was no way for him to prove all the things they said about him weren't true.

As if all this wasn't bad enough, Sharri added, now they had to go back into court and listen to more testimony from Dr. Herrmann, who was being recalled to the stand by Golde.

Sharri's mouth snapped closed and she shuddered. Her hands felt cold in spite of the warm summer day. She wondered how much more she could take.

Inside the courtroom, Golde muddled through setting up the slide projector and screen for his rebuttal witness. He wasn't very good at mechanical things.

After his auspicious cross-examination of Dr. Warnock, Golde had known he would have to recall Dr. Herrmann to the stand. Now, after Dr. Lawrence's testimony, it was even more important. His upcoming task was twofold—to poke more holes in the defense witnesses' findings, particularly those of Dr. Lawrence, by leading Dr. Herrmann through an

exacting revisitation of eosinophils, sloughing of the epithelium, petechial hemorrhages, and the like; and to close the
lid on Dr. Warnock's testimony by allowing the court to hear
from Dr. Herrmann's lips the real answer he gave to Shelley
Antonio's inquiry about hyperinflation of the lungs.

After the unexpected recesses of that week, Margulies appeared anxious to keep the trial moving. Although at an
eleven-thirty break she normally would call lunch recess until
two, today she'd declared that they would resume proceedings
at noon.

At twelve, as Michael reclaimed his seat in the second
row, Serena was led unsmilingly into court. Sharri, unable to
bear hearing Dr. Herrmann's testimony, sat on a bench in
the hallway.

As before, Dr. Herrmann perched forward in the witness
chair, hands resting on the podium. He drummed his fingers
expectantly as he watched Golde page through his notes.

The Deputy D.A. quickly established that Dr. Herrmann
had experience with asthmatic deaths. In 1990 to 1992, the
doctor noted, he had personally autopsied four of them, but
had "seen" quite a number more. Golde then moved to the
case at hand. First, in a prompt to rebut testimony from Dr.
Lawrence, he wondered about the petechial hemorrhages
found on the deceased. Could Dr. Herrmann have confused
them with lividity spots?''

Dr. Herrmann answered with a definite "no," then
launched into a three-paragraph explanation of his conviction.
As far as the hemorrhages being caused by right heart failure,
as Dr. Lawrence had suggested, "this girl" had not died of
that, nor were they caused by simply grunting for air. In
a long-standing episode of asthma—"status asthmaticus"—
during which the heart began to fail, theoretically petechiae
could occur, but he had never seen it. They perhaps could
also appear when "markedly hyperinflated" lungs prevented
a person from sucking in any more air, which would indicate
a lot of pressure in the chest.

Blood pounded in Michael's ears. He could hear his own
breathing, and worked to force it into steadiness. His daughter
wasn't "this girl." She had a name, he thought. Mallory.
Mallory Moore.

The answer provided Golde a transition into the "hyperinflation'' subject. ''And were the condition of the lungs in Mallory Moore [hyperinflated]?''

''There was no hyperinflation in this case,'' the doctor replied in monotone. Mallory Moore's lungs were like those of ''anyone who has died.'' Once breathing stops, the lungs remain static, he noted, the pressure inside them equal to the air pressure on the outside; no air leaves and none goes in. As the chest then relaxes with death, the size of the lungs corresponds to the size of the chest cavity. That is what he meant when he stated that ''the lungs fill the pleural space.''

Margulies's head came up from her notes. ''Is that synonymous with inflation or hyperinflation of the lungs?''

''No. The lungs remain inflated because there's nothing pushing the air out.'' If the lungs did not fill the pleural cavity, then there would be signs that something was wrong, such as a lung rupturing from hyperinflation ''in asthma.'' Lacking such evidence, in *all* his autopsies, Dr. Herrmann declared, he would normally say the lungs filled the pleural space.

''Now,'' Golde narrowed in, ''at some point before the trial did you meet with Miss Antonio?''

''Yes.''

''And did she ask you whether or not the lungs filled the pleural spaces?''

''Well, it's the same thing I told you. The lungs fill the pleural space; that's what they're supposed to do.'' They were not hyperinflated because they did not ''bulge through the pleural space.''

As Dr. Herrmann jumped into another explanation of asthma, Margulies interrupted. ''What we're interested in is what you told Miss Antonio. Did you tell her that the lungs were not hyperinflated?''

The pathologist's head swiveled left to address the judge. ''Yes. She asked me if the lungs were encroaching in the front of the chest cavity around the heart and I said no.''

''You did not say 'I don't know' did you?'' Golde nudged. ''No.''

Antonio objected—leading the witness. Margulies sustained.

Golde rephrased the question and elicited the same response, this time without objection. He'd gotten what he needed and the implication was clear: Antonio had lied to Dr. Warnock regarding Dr. Herrmann's answer to a question that, in Dr. Warnock's mind, had been key to her conclusions and, in fact, to her even agreeing to testify about the case.

Dr. Herrmann disagreed with Dr. Warnock that nonasthmatic, normal lungs should deflate after being removed from the body, saying instead that lungs typically retained their shape because of the balanced air pressure inside and out. In a harsh, seemingly unnecessary explanation, he went on to detail his routine autopsy procedure. First he took out "the heart," then "the lungs," etc. He would leave the lungs on the table "lying in a pan" while he removed all other organs.

Serena's head went down. Seeing it, Michael felt a surge of anger and pain. He wanted to jump up and scream, but forced himself to sit still, clenching his jaw.

Golde took up the next subject—sloughing of the epithelium. With little prompting, Dr. Herrmann opined at length that this falling away of the elongated cells that line the bronchial tubes was a natural phenomenon that he witnessed "all the time in postmortem material" and did not detract from his conclusion of traumatic asphyxia. The presence of eosinophils in "this girl" was an indication she suffered from asthma, Dr. Herrmann continued, but did not mean she was in the midst of an asthma attack at time of death. He'd seen just as many eosinophils in other asthmatics who had died of various causes. Similarly, the mucus plugs indicated asthma but not as a cause of death.

As Michael willed himself to listen, Dr. Herrmann answered questions about the anal scarring and dilation, reiterating how he "removed the anus and genitalia together" to "look at them without having to manipulate the body any further." Reexamining autopsy photographs that Golde handed him, he responded in graphic detail, adhering to his original conclusions that the symptoms did not occur naturally.

Golde leaned over the counsel table to flip a page in his notes, then suggested to Margulies that this would be a good time to break for lunch.

In a darkened courtroom after an hour's recess, Golde took Dr. Herrmann through slides of lung tissue from deceased patients, ranging from a stab victim to sudden infant death syndrome—SIDS. These, he compared to slides of Mallory's lungs. With head down and eyes closed, Michael continued his silent protest. He could not look at slides from Mallory, and did not know, as Golde clicked from one to another, which person's magnified tissue samples would next fill the screen until Dr. Herrmann identified it.

The slide show dealt another blow to the defense. Dr. Herrmann pointed out various examples of mucus plugging, eosinophils, and epithelium sloughing in people who had died of causes other than asthma. The overall effect was to eviscerate the conclusions of both doctors Warnock and Lawrence regarding cause of death. In closing, Dr. Herrmann projected slides of the "the little girl's" anus and genitalia and proceeded to point out internal scarring. As the last picture whirred off the screen, he glanced toward the judge.

"That's it." His tone was matter-of-fact.

"All right." Margulies's expression was unreadable as she called on Antonio for cross-exam.

The defense could gain back little ground. Under Antonio's questions, Dr. Herrmann was able to readdress key points, such as the fact that Dr. Lawrence was "at a disadvantage" for not having been present at autopsy. Dr. Herrmann's refusal to mitigate even the slightest in any area perhaps could have led to his undoing, but Antonio's frustration at his pompousness could not seem to find appropriate expression.

"Dr. Herrmann," she finally exploded, "you're sitting there disagreeing with Dr. Warnock, who is a pulmonary pathologist, in her determination regarding this, the cause of death but you've never *seen* a sudden asphyxic asthma death?"

"Objection," Golde called. "Argumentative, assumes facts not in evidence."

Margulies agreed that it was argumentative "as phrased," giving Antonio the chance to try again, but Dr. Herrmann only succeeded in whirling the attorney through another dervish dance. Antonio believed that he had seen very few deaths from asthma, and knew little to nothing about sudden asthmatic death. Did he know that an emotional trauma could precipitate an asthma attack? she asked.

Yes, he replied, it was "well-known in the literature such happens." When pressed to name a piece of literature in example, he responded that he had read about it in a pediatric textbook somewhere, the author of which he couldn't remember, but that author no longer wrote the textbook anyway.

"And in the textbook of pediatric medicine referring to emotional trauma precipitating asthma, did that end in death?"

"I'm sure it can. Any asthma attack has that propensity or has the potential for ending in death."

Belli pulled on Antonio's sleeve. She bent down, her facial expression changing from angry to amused as she listened, then straightened again. "Did the author die of an asthma attack?"

That stopped Dr. Herrmann cold, if only for a second. "Did I say the author died of it?"

"No."

"That was my fault," Belli volunteered. "I apologize."

Margulies pressed her lips together. "That was Mr. Belli's sense of humor."

Yeah, agreed Antonio, he "had to lighten things up, you know."

Dr. Herrmann did not appear amused.

The "lightening up" quickly passed. Dr. Herrmann was off and running again, pointing out contradictions in the paper from Wayne County, Michigan, that Dr. Warnock had cited in her explanation of sudden asphyxic asthma. Antonio tried to turn him around. "But *you* cited this as part of the literature you've seen regarding sudden asphyxia asthma, right?"

He had done exactly that, but would not admit it. "I don't think the term 'sudden asphyxic asthma' is even used in here. If it is, you point it out to me."

Throughout the afternoon, Antonio hammered away at Dr. Herrmann without success. According to him, Dr. Warnock's statement that lungs filling the pleural spaces meant the same as hyperinflated lungs was "totally nonsense." And, he had *never* seen petechiae from an asthma death. Furthermore, someone silently dying in a sudden asthmatic death was "almost beyond the realm of possibility." Lastly, he had no doubt that this cause of death was traumatic asphyxia.

Margulies posed additional questions for her own clarification. Golde was silent through much of the defense interchange.

Returning to the anal dilation, Antonio asked Dr. Herrmann if that finding "entered into his analysis that this was a death at the hands of another."

"Well," Herrmann acknowledged, "to some extent it does, yes."

It was a startling remark. Dr. Herrmann had just admitted that his finding of molestation had *helped guide him* to the conclusion of traumatic asphyxia. What did he mean? What did one have to do with the other? Did he believe the alleged sodomy happened concurrently with death? If so, how did that fit with Serena's committing the crime and confessing that she put a hand over Mallory's mouth? If Dr. Herrmann *hadn't* found what he believed to be evidence of molestation, or if it could be proven that he was wrong about the abuse, would his finding as to cause of death have been different?

Antonio did not pursue the matter. Inexplicably, she switched to the subject of petechial hemorrhages.

Amid the crucial testimony, Margulies allowed court to run over her typical closing hour of 4:30 P.M. Shortly before five, Antonio completed her cross after going over in detail the anal symptoms once again. In closing, she managed to leave the court with one cause and effect. Dr. Herrmann did agree that "something up the anus of this girl" could have been "stressful enough" to trigger an asthma attack.

But the most interesting cause and effect questions remained unasked and unanswered.

Attorneys, defendant, reporters, and spectators assembled Wednesday, June 9, shortly before 10:00 A.M. only to hear that the defense's one surrebuttal witness, Dr. Martha Warnock, was not available to testify until the following day. It was another frustrating delay for everyone. Court recessed until Thursday morning, leaving the Moores with an unexpected day off. They spent it at home, Sharri whisking about in a frenzy of cleaning, Michael parked in near catatonia before a series of meaningless television programs he neither saw nor heard.

Antonio used the time to prepare for Dr. Warnock's direct and for her closing argument, which she honed under Belli's direction. "Wait 'til you hear her closing statement—she's got a good one," he would proudly inform a journalist the next morning.

Golde was writing his final argument as well. He thought that Dr. Warnock's being recalled to the stand posed the prosecution little threat. On the contrary, it would allow him to confront the woman with Dr. Herrmann's real answer to her question regarding hyperinflation. Then he could watch her wriggle.

For the second day in a row, Serena's entrance in court Thursday morning was markedly lacking in smiles. Wearing a blue-and-white dress, her hair in a ponytail, she fell rather ungraciously into her chair next to Antonio. Her behavior was the same old sign of nervousness and boredom to Sharri. So much of the testimony, she knew, was beyond Serena's understanding.

A strange sense of weakness passed over Sharri as she jealously watched Antonio and Belli greet Serena with familial warmth. She realized fleetingly that she had not eaten for two days. The very thought of food still made her sick. Unconsciously, she groped for the penny necklace lying against her maroon blouse and breathed a quick prayer.

On the heels of Dr. Herrmann's testimony, Dr. Warnock's quiet, almost timid posture on the witness stand was particularly apparent. Antonio may have recognized the unbalanced comparison but she wanted Dr. Warnock's conclusions, not Dr. Herrmann's, to be the last ones Judge Margulies heard before the trial drew to a close. She hoped also to show that Matt Golde's calculated display of incredulity at the "misinformation" between doctors was a red herring. Regardless of what she had told Dr. Warnock, Antonio would later argue, Dr. Herrmann himself had answered Dr. Warnock's questions on the stand the previous day. Mallory Moore's lungs *had* filled the pleural cavity and *didn't* collapse upon removal. Which, as Dr. Warnock testified, was a sign of death from asthma.

Responding to Antonio's questions, Dr. Warnock restated that, as far as she was concerned, normal lungs collapsed upon removal from the chest, about to the size of a fist, but "when there's obstruction as in asthma, the lungs will remain expanded," as in Mallory Moore's case. Further, lungs did not need to meet over the midline of the chest in order to be "hyperinflated."

Referring to an article on autopsy pathology, she noted that petechial hemorrhages were known to be caused by asphyxia, not necessarily traumatic. She stood by her conclusion of death by asthma in this case, and felt that in general a sudden asthmatic death could preclude someone from calling out for help.

After only one half hour, Antonio turned her witness over to a ready and waiting Golde. Clad as usual in a light gray suit, he rose behind the counsel table purposefully, as if embarking on a mission. He wasted no time in reminding Dr. Warnock that she had previously testified about the necessity of understanding what "the lungs filled the pleural spaces" meant. She agreed that she "would not have taken the case" had the lungs not been hyperinflated. She also agreed with Dr. Herrmann's opinion that in a nonasthmatic death, pressure inside the lungs would equal the pressure outside. But, her agreement ended there. Those lungs would shrink when removed from the chest, she insisted.

Well, Golde countered, if she knew that Dr. Herrmann described Mallory's lungs as similar to those from any other nonasthma death, would that have affected her opinion?

"Objection," Antonio called a little too loudly, her voice holding an edge of anxiety. The question was "an incomplete hypothetical and not a complete restatement of the facts in evidence."

Margulies overruled.

Dr. Warnock replied that the other evidence—a history of asthma, the eosinophils, mucus plugging, etc.—would still point to death by asthma.

Golde saw his chance. Just a few moments before, she'd stated that, without hyperinflation of the lungs, she would not have been sure of an asthmatic death and would not have agreed to testify in the case. Now she was wavering, and he wasn't about to let it go. "Are you now saying then, that you can *completely* disregard the lungs and you would still find an asthmatic death in Mallory Moore?" Stretching her meaning to an extreme.

She hesitated. There was controversy on the part about the lungs collapsing, she admitted, but the other symptoms still indicated an asthmatic death.

Controversy aside, Golde pressed, *if* she disregarded the condition of the lungs *altogether,* would she still conclude death by asthma?

Dr. Warnock seemed to realize that Golde was trying to lead her in circles. As he threw out his convoluted questions, she would stick to her simple answers. "I think that there's a strong—I think it's a strong conclusion that she died of an asthmatic death even without that piece of information." Her voice was quiet but firm.

For Golde, it was the nail in her coffin. Confronted with the truth, he would maintain, the doctor was changing her story to save face in court. In so doing, he believed she had lost all credibility. He almost felt sorry for her, misinformed and unprepared for cross-examination as he felt she was. Belli and Antonio, Golde thought, had undeniably engaged in unethical conduct by relaying false information to her. All the same, now that she knew the truth, Dr. Warnock was still sticking by her first opinion as to cause of death. To Golde's way of thinking, she was displaying testimony biased toward the defense, and that was inexcusable.

After Dr. Herrmann's recall, Golde had been fairly certain he had proven beyond reasonable doubt that asthma had not caused Mallory Moore's death. Now with Dr. Warnock's demise, he was one hundred percent sure.

It was over. There was no question.

Thirty-two

THE REMAINDER OF Thursday morning was filled with "housekeeping," as Margulies called it—discussions as to which marked pieces of information, police reports, medical documents, etc., they wanted placed into evidence. It provided a half hour's lull in the action, an eye amidst the storm.

Sharri and Michael sat woodenly throughout the proceedings, wrestling with their emotions. They felt intense relief that the trial was nearly over and a strong hope that their daughter would be acquitted. The medical evidence packed a strong argument, they believed. The judge would have to completely discount the testimonies of both doctors Lawrence and Warnock in order to find Serena guilty.

Swirled with the Moores' hope was a gnawing fear of the trial's outcome. What if Serena *was* found guilty? She most likely would be shipped away to California Youth Authority for as long as ten years. Sharri didn't know how she could live through losing a second child. Added to their fear was the stress and anguish of being publicly labeled as child abusers. They could almost manage that humiliation if it helped free Serena, although Michael was incensed that Golde could make such accusations "only in hopes of winning his case," and then simply walk away from it all. Judging from his numerous quotes to reporters, he wasn't going to pursue the matter or press any charges.

At eleven-fifty, the "housekeeping" was done. It was time for the prosecution's closing argument. Michael felt himself tense. Here it came, right in his face.

Margulies raised her eyebrows at Golde. "Are you ready to go?"

He shuffled some papers. "Yeah." Rising confidently, he adjusted his suit coat with a slight shrug. Golde's closing argument would be the final summation of the many pieces of evidence he had presented and his theory of motive, to which he previously had only alluded. For a brief moment, the courtroom was silent. Reporters' pens were poised. Antonio's head was cocked back and to the right, allowing her an easier view of the prosecutor. Belli was leaning back in his chair, staring at the ceiling, his fingers pressed together. Serena was jiggling her right foot. Golde glanced at his notes, then raised his chin to look directly at the judge. Despite the courtroom's collective air of anticipation, in truth, his was an audience of only one. Sandra Margulies.

"Your Honor, over the last two and a half weeks, we have discussed the many dynamics of this minor's life and that of her family. Experts have testified, but there's one common thread that I think is still undeniable and is in evidence without question. This minor confessed to murder. People," he stated with emphasis, one hand supporting himself as he leaned over the table, *"do not just confess to murder.*

"Where did the minor confess? She confessed to her *diary.* She confessed to the most personal place she has. She confessed to the person or the thing that she can talk to. It's a diary that she locks. It's a diary that she hides the key after locking it."

Consider the accuracy of the confession, he challenged. Serena says she took Mallory into her room, that she told her she loved her. "And she probably did. I don't believe that the evidence shows the minor killed Mallory out of vile hate, although I'm sure there were times where the four-year-old annoyed the minor to no end. Most killings are not done out of hate. People kill people they love all the time."

Sharri sucked in a ragged breath, her heart thumping in a funny, offbeat rhythm. *God, please get me through this,* she prayed.

How did Serena say she killed Mallory? Golde continued. By covering her mouth and suffocating her. Suffocation was certainly consistent with testimony from Dr. Herrmann. Granted, Serena did not speak of lying on Mallory's chest. But "if a person were sitting on another's chest," he argued, "would you expect them to write, 'I was sitting on the chest and suffocating them'?"

Golde paused to search his notes before transitioning into the subject of the vast and often confusing medical evidence. First, Dr. Lawrence's testimony.

"I almost wonder how many pathologists the defense went to before they found someone in San Joaquin County," he commented. "I'm curious as to why we didn't hear from a big-city peer of Dr. Herrmann." Dr. Lawrence, Golde charged, really "knew very little about asthma," and in fact, had changed his diagnosis in the middle of his testimony, waffling from "death from asthma" to "well, if it's not death from asthma, then there's just not enough to say traumatic asphyxia." In addition, some of the basis for his argument was completely wrong, as shown by Dr. Herrmann. He didn't seem to know what petechial hemorrhages really were, nor did he bother to call Dr. Herrmann with questions about that or any other finding.

Dr. Warnock was a different story. Golde admitted she was "very knowledgeable about the lungs," although "asthma is not her specialty." Certainly, she lacked expertise in performing routine autopsies. And when one compared the testimonies of Doctors Lawrence and Warnock, things didn't add up. Both of them couldn't possibly be right. Dr. Lawrence based his conclusion of death from asthma on mucous plugging and eosinophils, while Dr. Warnock rested her findings on inflation of the lungs and sloughing of the epithelium. While "Dr. Lawrence did not consider the lungs at all, Dr. Warnock considered the lungs to be the most important element."

Then there was the petechial hemorrhage problem. "It's interesting," remarked Golde, "that Dr. Warnock and Dr. Lawrence have never seen petechial hemorrhages in asthma cases, yet they are basing their decision on these hemorrhages." He raised his voice. "I find that outrageous!"

After working for another ten minutes to pick apart every piece of the defense's medical evidence that he could, Golde turned to the defense's "impairing of the truth." Dr. Warnock needed specific answers, and "the defense wouldn't let her get that information." He spread his hands for effect. "You know, I'm not in the practice of commenting on defense counsel, but this is *absolutely outrageous* conduct. And while this is an adversarial system, there should be some concern for the truth by the defense counsel. Belli and Antonio have disregarded that. I find that to be outrageous."

Equally troubling was Dr. Warnock's testimony earlier that day. "Previously she said the lungs are the key, that 'if I had known that they were not hyperinflated, I would not be in here testifying.' Yet today, when confronted with the fact that these lungs were just normal, she says asthma anyway." His voice took on sheer disbelief. "It is beyond me why these experts would come in here and *lie*."

In the end, Golde concluded, Dr. Herrmann alone was honest and consistent. Therefore, it was clear that Mallory was killed. So, question was, who was the killer?

The Deputy D.A. then launched into an all-out attack on the Moores.

"Consider the minor's background, her model for behavior. Her mother has created an environment where this minor has been sexually abused, physically abused, and emotionally abused. As a child, the minor was abandoned by her mother, left without food, dumped on relatives, left in urine-soaked beds, witnessed men coming and going, witnessed men beating her mother up. Her life, her world, is abuse and violence. There's no love, no nurturing. There's no question Sharri Moore has surrounded this minor by such awful things that you have a violent person here.''

Golde looked back over his right shoulder at the Moores, as if checking for their reaction. Michael glared at him unflinchingly. Golde swiveled back toward the judge.

Without turning her head, Sharri sensed the moving pens of reporters clustered to her left. Her skin felt prickly, her hands cold.

Golde reminded Margulies of Dr. Wong's testimony about Serena threatening to kill her sister. That was how Serena reacted to problems—she threatened to kill.

And what of Dr. Berg's testimony of Serena's being mentally ill? ''I think it is unfounded,'' he announced. ''I think that he has a bias in favor of making a diagnosis. I think he can virtually diagnose anybody on the street with some form of an illness.''

Nevertheless, even Dr. Berg admitted that Serena was ''violent.'' And ''when Mallory Moore started to get molested, things took a drastic turn.'' Serena tried to stop her own and her sister's abuse, but no one listened. What did Sharri Moore do after Serena told the Carson City authorities about her molestation? Golde shot another glance in the Moores' direction. ''Was it love, compassion, understanding? No. Sharri's reaction was 'if you don't recant that, you'll have no family. You will be an orphan and you will *never* speak to your sister again!' ''

Sharri flinched, as though she'd been hit in the chest.

What happened when Serena tried to take Mallory away in the truck in order to save her? Mallory ended up back in the house, and Serena was taken to a psychiatric clinic. (In actuality, Serena had been sent to Truckee Meadows psychiatric facility *before* stealing the truck.) ''At that point,'' Golde alleged, his tone of voice climbing, ''I think it's clear that she knew she couldn't do anything to get Mallory out of there. She couldn't take her away. She couldn't go to the police. She couldn't go to her mother. She had tried *everything.*"

Golde went on to blast Serena's testimony, noting particularly the "absurd and total lies she told up there, the complete acts of perjury she committed. Just a classic 'I don't recall.' She refuses to say why and she won't answer the question."

Neither would Serena give clear answers about the molestation. "It was hard for her to admit here," Golde asserted. "She says, 'Well I thought it was happening, I'm not so sure now.' It was clear that the molest happened, from the manner in which she testified."

At the counsel table, Serena could not keep still. Appearing nonchalant, she swiveled in her chair, throwing smiles over her shoulder at family and friends. Sharri eyed her, knowing what her behavior indicated. Margulies seemed intent on watching Serena as well, occasionally flicking her eyes in Golde's direction between long apprising stares at the defendant.

Golde, showing no sign of noticing the undercurrent of activity, pressed on. Regarding the diary entry, he continued, Serena gave various answers about why she wrote it—for attention, to answer her mother's questions, etc.

Another point—Serena asked to get rid of her mattress. "I find that quite strange that the minor would have such problems keeping her mattress, but there would be no problem at all in keeping Mallory's mattress. They just kept that one there." And regarding Mallory's room—she had "nightmares in there," which led him to conclude, "I think it's clear she was being molested as well."

If Golde had already thrust a knife into the Moores, he was about to twist it with his conclusion.

"The stepfather could molest with impunity because certainly Sharri Moore would never say anything," he pronounced. "Michael Moore was her support. Gave her a house. She *never* had to have a job." Neither did Michael Moore "have to worry about the police. If the minor went to the police, she'd be threatened with 'you got no family; you're an orphan if you don't recant what you say.'

"At the time of the killing," Golde continued, "I think the evidence suggests that this minor had reached the end.

There was nothing she could do. So . . . she did the only rational thing in her mind. She killed Mallory Moore.''

Golde's voice dropped theatrically. ''Ironically enough, Sharri and Michael believe she killed Mallory too, because when they saw this diary, they didn't confront her. They went right to the police.'' His voice rose again. ''Because they *knew* it. They *always* knew it.

''I think,'' he concluded, placing emphasis on each word, ''the evidence is true beyond any possible reasonable doubt that this home, *that family,* created a person who killed her sister. And she is *guilty* of the murder of Mallory Moore.

''Thank you.''

Golde sat down. In the sudden silence, his chair scraped loudly across the floor.

Margulies's face remained a mask as she checked the clock. Twelve-forty P.M. ''All right. Thank you, Mr. Golde.''

Court was adjourned until one-forty-five.

During the lunch hour, Serena's hair had been gathered into one thick braid hanging down her back. She threw her parents a smile as she walked toward the counsel table, then sat quickly. Now that her attorney would be speaking, she seemed more relaxed. The chair-swiveling and fidgeting were gone.

Belli adjusted his hearing aids as Antonio stood up. As she formally addressed Margulies, the Deputy D.A., and spectators, her voice held an edge of nervousness. ''This case is a search for the truth,'' she began. ''And that truth lies in the love that was shared by Serena and Mallory. And this is a love between two children who had each other amidst the chaos of a world that unfortunately too often failed them.''

Here it comes, thought Michael.

''They were surrounded by ugliness and evil, violation and cruelty. A kind of cruelty that they were not responsible for. Serena and Mallory loved each other. For Serena, Mallory became the one and only person she could rely on for unconditional and heartfelt love. And for Mallory, Serena was the nurturing sister, the second mother who tended to her needs and gave her attention. She was the guardian. She was the teacher.''

Michael closed his eyes. He heard the relationship of Serena and Mallory depicted as "an oasis in the center of a storm, of the hurricane of pain, what the D.A. has described as a dysfunctional and unhealthy family life, filled with drugs sometimes, molestation maybe, abuse, physical and sexual.

"The final outrageous statement becomes the theory of the prosecution's case that the ultimate act of love is murder," Antonio declared. "The prosecution would make profane the sacred love between these two children."

And what about the diary entry? Antonio's words jumbled as she tried to explain why it was written. "Serena, in response to a very emotional time at Christmas, having lost her sister, a child, a child to whom Christmas is very important, this is the first Christmas following the death, wrote in her diary that she was, taking responsibility for that death. It was a desperate attempt, a dramatic attempt to get her mother's attention, to tell her mother to stop the questioning. She had to stop the pain."

There *was* a killer in the Moore house, Antonio conceded, her tone gathering strength. The killer was asthma.

As Golde had done, Antonio reiterated the words of the expert witnesses, trying in particular to buttress Dr. Warnock's damaged testimony. Dr. Herrmann made his findings, she pointed out, because he did not know enough about asthma and knew *nothing* about sudden asthmatic death. "The prosecution," she charged, "in its attempt to slur the case of the defense and impugn them, both the attorneys for the defense and Dr. Warnock, stated that, that we somehow injected some bias into Dr. Warnock. Well, Dr. Warnock was never paid for this case."

"Well, I object," Golde interrupted. "There's no evidence for that statement."

Objections occur rarely during opening and closing arguments. By definition, during those portions of a trial, attorneys are stating their opinions based on facts introduced on record, and so are alloted leeway in their logic. Antonio, however, had not elicited testimony from Dr. Warnock that she had not accepted money.

Margulies sustained.

Antonio's rhythm was thrown. She looked over her notes, five seconds ticking by before she continued.

In fact, she alleged, any "built-in bias" rested with Dr.

Herrmann, who is employed by the county and, therefore, "has to testify for the county."

And what about Herrmann's report? The doctor stated that someone would have had to apply pressure to Mallory's back or chest in order to cause the petechial hemorrhages. Merely putting a hand over the little girl's mouth wouldn't kill her. "If the diary is going to be used by the prosecution to show that Serena committed some crime," Antonio declared, "then it has to fit with the physical findings. And it doesn't. Dr. Herrmann said it couldn't have happened the way Serena wrote in her diary that it happened."

(Antonio was making a jump in logic, having asked Dr. Lawrence to compare Serena's confession with the initial coroner's findings, but not Dr. Herrmann himself.)

Add to that fact, Antonio went on, that Serena's grandmother slept in her bed the night after Mallory's death and saw no evidence of blood or saliva on the sheet. The blood and saliva were found on *Mallory's* sheets.

Silence reigned in the courtroom as Antonio paused at length, eyes poring over her notes. She turned to the sexual molestation.

"Now, the trauma to the anus is quite troubling. What do we make of that? The prosecution wants to create some strange and twisted story that—that the stepfather, Mr. Moore, was molesting Mallory and that Serena must have heard it and then rushed in within twenty minutes, because Dr. Herrmann says that the size of the anus was not large enough to accommodate a penis at the dilation that he found, but that it could have been within a half an hour.

"So we have Serena hearing molestation, running in suddenly, a half an hour later, taking her and putting her in her own bed and killing her and bringing her back. Well," Antonio shook her head, "that's a lot of activity for that night. The mother testified she was up every fifteen minutes with an earache. If all this activity was going on in the house that night, someone must have heard something. And nobody heard anything that night."

On the other hand, Antonio asked rhetorically, what was the court to do with the fact that Dr. Lawrence called the anal dilation found in Mallory within "normal limits" and that "he didn't really even find any evidence of tearing or scars?'' It was yet another dispute, she charged, ''two experts disagreeing.''

Antonio strove to ''crawl into the mind of an emotionally disturbed child'' in order to explain why Serena, distraught over Mallory's death and wanting her mother to stop asking ''why?'' impulsively scribbled such a ridiculous lie in her diary. It was a place in which she had written lies before. Perhaps Serena even felt guilty because she had not allowed Mallory to sleep with her that night. The diary, insisted Antonio, was ''the product of someone that was hurt because she wanted her mother to stop and to listen to her.''

The defense attorney threw in a hint at the ''other perpetrator'' theory that she had mentioned in her opening statement.

''The prosecution mentioned that the killer was in the house. But there's no competent evidence that links Serena to that. In fact, the prosecution raises enough doubt in their case that maybe it was someone else in the house. Maybe it was whoever was molesting Mallory. They're the one that has inflicted the trauma that Dr. Herrmann found.''

Antonio stumbled in her conclusion. ''Yes, this is a tragic family, but it doesn't prove that Serena murdered anybody. We can't blame the victims of sexual abuse because our society failed to protect them. I think this is a witch-hunt. And Justice Brandeis stated in his opinion in 1936—I think we have the same thing here, and he stated that men feared women—I'm sorry. Men feared witches and burned women.''

The reference fell flat. Antonio resumed her seat.

Belli leaned over to whisper a congratulation. Margulies said, ''Thank you,'' her face expressionless, then called a twenty-minute recess.

Following the break, Golde was allowed his rebuttal. Again, he reminded the judge of the medical findings and attacked Sharri as a reliable witness. So what if she had stated she was awake most of that night and didn't hear anything? ''There's no question,'' he charged, ''that Sharri Moore lied up here. She lied about what was really going on in that house. When Sharri Moore got off the stand, you would think she had described a perfectly normal house with a slightly troubled teenager. The defense, themselves, certainly demonstrated a certain amount of unbelievability of the testimony of Sharri Moore. It was clearly, clearly untrue.''

Sharri grimaced. "Thanks a lot, Shelley," she muttered under her breath. "That's what you get for impeaching your own witness."

In conclusion, Golde went back to the prosecution's one piece of evidence—the diary. "The fact is, for her own reasons, and as tragic as they are, this minor killed her sister and confessed to it. It's as simple as that."

Suddenly, the trial was over, and only the verdict remained. Spectators had known it was coming, yet at the moment seemed frozen in their seats, as if not yet able to separate themselves from the proceedings and resume their own suspended lives.

"All right. Thank you," Judge Margulies said smoothly. "That concludes arguments in this matter. The court will take the matter under submission. We will be adjourned until ten o'clock tomorrow morning."

Before anyone else could move, she swiveled in her chair, arose and left the courtroom.

Ten A.M. *tomorrow.* Shelley Antonio sighed as she grasped her briefcase with both hands and dangled it against her legs in the crowded elevator. She glanced at Belli. He was silent, staring at the floor. "Tomorrow morning," she said to him, oblivious to reporters around them. "That's too soon. It's not a good sign."

Belli grunted his assent.

Thirty-three

MICHAEL AWOKE FRIDAY to an overcast morning. Rolling quietly out of bed, he padded into the kitchen to make coffee. With a little luck, some caffeine would clear his head. The night before, he and Sharri had fallen asleep watching television, she on one end of the couch and he at the other, their feet meeting in the middle under a shared blanket. Vaguely, he remembered staggering to bed around two. Sharri's last words haunted him as he measured grounds into the plastic coffee urn. "I don't want to go to bed," she had protested. "Because when I wake up, it'll be tomorrow. And I'm scared."

Misty jumped onto the counter to rub against his arm. Absentmindedly, he smoothed her black fur. "Your buddy's coming home today," he whispered.

Sharri stumbled sleepily out of the bedroom around seven-thirty. "Oohh, coffee," she moaned, heading for the kitchen as though it were a desert oasis. For three days now, the dark, strong drink was all she'd managed to swallow. The thought of eating still made her sick.

A moment later, cup in hand, she entered the living room to find Michael busily flipping television channels.

"What do you watch this time of day, anyway," he muttered impatiently. Cartoons and "Sesame Street" he didn't need; news shows were too segmented. Scanning through cable channels, he settled on a rerun of "Little House on the Prairie." Soon entranced in the problems of Laura Ingalls, he managed temporarily to shut out his own. Sharri busied herself with small tasks—feeding the cats, emptying the coffee grounds, straightening towels in the bathroom, making the bed. Straightening the towels again. Vainly, she tried to block the fears nibbling up and down her spine. They'd endured over six months of separation from Serena. Six months of policemen, attorneys, court dates, and witnesses. Six months of frantic phone calls, gathering documents, scheduled visits to juvenile hall. Disappointment after disappointment. The shock of accusations flung in their direction.

Now it was D day.

By noon, Serena could be home. *Home.* Sharri choked back tears as she fluffed her pillow. She stopped to finger Mallory's chocolate-stained *101 Dalmatians* dress, then gently placed the pillow over it. To see Serena walking through the house—this house that she had never even lived in. To watch her petting Misty, exploring her own room, eating a home-cooked dinner. To be able to tuck her in bed this very night. "Oh, God, *please,*" Sharri whispered. They could start over, find help for Serena, be a family again.

As she stopped to wipe her eyes, her mind switched gears, distancing itself from emotion for an instant's cold, philosophical view. It was sort of like dying, she reflected, when your whole life flashes before you. At this hour, their entire lives were at stake and all they could do was wait for a higher authority to decide their fate.

Six months, and it all came down to one sentence.

Like a predator, a Channel 7 news truck lay in wait for the Moores in front of the courthouse. Sharri blanched, then steeled herself. She and Michael had known the cameras would be back with a vengeance. It was feeding time in the jungle, she thought, and they were the prey.

They stepped out of the elevator into a melee of reporters and cameras. Machines whirred; the crowd jostled. The return of the CBS crew added to the fray. "There they are," someone whispered loudly. As always, Sharri ducked behind her long hair, watching the scuffed floor slide underneath her feet as she hurried toward the courtroom door. That they never once had managed to get her face on camera remained her sole source of vindictiveness—her personal vendetta against the media's prying eyes. An odd quaking rumbled through her stomach, and she shivered in her thin ivory silk blouse and skirt as the large wooden courtroom door closed off their pursuers.

More reporters crowded the courtroom, many whom Sharri did not recognize. And, of course, the regulars. Catherine Bowman from the *Chronicle,* Bob Salladay from the *Argus,* Raoul Mowatt from *San Jose Mercury,* Channel 7's Anna Garcia. Joan Lynch, a dozen colored pencils in her left hand, was already engrossed in sketching the three attorneys as they milled nervously around the table. Antonio, as usual, was clad in black. Belli was shuffling toward his seat in a dark suit, beige shirt, and matching tie.

Sharri stopped cold as her eyes slid toward the judge's bench. There were too many bailiffs. She counted three, no— four. She did not know that extra bailiffs typically would be present during a verdict. A block of ice surfaced in the pit of her stomach. Serena was going to be found guilty, that was it. All those bailiffs were there to restrain her when she freaked out, when she jumped up and starting screaming. . . .

"Michael," she dug her fingers into his arm, "look at them all! Why are they here? Something's *wrong.*"

"No, no." His voice was calm, matter-of-fact. "They're just here to help us deal with all the reporters."

Sharri gazed at him, eyes darting across his face. He gave a slight, reassuring nod, then guided her toward their usual seats at the far end of the courtroom. She let the subject drop but wasn't convinced.

Pastor Doug and Sheila, one row behind, leaned forward to give them each hugs. Esther Corren and her boyfriend, Greg, soon entered, trailed by Mary. They sat on Sharri's left. Michael's parents also greeted them. Lana Bridges, their ex-neighbor from Lucia Street, held Sharri tightly before claiming a seat.

"It's going to be all right," she said. "It's going to be all right."

Sharri's lips curved into a thin, tense smile. "There's too much reasonable doubt," she said, working to keep her voice firm. "No way can they find Serena guilty." She sat down to wait the last few, interminable minutes, refusing to admit to herself that she'd made the statement not for Lana, but for her own peace of mind.

Hearing the exchange, Doug nodded in silent agreement, confident that Matt Golde had not made his case. The kid was grasping at straws, for heaven's sake, he thought. He hadn't proved anything. Yesterday, he'd come up with a motive resting on a sexual crime that nobody had even been charged with. That wasn't a real motive; that was just a Deputy D.A. trying to prove a shallow case.

"Our main concern," Michael was speaking in low tones to a journalist on his right, "is what to do with Serena after it's over. She's been so damaged through all this. We have to get her help."

A commotion up front announced Serena's entrance. Clad in a casual blue flowered dress, her hair in a ponytail, she smiled and waved at her parents. The teenager carried herself easily, almost jauntily, feeling a mixture of anxiety and happiness. Sitting in juvenile hall the past week, she'd skimmed over her undulating tension about her fate, choosing to land on what she decided was stable ground. She'd said all along she was innocent. Today, the judge would agree.

She was going home.

As Serena settled into her chair, Antonio leaned over and

hugged her. "Everything will be all right," she whispered, "no matter what happens." Briefly, Antonio played with Serena's hair and held her hand. Belli patted Serena on the shoulder before sliding into his seat.

Watching them, Sharri felt her heart lurch. It was unfair having to watch Serena being hugged by the very attorneys who'd turned against her and Michael, when she hadn't been able to visit her own daughter during the entire trial. She longed to put both arms around Serena, to kiss her and smooth her thick hair. When the judge announced the acquittal, she would run up and grasp Serena in a bear hug, whether Shelley Antonio or the bailiffs liked it or not.

Margulies's walking in, her face impassive, jerked Sharri back to the present. She sensed Esther pulling at her left hand; automatically their fingers entwined. Michael rubbed a moist palm on his blue jeans.

"Remain seated and let the court come to order," called a bailiff.

The judge wasted no time. "Let the record reflect that both attorneys are present and the minor is present ..."

It's going by too fast, panicked Sharri. *I can't keep up with it. What is she saying?* Unconciously, she gripped Esther's hand until her knuckles turned white. A sudden shiver ran from the top of her head down her spine, through her legs and out her toes, leaving her weak and disoriented. Vaguely, she registered the rustling of paper around her as reporters scribbled in low-volumed stereophonic sound.

"... The court finds that the district attorney has proved ..."

Someone nearby sucked in a gasp. At the word "proved," Sharri bent her head down. She couldn't make a sound; she couldn't cry, she couldn't *breathe.*

"... beyond a reasonable doubt that the cause of death of Mallory Moore was traumatic asphyxiation ..."

Serena pressed herself rigidly against the back of her chair and froze.

"... and that the minor ..."

The instant seemed lost in time to Sharri. She felt as if she were floating in outer space. Only the painful pressure of Esther's grip on her hand pulled her back down into the wooden seat.

". . . caused the death of Mallory Moore. The court finds that this is murder in the second degree."

Serena could not move a muscle, as if a ten-ton weight had been placed on her shoulders. How could the judge say she was guilty? And in front of all these people! She was so *humiliated*.

At the final words, Pastor Doug was flooded with anger. As he would later tell a reporter, God was perfect; the system was not—justice surely had not been served that day.

A long, hard sigh seeped from Michael's throat as Sharri fell, sobbing, on Esther's chest. Judge Margulies continued to speak, noting she needed longer than the normal ten days in order to "explore all options," including psychiatric facilities, in placing Serena. A pall hung over the courtroom as she called Antonio and Golde out for a conference, leaving Serena to sit, back ramrod straight, at the defense table. Belli remained seated to her left, with Antonio's empty chair between them. They did not speak.

Most reporters were surprised at the verdict. Bob Salladay did not think Golde had proven murder beyond a reasonable doubt. Wagers in the Channel 5 newsroom had run strongly for acquittal. In light of the media's typical competition-oriented scurrying, the reporters' silent reaction was glaringly uncharacteristic. No press member rushed for the door to be first bearer of the verdict; no one whispered or jostled a neighbor. Each one's demeanor reflected the grim expressions on the faces of Sharri, Michael, and their friends.

After crying on Esther's shoulder for several minutes, Sharri pulled away, only to sense the tug of eyes on her from further left. One row in front and four seats down, Catherine Bowman from the *Chronicle* was staring over her shoulder, observing Sharri's reactions. They locked eyes. "It's not true," Sharri whispered. "It's not true!" Bowman lowered her chin and turned away to write.

Sharri twisted to look at Michael. His face was set in a faraway gaze, one hand continuously rubbing his leg. She could hear his pained breathing. "Oh, Michael," she cried, grabbing his hand as she leaned against him. She began to shake. He held her and closed his eyes.

The bench conference dragged on, the courtroom quiet except for Sharri's muffled sobs. Serena still had not moved. Finally, both attorneys and the judge returned to their seats.

"Counsel and I have agreed on a hearing date of three weeks from today," Margulies stated. She looked at Serena. "You have a right to be sentenced in ten days. Do you agree to waive that right, postponing disposition for three weeks, in order to give me some extra time in looking for appropriate placement?"

Serena's voice was barely audible. "I don't care. Fine." In her first movement since the verdict, she turned her head to her left and mouthed one word.

"Bitch."

Judge Margulies did not notice. "Let it be known for the record that the minor has waived her right. Disposition will be Friday, July 2 at 2:00 P.M."

Before Sharri could protest, Serena was led away by a bailiff. The still, suspended moments were suddenly over as reporters began hustling for the hallway, where they would throw questions at the attorneys. Sharri and Michael, with their friends and family, lingered in the emptying courtroom.

"Mr. Grimes," Sharri pleaded to a probation officer, "I know it's not regular visiting hours today, but *please* could you see if we could visit Serena this afternoon?" She stopped to catch a ragged breath, tears etching lines in her face. "We just need to hold her. She needs to know we still *love* her."

Reassuring, respectful, Grimes promised to do what he could.

Friends moved in quickly to help Sharri, who was shaking uncontrollably, her arms and legs smacking against her wooden chair. Michael quietly pulled a folded document out of his pocket, handwritten on two lined yellow pages. He reviewed it carefully, mentally practicing how he would read the words aloud.

"Why don't you sneak out the other door—the way they took Serena," a friend suggested. "You don't want to face that mess outside."

He shook his head. "We have a statement to make. We have to go out there so I can read it." His gaze fell again on the words he and Sharri had so carefully constructed the night before. Even though they had expected an acquittal, the

Moores had agreed they couldn't leave the courtroom without addressing all the accusations that still remained unanswered. They felt that Serena's attorneys had thrown them to the wolves and that Golde should not be allowed to defame a man's character and just walk away.

The press would finally get their wish. Serena's parents were about to face the cameras.

The Moores' tight group moved into the courtroom foyer, listening angrily to the muted sounds of scrambling bodies filtering through the wall. Someone opened the door, allowing in a flood of argumentative voices and commotion. The foyer filled with brightness from a television crew's spotlight. Sharri shrank back, her eyes bugging.

"Shut the door! Shut it!" Lana commanded.

"As far as I'm concerned," Matt Golde was announcing to the crowd of reporters, "she killed another person, and that is a very serious crime. I do consider her to be a potentially dangerous person. I think that the family, particularly Sharri Moore and the stepfather, is very much responsible for creating an environment where this girl has become a killer. . . . She gave an accurate and detailed confession." He spread his hands. "The asthma factor was something that was manufactured by the defense. People do not just confess to murder."

"I'm outraged," Antonio shot back. "If there isn't reasonable doubt in this case, then it doesn't exist. Our client cannot *believe* that a crazy diary entry she made four months after her sister's death would be the thing that convicted her for something she didn't do."

Belli's gravelly voice boomed above the din in a disgusted tone. "She wasn't guilty of anything here. Why the hell did they have these people come in here and intimate that there was molestation on all the rest of those cases, throw in more mystery, more who-dun-its, and then come up with a verdict like this?"

"What about the sexual abuse?" One reporter flung the old question at Golde. "What are you going to do about it?"

"If Serena comes forward and wants to press charges, wants to give us a statement," he responded, "we will investigate this as we would any other case. I am very interested; my door is open and the door of our office is open."

Inside the foyer, Michael waited numbly for the attorneys' publicity batteries to wind down. He was nervous about facing the cameras, dreading having to read in front of so many people. Between the two of them, Sharri was the one with the better communications skills. Putting words on paper had always been difficult for him, in concept as well as logistics. He couldn't spell worth a damn. For the most part, Sharri had authored their statement the previous night. Reflexively, he fingered the yellow sheets. Sharri was in no shape to speak her own words today.

"We've got to hold her up," he heard someone insist. "She's gonna faint."

He glanced at his wife. Her face was gray-white as she leaned weakly against a wall. "I'll read the statement," he whispered to her. "You go on and duck the cameras."

Resolutely, Sharri shook her head. Not this time. He needed her. The words he was about to read were written by her own hand. They reflected the weeks of pain they'd come through as their private lives had been soiled, stained at the hands of attorneys and the media. Today, the reporters would see her face, all right. They'd see her standing beside her husband where she belonged, supporting him with bare-faced defiance.

"No. I'm going with you."

"They're like vultures out there," a friend protested.

Lana put an arm around her shoulders. "We'll be with you. We'll be right there beside you."

A surge of bitterness ran like a shock through Sharri, leaving her mouth tasting of metal. "I'll have to tell my mother the part she played in all this," she spat. "The D.A.'s stellar witness."

Doug patted her arm. "That won't help."

"Oh, God," she wailed suddenly as both knees buckled, "I don't want to *be* here anymore."

Lana struggled to pull her up. Sharri huddled as waves of grief rolled over her, dashing themselves against her body. Mallory's death, the weeks of not knowing why she died, losing Serena, the trial, the accusations and horrible rumors. All those tortured days and nights of dealing with Serena's problems had left her without time to heal herself. She clung to Lana and Esther, fighting vainly to get herself under control. She *had* to; there was no choice. She had to face the cameras.

Outside the foyer, the muffled shouts grew quiet.

"Come on, it's time to go," Michael urged.

The door opened.

Sharri was hit instantly by a glaring whiteness in her eyes, as if facing a locomotive in a black tunnel. Vaguely, she was aware of people in front of her, talking, writing notes. She was propelled forward toward the light, into a melee of whirring black boxes and strange faces. Zombielike, she moved beside Michael until she sensed him coming to a halt. She could not feel Lana's arm around her shoulder, or the hands of another friend lending support under her shaking elbows. She didn't know that her mouth was trembling, her face tear-stained. She couldn't feel her feet on the floor. She was a disembodied head bathed in white, bobbing here and there in front of the cameras.

Then, beside her—or was it miles away?—she heard Michael begin to speak.

"We greatly appreciate the help, work and support my stepdaughter has gotten on her behalf by Miss Antonio and Mr. Belli," he read in a flat tone. "We have worked side by side with them for the last five and one-half months, and their concern for her is obvious.

"However, we are wounded and disillusioned by a judicial system wherein the truth alone does not seem to be enough to set you free. We have watched, hurt and bewildered, as both the D.A. as well as the defense attorneys victimized us with vile and blatantly untrue characterizations of the environment we created for our children—each for the sake of winning their case."

Without looking up, he pressed on.

"Our daughter is, has been, emotionally disturbed for many years. We have spent those years trying to help her, bringing us to the point of financial as well as emotional ruin. Both counsels in this case have chosen to support their opinions with the ravings of an equally disturbed family member who lives in another state and has little firsthand knowledge of how we live, rather than to heed the observa-

tions of friends, family and clergy who know from experience
that our little girl was surrounded by love and afforded every
life-enriching experience we could offer, and our older daughter fared as well. Both counsels in this case chose to ignore
the views and experiences of other teens who had spent many
hours in our home since they were children and could attest
to the supportive and generous lifestyle contained there. Our
older daughter's mental illness precluded her from benefitting
from these things, despite our efforts.''

Michael stumbled. Sharri looked at him through a fog and
noticed for the first time that he was wearing sunglasses.
Behind their lenses, tears welled in his eyes. For an instant,
she was afraid he could not go on.

"Our hearts will break for the rest of our lives for the loss
of our little girl," he managed. "And with God's help, we
will try to forgive those who assaulted and soiled our character, as well as our memories of the brief but precious time
we had with her. Our love for our older daughter, likewise,
does and will remain as strong as ever.''

He lowered the paper, glancing up for the first time.
"Thank you," he concluded, momentarily bewildered at the
expanse of people and cameras before him.

Sharri felt her own mouth move. "That's it.''

Suddenly, her floating head was whizzing toward the balcony exit. Pandemonium broke out as countless cameras and
reporters shoved for questions, fighting for expanded footage.
Futilely, Pastor Doug tried to block their path. They chased
Sharri as she flew like a frightened bird down the hall. In
that instant, warmth gushed through her body, and she gained
sensation in her fingers, her hands, her arms, chest and legs,
like the invisible man slowly fading into view. Her feet were
running, running as she was pulled along, Lana's blond head
rushing before her. Double glass doors loomed ahead, with
a concrete patio beyond. Get to the door, get to the door!
she told herself. Michael was in front of her, friends on either side.

They were the foxes, she thought crazily; behind them, the
hounds were closing in.

She saw the door open, Michael dash through, felt a breeze
tickle her face. Then the world darkened. "I'm not gonna
make it!" she swooned.

Lana turned just as Sharri collapsed on the concrete balcony. "Michael, help!"

Michael, Lana, Esther, and Mary crowded around Sharri, trying to block her from the onslaught of the media fighting their way through the door. In a moment, they were surrounded by cameras, tapes eating up the medical emergency like sharks in a feeding frenzy. Only the young cameraman from Channel 7 put down his equipment to try to help. He used to be an EMT, he told Doug; he knew what to do. They needed to elevate Sharri's feet, give her room to breathe.

All other cameras kept rolling.

Doug was outraged. "For God's sake, let her go!" he yelled, his voice thick with anger.

Esther, kneeling beside Sharri, swiveled toward the cameras at his shout. "Leave her *alone!*" she screamed.

Again and again that day, her words would be replayed on television newscasts across the Bay Area.

Doug peered anxiously at Sharri. She wasn't moving. "Someone call 911!" Judy Schaeffer, producer of "Eye to Eye," ran to the phone.

Sharri awoke to the babble of voices overhead. *Oh, God,* she screamed inside, *get me out of here!* The vultures hunched in their branches, leering down at her while she lay, helpless, at their feet. Michael squatted on the floor at her right. She could see Doug, Mary, Lana. A strong hand began stroking her hair gently. Who was that? Slowly, her eyes grazed across a pair of khaki-covered knees to a chest, a badge, the face of a young blond bailiff beside her, guarding her. She struggled to say something, but sleep overtook her and she closed her eyes once more.

"Sharri! Mel Belli here!" a voice boomed through the clouds. Her eyelids fluttered open to see the attorney's broad figure looming above. "There's a lot we can do," he declared, "and we will."

Sleep and wake, sleep and wake. Exhaustion undulated through her body, followed by moments of heightened awareness. Esther was telling her to hold on, help was coming. "I don't *want* paramedics," she begged. "I just want to go home. Take me home." Her chin wavered and she began to cry as, somewhere in the distance, a siren wailed. Not until it stopped did she realize it was for her. "No," she protested again, "just take me *home*."

Reporters hung back, watching. "This is awful," Channel 7's Anna Garcia remarked. A colleague nodded his assent.

"Everyone stand back," a voice commanded as first firemen, then paramedics came through, rolling a gurney. The crowd shuffled a few feet. Sharri felt a mask being placed over her face, then a rush of cool air through her lungs. Her sleepiness quickly abated under the oxygen. "I don't want to go to the hospital," she protested to the paramedic at her side.

"I know, I know," he soothed. "But we just need to make sure you're okay."

Strong arms on each side pulled her up. She saw a portable bed's steel legs lower themselves to meet her, but she collapsed again before reaching the top. She sensed more cameras clicking, more hands reaching out to help. Then she was rolling away, both eyes squeezed shut against the gawking world. She was in an elevator; she was rolling again; they were lifting her into an ambulance. Michael and the paramedic crowded in.

"Please. I'm all right now. I promise."

The paramedic smiled wanly. He looked in his mid-thirties, kind of chunky, with glasses. He patted her head. Her blood sugar was probably down because she hadn't eaten, he told her. She also looked dehydrated. Probably, all she needed was food and rest, but he wanted to be sure.

As soon as Sharri was wheeled into St. Rose Hospital in Hayward, nurses began scurrying to attach a heart monitor and take blood. She pushed the oxygen mask from her face until they finally took it away. She refused to eat.

"Will you eat at home?" a nurse pressed. Michael promised to see that she would.

Doug, Michael's parents, Lana, Mary, Esther, and Greg hung about the lobby, idly watching television as they waited for Sharri's release. At 11:30 A.M. on Channel 7's midday news, they saw what they had prepared themselves for. The verdict and Sharri's collapse were the top story, complete with hastily edited footage of the melee. Anna Garcia was standing "live" in front of the now-quiet courthouse steps.

"The so-called 'Dear Diary' case ended today in the East Bay with a guilty verdict. And hearing that, the mother collapsed.

"It was an emotional end to an emotional case. . . ."

PART IV

Fighting Back

June 1993-November 1993

You wait. We'll get Serena back. We will. We can't let her sit in jail for something she didn't do; we can't let that hang over her head for the rest of her life. We'll do everything we possibly can to help her. We're only just beginning to fight.

—SHARRI MOORE

Thirty-four

June 14

Hey Mary,

How are you doing? I'm doing okay! Well the shock is still here! i can't really believe it. Well I miss everyone so much. your still gonna help me [decorate] my room when i get out. I miss you so much. the heart means me and you will always be together in our hearts. We will always be best friends. Call my mom and tell her i said "I Love her." Well i gotta go!

Love ya Always, Serena

SERENA READ OVER her words. They read okay—not too gloomy, not too happy. Too happy wouldn't be good; Mary would see right through that. Before sealing her letter, Serena filled a second sheet of paper with a large heart divided lengthwise by a ribbon bearing the word "Love." In the heart above the ribbon, she wrote "Mary" and below, wrote her own name. As she folded both pages and slid them into a plain white envelope, she tried not to cry.

She wanted to go home so bad! She longed to sleep in her own bed, wear her own clothes, see her friends. Most of all, she wanted to be near her parents—every day. They'd stood by her through everything. Especially Michael. After all the years, she was grateful for their support.

At least now that the trial was over, she could see them again.

If life in juvenile hall had been difficult for Serena before the verdict, now it was sheer hell. With the judge's few short sentences she had crossed the line from a minor charged with a felony to a criminal convicted of killing her own little sister—an act to be despised by other inmates. She began receiving hate mail, and some juveniles in the hall threatened to "get her" if and when she was released. The hate mail would prompt heightened security around Serena's future hearings in the form of body scanning of spectators in the courtroom foyer. Apart from the reactions of her "juvey" peers, the conviction itself relegated her to a continued solitary status. Because of her crime, she typically would be allowed a roommate only when the girls' ward was full. With no one to talk to during room time, she found herself face-to-face with painful memories of Mallory and a hopeless future.

Despite her tearful plea at court, Sharri had not been able to visit Serena the evening after the verdict. She spent the weekend trying to regain her physical strength. Michael hovered over her, making sure she ate. On Monday the fourteenth, during regular afternoon visiting hours, she finally was able to see Serena.

After taking off for three weeks during the trial, Michael returned to work that Monday morning, grateful that his supervisor and friends there were supportive. Not one of them "believed that crap," as he was told. Staring mindlessly at his desk for the first few minutes, he fought to pull himself out of the stupor that enveloped him. His sense of responsibility, plus a good dose of his old defense mechanism, repression, enabled him eventually to conduct his plastics experiments.

As the warm, continuously sunny June days passed, Sharri wondered how she would face each new day. With both children gone, she had lost all purpose in life. She was going crazy knocking about the house with nothing to do but think and remember. Her schedule began to revolve around the Monday, Wednesday, and Saturday visits to juvenile hall.

Mallory's *101 Dalmations* dress still lay beneath her pillow.

Financially, the Moores were facing ruin. On top of having to pay Dr. Lawrence and Dr. Berg a total of around $5000, they had lost over $2000 more through Michael's unpaid work leave to attend the trial. Even worse, the house on Lucia, which they had placed on the market, wasn't selling.

Although it was rented, those monies still resulted in a negative cash balance after paying mortgage on the property. They had borrowed money from Michael's brother Ben to open the pet store several years ago and to pay for Mallory's funeral, then more recently to help pay the Lucia mortgage. Now, they owed him a total of $16,000 and did not want to ask for more. By August, they would have lost their Lucia renter, be two mortgage payments in arrears, and face foreclosure.

They were grateful for the help received from their church, which had set up a fund for Serena. One thousand dollars of that fund had helped pay Dr. Berg. The rest was designated for Serena's psychological treatment whenever she was released from jail.

Despite their monetary woes, the Moores remained adamant on two points. One, they would not sell their story rights to any production company bent on making some sensationalistic movie about Serena Moore, the murderess. Luckily on that point, they had heard that Lorimar had put its plans for a movie on hold. Second, much as she needed a job for both practical and emotional reasons, Sharri would not take one that precluded her from visiting Serena. As during the six months before the trial, she planned to miss not one session. Eventually, she was able to land employment as a weekend waitress in a bar, telling herself through gritted teeth that she could stand the deafening rap music, but quit only after two weeks when the clientele refused to "treat her with respect." The last thing she needed was more denigration.

Shortly after the verdict, the Moores flew to New York at the expense of CBS's "Eye to Eye" show for final meetings with Connie Chung, whom they thought both sensitive and delightful. Given $400 to spend, they managed to enjoy two nights of fine dinners and a Broadway play. The change of locale afforded them a brief respite checkered with grim reminders of reality during their two interviews.

"I try hard not to consciously mourn Mallory in the same instant that I'm missing Serena," Sharri told Chung. "I try to separate it. Because if I were to mourn both of them at once, it would be too much. I would not survive."

When Chung asked about their future, Michael hesitated,

then replied, "We don't have one at the moment. We haven't been able to see beyond this."

"I have to try to help Serena now," Sharri added, "because where there's life, there's hope."

Life for Matt Golde postverdict was fantastic. The halls of the bleak county building that housed his office were full of back-slapping, congratulatory colleagues. He was the Golden Boy of the hour, the David who'd gone up against and slain Goliath. Wisely, he would keep any crowing to himself. Unlike his father the judge, he would insist, he had no political or judicial aims. Therefore, wins and losses meant nothing to him, he said. He wasn't scrabbling up any career ladder; he was just doing his job.

In Golde's eyes, justice had won. Serena Moore was unquestionably guilty of killing her sister. Now convicted, she would soon be on her way to CYA, where she could remain until her twenty-fifth birthday. There, perhaps, she could receive the psychological counseling she needed. Locked up in juvenile hall, with its inadequate facilities and its persona as more of a holding tank than a jail for long-term inmates, her treatment was positively nil. Although her attorneys were likely to fight a sentence at CYA, they had little chance of succeeding, thought Golde. As they had discovered soon after Serena's arrest, no psychiatric hospital seemed to exist that could satisfy the state's unyielding requirement to secure a defendant. If the defense attorneys hadn't prevailed then, they certainly wouldn't now, after their client had been convicted.

Equally important to Golde was the fact that Serena would not have to return to her unstable home and abusive parents. In an interview a week after the verdict, he contended that the Moores were mere pretenders in claiming their marriage was strong. It was "absolutely untrue that they [were] a tight couple." There was "no love in that marriage whatsoever." Odds were, Michael would soon be out of there. As for Sharri, she had chosen Michael over Serena, allowing him to "abuse with impunity" while she rested in the financial security that he provided her. Michael was Sharri's "meal ticket." She "wanted to be on easy street, and if it meant sacrificing her daughters to a man that molested them, it was all right." Most of Golde's anger regarding the case rested with Sharri, whom he called "one destructive person in her daughters' lives."

Further, the Moores seemed to want publicity from the case more than they cared for the welfare of their own child, he accused. It was "pure money" with them; they aimed to make a buck off the ordeal however they could.

As Golde had told reporters after the verdict, if Serena wanted to file charges against Michael for the sexual abuse, his door was open. He doubted, however, that she was capable of doing that at the present time. Maybe in a few years, as long as it fell within the six-year statute of limitations. It depended on how she recovered from her ordeal and where Michael was in her life. Golde was convinced that whenever she did find the strength, Michael would not be married to Sharri.

Shelley Antonio could not let go of the case. She was, in her own words, "obsessed." What could she have done differently? The Deputy D.A. was wrong in claiming there was no way Serena could be innocent, she would say, given the fact that there were two story lines that fit perfectly for the same information. There was nothing to say "this is convincing" one way or another. If Serena had been allowed a jury, most surely she would have been acquitted, Antonio believed. Gauging from disinterested parties at court—the clerks, guards, even reporters—who had been so amazed at the verdict, Antonio was convinced that a jury would have found plenty of reasonable doubt. A reporter from Channel 5 news (CBS) had told her "everybody in the newsroom couldn't believe it."

For that reason, Antonio still felt the sensational case had helped her career, even though she had lost. Other people seemed to know it wasn't a just decision. The judge, with her prosecutorial background and a husband who was currently a D.A., simply had not been able to justify to her colleagues acquitting a juvenile who had "confessed," Antonio rationalized. Add the judge's background to the paradigm of the "paternalistic juvenile system, which tended to view any kid that entered it as bad and/or needing protection," Antonio maintained that Serena had not been given the same constitutional deference afforded to adults. She and Belli had faced an uphill battle from the start, she now thought, and had never been allowed to rise above it.

In her less cynical moments, Antonio felt Sandra Margulies simply did not understand the pathology and evidence of asthma enough to verify Serena's innocence. Plus, Golde had made such a big thing of her own refusal to allow Dr. Warnock and Dr. Herrmann to speak with each other. Maybe she had given the judge too much credit for figuring it all out, but what really happened, Antonio said in an interview, was that Dr. Herrmann had "lied" on the stand. She had placed herself as a go-between because she had not wanted to expose Dr. Warnock to Dr. Herrmann before she, Warnock, reached her conclusions. (Antonio perhaps was remembering how convincing Dr. Herrmann had been in her own conversation with him regarding the anal findings.)

According to Antonio, Dr. Warnock had given her three questions to pass along to Dr. Herrmann. To the first question—what was meant by the lungs filling the pleural cavity?—he had responded that they went right to the edges, there was no space between the lungs and the chest wall. Second, did the lungs cross over the heart? To which he replied, "I don't remember, but if they had, I probably would have written it down." Antonio said she had related to Dr. Warnock that complete answer. Dr. Warnock was wrong when she testified that the answer given her had been "I don't know." Antonio reasoned that "I don't know" and "I don't remember" were easy to mix up. And Dr. Herrmann had definitely "lied" when he stated in rebuttal that he had told Antonio the lungs did *not* cross over the chest, she said. He had answered, "I don't remember." Third, Dr. Warnock had wondered if the lungs collapsed when he opened the chest. And that answer was no.

After Dr. Herrmann's rebuttal, Antonio claimed, she had caught him in the hallway outside court, reminding him of their conversation and his "I don't know" answer. That exchange jogged his memory, said Antonio, and he agreed that's what he had said.

At any rate, that was all behind her. Now she had an appeal to worry about. Belli wanted to appeal on the grounds that a juvenile should have a right to a jury trial. Such an appeal, based as it was on constitutional grounds, could potentially change the system for other juveniles, but would do little to help Serena, probably taking years to reach the state supreme court.

With little other grounds left on which to appeal, Antonio was excited to receive a call less than a week after the trial from a consultant to the San Francisco Center on Juvenile and Criminal Justice, Jim White-Gellepes. He had been following the case, Gellepes told her, and was calling at his own behest, not that of the Center's. He felt Serena Moore "got a rotten deal." Gellepes offered his help in two areas. Regarding an appeal, he suggested an argument could be made that Serena should have been granted a judge from the juvenile system instead of from the superior court calendar. She had in effect been given a double whammy, denied a jury because she was a minor, then tried before a judge from the adult system. Second, he would prepare an alternative sentencing report for free. Serena Moore certainly would get no help at CYA; in fact, if she wasn't a murderer now, she'd most likely become one in that awful place, he felt. According to Gellepes, there were many alternatives in residential treatment programs.

With a report in hand at the July 2 hearing, Antonio and Gellepes could challenge the probation department's almost certain recommendation to send Serena to CYA. Antonio had located several locked psychiatric facilities since Serena's initial hearings on the matter six months earlier. She hoped to propose that Serena receive a stipulated period of treatment in one of those facilities, then be placed in the custody of a foster home or her grandmother, Tessie Dornellas.

Even as she reread police reports in her "obsession" and second-guessed her decisions in the case, Antonio still felt she had done a better job than anyone else could have done. She had brought passion and compassion into the courtroom; she had championed Serena's cause like no other. She did not regret for one second taking the case, only that she did not win. But, she consoled herself, if she had, the girl would now be back with her family. At least this way Serena did not have to live in an abusive household.

At the July 2 hearing, Golde arrived with a new short haircut, looking somewhat like a shorn sheep. Court employ-

ees and spectators giggled. Sharri chortled the hardest. He
looked around the room with a good-natured grin. "What's
so funny?"

Antonio entered court without Belli ten minutes late, chew-
ing gum. She wore black. Serena slouched in, wearing a
blue-, green-, and maroon-striped jacket, hair in a ponytail.
She smiled at her parents.

With court called to session, Antonio formally requested a
continuance until July 16 in order to allow Jim Gellepes time
to prepare his report. Serena, meanwhile, would remain in
juvenile hall.

In a *déjà vu* of Serena's trial, Golde noted that he had not
received any notice of the continuance, and asked that he be
given copies of any written documents before the next hearing. His complaint prompted Margulies to deliver another
short lecture to Antonio.

After the ten-minute proceeding, Serena was led out of
court, blowing three kisses to her parents on the way.

Serena could not understand why her Grandma Tessie had
testified for the prosecution. She had always been close to
her grandmother and loved her dearly. But once again, even
in juvenile hall, she found herself caught in the middle of an
ongoing feud between her grandmother and parents. Neither
side had spoken to the other since the trial. Her mom would
say that Grandma should just leave the three of them alone.
Grandma, meanwhile, was writing Serena letters filled with
X's and O's, words of support and, as the Moores viewed it
after reading them, "pressure" on Serena to live in Carson
City whenever she was released. Michael and Sharri might
be Serena's parents, but, according to the letters, Tessie and
her husband, Kirk; Aunt Roxanne; Great Aunt Laura and
Uncle Phil were her "blood relatives" as opposed to a "step
family," and Tessie's house was Serena's "home." Furthermore, Serena was not to trust a certain friend from Tahoe.
That person was "on [her] mother's side."

Serena was not to give up, wrote Grandma; they would be
together soon.

Serena knew very well they *couldn't* be together. She was
about to be shipped off to CYA, and Grandma's testifying
for the prosecution just may have had something to do with

it. Angrily, Serena wrote to her grandmother and told her what she thought, receiving a feisty letter in return, saying that Tessie didn't know what Serena was talking about. Tessie told her granddaughter that she had no say in Serena's sentencing; that power lay with the attorneys, the judge, and Serena's mom. The very same day Serena received the letter, she was to call her grandmother with an explanation for her harsh words. Tessie would not spend the money to visit Serena until she called.

Serena read the letter, slapped it down on her lap, and sighed. Call the same day she got this reply. Like she could just pick up the phone. Where did Grandma think she was, Holiday Inn?

At seventeen, Jim Gellepes had spent ten months in the California Youth Authority for running up an unauthorized bill worth thousands of dollars on a friend's credit card while he worked on the campaign to elect Dianne Feinstein for governor. In CYA, he'd quickly learned the error of his ways. Knowing he "wasn't a bad guy," he decided upon his release to turn his negative experience into good by helping juveniles in the "System."

Gellepes was diminutive in stature, with dark hair and brown eyes framed by thick-lensed glasses. Unashamed of his openly gay lifestyle, he shared with his partner, Romaldo Allen, living and office quarters on the twenty-seventh floor of the highest building in Emeryville, just across the Bay Bridge from San Francisco. Now at just twenty-one and a lobbyist, he was still interested in politics and was already working toward goals in that arena, seeking at the time a seat on the Emeryville School Board with plans to run for state assembly in 1996.

In working on his sentencing report of Serena, Gellepes gleaned information from Shelley Antonio. She, in turn, connected him with Tessie Dornellas, who, along with Roxanne and Laura, quickly became his ally. The social history of Serena as depicted in his report, then, would be based on input from those women as well as documents given him by the Belli firm, including probation files, police documents, and psychiatric evaluations. He also interviewed Serena on one occasion. Gellepes spoke with Sharri Moore a few times on the telephone, but did not interview her in depth. Put off by her talkative nature and excitability, he was left with the sense that she was almost flippant about Mallory's death.

Adding to his opinion of the Moores was a partial copy of Fremont Officer Lamb's September 1992 police report, filed in response to Serena's allegations that Michael had caused bruises to her neck and thighs. Apparently, Antonio had given Gellepes only the pages detailing Serena's accusations. He unknowingly was missing Lamb's accounts of interviews with all parties involved and the officer's final analysis that Serena's claims were "unfounded." Gellepes's attempts to contact Officer Lamb for his viewpoint on the report were unsuccessful. Referring to the incident in his report, Gellepes paraphrased, "On one occasion the Fremont Police Department documented Michael Moore brutally beating Serena Moore while her mother watched."

For Gellepes, his conversation with Sharri, the partial report, additional research, plus the other documents and what he had heard from Tessie and Roxanne and Laura, were enough for him to conclude the Moore household was dysfunctional. He backed up his depiction with Golde's statement from the trial that "the minor had suffered a lifetime of physical, emotional, and sexual abuse."

Months later, Gellepes would be dismayed to hear that the information he received regarding the alleged sexual abuse, particularly the pages from Officer Lamb's report, had been incomplete. He believed that *he* had made "all reasonable attempts to research" the case and "be thorough," but felt that the "process was somewhat impugned by the insufficiency of the file" give him by the Belli firm.

Regarding sentencing for Serena, Gellepes noted in his report that the probation officer and Deputy D.A. had recommended placement at CYA, claiming she would have access there to the adolescent psychiatric wards at Napa State Hospital. Not so, he countered. Rosa Rivera of the CYA Population Management Division had informed him that CYA only had access to eight beds in the hospital. All beds were occupied until 1994, with four youths on a waiting list.

As an alternative, Gellepes recommended Excelsior Youth Center of Aurora, Colorado, a thirty-three-acre site that offered an "intense, qualified residential treatment program" for girls from age twelve to eighteen. Admissions Director Terry Hoffman had issued a formal acceptance of the minor into the program, and could accommodate her beginning the first week in August.

Gellepes was pleased with his sentencing report and excited about arguing on Serena Moore's behalf at the July 16 hearing. Little could he know that, for all his *pro bono* consultation, the report would never be discussed in court.

As they had done since Mallory's death, Sharri and Michael continued visiting her grave every other Sunday, leaving behind new pinwheels and watering the grass. Although Mallory's grave was in a family plot at Skylawn, occasionally after "seeing" her, they would drive over to the children's section. Many of the sites there were pitifully neglected, barren of flowers, and full of weeds. Sharri would cry for the forgotten children, sometimes placing an extra toy or flower on a small marker. She wondered if their parents didn't come because they had moved away. She would love to get away from the Bay Area, too, if Serena were ever released from jail. There were too many bad memories here. But she knew she couldn't leave her daughter's grave. Sometimes, the thought that a burial place tied her and Michael forever to the area made her bitter. Then she would remember Mallory and feel guilty for her bitterness.

July slowly was ticking by, and August was approaching— the dreaded month that held anniversaries for both Mallory's birth and death. After everything else, they did not know how they would get through it.

In the midst of their grief, the Moores viewed continued attention from the media as adding insult to injury. Movie producers were calling the Belli firm, as were scouts for national talk show hosts such as Phil Donahue, Sally Jessy Raphael, and Larry King. Reportedly, Shelley Antonio and Matt Golde were willing to appear on "Larry King Live," but King didn't want to cover the story without the Moores. Sharri and Michael were not the least bit tempted. No way were they going to put themselves through that. Strapped as they were for cash, they decided that maybe they would consider a movie that told their side of the story, but only as long as they had script approval.

In a telephone conversation, Sharri later reported, Antonio tried to talk her into appearing on King's show. It would be easy, Antonio encouraged. She and Michael would not even have to travel to the studio; they could sit right in their own living room and participate via monitor. Antonio and Golde would do most of the talking.

"All you have to do," Sharri recounted Antonio saying, "is play the distraught mother."

With the shock beginning to wear off, anger set in—anger deep enough to pull the Moores out of their lethargy. Exhausted though they were, a new undercurrent of energy began slowly to seep into their bodies, and they vowed to fight anew for their daughter. Alternative sentencing report or no, Serena most certainly would soon be transferred to CYA, a place full of *real* criminals. She would still receive no psychiatric help, plus she would be two to three hours' drive away. Sharri did not know how she could live through separation from her one remaining child. The thought made her physically ill.

Not knowing what to expect, or if any plausible options existed, Sharri and Michael made an appointment with Doug Horngrad, the San Francisco attorney whom Sharri had contacted before Belli came on the scene. Their first meeting took place in early July. Horngrad's office on Stockton Street at the edge of North Beach, the section of San Francisco noted for its Italian restaurants and bistros, was instantly inviting with its white wood walls and furniture covered in shades of dark rose. Tapestries from the country of India added a touch of the exotic. Smack-dab in the middle of an imposing-looking couch rested a small pillow embroidered with the quote, "There is no situation of human misery that cannot be made worse by the presence of a police officer."

The Moores knèw they'd found their man.

Standing six-foot-two, with closely cropped dark hair and glasses, Horngrad first appeared to the Moores the picture of formality. As they came to know him, they would see his "other side." Horngrad was, indeed, a complex person, at times coming across as standoffish, perhaps because of his strong sense of privacy. As he would put it, "I'm a pretty personal guy." Of Jewish descent and hailing from the East, he had majored in political science at Boston University, then attended graduate school in Washington, D.C., followed by law school at San Francisco's Golden Gate University from 1976 to 1980. He had been a public defender in Marin County, across the Bay, until opening his private practice in August 1989.

The attorney's formal air and exceeding politeness no doubt had its origins in his Eastern prep school days, when teachers demanded the utmost respect and beds were made with hospital-cornered precision. At the same time, he carried a certain aura of California free-spiritedness. He might remark that something pleasant was "groovy" or tell a nicely dressed woman, "Great getup." He was apt to play any number of music styles loudly in his office, including Spanish tunes with lots of marimba and maracas. The shelf in his waiting room was filled with an equally eclectic assortment of books, their topics ranging from flowers to astronomy, coins to comics, the law to *Rolling Stone's Illustrated History of Rock and Roll.*

Not one to self-aggrandize, Horngrad would nevertheless employ an amazing facility of the tongue when deemed necessary for a client's best interests, often delivering memorable one-line zingers that at once befuddled the opposition and amused the press.

Horngrad, "as cynical as the next guy," listened to the Moores' tale of their debacle with interest. At first blush, it sounded like something had definitely gone wrong in the trial of Serena Moore. And, according to Sharri, the Belli firm was now acting not only as defense counsel for Serena, but also as the family's media agent, negotiating with various movie producers willing to tell the Moores' story with the intent of earning a fifteen percent commission on any finalized deal. Horngrad thought the arrangement underhanded. Belli and Antonio had apparently only added to the sensationalism of the trial, and should not reap any resulting monetary benefits. He gave the Moores the name of a respected media attorney in the city, whom they promised to call.

As for Serena, a move that could occur after a murder conviction, Horngrad explained, was to make a motion for new trial, which had to be filed before sentencing. A motion for new trial was a request that the verdict be set aside based on a variety of factors such as wrong evidentiary rulings, insufficient evidence, or ineffectiveness of defense counsel. They rarely were granted. They acted instead as a "road map" for the appellate court, introducing new items of information into the record that could support arguments for overturning the verdict on appeal.

Making no promises, Horngrad agreed for $5000 to become Serena's new defense counsel and look over all trial records in an effort to see how plausible such a motion would be. The Moores could pay him over time. If only an appeal were in order, he would refer them to the best appellate attorney he knew. If he did make a motion for new trial, he would charge an additional $5000, and if they were lucky enough to win, his fee for a second trial would be another $5000 for a total of $15,000.

After the meeting, as they walked down one of San Francisco's many hills toward their car, Sharri fairly pranced. The sky was fogless, the slight breeze was warm, and they were doing something to save their daughter!

Michael hoped she was right.

At the July 16 hearing, Horngrad "substituted in" as defense counsel, the Belli firm thereby being publicly "fired" from the case. Antonio had been highly upset when she learned that she was being replaced. Serena was almost like her own daughter, she felt; she couldn't give up the case now. Desperate to change Serena's mind, she phoned juvenile hall numerous times, pleading to speak with her, only to be told that she was no longer legal counsel and had no rights in that regard.

For her part, Serena felt well rid of Shelley Antonio and Mr. Belli. They'd let her down, gotten her convicted, plus said awful things about her family. Mom was visiting every chance she got, Michael came regularly on Saturdays, and they all were becoming reacquainted. Her parents were still supporting her one hundred percent and that was more than she could say for a lot of people.

Sharri was furious over Antonio's actions. She saw it as a surefire indication that the woman was led willy-nilly by her emotions, not her head. It was just too bad if she "missed"

Serena. And an attorney had *no business* trying to talk a client out of changing counsel when it was in her best interest.

During the July 16 hearing, Horngrad requested that the court grant him a free copy of the trial transcripts so he could study them and see how to proceed. Margulies balked, saying that she was concerned as to "what the nature of the motions" and "the end result of those motions" would be.

"Hard to say," responded Horngrad, until he could look over the transcripts.

Margulies acquiesced.

Allowing time for preparation of the transcripts, Horngrad's perusal of them and Golde's vacation out of the country, Margulies scheduled the next hearing for September 3. In the time being, Shelley Antonio was to see that new counsel received all discovery materials on the case.

Sentencing of the minor was temporarily postponed.

Thirty-five

"HAVE YOU EVER read your daughter's diary?" Connie Chung asked. "Sharri is one mother who did and may be sorry for the rest of her life."

"Eye to Eye's" recounting of the "Diary Girl's" story aired in mid-August. After watching the show, Tessie wrote Serena, assuring her that those who saw it would believe she was innocent. Tessie was dismayed that Serena hadn't written or called and knew that could only be because she was being "pressured" by "outside influences." But "they" couldn't keep Serena away from her "true family" forever. Grandma still hoped Serena would live in Carson City and was sorry that Serena was running into opposition regarding what she wanted to do. Serena, suggested Tessie, just might have to "put her foot down."

Horngrad was having a heck of a time obtaining discovery files from the Belli firm and when he finally did, they were not complete. He made a couple of phone calls to Antonio, then was forced to wait for her response. Meanwhile, the date on which he was to receive trial transcripts rolled around. On August 19, as he delved into reading them, he told Sharri over the phone that he was "getting very excited" at the prospects of filing a motion for new trial based on ineffectiveness of counsel.

After taking the case, Horngrad had heard that Phyliss Winters, who had been Antonio's legal secretary during Serena's trial and was fired shortly afterward, was claiming that Antonio "hadn't known what she was doing day to day" on the case. Horngrad told Sharri that he would try to speak with Phyliss Winters for further information and hopefully get an affidavit of her statement. (This would not come to pass. When Horngrad tracked down Winters, she told him she would not talk to anyone about the Moore case without payment. Horngrad declined.)

Reading the transcripts in the next few days, Horngrad believed Winters's claim. Antonio didn't seem to know how to introduce evidence around the prosecution's objections, he thought, and her own objections often had been overruled. According to Golde's argument, she had destroyed her own expert witness's testimony. And she had failed to ask key questions. In the latter point, Horngrad particularly noted her cross-examination of Dr. Herrmann, believing that the pathologist had not been allowed to state what he really thought about the case. Antonio should have asked him, for example, whether his physical observations at autopsy were consistent with Serena's confession and committing the crime. She should have inquired if the molestation Dr. Herrmann spoke of could have been contemporaneous with death.

The entire sexual abuse issue had been misused, Horngrad felt. Antonio had hemmed and hawed in her suggestion that the stepfather could have committed the crime, but never adequately pursued it. She should either have fought to disprove the molestation and rebut Dr. Herrmann's finding on the matter or gone "full-tilt boogey" in arguing the potential for a perpetrator other than the defendant. By not pursuing either course effectively, Horngrad believed, she had played directly into the hands of Golde, who needed proof of sexual abuse as a foundation for his crazy motive.

In Horngrad's eyes, Antonio's neglect of the matter raised another serious problem. Lacking the "Plan B" argument of another perpetrator, the Belli firm had rested its defense solely on the medical evidence in hopes of convincing the judge that Mallory Moore's death was due to natural causes. When, through the testimony of "hometown boy Herrmann," Margulies had been convinced that a homicide *had* occurred, she was left with only one suspect—Serena.

Horngrad was well aware of the Moores' anger and sense of betrayal at the Belli firm's implication, weak though it was, that Michael could have molested and even killed his own daughter. On a personal level, Horngrad knew he could not fully understand their feelings, not having children himself. But sensitivity was not the issue here. At issue was the ancient ethics code upon which legal representation was based—the client comes first. Serena Moore was now his client, not her parents, regardless of who paid the bills. However unpleasant, if he had to pursue the "other perpetrator" argument, whether it was true or not, in order to secure his client's acquittal, so be it.

Another major mistake committed by the Belli firm, Horngrad felt, was Antonio's failure to introduce adequate evidence of Serena's propensity to lie in order to expose the confession as false. When Margulies did not allow Dr. Berg to testify that the diary entry wasn't true—a ruling that should well have been expected—Antonio seemed to have had no recourse. The upshot of her error was that the judge was left with no clear reason to view the confession as anything but accurate.

His reading of the transcripts accomplished, Horngrad had a much clearer sense of why Serena had been convicted. Bottom line was, Horngrad would later say, Golde had "seriously outlawyered" Belli and Antonio. He'd "outsmarted, outwitted, outplotted, and outschemed 'em." He'd "spun 'em like tops," making all the right evidentiary objections and eliminating part of their defense. He'd been "five times the lawyer they both were combined."

If Horngrad thought the transcripts revealing, he was completely astounded after reviewing discovery materials finally received from Antonio. One of the documents was a copy of Serena's first journal, kept over a number of years. Horngrad noticed that the first page of his copy of the journal was numbered 118. He didn't know what the number referred to, but had been assured by Antonio that she had sent him everything she had on the case. A synopsis of the journal, written by the Belli firm, began with the first entry Horngrad had, reinforcing his belief that he indeed possessed all the contents of the journal. Scanning through Serena's notations over the last few years, he was most interested to see what she had written around the time of Mallory's death. To his utter disbelief he read her entry of August 23, 1992, numbered page 143:

> sorry I haven't written in a while! well, i got tuns to tell you. you remember my little sister Mallory she was 4! well on Monday night between midnight Mon. and 7:00 Tues., she died. i woke up, went in there and something was wrong. she wouldn't move or breath or anything. so i went into my mom's room and told her so she went in there and she was dead.

Horngrad blinked, backed up, and read it again. Here was an innocent version of events! It out and out negated the confession. Neither Antonio nor Belli had ever so much as *mentioned* it. And to not use it in court as a rebuttal to the confession diary! The entry in Diary #1, as Horngrad quickly dubbed it, would be a major break in the case. With that diary, he hoped to undermine Margulies's confidence in her verdict by demonstrating that she had not heard all the evidence.

In a subsequent phone conversation, Horngrad informed the Moores that there was no question he would file a motion for new trial based on ineffectiveness of counsel. They had what he would term a "righteous claim." Nevertheless, even though he had more ammunition than most motions of that sort carried, he cautiously warned them that it would be "a long shot." If he had to guess, he'd say that out of five hundred such motions, maybe one was granted.

Horngrad's caution was well founded. California law specified inadequate counsel as lacking any "rational, tactical reason" for decisions made in court.

As far as Horngrad was concerned, there could be no rational, tactical decision for not introducing Diary #1 into evidence. But would Sandra Margulies agree?

Further diminishing Horngrad's chances for winning the motion was the fact that granting it would require Judge Margulies to overturn her *own* decision, not that of a jury. Few judges had the fortitude to reverse themselves, particularly under the kind of media scrutiny that this case had generated.

In his "heart of hearts," Horngrad thought the motion should be granted. Serena Moore had not received adequate counsel and as a result had been convicted of a crime she did not commit. But as much as he wanted to win, he doubted that would happen, and consoled himself with the fact that he was setting up a proper appeal. The problem with appeals was that they took so long; Serena could serve a year or more at CYA before her case would reach the appellate court.

At the September 3 hearing, Horngrad informed Judge Margulies of his intent to file a motion for new trial. He needed at least five weeks before the next hearing date in order to complete another murder trial in which he was involved. Golde, facing the situation with stoic acceptance, had no objection to waiving time, but noted that "there is a certain concern for the minor being in the hall, just sitting there, all this time."

Sharri couldn't repress a snort at the remark. Fine time it was for Matt Golde to be worrying about Serena's well-being, she hissed to Michael.

Point well taken, Horngrad responded to Golde, but if he couldn't do his homework properly and the motion wasn't granted, "the minor was facing ten years." To the judge, he commented that "hope springs eternal" that he would prevail.

Margulies allowed herself a brief smile. "I never know what I'm going to do until I read the papers."

That was certainly apparent from the transcripts, Horngrad replied solicitously.

Agreeing to a due date for Horngrad's filing his arguments in mid-October, Golde submitted that he could respond by November 1. The hearing was set for November 12, giving Horngrad adequate time to answer Golde's opposition and still leave Margulies a few days to review all the documents.

During these proceedings, Serena, her hair brushed prettily and hanging down her back, sat motionless beside her new attorney. She was so glad he didn't make her wear a ponytail like Shelley had! Afterward, as she was led out to be handcuffed and shackled for transport back to juvenile hall, she threw her parents a brilliant smile. Her hope sprang eternal, too.

The Moores' financial problems were coming to a head. Desperate to get out from under their debt on the Lucia property and to Michael's brother Ben, they negotiated an agreement with him. As payment for the $16,000 he'd lent them, Ben would take ownership of their house on Lucia. Both parties would benefit. Ben was assuming a long-term investment that eventually would pay well since equity in the house was far above $16,000. Sharri and Michael would lose the equity, but be out from under the hefty mortgage payments. Ben even agreed to cover the two back payments they owed.

That done, the Moores still needed to come up with about $3000 to pay Doug Horngrad's investigator, Stuart Kohler, who had interviewed a dozen or so of Serena's friends. He billed on an hourly basis and it was adding up, although Horngrad had persuaded him to work for half his usual wage. Horngrad himself needed $5000 to cover his motion for new trial. If the motion were granted, he would require another $5000 to try the case.

Sharri began scanning the want ads for employment. Despite their financial difficulties, she still insisted she must find a job around visiting hours at juvenile hall. That negated the normal 8:00 A.M. to 5:00 P.M. weekday schedule. She applied for a weekend bartender's job, sure she wouldn't get it since she'd never tended bar before. But the owner took special notice of her upbeat letter of introduction and announced that he would train her on the job. She was thrilled suddenly to be working Thursday through Sunday, 10:00 A.M. to 6:30 P.M., the only downside being that she missed church. She not only was earning money, but she had something to do other than clean house and worry the days away. She made a good hourly wage, plus tips, and the bar had a friendly clientele.

Proudly, she began bringing home pocketsful of dollar bills, counting them out on the coffee table while Madison and Misty sniffed them curiously. With her earnings, she could pay numerous bills, allowing a good chunk of Michael's paycheck to be sent to Horngrad.

On the job, Sharri would turn up the music and work at an often feverish pace. That, and listening to the love life problems of the clients, helped keep her mind off her troubles, at least for the moment. She continued seeing Serena Monday and Wednesday afternoons. Michael visited alone on Saturday, his relationship with Serena continuing to strengthen as a result.

Still needing more money, the Moores decided to sell Michael's Ranger. Sharri still had her Chrysler, and an old Chevy convertible sat in the garage that Michael could drive to work. They fixed up the Ranger, had it painted, and placed ads in the newspaper. After a number of weeks and a few price reductions, it sold for $3000, all of which they sent to Horngrad.

While the attorneys were preparing their documents and Sharri and Michael shored up their and Serena's spirits as best they could, Jim Gellepes quietly continued his communications with Tessie and Roxanne. Gellepes and his partner, Romaldo Allen, had discussed their own theories on the case, Gellepes posing "the-mother-did-it" scenario, based on input he had heard that mothers sometimes took it upon themselves to remove their children from abuse in that manner. He posed the theory to Tessie and Roxanne. They didn't agree, asserting that they felt Michael was responsible.

Tessie and Roxanne still had not spoken with the Moores since the trial. Although Doug Horngrad was seeking to have Serena's guilty verdict overturned, Gellepes felt they did not view the attorney as an ally, most likely because of their belief that Horngrad would protect the Moores against any further allegations of abuse. Indeed, Gellepes had told the women that "Horngrad had a reputation for defending child molesters," referring to a nationally publicized case in which the attorney had been involved three years earlier.

Roxanne was planning to drive to the Bay Area from Lake Tahoe on October 21 for a rare visit with Serena during the weekly Friday afternoon session reserved for friends and extended family. In a phone conversation with Roxanne a few days earlier, Gellepes suggested that the two of them hold a press conference to draw attention to the fact that Serena was languishing in juvenile hall with no medical help.

It was terrible, he complained, how the system was treating this teenager. Equally disgusting, he thought, was the Belli firm's obvious incompetence in defending Serena. Gellepes told Roxanne he'd been talking to Phyliss Winters, who said that Antonio hadn't known how to handle the case.

Roxanne agreed to participate in the press conference, which they set for Friday morning, the twenty-second, Gellepes faxing notifications to newspaper and TV reporters. Roxanne would be their draw. Save for Michael's statement to the press, the defendant's family had remained tight-lipped. Now, the aunt would speak. Regardless of his own political aspirations, he was not doing this for the publicity, Gellepes would insist, but only for the cause of Serena Moore.

He saw no reason to check with Doug Horngrad before making the arrangements.

"What! That's it, I'm pulling her visitation pass!"

Horngrad was furious. Two phone calls from the media Thursday morning were his first indication that a family member and a political lobbyist were holding a press conference about *his* client. Jim Gellepes was no stranger. When he first took over Serena's case, Horngrad had spoken with Gellepes about working together on her sentencing. So why in hell hadn't the guy bothered to call him now? Horngrad immediately dialed Gellepes's office, got his answering machine, and launched into an acid-tongued lecture.

"Jim, I think common courtesy would dictate your calling me before you hold some out-to-lunch, unguided missile press conference without bothering to consult the attorney for the juvenile whom you purport to speak for. Unless this is some exercise in some ego gratification or self-aggrandizement, I'm not entirely clear as to why you wouldn't call me before you faxed your press conference releases around the state." Horngrad's voice remained cold. "I encourage and urge you to call me before you go forward with some numb-skull venture . . . [or] publicity campaign. I don't think what you're doing is right or ethical. You're purporting to defend the interest of my client, which I certainly do, and when you go off on a romp and frolic of your own to get yourself on television or whatever it is you're doing, you are not serving [her] interests."

Next, Horngrad phoned juvenile hall to demand that Serena's Aunt Roxanne no longer be allowed on her visitation list. As far as he was concerned, anyone who would dare participate in an unauthorized press conference at the potential expense of Serena's welfare should not be allowed near his client.

The Moores were even more livid than Horngrad when they heard the news. That's what Roxanne wanted all along, Sharri railed, a spot on television—neither she nor Tessie cared *one whit* for Serena. If they did, they certainly wouldn't be jeopardizing her case by stirring up unwanted publicity. Nor would they count Serena's attorney, who was trying to get her conviction reversed, among the enemy camp just because he was civil to her parents.

Serena was also bent out of shape. Grandma had promised that she'd mind her own business and stay out of things! And after hearing about the press conference, she didn't even *want* to see her Aunt Roxanne.

Most disturbing to Horngrad and the Moores was the unknown content of the press conference. If Gellepes, Tessie, and Roxanne were bandying about such despicable theories as to which parent murdered Mallory, what on earth would they say to the media? With a hearing on Horngrad's motion just over the horizon, any talk of sexual abuse could only help support the prosecution's case.

Later Thursday morning, Gellepes returned Horngrad's call, assuring him that he and Roxanne would only speak about the conditions Serena faced at juvenile hall, using her case to make a plea for overhauling the juvenile justice system in general. If Roxanne so much as mentioned sexual abuse, Gellepes promised, he himself would "pull the plug."

The conference turned out to be an awkward event, attended by only two newspaper reporters (Bob Salladay from the *Argus* and Raoul Mowatt from the *San Jose Mercury*), a journalist and a television crew from Channel 5. Roxanne kept her word, focusing her brief statement on the fact that her niece was "sitting in juvenile hall basically to rot."

In a rambling diatribe against both the juvenile system and the Belli firm, Gellepes jumped between denouncing the court's denial of psychiatric help for Serena Moore to accusing Belli and Antonio of unprofessional conduct, such as "creating a circus atmosphere" around the case. Kicking off the session, he played a brief statement recorded over the phone from Phyliss Winters, who claimed that Antonio had no trial experience before the Moore case. "I believe that Serena Moore did not receive appropriate legal representation," Winters said. "The Belli firm has no experience in juvenile law, nor had Shelley Antonio. She did not do her homework." Gellepes added more fuel to the fire, pronouncing that Belli could be sued for malpractice and should never have extended his services to the Moore family.

He and Roxanne also blasted Doug Horngrad for arbitrarily pulling her visitation pass. It would be such a disappointment to Serena, Roxanne noted.

Salladay left the conference shaking his head. The opening paragraphs of his Saturday, October 23 article would call it "another twist in a bizarre case of soap opera proportions." Later that day, he phoned Antonio to elicit her responses to Winters's and Gellepes's "defections":

> ... She called the allegations "patently false" and defended her work on the case, which she said consumed the Belli office.
>
> "She had representation from one of the best attorneys in the world," Antonio said, referring to Belli. "I graduated from Stanford Law School and I have plenty of trial experience ... I just felt that we did everything we could."
>
> Antonio ... laughed at what she called the "circling forces of evil" that have attached themselves to the case. "I think it's really unfortunate," she said, "because it's not helping [the teenager]."

Belli, not laughing one bit at Gellepes's remarks, responded with threats of a lawsuit.

When Gellepes got wind of the threat, he called Paul Monzione, one of Belli's ex-partners, and asked if Monzione would represent him if Belli went ahead with the threat. Monzione, already involved in the ex-partners' lawsuit against Belli, said yes. Gellepes was also dismayed to hear that the Moores were angry with him over holding the press conference. He had "worked very hard on Serena's behalf for free,'' he said, and was only doing what he believed to be in her best interests.

Earlier that month, Horngrad faced the deadline of filing his motion for new trial. One night as he sat at his desk, piled neatly with various documents and transcripts from the proceedings, the Deputy D.A.'s motive theory played over and over in his head. It was so whacked out. He needed a few choice words that would effectively capture the essence of its kookiness. Faced with the challenge, Horngrad's wittiness soon surfaced. He picked up his pen and dashed off a line.

"Euthanasia by sororicide."

That was it? Those three words, placed by themselves in a paragraph, would smack the most casual reader into brisk attention.

Twenty-four pages and a number of days later, Horngrad's motion was complete. Serena Moore, he charged, had been wrongfully convicted by a verdict that was contrary to law and evidence, and had been deprived of effective assistance of counsel as guaranteed by the Sixth Amendment.

Five main arguments supported Horngrad's contention. First, because of defense counsel's "inaction and incompetence," the court was not shown "overpowering and exculpatory evidence that Serena was a chronic and compulsive liar." ("Exculpatory evidence" referred to information that would help prove the defendant's innocence, as opposed to "incriminating evidence.") Attached to the motion were affidavits from thirteen of Serena's friends and family members who could testify under oath to the various lies she had told them—that she had leukemia, had given birth to one or more children (including Mallory), had undergone abortions, had been raped by a boyfriend, etc. Horngrad argued that, had the judge been allowed to hear such testimony, the veracity of the diary confession would have been brought into serious question. The prosecutor had "celebrated this lapse" in his closing argument by stating, "There really is no evidence that this minor is a chronic liar. It's not in the record."

Second and even more incomprehensible, Horngrad continued, was defense counsels' failure to offer "crucial rebuttal evidence" from Serena's first diary, which contained an entry about her discovering Mallory's body. Horngrad quoted the text, asserting there could have been "no tactical reason to refrain from making the trier of fact aware of its existence."

Third, the prosecution was allowed to elicit, without objection, "substantial testimony concerning abuse and neglect on the part of Serena's parents and concerning Serena's own 'beyond control' behavior." Admission of such evidence, Horngrad contended, might be appropriate in Section 300 proceedings, which dealt with protecting children from abusive parents, but was "absolutely prohibited" in a criminal proceeding. The "aggregate effect" of allowing testimony about such issues as the parents' drug use; arguments with and alleged violence against the minor; the defendant's being caught masturbating; and other information "calculated to produce repugnance toward her and her family" was to "let in so much negative character evidence ... that the minor was irretrievably prejudiced." Defense counsel itself had elicited testimony that Serena's family was dysfunctional and that she had probably been molested, which was "consistent with the prosecutor's theory, but departed from the minor's testimony." Horngrad went so far as to suggest that the judge, after hearing the many allegations of an unfit home, had been left with a "compelling case for out-of-home placement of the minor." Any authority to do so would have been relinquished through an acquittal.

Fourth, trial counsel "fatally undermined" the testimony of their own witness by "improperly and prejudicially inserting themselves as conduits of information" between doctors Herrmann and Warnock.

And fifth, the defense "orchestrated yet another evidentiary disaster" and reached its "zenith of incompetence" as a result of Serena's testimony. Deciding whether or not to call a defendant to the stand was often one of the biggest dilemmas faced by defense counsel. Horngrad realized that Belli may have felt the necessity to do so in order to rebut the diary confession. But under the "fiasco" of Belli's questioning, which was often fraught with "non sequiturs," Serena's testimony had been woefully inadequate, even harmful.

In sum, Serena's defense was "unprepared, unfocused, haphazard, and ill-conceived." The court "was only permitted to hear the sound of one hand clapping."

*   *   *

Sharri and Michael were delighted with Horngrad's motion. Finally someone was publicly saying what they had thought all along!

On the day of its filing in mid-October, the document was immediately a hot property. Horngrad's phone rang off the hook with reporters' requests for a copy. Carol Moor, an acquaintance of Horngrad's who worked for Richard Brown, one of Belli's ex-partners, also wanted one. Horngrad obliged them all, including Moor.

After the press conference, Gellepes, fearing that Horngrad was "serving a dual interest" by protecting the Moores from allegations of molestation as well as representing Serena, issued a press release alleging that Horngrad had a reputation for defending child molesters. "At the time, I was trying to cover all ends and make sure that his representation was *only* for Serena, as it should be," he later explained.

Horngrad again was outraged, considering this second affront profoundly gratuitous. The attorney called Gellepes, "mad as hell," only to be informed that he was now represented by Paul Monzione. Phoning the attorney, Horngrad warned Monzione that he'd better "rein his boy in" or he, Horngrad, was likely to "mop the floor" with Gellepes.

The lobbyist, Horngrad would later declare, "was serious bad news."

Horngrad's filed motion for new trial placed Golde in an interesting position. To protect the conviction for Serena Moore and, of course, his victory in the case, the Deputy D.A. now had to uphold the very counsel's arguments that he had so sought to destroy during the trial. This mandated turnabout in position would seem curious to those outside the legal community, but Golde took it in stride as a natural occurrence in the often-convoluted machinations of the law.

In his written opposition to Horngrad's motion, he reminded the court of the difficulty in meeting the requirement to prove ineffectiveness of counsel. "Unless counsel was asked for an explanation [regarding why they presented the case in the manner chosen] and failed to provide one," he wrote, "or unless there simply could be no satisfactory explanation, [the convictions in any such] cases are affirmed." One by one, Golde argued against Horngrad's major points. For example, the issue of Serena's lying. In an unabashed 180 degree turn from his closing statement at trial, Golde claimed that "evidence of the minor's propensity to lie was clearly before the court" and quoted pieces of testimony in which Sharri Moore, Serena, and others talked about the defendant's storytelling. As for Diary #1, it was not a denial of the crime, was "not inconsistent" with the confession, and expressed no shock at Mallory Moore's death. In addition, other entries in that diary contained information of a "graphic sexual content" that defense counsel may well have not wanted known. Counsel, therefore, had "plausible, tactical reasons" for not offering Diary #1 into evidence.

Regarding information on the family history, all testimony about any past events were relevant once a psychologist was called to the stand. Whereas in his closing argument, Golde had called Dr. Berg's testimony "unfounded," alleging that the doctor could "virtually diagnose anybody on the street with some form of an illness," he now averred that the "minor's erratic and sometimes violent behavior was consistent with the psychiatrist's [sic] diagnosis of a manic-depressive."

Even with the turn-about-is-fair-play arena afforded him under the situation, Golde did not address the issue of defense counsels' "fatally undermining" Dr. Warnock's testimony. All he noted on that matter was that they "called two experts to show death was from asthma."

On another point, he called it "disingenuous" to blame defense counsel for the minor's perjury on the witness stand. How could the minor's new attorney claim she was inadequately prepared to testify? "How do you prepare someone to tell the truth?" Golde asked rhetorically.

Horngrad's rebuttal to Golde, filed just two days before the hearing on November 12, took the Deputy D.A. to task over Diary #1. "It is hard to imagine," Horngrad wrote in a footnote, "arguing with a straight face that the contemporaneous diary entry is irrelevant." The government had insisted that, in the entry, the minor did not deny committing the crime. "The minor," he countered somewhat disgustedly, "does not contend that her contemporaneous diary was a denial of a lie yet to be made." On the same matter, in its "most preposterous assertion," the government had noted that the diary contained sexual material and "speculated that effective trial counsel would censor exculpatory evidence in a murder trial rather than share details of Serena's sex life." That was to say, they would "rather have their client convicted of murder than allow her reputation for chastity to be besmirched."

Horngrad was also quick to point out Golde's flagrant reversal on the issue of lies being introduced into the record.

In his original motion, Horngrad had not mentioned the Belli firm's failure to pursue the "other perpetrator" theory. He felt the judge was already aware of it, and had concentrated instead on information that she could not have known. He nevertheless fully expected to argue the point in court. Now in his rebuttal, he noted that the defense was lacking by sidestepping the issue. Either the alleged molestation shortly before Mallory's death happened, in which case the stepfather should be a suspect, or it didn't, which would shatter the central premise in the government's theory of motive. Serena's attorneys had not adequately pursued either course.

The Moores liked Horngrad and were grateful for his fine performance, so far, in helping their daughter. But the "Michael-did-it" argument was a continued thorn in their side. Horngrad explained that, upset as the Moores may have been at Belli and Antonio for even mentioning the matter, the attorneys in actuality had not pursued the line of defense *enough*. Sharri and Michael listened and, in spite of themselves, slowly began to understand. With Horngrad's patient communications—an important ingredient they felt was lacking in their relationship with the Belli firm—they came to accept the fact that the subject would not go away until Serena was freed. If Horngrad said the point must be argued in order to have any chance of winning, they were willing to sit silently by and let him do his job. At least he was talking to them and being honest about it.

"All I can say," Sharri muttered to Michael one evening, "is it better work."

Horngrad needed all the help he could get in fighting for justice in *The Matter of Serena M.* Stating his own arguments and opinions about the Belli firm's alleged incompetence was appropriate for writing his motion, but at the hearing, he needed an expert witness—a high-caliber attorney who could testify that defense counsel had been ineffective.

Horngrad called Penny Cooper, a highly respected attorney in the East Bay. She had heard about the case, she said, and was interested in looking at it. After talking with her at length, Horngrad knew she was the right choice. She was highly intelligent, experienced, and spoke with precision. Because she had practiced in the East Bay for many years, Cooper was well known in Alameda County and, in turn, knew many of the area's judges. In fact, she counted Stanley Golde, Matt Golde's father, as a close friend. She also knew Dr. Herrmann well.

Horngrad made arrangements to send Cooper copies of the transcript and everything in his file.

After taking three days to review all the documents, Cooper called back. He had a strong case for proving ineffectiveness of counsel, she thought, but posed a critical question. Were there other lies in Serena's diaries? It was one thing to tell lies, but quite another to write them in such a private place. Other written lies would certainly bring the validity of the confession into suspicion. Horngrad responded that he believed there were, but needed to go through the diaries page by page to see to what extent.

By the end of the conversation, Cooper had agreed to testify as an expert witness against Belli.

"Groovy," said Horngrad.

As opening day of the hearing approached, Horngrad felt charged and ready, loading up his righteous indignation as an offensive weapon to be displayed in court. Even though he believed Serena was innocent, he knew the cards unfortunately were stacked in Golde's favor.

He badly wanted to win.

Adding to his anxiety was the fact that Belli was apparently taking the whole thing poorly. Rather than cooperating, Belli seemed to be fighting the motion, which Horngrad considered "all wrong." The Belli firm should be on *his* side, doing whatever they could to help their former client.

Horngrad would not be alone in his opinion that former

counsel should cooperate. Within the legal community there exists, for the proceeding that was about to take place, an unwritten rule of required conduct based on the defense ethics code, "the client comes first." In the rare instance of such attorney's defense tactics being called into question, according to the rule, he or she should cooperate fully for the sake of the former client, whose advocacy once rested solely in his or her hands. Attorneys in such a situation should "take their licks," as it were, for if incompetency of counsel is proven, the former client is awarded a new trial, and the guilty verdict is set aside. An ultimate defense victory, albeit ill timed and perhaps humiliating for reprimanded counsel.

By definition, then, a motion for new trial can evoke an internal battle for the lawyer in question, a battle pitting pride and reputation against the unwritten rule.

In the face of the Belli firm's apparent hostility, Horngrad doubted that he could count on previous defense counsel for help and decided to subpoena Belli and Antonio to the stand in order to ask them about their decision-making process in Serena's case.

Horngrad kept the subpoenas a secret in order to hold the press to a minimum at the hearing. Reporters and cameras would have a field day if they had any notion of the fight at hand.

Things could get downright ugly.

With just three days to go, Horngrad knew something was wrong. During his third reading of the trial transcripts, he noticed that Golde had asked Serena numerous questions evidently based on information from Diary #1—information that he, Horngrad, did not have. He began to realize that the diary's pagination, beginning with 118 in his file, meant that he was missing a little something—like the first 117 pages.

He phoned Antonio, requesting the missing pages. A day went by without a return call. By then it was Wednesday, November 10, two days before the hearing. Antonio spoke with him that afternoon, saying she didn't know where the document was, and sent a law clerk on a harried mission to find it. Meanwhile, Horngrad called the Moores. Had the Belli firm *ever* had this portion of Serena's journal? he asked Sharri.

"Absolutely," she replied. "I know for sure they did, because I went through *all* that stuff. I even put those little sticky yellow tabs on all the pages that contained lies. I was trying to help Shelley prove that Serena wrote other lies in her diary besides that confession."

Horngrad sorted through his files until he came up with the synopsis of Diary #1 prepared by the Belli firm. If his memory served him right, that synopsis began with information gleaned from page 118. Sure enough, it did. My God, he thought, they'd *lost* the first 117 pages months ago, before Serena's trial ever took place, and didn't even seem to know it! By the time that synopsis was written, the pages were long gone. All that evidence of Serena's other lies!

Thursday dawned. Still nothing from Antonio. Horngrad called Sharri, asking her to come to his office to review what parts of the journal he did have and to underline any lies. He also called Matt Golde, requesting that the Deputy D.A. send a copy of the first 117 pages of Diary #1. It was too late to rely on receiving it from the Belli firm, although Horngrad planned to give them hell about it anyhow.

Sharri, with Esther Corren along for the ride, arrived at Horngrad's office at 6:30 P.M. to find him pestering the Belli firm with phone calls. Where in the hell was the rest of his discovery file? Perturbed as she was at Belli, Sharri found herself giggling at the scene. Horngrad was dressed in purple—purple corduroy shirt, purple socks, purple high-top sneakers. His slacks, at least, were tan. He was writing with a purple pen filled with purple ink. "I love purple," was his cryptic explanation.

Sharri almost felt sorry for "the poor guy" answering evening phones at Belli's office. After putting Horngrad off in numerous calls, he finally admitted that Belli, Antonio, and another attorney named McLean were huddled in a meeting, discussing their strategy for the next day's hearing, and could not come to the phone.

Well, stick your head in the door! Horngrad railed. He needed to talk to Antonio *now*—it was inexcusable that less than twenty-four hours before a court proceeding he still lacked complete discovery materials.

The receptionist told Horngrad to hold on. A moment later, his apologetic voice came back on the line. "Mr. Belli told me if I open that door one more time I'm fired,'' he said. ''I *can't* go in there again!''

Horngrad let ''the poor guy'' be and phoned Antonio's answering machine, leaving her a message that he needed those 117 pages of the diary and she had just better find them. He never would receive the balance of Serena's journal from Belli or Antonio. Before the day ended, Golde faxed him the pages he needed.

Two days later, Belli's receptionist reportedly was fired.

Thirty-six

WITH THE TWO original factions in *The Matter of Serena M.* now expanded into an animosity-filled triad, Friday's hearing promised to be the epitome of a three-ring circus.

In one ring was Belli, clad in a dark suit with his trademark matching shirt and tie, these in ice blue. A red kerchief hung brightly out of his suit pocket. Antonio sported her typical black suit over a teal blouse. Representing them was a third lawyer from the Belli firm, Kevin McLean, a solidly built man with a black mustache and a near completely receded hairline. His face was full, his nose somewhat hooked. He looked to be in his mid-forties.

In the second ring stood Horngrad and Penny Cooper, the expert witness ready to testify as to Belli's and Antonio's ''incompetence.'' Cooper's brown hair was cut in a short, masculine style. She wore glasses and no makeup; her dark gray pantsuit was strongly tailored. She moved in a no-nonsense, decisive manner as she conferred with Horngrad. During the proceedings, she would act more as second defense counsel than expert witness, suggesting questions and tactics for Horngrad's examinations of Belli and Antonio.

Solo, and clearly upstaged, in the third ring was Matt Golde, a leery expression on his face as he watched the Horngrad/Cooper duo and the Belli firm prepare for their performances. He had retained his preppy-style haircut. His suit was gray.

Throughout the hearing, Golde's performance would be inexplicably halfhearted, a far cry from his aggressiveness during Serena's trial. He would explain his actions on the first day of the hearing in terms of practicality—that with Belli and Antonio subpoenaed to testify,·the fight was really between them and Horngrad. But that explanation would not suffice for subsequent days, when Belli was no longer present and Golde was responsible for defending the conviction he'd worked so hard to acquire. Only months later would he admit that his actions had reflected an unshakable inner sense. He knew he was going to lose.

Reporters were slow in arriving, and only a television camera from Channel 2 panned the hallway, thanks to Horngrad's keeping his subpoenas quiet. The Moores were grateful. As media representatives spotted Belli, news of the subpoenas spread among them, until the courtroom bristled with anticipation.

Catherine Bowman from the *Chronicle* hustled over to Antonio for a reaction to the subpoenas. The attorney obliged, "It seems like a publicity stunt to me."

Sharri, seated two rows back, poked Michael with her elbow in a silent "Did-you-hear-that?" She looked overwarm in·her burgundy blouse and gray wool suit. At her request, Horngrad had issued her a subpoena to present to the owner of the bar where she worked in order to receive the day off. To her boss, she'd been vague about the reason for the court proceeding. Around Michael's neck was a large handmade cross, vying for attention with a blue- and purple-flowered tie. Next to Sharri sat Mary and Esther; Pastor Doug, Sheila Evans, and the church secretary were one row behind. The entire group looked nervous.

At 9:20 A.M., the side door opened. All eyes fixed upon it as a bailiff led Serena in. She looked slimmer in a new black jumpsuit, brought by a family friend as a good luck gift. Belli hoisted himself up from his seat along the courtroom's side wall and shuffled over to give her a hug.

"How are you?" he mumbled. "Good to see you."

Serena turned toward her parents to roll her eyes and make a face. Belli didn't notice. Antonio sat woodenly in her seat, looking for all appearances like the rejected parent as she swiveled her head away from Serena.

Margulies appeared, calling Golde and Horngrad to side bar. She ignored McLean. With court in session three minutes later, she asked that McLean identify himself, then moved on. Horngrad called Belli to the stand.

Kevin McLean immediately made a motion to quash Belli's and Antonio's subpoenas. (Aha, thought Horngrad, so *that* was what they were up to in last night's meeting.) When Margulies agreed to hear McLean's arguments, he approached the counsel table, positioning himself between Golde and Horngrad. One basis for the quash, he noted, was attorney-client privilege.

That was no problem, Horngrad responded. For the record, he turned to Serena. "The court wants me to tell you that we will be putting your former attorneys on the stand. Are you willing to waive your rights to attorney-client privilege?"

With lips pursed in half amusement, Serena replied that she was. Margulies wasn't satisfied.

"Mr. Belli and Ms. Antonio will be able to testify about conversations with you and your family. Do you understand that any such conversations may come out in their testimony?"

"Yes."

"The prosecutor will be cross-examining regarding those conversations," Horngrad added. "Are you willing to waive your privilege for that?"

"Yes."

"Are you doing this of your own free will?" Margulies pressed.

"Yeah." Serena's voice was low. "Nobody influenced me."

McLean threw out another argument. Perhaps the judge should consider the fact that the testimony being offered under subpoena was irrelevant, he argued, "Since it looks like my motion is about to be denied—"

Margulies interrupted sharply. This judge did not rule on motions until she had heard all arguments, and "resent[ed] any inference drawn from [his] comments."

Busily shuffling papers, McLean opened his mouth only to insert a second foot. Horngrad was "working underground with

Mr. Belli's ex-partners," he accused, the same ex-partners who were now suing Mr. Belli and smearing his name in the media. "I don't know if the court is aware of that—"

"The court is *not* aware of that," Margulies shot back, "because the court has not read any newspaper articles."

Horngrad was disgusted. "Your Honor, Mr. McLean's statement is patently false."

McLean tried again. All information gleaned from attorney-client conversations were the lawyer's "work product," its privilege resting with the attorney and, therefore, not waivable by the client. Mr. "Hornblatt" knew that. "The only reason he's doing this is to smear Mr. Belli, and I can't imagine the court ever agreeing to hear it."

Ignoring the intentional name-calling, Horngrad countered that case law held the courts could override such privilege when in the best interests of the client. "I would ask the court to balance any reason for withholding work product against obtaining a fair trial. It's a qualified privilege."

No, McLean insisted, it was an absolute privilege, and cited two civil cases. Margulies asked him for a criminal case. There is none, he conceded, then hurriedly shuffled through his file again. There was a case, he added as he grabbed a piece of paper, regarding denying the use of an attorney's notes.

"We're not seeking writings here, Your Honor." Horngrad sounded impatient.

"Are you preparing to ask questions regarding the defense's tactics?" Margulies asked Horngrad.

"Yes, to an extent."

"That involves work product, Your Honor," McLean interjected.

Horngrad said he was seeking to show there were "no rational reasons" behind some of the defense team's actions, that their decisions could not have been "tactical."

Watching from his seat on the sideline, Belli swayed toward Antonio and whispered loudly, "We'll be here a couple of days."

McLean gestured in frustration, as if Belli's complaint was directed at his performance. "This is a setup—"

Margulies cut him off to read a case citation that allowed the introduction of work product. That was only in malpractice cases, McLean retorted, not at issue here. To which Horngrad countered, malpractice could *well* be the case here, given the circumstances. McLean's response was spiced with another "Hornblatt."

Golde stood up. The materiality and evidentiary issue should be determined, he said. If the judge saw Horngrad's purported "new evidence" as not tending to overturn her verdict in the case, then the subpoenaed testimony would be irrelevant. Furthermore—

"The court's position," Margulies interrupted, "is that I cannot make a decision regarding the outcome of this hearing based on the moving papers. I must hear all argument first." Golde was, in essence, asking her to put the cart before the horse.

The Deputy D.A. sat down, looking quickly beaten.

Well, there were other reasons, McLean contended. This was not a proper forum for such a hearing, for one thing.

Margulies was having none of it. It was a "proper forum"; she had ruled over similar such cases. She called a half hour recess to render her decision.

As the courtroom emptied, Horngrad accosted McLean face-to-face. "You call me 'Hornblatt' again, and I'll call you 'McClown!' "

At 10:25 A.M., Margulies reentered a near-empty courtroom. None of the attorneys was present; the court clerk was munching quietly on a candy bar. Margulies left. Horngrad and Golde appeared momentarily, making an effort to break the tension by good-naturedly sparring over who had been more patriotic on November 11, Veterans Day. At ten-thirty, court came to order. Margulies began reading through the civil cases cited by McLean, reiterating that in criminal cases, the issues were different. McLean jumped to his feet, bursting with argument.

"*Excuse* me, Mr. McLean! I allowed you and Mr. Horngrad to argue, now I'm in the process of ruling. Please allow me to do that." She ordered him to sit down.

Balancing the three cited cases against the defendant's rights, Margulies ruled that "public policy and due process mandates an exception to the work product issue." In this particular situation, it seemed there could be no work product privilege since that very work product was being questioned. "It appears that this information is necessary for the minor to put on her motion for a new trial; the minor's rights would be violated in not doing so."

McLean's motion to quash the subpoenas was overruled, and Margulies made a point of excusing him from the counsel table. He obeyed, with the *quid pro quo* that he would be back when his clients were on the stand.

"When that time comes," Margulies said wryly, "you may sit right by your clients, if you wish."

No, McLean replied unabashedly, he planned to make objections, and so would sit at counsel table.

Golde had his own objection—Horngrad's affidavits about Serena's lies were "hearsay." The judge agreed that was a problem; she might need to hear the testimony of the people who signed the affidavits. They could be subpoenaed, Horngrad offered. Margulies suggested that during a recess he and Golde discuss which affidavits the prosecution would be willing to stipulate—allow into the record without testimony. If Golde was not willing to stipulate to a certain affidavit, then the person who signed it would have to testify in court. This would allow Golde a chance to cross-examine.

All precursors aside, it was time for Belli to testify. Michael studied every move as the elderly man made his way to the stand. He and Sharri had waited a long time for this moment. McLean positioned himself at the counsel table. Horngrad rose. His first question, establishing Belli as previous attorney for Serena Moore, sounded innocuous enough, but unleashed a floodgate of contempt from Belli.

"I'm still counsel *pro bono*," he growled, "and I'm going to take an appeal to the Supreme Court with your consent or not." He reminded the court again that he had taken the case *for free* and had paid all expert witnesses on behalf of the defendant.

Sharri gasped under her breath. "That *liar*."

He had personally appointed Shelley Antonio to the case, Belli continued, because "she's one of my best girls."

Horngrad tried futilely to clarify which of the two had been lead counsel. Each time Belli replied with a roundabout answer, Horngrad posed the question in a different way until

Belli refused to speak anymore on the subject. The judge intervened, calmly but firmly ordering him to answer.

Yes, Belli responded, Antonio was responsible for research in the case.

"Had she ever been lead counsel in a juvenile case before?"

"I don't know."

"Are you aware of any juvenile cases she handled?"

"I'm not aware."

"Are you aware of any criminal trials that she handled?"

McLean objected and was overruled. Belli shifted sideways to throw his own objection about the entire proceedings at the judge. "You're aware, Judge, that we sought to oust you from this trial—"

His complaints met with sharp reprimand. Margulies's voice remained steady, her face expressionless, but her irritation was clear. She would "tell [him] just this once." He was to answer all questions and he was not to object; that was what McLean was for.

Did Mr. Belli know of any criminal trials Antonio had handled? Horngrad inquired again.

"Not specifically," Belli conceded, reiterating that the case had been *pro bono*.

Horngrad regarded him silently for a moment, as if processing the answer. "Well, is there a distinction in your mind between *pro bono* cases and those that are paid?"

Absolutely not, Belli shot back, he was particularly careful in *pro bono* cases.

Horngrad rocked on his heels, arms folded. "How old are you, sir?"

Another objection from the witness stand, another reprimand from the judge. Belli eventually obliged that he was eighty-six, then refused to answer the following question as to his level of responsibility in the case. "Why were *you* so strong in taking this case," he challenged Horngrad. "We should deal with *that*." He wasn't going to answer these questions, he told the judge. "You can hold me in contempt!"

Margulies formed her words succinctly, as though talking to a belligerent child. Belli *would* answer, would *not* make further objections and—when the attorney lashed out with yet another argument—he would *not* interrupt her again.

Horngrad restated his query.

My responsibilities were varied, Belli allowed—supervision of Shelley Antonio, making objections in the courtroom, acting as senior counsel and seeing that the minor received a proper defense. He angled his head toward Margulies. "Such as having Your Honor removed from this case."

"Your Honor" ignored the barb.

"Was this then *your* case?" Horngrad pressed.

He had already answered that, Belli retorted.

Margulies stepped in. "You were called first, then you engaged Ms. Antonio?"

Yes, Belli said, he had taken the case, then personally appointed Shelley.

Horngrad paused. He had uncovered credible information to the contrary. Wasn't it true that Shelley Antonio had come to *Belli,* Horngrad pressed, asking if she could help on the case?

"No."

Another pause, allowing the answer to resonate. Horngrad had scored a point. The issue of how Antonio became lead counsel was relatively minor, but Belli had just aggrandized it by not telling the truth. He let the matter rest for the moment, moving on to discuss the three expert witnesses used in the case. Horngrad wanted to show that Sharri Moore, not the Belli firm, had done most of the work in finding and dealing with the experts.

The mention of Dr. Berg's name precipitated a lengthy response from Belli. Leaning back in the witness chair, with fingers folded together, he gazed at the ceiling while extrapolating that the psychologist had not been able to testify regarding Serena's being a pathological liar—a "principal point" in the case. The judge had ruled unfairly in precluding Dr. Berg from offering his opinion as to the validity of the diary confession—"the final truth of the matter"—and Belli planned to appeal based on that unfair ruling.

Horngrad passed over the diatribe against Margulies, asking Belli if he knew a few of the witnesses who had signed affidavits. The lies Serena had told them were fantastical— that Mallory was her own daughter, that she had given birth to other children, etc. Belli's manner suggested that he thought Horngrad's question pointless. No, he said, he could not recall the names. Finding witnesses had been Antonio's domain.

Again, Horngrad pondered the answer. "Did you think," he said slowly, "that because the judge ruled Dr. Berg could not testify as to the final truth of the matter, did that mean you couldn't bring *other* people in regarding the defendant's lies?"

"We put that aside for appeal grounds," Belli averred, "and would have appealed *pro bono* had you not come into this case for the publicity of it." What's more, he declared, "our feet were pulled out from under us" when the judge ruled against Dr. Berg's testifying that the defendant was a pathological liar.

Margulies would not allow the question to go unanswered. Had Mr. Belli not used any of these other witnesses because of his interpretation of her ruling? she restated.

Yes.

Horngrad was amazed at the answer. It was so completely, utterly, horribly *wrong,* he would contend. Margulies's ruling that Dr. Berg could not testify regarding the truth of the diary confession covered no more than that narrow territory. It had nothing to do with allowing Serena's friends and family members to testify about her lies. Belli knew that. He was grasping for excuses, thought Horngrad, and this one was pathetically transparent.

Margulies apparently was surprised as well. "Mark that answer in the transcripts," she said to court reporter Nancy Cardoza, then asked for a moment to catch up on her notes.

"I'll note that too," Horngrad commented wryly.

At the counsel table, McLean sat hunched forward, ready to pose objections, if Belli didn't beat him to it.

At a "continue" nod from Margulies, Horngrad named the balance of potential witnesses who had signed affidavits. Leukemia, pregnancies, rapes—the lies they had been told were extensive. Belli admitted a few of the people had been called but ultimately not used after he and Antonio decided not to "go into the issue of Serena's promiscuity."

Horngrad allowed disbelief to creep into his voice. Wasn't

Serena's sex life "gone into" in great detail, often at the prompting of the defense team?

Some, Belli agreed, the anal abrasions on Mallory and the sexual assault on Serena. But then they had backed off, because "the father came to me and wanted to be sure I wouldn't go into the sexual abuse."

Both Horngrad and Margulies blinked at that one, unvoiced reactions of "Whoa, wait one minute!" written across their faces. Golde appeared to shake his head, then caught himself.

In implying that a father's request could supersede an attorney's responsibility to his client, Horngrad knew, Belli had committed a second serious error. As far as Horngrad was concerned, the statement was symbolic of Belli's "egregious breach" in preparing a thorough defense. His evident lack of involvement in the case, plus Antonio's inexperience, had added up to a completely "wrongheaded and unlawful" response to the situation.

"And did you abide by Michael Moore's wishes?"

We decided not to go into that, Belli contended. It would paint the defendant in a difficult light, particularly since the judge was a former district attorney. Because of that, he and Antonio had not wanted her on the case in the first place—

"You said the stepfather asked you not to go into the abuse," Horngrad interrupted. "Did you discuss the matter with Ms. Antonio?"

"No, I did not discuss it: I would do what was best for my client. I was ambivalent about it—I let some come in where it would help us, but kept a lot of stuff out."

"But you said, 'better not go into the situation with the stepfather.' "

He was in a "catch-22," Belli replied, not knowing what to do. He "had resented what was being done" to besmirch Serena and paint her as promiscuous.

"Did you think evidence of *molestation* would show Serena as promiscuous?" Disbelief again.

"I thought that trying this case before a former district attorney and a *woman*—she wouldn't appreciate it."

Sharri and Michael exchanged a glance. Pastor Doug shook his head as if to clear it. Margulies showed no response.

Horngrad would not back down. "Did you ever pursue a

defense that there was an alternative suspect in this case—the stepfather?"

No, it wasn't developed. Not enough evidence.

But, Horngrad reminded, Dr. Herrmann testified that he had found anal dilation and scars. Didn't Mr. Belli believe it would have been a viable defense to pursue death during molestation by the stepfather?

They couldn't "switch their defense in the middle of the trial from fantasy to another person causing death," Belli said. Surely the judge—a former district attorney—would see that.

Horngrad paused. "Was that the right decision?"

"Yes it was. But it was before the wrong judge, and should have been before a jury." Belli returned to the issue of the defendant's promiscuity, adding that he had not wanted to "bring out" testimony of her pregnancies and abortions as it might prejudice the court.

"There never *was* an abortion!" Horngrad exploded.

The outburst earned him a reprimand from Margulies. "Just ask questions," she reminded.

"Very well," Horngrad nodded. "Did you ever see any writing of the defendant's that indicated she has had an abortion?"

Yes, Belli replied, he had seen it in one of Horngrad's own affidavits.

"That was a fantastical lie!"

Belli chuckled under his breath. "I don't know about that. Maybe *you're* fantasizing now."

Temper in check, Horngrad changed the subject. "You are aware of Diary #1 and its entry regarding the defendant's finding her sister."

"Yes."

"What were your reasons for not introducing it?"

They had a sound defense already, Belli said, based on Dr. Warnock's testimony that Mallory had died of asthma.

"Well, were you aware of any *lies* in Diary #1?"

No, Belli was not. He was aware, however, of "things in there that would show her in an unbecoming way, particularly in a trial before a former district attorney." In his and Antonio's judgment, the best defense was to "try the case on what Dr. Warnock gave [them]—that it was a sudden death."

He chose not to "bring in irrelevant stuff" such as this diary before a judge who was a woman and a former district attorney. Some of the entries repulsed him, he added, such as the defendant's writing she was "awful dry" while trying to have sex the day of her sister's funeral. He hadn't wanted to bring up these things, Belli claimed with a condescending air, but Horngrad was forcing him to do so now.

At the counsel table, Serena hid her face in her hands. Sharri sucked in an audible breath. The *bastard*. He didn't care how much he embarrassed Serena, or how much he stretched the truth as to what was in that diary, she railed to herself. He just wanted to save his own hide.

Horngrad veered away from the statements, rephrasing Belli's testimony to conclude that his defense team had "put all its eggs in the asthma basket."

Not so. Picking up on the metaphor, Belli replied that he "couldn't have eggs and hamburgers together." Leaning back in his chair, he gazed upward, as if engaging the heavens. "I don't make these cases, I just do the best I can with them." He thought Serena Moore innocent, thought she should get a new trial, and would take her case *pro bono* to the Supreme Court if he had to, on the basis that Dr. Berg should have been allowed to testify about the confession diary's "truth of the matter."

Margulies called a short recess.

In the hall, Belli continued his disputation to the Channel 2 news camera. "I worked like a dog on this case," he said to KTVU reporter Randy Shandobil, "and this is the way I've been repaid by the father, who is resentful of me for letting in this evidence of his sexual actions with the family." Belli hadn't wanted to bring out all that sensitive information; it was a shame Horngrad was making him say these things now. He would carry the case through appeal regardless of what Horngrad did. McLean jumped in, assuring the reporter they wanted their former client to "get a new trial," but that this proceeding was "just a ploy from a known publicity hound."

At 11:50 P.M., the judge and all attorneys, except Belli, were reassembled. *Where is he?* Margulies wondered.

"There's a camera," Horngrad replied, rolling his finger in the air.

Back in the witness chair, Belli again turned Horngrad's questions into a means for attacking the judge. Watching in amazed anger, the Moores wondered why Margulies put up with it. "She should *shut him up!*" Sharri hissed to Michael.

"Didn't you think," Horngrad was countering, "that a 'former district attorney' would be sensitized to hearing information on sexual actions?"

"You mean did I think she would bend over backward to be fair?" The sarcasm was thick. "No, that didn't occur to me."

"Well, did it occur to you to use the previous diary's lies in order to impeach the defendant's confession?"

"I don't recall any previous lies."

"Did it occur to you that Diary #1's entry regarding the morning of August 18 would impeach the second Confession Diary?"

Using that diary had to be weighed against a "horrible test," Belli answered. The defendant had written that she had intercourse some six times after the funeral and other such things. At the sight of Serena covering her face, Belli accused, "*You're* forcing me to do this, counsel, and *you're* making my client face this embarrassment." He had an "absolutely ironclad case on causation" with Dr. Warnock's testimony, more so if Dr. Berg had been able to testify properly. "That's what I will appeal on." He cast a withering look at Horngrad. "I think once the publicity dies down, you won't be in there doing anything for her!" Smiling at Serena, who was still hiding her face, he added that he was "very fond of the little girl."

Horngrad moved on. The defense team had shown Serena as a member of a dysfunctional family. What purpose did that serve?

Belli didn't agree he and Antonio had done that. A dysfunctional family would have "turned the judge off" against them, he believed. Had there been a jury, however, the ruling would have been more "intelligent."

Throughout the courtroom, eyes flicked toward the judge. Was she going to let *that* go? Margulies remained deadpan.

Wait a minute, Horngrad said, leaning his knuckles on the counsel table, didn't Belli and Antonio themselves elicit the information on dysfunctionality?

No, no, said Belli, they "let the D.A. do that."

Well, they certainly hadn't objected to the dysfunctional information, Horngrad commented.

"I did object once, and I was overruled."

"Didn't you elicit such information from Dr. Berg?"

True, they had to, Belli replied, in order to show why the defendant fantasized.

In "using" the dysfunctional family information, including Dr. Herrmann's testimony of sodomy on Mallory, Horngrad alleged, shouldn't the defense team have pursued the fact that someone *else* may have committed the murder? And on the other side of the coin, if he could prove Mallory had *not* been sodomized, wouldn't he agree that would have undercut the prosecution's theory?

McLean objected and was overruled. Belli refused to answer, proceeding instead to lambast Horngrad's questioning his competence and judgment on this *pro bono* case. "Thank God I'm hale and hearty at eighty-six and I'm going to do a lot more *pro bono* cases, including this one on appeal!"

Hands clasped in front of him, Horngrad allowed what he would later call "the ramblings of an old man." Belli's testiness only increased as Horngrad asked him how much time he had spent with Serena prior to trial.

"I have no way of estimating that. It was adequate time."

"Didn't you visit her at juvenile hall only *once?*"

Belli's facial muscles flexed in anger. "I can't recall."

"Isn't it true you spent a maximum of one-half hour with the defendant before she testified?"

Belli denied it vehemently, calling Horngrad "insulting" and a "jughead."

On that note, Horngrad turned the witness over to Matt Golde.

The Deputy D.A. remained seated during his one cross-examination query. Was it accurate to say that Ms. Antonio was responsible for finding witnesses?

Yes, Belli said, he did not handle initial interviews.

"Did you talk to any witnesses at all?" Horngrad asked in redirect.

Belli couldn't remember; he'd "had too many cases since then."

As Belli stepped down, Horngrad, feeling both derision and triumph, engaged in a short side bar conference with Golde and Margulies. He managed to contain his glee. For the first time since he had decided to file his motion, Horngrad felt he might prevail. The whole gestalt of Belli's performance, Horngrad would say—his accusations against the judge, his "off-the-wall" answers and obvious priority of saving his own reputation over that of his client's—had afforded the court visible, firsthand proof of his unreliability and incompetence.

Shuffling past Serena, sitting by herself at the counsel table, Belli leaned over to apologize for the embarrassing things her attorney had forced him to say.

Serena swiveled toward her parents and rolled her eyes.

Shelley Antonio's direct testimony that afternoon would be shorter than Belli's. Called at two-fifteen, she assumed the stand with a resolutely defensive air.

McLean hunched forward in his seat at the counsel table. Sharri glanced at him and humphed to Mary that he looked "like a pit bull ready to attack."

Horngrad's wondering about Antonio's trial experience was soon laid to rest. When had she started working at the Belli firm? he began.

Her first day was December 28, 1992, Antonio answered, trying to appear nonchalant as she poured herself a glass of water and took a sip.

Catherine Bowman, Bob Salladay and John Dillon *(Valley Times)* all scribbled in their notebooks. December 28 was the day after Serena's arrest.

"Have you ever been involved in a juvenile criminal case?" Horngrad queried, clasping his hands in front of him.

"No."

"Have you ever been involved in a criminal case in a jury trial?"

"No."

"How about a criminal case in a court trial?"

"No."

Horngrad feigned a surprised hesitation. "Have you ever been the counsel of record in a criminal proceeding?"

Yes, Antonio replied, in cases, plural.

"Have you ever attended an evidentiary hearing in these cases."

"No."

Another moment of silence. "So this was your first juvenile case, your first criminal trial, your first evidentiary hearing."

"Yes," Antonio replied in a challenging tone. But in this case she had been supervised by "an attorney who is one of the best in the States."

Horngrad rocked on his heels. "So you lacked experience, but your association with Mr. Belli made up for it, is that right?"

That and counsel with all the other attorneys in their office, Antonio noted, including Kevin McLean.

Bowman, Salladay, and Dillon continued scribbling. They, along with other reporters, would note in their articles that Serena Moore's case had been Antonio's first. Dillon would make the point after quoting Belli—"She's one of my best girls."

On the subject of expert witnesses, Antonio conceded that Sharri Moore had been "very involved in finding them, giving her the names of Doctors Berg and Warnock. And in a quick pivot, Horngrad asked how she became lead counsel on the case.

Antonio hedged. "Nobody gets a case in that office without Mr. Belli's assigning it."

"Didn't *you* in fact, ask for this case?" Horngrad asked casually. "Didn't you call Mr. Belli at home and ask him if you could attend a hearing the next day. To which he replied, 'Which one of those expletives can I get to appear on that?' And didn't you say, 'I don't know, but I'd be willing to?' "

Foreseeing the moment, Horngrad had memorized Antonio's own words as they had been quoted to him. It was a calculated tactic, designed to loosen her footing, an I-know-more-about-you-than-you-think-I-do approach. It seemed to work. She blinked, then admitted it was true. Horngrad turned his witness over to Golde, thinking Antonio would be more careful, lest he trip her up again in redirect.

Golde again remained seated, leaning on both arms over

the table as he invited Antonio to describe her decision-making process in not using Diary #1.

There were two reasons, Antonio maintained. First, that it was "not inconsistent" with the confession entry.

Horngrad couldn't help but notice the statement's similarity to Golde's argument in written rebuttal to his motion. Cooper, standing in the back of the courtroom, was incensed. How any *defense* attorney could think that entry "not inconsistent" was beyond her understanding. Furthermore, she felt, Antonio's statement, reiterating as it did Golde's contention, was a blatant argument against her own former client's guilty verdict being overturned.

Second, Antonio continued, that the entry's "matter-of-fact, dispassionate tone" would not help the defendant. She and Belli chose instead to allow Serena to testify, thinking that the minor's emotional, tearful response to her sister's death would best indicate her innocence. The Confession Diary was to be shown as "fantastical," written for crazy reasons by a girl in a dysfunctional family.

McLean, champing at the bit, interrupted, asking to pose questions to Antonio. That was "wildly inappropriate," retorted Horngrad. Margulies agreed, indicating that McLean "had no standing" in eliciting testimony.

The Deputy D.A. proceeded. Hadn't Antonio in fact presented evidence of Serena's past lies, such as in calling Dr. Berg to testify?

Yes, Antonio agreed, Dr. Berg's testimony was offered to contend that the confession was a lie, written in context of a psychological disorder. It was unfortunate, she added, that she had to depict the Moores as dysfunctional, but she had warned them about that from the start. They had "relied heavily on Dr. Berg's testimony" that Serena was "histrionic" since the judge had ruled they could not introduce such testimony from others.

Golde had opened Pandora's box.

Redirect by Horngrad. If Antonio had not been able to present evidence of Serena's lies through other witnesses, and if Dr. Berg's testimony was all-important, had she at least provided information of such lies *to him* to help in his diagnosis?

She and the doctor had held "many discussions" on the topic, Antonio said.

Well then, Horngrad wondered, had she given him Diary #1, which also contained fantastical lies? Horngrad knew that she had not.

Yes, Antonio said, she'd "read it to him over the phone."

"*All* of it?" Openly cynical, he reminded her that it was a lengthy diary.

Well, Antonio had "talked to him about it." But she had chosen not to use it as an impeachment of the Confession Diary. Their defense was twofold—to attack Dr. Herrmann's medical evidence, and to impeach the confession by the testimonies of Dr. Berg, Sharri, and Serena. The main focus of the defense was death by asthma, and if it *was* a homicide, they would "let it come in that maybe it was someone else."

Horngrad clasped his hands. "You mean Michael."

"Yes."

"But you never argued that in court."

"I believed in reasonable doubt!" Antonio's voice rose. "We had no direct evidence on Michael, but with evidence of anal penetration, it was more likely than not that that person could do it. It was up to the court to decide."

Horngrad let the issue rest for the moment. "Did Diary #1 have untrue stories?"

"Yes, regarding pregnancy and abortion."

Horngrad reminded Antonio of her failing to supply him with the entire contents of Diary #1. That was because of the "partnership fight," Antonio retorted. Mr. Belli's ex-partners (who still shared office space in the Belli Building) were "stealing" things from them, among the items the first 117 pages of that diary. The *same* ex-partners that were "in part responsible" for Horngrad's motion.

"Do you have any evidence of that?" Disgust again.

McLean's objection was sustained.

Thumbing through his copy of Diary #1, Horngrad read an entry about Serena's being raped. Was that page in the file Antonio had given him? She couldn't remember. Horngrad put down the diary, picked up another document. How about this two-page synopsis of Diary #1 that she had provided him. What a coincidence that it began at page 118. Did she have a synopsis for the first 117 pages?

Antonio launched into the same defense—Belli's ex-partner's stole the missing pages. Margulies cut her off.

"*Do* you have a synopsis for pages one through 117?"

"No."

For Horngrad, it was an admission to what he had suspected—the Belli firm had lost those critical pages early in its defense preparation and had scuttled about trying to cover the error. He studied the judge, trying to determine whether her inference was similar.

He leaned over to pick up the diary again, reading other lies it contained. Didn't Antonio think she should have shown these other lies as an impeachment for the diary confession?

"You may have chosen a different strategy," Antonio argued. "We could have ten attorneys in here, and they could all disagree."

"I doubt that."

Margulies pursed her lips. "Mr. Horngrad."

"Sorry."

Over McLean's stringent objections, Horngrad continued his line of questioning, offering into evidence other examples of lies in Diary #1. Heated arguments ensued—between Antonio and Horngrad, between McLean and Horngrad, and sometimes among all three. Twice, the court reporter threw up her hands in frustration as they tried to outtalk each other, forcing the judge to intervene.

"Wouldn't you agree," Horngrad hammered away, "that these diary entries were important to this case? That it was an important part of your job to impeach the diary confession?"

"I can tell you what we did," Antonio rejoined. Their first defense was asthma, the second was that the confession was a lie. They had considered everything in deciding what evidence to put on record. She and Belli believed an appeal could be made based on the judge's ruling on Dr. Berg's testimony, while Horngrad hadn't mentioned that in his motion. Who was to say who was right?

Horngrad thought the answer ridiculous. Why would he argue with the judge about a ruling she had made when she held the power to grant a new trial? Allowing Antonio's rhetorical question to hang in the air, he indicated his redirect was complete.

With Golde wanting to call Antonio as his own witness, Margulies agreed to allow him direct examination while she was on the stand. His relaxed questioning helped calm the proceedings until Antonio made a statement that angered both Serena and her parents. Serena had told her that the molestation *did* occur, Antonio said, but Sharri Moore's influence over Serena caused the story to change from day to day. For that reason, she had "tried to keep" the mother away from Serena during the trial.

Serena's jaw dropped. She shook her head firmly and mouthed "No."

With the coroner's report on the anal abnormalities and with Serena's lies, Antonio maintained, she and Belli "had to show abuse of the minor that would make her write such a confession." The abuse had created a psychosis. Also, the mother had turned over the diary to police, and there was "no way to show why a mother would do that. There was an underlying difficult, twisted relationship there."

Pastor Doug couldn't repress his own headshaking at Antonio's "forgetting" of his presence the night Serena's diary was found. Why hadn't they just let him testify about what happened?

On cross, Horngrad summarized his perceived inadequacies of Antonio's defense in a nutshell. "You testified that you had to show that Serena's household was a tumultuous one. Wouldn't it have been a less circuitous route to prove she was a pathological liar?"

More heated arguments between Antonio and Horngrad, with McLean popping up to object. Golde sat passively throughout the exchange. Margulies intervened, stating that the witness had given sufficient reason for not using Diary #1; please move on, Mr. Horngrad. Her impatience served as a grim reminder that the *Strickland* standards were hard met; Antonio's answers were at least depicting a course of tactical decision-making, whether that course was the best one or not.

"Very well." Horngrad returned to the equally volatile topic of the missing diary pages, which prompted more arguments. Finally, as the clock on the courtroom wall neared 4:30 P.M., Horngrad said he was through.

When McLean jumped to his feet, demanding to ask his own questions, Margulies dressed him down, announcing that he was "only present here as an attorney for motion to quash the subpoenas."

"That's not so," McLean argued. "I am here as counsel

for Ms. Antonio and Mr. Belli because 'Mr. Hornblatt' stood up and said he was going to sue!"

That did it. Doug Horngrad had a promise to keep. "Mr. *McClown*," he announced, "it's Horn*grad*."

Margulies recessed court until Tuesday morning.

Thirty-seven

TUESDAY, NOVEMBER 16. The day's proceedings would be calm and orderly. Neither Antonio, Belli, nor McLean was present. Not a camera in sight.

As the Moores and their entourage claimed seats on the right side of the courtroom, a young, meticulously groomed man in a dark suit surreptitiously slid into a chair near the reporters' group on the left. He carried a notebook and pen. The reporters, ever curious and competition-minded, sent silent questions to one another. Sharri and Michael also looked him over. Who was he? No one knew.

Serena appeared cheerily, wearing a short-sleeved flowered pantsuit made by her mother. She had decided to wear a ponytail. Her fingernails were painted blue.

As court was called to order at 10:30 A.M., it was Penny Cooper's turn to take the stand. In legal circles, Cooper was a "heavy," having practiced criminal defense law since 1969. In her *voir dire,* she told the court she had been certified as a specialist in criminal law in 1973. She had lectured numerous times on trial tactics and had provided "sample closing and opening statements" at numerous legal conferences. In 1989, *California Lawyer's Magazine* had named her one of the four "most respected attorneys" in the state. She had tried cases in New York, Washington, Iowa, Illinois, Puerto Rico, and at least half of the counties in California, and had argued before most divisions of California appeals and in the U.S. Supreme Court. As for homicide cases, she'd handled "a couple hundred," only twenty to twenty-five of which went to trial, meaning that she'd managed to settle the rest of them or have them dismissed.

What she did not tell the court was that she normally billed at $325 an hour, but was taking part in Horngrad's motion for new trial *pro bono*.

Cooper's *voir dire* was interrupted with the timely arrival of Dr. Berg, whom Horngrad had called in response to Antonio's statements the previous Friday. Dr. Berg's testimony, Horngrad told Judge Margulies, was being offered as impeachment of Shelley Antonio. Cooper stepped down, and Dr. Berg took the stand. Horngrad leaned over the defense table, resting on his hands. Had Ms. Antonio given the witness a copy of Diary #1?

"No."

"Did she ever tell you about the lies contained in that diary?"

"No."

"Ever tell you of that diary's innocent version of events?"

"No."

"It was never shown."

"Correct."

"Were you aware of that diary's existence?"

"No."

"When did you become aware?"

Dr. Berg shrugged. "When you called me, about a week ago."

Sharri couldn't hide a smirk.

Dr. Berg could not recall Antonio's giving him examples of Serena's lies, although they had discussed the propensity of the minor to do so.

Had he ever heard of Serena's claim of suffering from leukemia? Horngrad wondered.

Dr. Berg couldn't recall that.

"That she gave birth to Mallory?"

"No."

"That she was going to be artificially inseminated by Michael in order to produce another child for the family?"

"No."

"That she claimed rape or molestation by seven or eight people?"

"She may have said the defendant claimed having involuntary sex," Dr. Berg replied, "but seven or eight people? That doesn't ring a bell."

Golde's cross was short. Suggesting that Dr. Berg and Antonio *had* discussed Serena's lies, he was informed that they had only discussed the lies Dr. Berg had brought up. At that, Golde had no further questions.

Horngrad dismissed the doctor with no redirect. He'd made his point before the judge; Shelley Antonio had committed perjury. "We'll have to pay him a couple hundred for appearing," he later told the Moores, "but it was worth it."

Cooper seemed the image of relaxation as she resumed the stand. Her answers were short and to the point, her demeanor a combination of judicial respect and barely contained outrage at what she deemed unprofessional conduct by the Belli firm.

She had read the transcripts in *The Matter of Serena M.*, all discovery materials, Horngrad's motion for new trial, and Golde's response, she noted. And she had witnessed Belli's and Antonio's testimony. She was "well aware of the facts at hand."

There were two aspects in this case, she told the court— the expert testimony and whether or not the "so-called confession" was correct. It was therefore incumbent upon counsel to prove that entry as unreliable. A critical step in so doing was to introduce evidence of other diary entries that were untrue. Matt Golde's closing statements had been good argument— "What we have here," Cooper quoted, "is a confession, and in a diary." Other untrue entries in a diary, therefore, were of utmost importance to the trier of fact. There could be no tactical reason not to use that evidence. Failure to do so was downright incompetent, unless there could be found a strong counterbalance for not using the information.

"Did you hear the tactical reasons stated in this courtroom?" Margulies asked.

"Yes." Antonio gave three reasons, Cooper noted. One, she and Belli did not want to bring out the defendant's sexual background. Such reasoning Cooper called "unimaginable" and "off the wall," since the record clearly indicated it was Belli who asked Serena about her sex life, opening up that area for Golde on cross. "Sex life," Cooper added, "has no bearing on a homicide." Second, Antonio called the entry in Diary #1 about Mallory's death "matter-of-fact." Cooper disagreed strongly, stating that those entries were the most feeling ones in the diary. "What was matter-of-fact," she contended, "was the 'confession.'" Furthermore, most entries within Serena's diary were dispassionate. Reason number two was therefore, simply "ludicrous."

Reason three—the entry in Diary #1 "was not inconsistent" with the confession. "That," she charged, "is the ultimate of Monday morning quarterbacking in trying to save your hide." Any reasonable person would find the two entries "terribly inconsistent." Someone who *finds* a person dead did not kill that person. Reason number three was "invalid."

Belli's testimony had been "puzzling." The "eggs-all-in-the-expert-basket" tactic did nothing to explain the diary confession. Furthermore, the defense team had completely undermined the testimony of their experts. Dr. Berg's testimony had been "gutted" because he wasn't given proper information on which to form his opinion of the minor, and because Antonio was so inexperienced, she did not know how to introduce the defendant's lies into the record after the judge's ruling that limited Berg's testimony. As for the situation with Dr. Warnock, Cooper declared, attorneys have a standing obligation to ensure that experts be given complete information and be allowed to talk to each other. "Any trier of fact would hold Dr. Herrmann's testimony as initial coroner in high regard. In order to refute that, the defense would need an expert totally unfettered."

Margulies was checking the clock. It was near noon—her lunchtime. She called a recess until two.

As the courtroom emptied, the mysterious man in the black suit hurried down the hall toward a pay phone. Strolling casually behind, Michael managed to pass him by as he spoke into the phone, and related his findings to the defense attorneys and Sharri. The reporters soon heard, as well. The guy was from Belli's office, and had been calling the firm to tell them what was happening.

"A *spy*," Sharri whispered theatrically. "All he needs is a raincoat with the collar turned up."

Horngrad had his own response. Sidling up to the "man in black," who was still speaking in low tones into the phone, he challenged, "Is that McLean on the line?" The young man answered somewhat hesitatingly that it was. "Give him a message for me," Horngrad replied.

"Tell him to go fuck himself."

* * *

With Penny Cooper back on the stand, Horngrad asked an open-ended question. Was the "eggs-in-Warnock's-basket" defense reasonable? Cooper's answer was meticulous.

At great issue, she explained, was the second diary—was it or was it not a true confession? Apart from proving that cause of death was not by criminal means, the defense should have impeached the confession using four arguments—first, that it was inconsistent with a prior entry written concurrently with the events of Mallory's death; second, that the person who "confessed" had written other lies in her diary; third, that the same person had also spoken many lies. Finally, Sharri Moore's testimony about the position of Mallory's body should have been used to impeach Dr. Herrmann. The natural position of lying on one's side with a foot sticking out of a blanket could have been argued as inconsistent with the defendant's confession of placing her sister back in bed. Most likely, Cooper surmised, in that scenario, the little girl would have been carefully placed and covered.

All told, "there was nothing more important than to impeach the diary entry." Failure to do so was incompetent, since there were no valid reasons not to bring Diary #1 before the court. *Strickland* spoke to the "totality" of performance and evidence. In Cooper's opinion, the defense "in totality" was not competent, and was deficient in affording the minor her Sixth Amendment rights.

Golde's cross would be benign, his body language indicating that he didn't feel his efforts worth the energy spent, his few questions lacking punch.

"Hi, Matt." Penny Cooper greeted him with a smile.

Golde returned the greeting, then began his cross. Did Ms. Cooper ever discuss trial tactics with other attorneys?

"Yes."

"Are there usually differences of opinion?"

"No question," she stated. "Often."

"Do you respect others' opinions?"

"Absolutely."

Golde asked if she were aware that various people had testified in the trial about Serena's lying.

"You argued in your closing that there was no such evidence in the record," Cooper reminded him. "I'm assuming you argued from the record."

Golde's expression remained neutral. As if to buy time, he shuffled through his notes. "Did you talk to Dr. Berg about this case?"

"Never. No."

In his redirect, Horngrad picked up from Golde's cue. "When you seek advice from other attorneys, if you were handling a case like this, would you ask the advice of an attorney who had never tried a case?"

"No."

Horngrad moved on. "Why was the decision to only attack the cause of death not a reasonable tactical choice?"

It was not reasonable, Cooper declared, because *if* the court did find criminal conduct, then the confession would stand and a guilty verdict would be rendered. Belli's claim that the "someone-else-did-it" avenue of defense would have been inconsistent was therefore incorrect. For if Antonio and Belli had accurately pursued that course, even with the court's finding criminal conduct, there would still have existed a reasonable doubt as to *who* was responsible for the crime.

"We could go on a long time about the inadequacies of the defense here," she commented a short time later. But the argument of worrying about the defendant's promiscuity was particularly wrong. What weight had promiscuity when the minor had been charged with the murder of her sister? One couldn't imagine "a more egregious charge."

Cooper leaned back in the witness chair. "It was a complicated case that raised a lot of issues."

With the completion of Cooper's testimony, court recessed until Monday, November 29, after Thanksgiving. At that time, Horngrad's witnesses to Serena's "fantastical" lies would take the stand. Matt Golde had refused to stipulate to any of their affidavits.

Golde rode down the elevator with one of the journalists covering the trial. She gazed at him and shook her head. "This wasn't your day, Matt."

He feigned surprise. "No?"

"Nooo. This was definitely not your day."

Thirty-eight

Justice—like a beam of light.

—HORNGRAD, TO A STUNNED REPORTER AFTER THE VERDICT

THE COURTROOM WAS nearly full with Serena's friends subpoenaed to testify, accompanied by their parents and other family members. Excitement and nervousness among the witnesses were almost palpable. Anxiously waiting for the session to begin, Sharri, dressed in red and black, sat between Michael and Sarah Moore, clutching her mother-in-law's hand. A steady rain, one of the first in California's wet season, had wreaked havoc on numerous freeways, causing an accident in which the court reporter was involved. She was unhurt, but had spun around in her car, becoming entangled in the melee. Court could not begin until she arrived, nearly one-half hour late.

At the counsel table, Golde casually mentioned to his opponent that he was thinking of asking for a continuance. Horngrad glanced over his shoulder at the room full of assembled witnesses who had been pulled out of work and school. "No-no-no-no-no" he replied. That dismissed, he rested his left elbow on the table, cheek in his hand, and began trading war stories with the Deputy D.A.

With the arrival of the court reporter, who looked remarkably unflustered, Serena was brought in, again wearing her new black jumpsuit. *"Dang,"* she mouthed, her eyes flitting about the room, "look at all these people!"

Golde made the precursory motion to exclude those prepared to testify from the courtroom. A general commotion followed as the witnesses emptied their seats, mincing their way past spectators' knees to file out into the hallway. Then, an objection. The scheduled testimonies were all "self-serving hearsay," Golde rose to tell the judge. Even if not "offered for the truth," they were still irrelevant as to the validity of the diary confession.

Margulies overruled. One, the testimony provided circumstantial evidence regarding the minor's state of mind as she wrote the confession, specifically speaking to her tendency to lie. Two, the testimony was necessary to hear in that they represented information that the defense was alleging should have been introduced in trial and given to Dr. Berg.

Silently, Golde sat down.

In rapid-fire succession, Serena's friends took the stand. Hillary Fraley testified that Serena told her she was Mallory's real mother. Mrs. Marilyn Clearing, Serena's former cheerleading instructor, had been told on separate occasions that Serena had leukemia and that she was pregnant and being forced into an abortion by her mother. Serena's best friend, Mary Corren, told the court of various lies involving rape, pregnancy, and abortion.

Throughout the parade of ten witnesses, an embarrassed Serena swiveled in her chair and played with her hair.

Tina Craig told the court of her readiness to testify at Serena's trial and her eventual returning to classes when she did not receive the subpoena she requested from Antonio. She also noted that, after hearing Serena's many lies, she did not readily believe that Mallory had died when Serena phoned her the morning of August 18, 1992.

In cross-examination, Golde asked each person no more than an obligatory question or two. The prosecution's refusal to stipulate to the affidavits seemed a mistake. Margulies was now seeing each witness in the flesh, and their presence allowed Horngrad to embellish the affidavits through further prodding.

Finally, Sharri was called to the stand to testify, over Golde's numerous objections, that Serena's statements weren't true. No, she said, Serena had not been treated for leukemia; no, she had never been raped, pregnant, or had an abortion. One last question, Horngrad added, apologizing that it even had to be asked.

"Who gave birth to Mallory?"

Her answer was barely audible. "I did."

The defense rested.

*   *   *

Following the break were oral arguments, Horngrad's as eloquent and clear as Golde's was ill prepared and stumbling. By this, the third day of Serena's hearing, Golde looked as if he'd had the fight knocked out of him. He hunched over the counsel table as Horngrad rose to address Judge Margulies.

"This case is not about what Melvin Belli was or is," he began, "although we can agree that he is over the hill as this case is concerned, period." Belli, Horngrad quoted, had told the court that Antonio was "handpicked" because "she was one of his best girls." Only in later questioning did the truth emerge. Through some last-minute volunteering, Antonio had become *de facto* lead counsel.

The defense was negligent for numerous reasons. It had failed to introduce evidence of the defendant's other lies. This failure could not "be called a tactical decision under the law." In addition, in offering medical evidence, the defense had "crippled" Dr. Warnock's testimony, a fact which the prosecution had argued strenuously. Antonio's inserting herself between medical experts had prompted the prosecution to call her "unethical." Horngrad agreed. She also had crippled Dr. Berg's testimony by not giving him Serena's first diary, although she testified that she had. Dr. Berg's own testimony had been offered for impeachment.

Horngrad was frustrated that he could not catch the eye of Judge Margulies, who was bent over a sheet of paper, taking notes. He paused until she raised her chin.

"Ms. Antonio lied to you. That was part and parcel of her effort to save her own hide. And the hide she saves is at the expense of this minor." He pointed to Serena.

"This trial was a mess," he declared. Any one of the Belli firm's errors could be enough to set aside the verdict, but taken together, they clearly pointed to the fact that the minor was entitled to a new and fair trial.

"I'm asking the court to give her a new chance. I *know* it's difficult." But in order to satisfy *Strickland*, Horngrad reminded the judge, she only had to find that there existed a fair to reasonable probability that the verdict might have been different had this evidence been first presented. She was not saddled with a definitive decision as to whether or not her mind would have been changed. Granting a new trial was not an acquittal; it was a ruling that trial counsel had been deficient, and that their errors prejudiced the minor.

At the hearing, Horngrad contended, Belli and Antonio "were not here to advance their client's interests as aggressively as possible. They were here for self-aggrandizing reasons." By trying to persuade the court not to grant the motion, they were advancing their own interests over their client's—an act which was "reprehensible." The judge should not countenance such shameful behavior.

"The only time I agreed with Belli," Horngrad remarked, "was when he asked you to hold him in contempt."

Belli's had been a "seat-of-the-pants" counsel, a perfect example of which lay in his direct examination of the defendant. At best it was "rambling," at worst, "thoroughly deficient." As for Antonio, she was chosen as *de facto* counsel even though she had no experience with a criminal trial or juvenile case. That was—to use one of Matt Golde's favorite words—"outrageous." Antonio was an earnest young woman who probably thought "the great old man would pull her through." She was enamored of Belli. But she should not have taken on this representation under such hope. Belli was unable to give her proper supervision. Further, it was obvious from transcripts that Shelley Antonio, due to her inexperience, did not know how to introduce key pieces of evidence. There was "no way" the court did not see that.

"Having sat through the thoroughly unpleasant presentation of Belli's counsel, Kevin McLean," declared Horngrad, "it was clear that they were most worried about a civil suit and their own reputations. They were not worried about their former client. They were here to violate confidences if they had to in order to make themselves look better and their client look worse."

How coincidental it was that the missing 117 pages of Diary #1 had not been accounted for in the Belli firm's synopsis given to Horngrad. Clearly, those pages were lost at an early stage of their preparation in the case. "To sit up here and say it was stolen by members of their previous firm is nothing more than a paranoid schizophrenic version of 'the dog ate my homework,'" he remarked.

Horngrad turned to the molestation issue. "There are two ways to look at the molestation. If there was evidence that

Michael is a molester, then he is clearly a suspect. That avenue shouldn't be shut down by Michael's asking that it not be considered. If Mallory *wasn't* molested, than the prosecution's theory of motive falls apart." Unfortunately, counsel had not carried either theory to its proper conclusion.

Horngrad's tone intensified. "I would ask the court to be mindful of Mr. Belli's testimony here. It was shocking, riveting." If the court had heard unfettered expert testimony, had seen Diary #1, had been aware of the pathological lies Serena had told her friends, there was a reasonable probability that the outcome of that trial would have been different.

"This is a stain that will follow this minor for the rest of her *life*. She deserved, and the Sixth Amendment demands, better representation than what she received. It was clearly deficient. I ask," he pronounced, emphasizing each word, "that you give this minor back the Sixth Amendment, and beseech that you grant the motion and give her a new trial."

Sharri could hear the *rat-a-tat-tat* of her heart as Horngrad sat down and gripped Serena's arm. Spectators and reporters let out a collective breath.

"Thank you," Margulies said tonelessly. "Mr. Golde?"

Looking ill at ease, the Deputy D.A. rose, leaning over the table momentarily to scan his notes. "All through this hearing, the overwhelming focus of the motion in unrelentless fashion attacked the character and integrity of Mr. Belli and Ms. Antonio. He is making an emotional, dramatic appeal and saying 'not fair.' The focus of a new trial motion must focus on the record." The brief filed by defense was a "general all-out attack without reference to specific reasons."

Golde flipped through his notebook. There were two things here, he said, lies and the diary. Belli "mostly did not have in his possession the lies." Should they have found out the lies? It was "purely cumulative evidence." At a certain point, the "defense attorney cannot be said to be ineffective for not finding more evidence of untruth. There was nothing remarkable in the lies—assuming they *are*."

Evidence of lies in the diary were "pure, unbridled, self-serving hearsay, not admissible. You can't have a confession and then the defense says the client is a liar. You can't prove it by other people saying they are lies." Same argument for the diary. In the trial, "Sharri Moore and the minor said that she lied. Evidence that the minor was a liar clearly was presented, particularly by Dr. Berg.''

The courtroom was quiet as Golde paused awkwardly.

"The issue here is not lies. The issue is a confession to a crime. Is there any evidence that the minor falsely confessed to a crime before? We all tell lies. We're talking about a confession to a crime. That's not lying. The defense produced no evidence that the minor regularly confesses to crimes regularly [sic].''

The first diary, probably not admissible anyway, was "not a denial unless you employ mental gymnastics. It goes on to talk of missing her boyfriend, sex with the boyfriend, she was dry, he wasn't coming.''

Serena hid her face again.

"I'm not saying this to embarrass the minor,'' Golde said, noticing her movement. Also, he added, the first diary entry about Mallory's death was consistent with the second.

Dr. Berg gave a detailed history of the minor's past so there was no possibility of a different result based on Dr. Berg. And yes, the defense should have allowed Dr. Warnock to talk to Dr. Herrmann, but "all it did was make our fact-finding process more difficult.''

Another long silence. Horngrad alleged general poor tactics, Golde floundered, such as eggs-in-a-medical-basket. "As to not presenting an inconsistent defense, Antonio shouldn't do that. However, the defense *did* indirectly offer that Michael Moore did this.'' Penny Cooper "gave four reasons for giving an inconsistent defense, saying there was no rational tactical reason for not going after Michael Moore. That is a tactical reason they made.''

Judge Margulies gazed quietly as Golde struggled for further argument. She had taken few notes.

"It was definitely demonstrated that she was a liar.'' He spread his hands. "When we talk of incompetent counsel, we should look at not experience, we should look at the record. There is no new evidence, no other false confession. All we have here is more lies. This is not the kind of evidence for a new trial.'' Horngrad should focus on the record, not on criticizing former counsel. "Look at the record and what they have as opposed to inflammatory attacks on the part of the defense counsel. There is no false confession, no third party admission.''

Golde appeared ready to say more, then abruptly sat down.

Horngrad's rebuttal was short and emphatic. He couldn't *believe* the same prosecutor, who had originally argued that there was "no evidence of lies in the record," now was charging that evidence of lies was "cumulative." The very phrase "no evidence" meant that the prosecutor knew full well the minor *was* a liar, and that such evidence was not *in the record*. Regarding Diary #1, if its sexual content was so helpful to the prosecution, why hadn't the Deputy D.A. introduced it?

As for Belli and Antonio, "They rolled in here, moved to disqualify Your Honor in an untimely manner, and never asked for an advisory jury. The notion that they could walk in here and persuade you that the hometown coroner is wrong was foolish. You have to be ready with a defense in case the court should find that it was a homicide." Their "preposterous" ideas "showed how little they knew what was going on over here."

Horngrad leaned his knuckles on the table, summoning every ounce of his righteous anger. "I play with the cards I'm dealt," he declared. "And I *will* criticize these lawyers until *this young lady*"—he supported himself with one hand and jabbed a finger at Serena—"gets another trial. I'll criticize as long as she is in a *living hell* due to a conviction because of their deficiencies. Then as soon as a new trial is granted, *I'll shut up and go about the business of trying this case!*"

He held his position like an actor after a dramatic scene, gray suit coat rising and falling with his breathing. Then, quietly, he resumed his seat.

Judge Margulies's expression remained unreadable. "All right," she concluded succintly. "We'll see everybody back here at four-thirty tomorrow afternoon for my decision." And she swept out the door without further comment.

It was a long twenty-four hours. Monday night, Sharri's restless sleep was punctuated with nightmares of prison cells and more cellophaned baskets. As Tuesday wore on, she clung to hope, at the same time reminding herself of Doug

Horngrad's "long shot" cautions. The motion for new trial was mainly to provide grounds for an appeal, he had often told them. They faced better odds then; three appellate judges were far more likely to overturn Sandra Margulies's ruling than she was to overturn herself. Even so, victory through that process could be a year in coming. Meanwhile, Serena most likely would be sentenced to the dreaded CYA.

Mary Corren, Pastor Doug, and many of Serena's friends from church accompanied the Moores to court Tuesday afternoon. The air was filled with grim anticipation as they waited anxiously for a late Judge Margulies. Outside in the hallway, television cameras stood ready to film immediate on-site coverage for the five to six evening news hour.

Matt Golde arrived at four-thirty, looking as if he'd been beaten up. His face was chalk white, his hands shaking.

"Gee," Horngrad blurted as they greeted one another, "are you all right? Ya look like hell."

Yeah, he was fine, Golde responded automatically as they both disappeared into the judge's chambers.

Margulies was all business. "I'm not going to tell you my decision, but I just want the family warned." She looked to Horngrad. "I'll have no outbursts, whatever the outcome."

"Very well." Horngrad reentered the courtroom, leaned over the front row of seats and quietly advised the Moores and their friends. Sharri felt a flicker of excitement. No one had behaved badly when the trial verdict was for the prosecution. Could the judge be afraid of their elation at a finding for the defense?

At four-forty-five, Serena was led in. Once seated, she immediately began to crack her knuckles.

As Judge Margulies prepared to begin, Sharri clasped Mary Corren's hand.

"I have reviewed the case law in this matter," Margulies stated. "In so doing, I find that there are two components to ineffectiveness of counsel—performance and prejudice." Horngrad tensed. "Regarding the first, I find that trial counsels, plural, fell below the required standard."

An electric shock seemed to race through the courtroom.

Serena searched Horngrad's face. "This is the easy one," he whispered, keeping a rush of hope to himself. If the judge thought this on point one, a similar point two might not be far behind.

"The defense has shown that trial counsel*s*, plural, fell below the standard in five areas. One, failure to introduce other lies told by the defendant. Two, failure to introduce the August diary entry. Three, the crippling of expert witness Dr. Warnock's testimony through the defense's interference in the communication process. Four, failure to pursue another line of defense, namely, that the stepfather, Michael Moore, could have committed the crime. And five, Ms. Antonio's becoming *de facto* lead counsel without having prior experience."

Horngrad was elated. She had granted every one of his arguments!

"Both counsels testified here regarding their strategies and tactical reasons. I have considered those reasons, and in light of the circumstances find that their choices were not in the range of professional reasonable standards."

In the brief silence that followed, just as during the first verdict, Sharri was acutely aware of reporters scribbling furiously around her. She began to tremble.

"As to the second point—prejudicial—I find that there is a reasonable probability that the outcome of this case would have been different. The motion is granted."

Triumphantly, Horngrad slapped his hands against the table and pushed back his chair. Serena grabbed his arm. "What?" The muscles in his face felt tight. "You got your new trial, love." Serena gasped as her hand flew to her mouth.

Margulies concluded, "The verdict is set aside."

Serena grasped Horngrad in a sudden, fierce hug. Sobbing wildly, she covered her eyes with a tissue, then soon recovered to throw brilliant smiles at her parents. Sharri and Michael embraced. Two television reporters made for the door. Salladay grinned; pastor Doug was nodding effusively, tears in his eyes. As Margulies called Horngrad and a silent Golde for a conference, the Moores and friends barely contained their jubilation.

"I don't mean to sound patronizing," Horngrad told Margulies in her chambers, "but that was a courageous thing you did."

Margulies's circumspection rested firmly in place. "I don't

know if it was courageous," she shrugged, "but it was my decision."

She informed both attorneys that she would remove herself from sitting on the case again. In Horngrad's paraphrase, she was "outta there." Back on record in the courtroom, she intoned that Serena Moore's new trial was scheduled for 9:00 A.M., January 21, presiding judge to be determined by the master calendar of Department 30.

As with the past verdict, the Moores and their friends clustered in the courtroom foyer, waiting for the right moment to emerge, this time intent on making a mad dash for the elevator. Sharri remained adamant about keeping her face from the cameras; she did not want anyone at work recognizing her from TV. Meanwhile in the hallway, reporters crowded around Horngrad. Shielding themselves and surrounded by Serena's friends, the Moores suddenly burst into the hallway and made a run for it, all cameras turning in immediate pursuit. Crowding into an elevator, the Moores shooed away the cameramen, who responded by piling into a second elevator and hastily punching the first floor button.

"Hit number two!" someone in the Moore contingent cried. Grinding to a stop on the second floor, they fanned into the hallway, skittered toward the outside stairs, and made their escape, visions of befuddled cameramen raising their spirits even higher. About time those vultures got their comeuppance!

With the Moores having vanished, video crews straggled back up to the third floor for shots of Horngrad as he answered reporters' questions.

"The judge did the right thing under the law," he was asserting. "I believe in the system, and the court vindicated the system." Based on Margulies's ruling, he was "absolutely positive" of an acquittal.

As for taking shots at Belli, Horngrad kept his word. He wasn't "into icon-bashing," he noted after a reporter's leading question. He'd said all he needed to say about that, and now he must turn to winning Serena's next trial.

Amidst all the commotion, Matt Golde managed to elude the press, slinking out of the courtroom through the judge's chambers. He remained unavailable for comment.

* * *

Melvin Belli had plenty to say. He lingered in his office that evening, taking calls from numerous reporters for the following morning's front-page stories.

"I'm satisfied I did a good job," he declared to Catherine Bowman from the *Chronicle*. "I think she (the judge) was completely unfair during the trial. She knew she'd made a mistake but now she's trying to blame me and blame Shelley."

To Raoul Mowatt from the *San Jose Mercury,* he admitted that, if he could try the case over, he could present additional evidence of the minor's lies from her diary. "The main thing is that the girl gets a new trial with a different judge," he said. "This judge was out to get this little girl, and to get me, too. For what purpose, I don't know."

The *San Francisco Examiner*'s Don Martinez printed Belli's further denouncements against Margulies, who he said was "trained in a district attorney's office." Perhaps the most denigrating remarks were elicited by Bob Salladay. ". . . Belli defended his work," he wrote in the *Argus,* "and blamed his former law partners for trying to discredit him by feeding spurious information to Horngrad. He also said Margulies was biased because she is a "former prosecutor and a woman.""

PART V

Turnabout

December 1993–April 1994

This trial is not necessarily a search for the truth. We're not trying to find out the truth; we're trying to defend Serena.

—Penny Cooper to Sharri Moore

Thirty-nine

To THE COMMISSION on Judicial Performance from Melvin Belli, regarding the Honorable Sandra Margulies:

> *Melvin M. Belli and Shelley Antonio . . . hereby complain of and request a formal investigation into the gross misconduct and incompetence of Judge Sandra Marguilies* (sic) *before, during and after the above-referenced juvenile trial of Serena Moore.*
>
> *The misconduct and incompetence of Judge Sandra Marguilies* (sic) *resulted in the illegal and unjustified conviction of Serena Moore for second degree murder . . . Judge Marguilies* (sic) *violated the Canons of the Code of Judicial Conduct . . . declaring that 1. Judges Should Uphold the Integrity and Independence of the Judiciary, 2. Judges Should Avoid Impropriety and the Appearance of Impropriety in all Their Activities, and 3. Judges Should Perform the Duties of Their Office.*

Belli's seven-page complaint against Margulies listed these contentions: 1. because "she coveted the minor's case," Margulies refused defense counsel's challenge against her presiding over it, so made because Belli felt her background as a district attorney would render the judge to "not have the requisite sensitivity for this type of case," 2. Margulies refused to allow "psychiatrist" (sic) Dr. Berg to testify that the diary confession was not true, which "undermined the defense." 3. "in her incompetence, the judge failed to understand and appreciate the technical and scientific evidence" that the deceased died of a sudden asthma attack, "which would have exculpated defendant," and 4. Margulies "com-

351

mitted numerous trial errors which compelled her, upon reflection, to reverse her errant verdict,'' at which time she
''deliberately and maliciously attempted to make former trial
counsel responsible and her scapegoats.''

Two pages of the complaint dealt not with direct accusations against Margulies, but defended Belli's and Antonio's
not using Diary #1, arguing that the diary would have depicted the defendant as ''a callous, insensitive and sexually
obsessive deviant, reaching almost nymphomaniac proportions'' even though, Belli admitted, such acts ''were not ele-
ments of the crime she was charged with.''

As a result of Margulies's ruling, it was mandatory that
the findings against Belli and Antonio be reported to the
California State Bar Association, which held the power in
deciding after an investigation what punishment, if any, was
appropriate. Repercussion, if any, against the attorneys could
range from a short-term suspension from practicing law to
''pulling their Bar cards'' permanently.

Belli's letter to the Commission on Judicial Performance,
dated December 8, 1993, was apparently designed to ''turn
the tables'' so to speak, to echo, formally, the statements he
had made to newspaper reporters immediately following the
hearing's outcome.

In essence, ''*She* did it.''

Highly pleased with Penny Cooper's performance at the
hearing, Horngrad pursued her as defense co-counsel for Serena's hard-won second trial, scheduled for January 21. Cooper agreed to join the case *pro bono,* although Horngrad
would end up sharing his earnings with her. (Horngrad's fee
for the second trial was $5000—bringing his total bill for
Serena's defense to $15,000—plus expenses for his investiga-
tor, Stuart Kohler. After reviewing the Moores' finances, the
court awarded them up to $5000 for medical experts plus
an additional $2500 for further investigation.) The Horngrad/
Cooper team-up created a dual force for the prosecution to
reckon with, but it also caused, at least in part, a series of
continuances that would stretch into the spring. Conflicts in
the attorneys' schedules were one factor. Horngrad had a
three-week trip to India planned after Christmas (he later

shortened the trip to a week and went to Paris instead); Cooper was trying a case in Tacoma, Washington, in March.

Numerous case-twisting events took place that also helped cause the delay.

Cooper's and Horngrad's first line of defense was an offense—to keep the case from being retried again. In the last week of December, they met with Matt Golde and his supervisor, Walt Jackson, in an effort to convince the D.A.'s Office to drop charges against Serena. Margulies's setting aside the verdict was in effect an acquittal, they argued. Implicit in the judge's ruling was the statement that, were it not for attorney errors made in the first trial, her verdict would have been different. How could the District Attorney's Office possibly expect to win its case after such a ruling?

Before the meeting, a suspicion, still not perfectly clear, had been germinating in Cooper's mind after careful perusal of Dr. Herrmann's testimony and his autopsy report. Like Horngrad, she suspected that the pathologist had not been given the chance in trial to state what he really believed. Raising their suspicions to Jackson, Cooper and Horngrad received a reply that, when relayed to the Moores, would strike them with all the force of a lightning bolt.

Dr. Herrmann *himself* thought Serena innocent.

Jackson's admission was a major turning point in the case's defense.

The pathologist's opinion was nothing new, Golde would argue with a shrug. Nor was it evidence that he in any way had tried to hide. Dr. Herrmann had told the prosecution this opinion long ago. And previous defense counsel had enjoyed equal access to the doctor; in fact, Shelley Antonio had met with Dr. Herrmann before the trial.

For her part, Cooper found it hard to believe that Dr. Herrmann would not have explained his beliefs to Antonio during their meeting had he been properly questioned. The doctor was a respected pathologist and "had no ax to grind."

Cooper left the meeting believing that Golde would not retry the case. The only two pieces of evidence—the diary confession and the autopsy findings—*did not match*, according to the pathologist. Once Dr. Herrmann's opinion was extracted effectively during trial testimony, the prosecution's case would be left in utter shambles.

Under the circumstances, Cooper and Horngrad continued to challenge Golde, the bravest thing he could do was to admit he was wrong to ever have prosecuted Serena Moore, given the conclusions of his *own star witness*. Admit he was wrong and drop the charges.

Golde challenged Horngrad in response. "Give me some new evidence that shows me Serena Moore didn't do this." As far as he was concerned, nothing had changed. He still had a written confession, he still had an autopsy conclusion of traumatic asphyxia. And he still firmly believed that the defendant was guilty.

During the month of January, Golde discussed with Jackson the issue of whether or not to proceed, but, as he later stated, "It was never a great debate topic." One week before the trial was slated to begin on January 21, Jackson delivered the final, anxiously awaited word to Horngrad. They would prosecute the case again.

Sharri and Michael, fervently hoping for Serena's sudden release, were crushed. Serena, mercifully, had been left in the dark about the possibility.

The defense team was not prepared to begin trial the following week. Serena's January 21 court appearance was no more than a short hearing before Alameda County Judge Ronald Sabraw, a man looking startlingly like a mature Clark Kent, down to the glasses and cleft in his chin. The case would be assigned a new judge, Sabraw indicated, who would hear any pretrial motions and preside over the trial. Serena, in a blue- and pink-flowered shirt, reluctantly waived time until February 9, when the motions would be heard.

As for the new judge, Horngrad and Cooper would be allowed one challenge if assigned someone they did not want. They would proceed carefully on that issue, not wanting to overly irritate the Alameda County judicial system, in which Margulies's ruling for a new trial would be viewed with collegial respect. "If you jam the hometown kids too hard," Horngrad warned the Moores after the hearing, "they might send us to Judge Horror Show in Oakland."

Gearing up their defense, Cooper and Horngrad scheduled another important meeting—this one in early February with Dr. Herrmann. Cooper had known Paul Herrmann for years, their paths having crossed in previous cases. She reviewed his testimony in Serena's first trial again before engaging, along with Horngrad, in a "warm, friendly" conversation about his conclusions from the autopsy of Mallory Moore. Admittedly, Herrmann noted, the medical evidence was weak. He'd had many questions at the outset, he told the attorneys, and had posed them to the police, who, according to Dr. Herrmann, had suspected Serena long before the diary surfaced. In the upcoming trial, Dr. Herrmann informed the delighted attorneys, he "would not rule out" that Mallory might have died from an epileptic seizure. However, believing as strongly as he did that Mallory had been sodomized, and concluding that cause of death was from chest compression, Dr. Herrmann's "best guess" was that Mallory had been killed accidentally while being molested.

The "other perpetrator" or, more bluntly, the "Michael-did it" theory, just took on new meaning.

Before the next court appearance there arose another bizarre twist in the case, which sprang from the mere ringing of a phone in Golde's office some months before. Michael Ballachey, an Alameda County judge and a friend of Golde's father, had been on the line. Gregarious and well liked, Ballachey nevertheless was laughingly known behind his back by some colleagues as "Radio-Free Berkeley" because of his love of gossip and intrigue. According to Ballachey, a young black student in his second year law class by the name of Danine Bailey told the class she had heard Serena Moore "confess." A "Group Custody Intermittent" employee of juvenile hall, Bailey had transported Serena to and from her first trial on two occasions, and it was during one of those trips, Ballachey said, that Bailey had heard the remark from Serena. After Serena was granted a new trial, Ballachey later explained, he felt "an obligation, right or wrong" to bring this to Golde's attention.

Golde intended to use this serendipitous information in the next trial, but apparently did not immediately alert the defense team in compliance with discovery procedures. By chance, Penny Cooper attended a dinner party at which Judge Ballachey was present and mentioned Serena's case to him. The judge replied that he could not discuss that case, as he most likely would be a witness. Cooper was stunned.

Meanwhile, Golde was running into problems as he and his investigator, John Samuelson, interviewed Danine Bailey about the incident in the last week of January. Bailey emphatically denied telling the judge that Serena had confessed to her. When Golde repeatedly questioned her, she stood her ground, even when informed that Judge Ballachey would also stand by his account of the events and would testify under oath to that effect.

February 9 rolled around. As the Moores and a smattering of reporters waited in the courtroom, Cooper and Horngrad argued heatedly in Judge Sabraw's chambers over the Bailey/Ballachey incident. How dare he not inform them, Horngrad and Cooper charged, and just when had he planned on letting them know—the day the trial started? In addition, they said, the testimony was worthless. Besides the fact that Ballachey's testimony would be double hearsay, Serena's alleged "confession" to Bailey negated itself. According to Judge Ballachey, the statement as repeated by Bailey was a confession, then a recanting—basically, "I did it; I didn't do it."

Occasionally, the muted sound of a raised voice drifted into the courtroom. The Moores were well aware of the situation, but reporters had no clue. Attorneys on both sides of the issue had kept a tight lid on this latest contention.

Arguments finally abating, Golde, Cooper, and Horngrad took their seats before Judge Sabraw. Serena was led in, wearing a green pantsuit, her hair brushed into a partial ponytail. Horngrad hunched sideways as soon as she sat next to him, whispering in her ear about the importance of another continuance while the issue at hand and pretrial motions were further pursued.

On record, Judge Sabraw indicated that he and the attorneys had "spent a long time in chambers discussing motions and other issues." Next court date—March 2, when pleadings and motions would be heard.

Serena waived time angrily. She was tired of sitting in juvenile hall day after day, hearing promises about scheduling that were never kept. She wasn't sure she could contain herself much longer, and was afraid of "losing it" in the hall, which would earn her a stay in the dreaded intake cell.

The session over, Serena was escorted back to juvenile hall to wait another month while the attorneys fought it out. The defense still maintained that Golde should not only forget Bailey and Ballachey, but should drop the case entirely. Pursuing it, in their eyes, was worse than just impractical. It was *wrong*.

The three attorneys were well aware that Judge Sabraw also had a decision to make. What to do about the prospect of an Alameda County judge, Michael Ballachey, testifying for the prosecution before one of his own colleagues?

Regardless of which judge presided over the second "Diary Girl" trial, Cooper and Horngrad intended to be fully armed in battling the Bailey/Ballachey testimony, which meant gaining information from the two potential witnesses themselves. On February 15, Horngrad's investigator, Stuart Kohler, interviewed Judge Ballachey by phone, then spoke with Danine Bailey in person. The stories he heard were vastly different.

According to Kohler's report, Ballachey recalled that Bailey, who was attending one of his trials in Alameda County Superior Court some months past, entered his chambers during a recess to chat, and their discussion turned briefly to Serena's case. To quote the report, the judge was "adamant" that Bailey said that "Moore told her (Moore) did it. She killed her sister. Then she (Bailey) said, in almost the same breath, she (Moore) later recanted." After hearing this, the judge continued, he told Bailey that she was a witness for the case, which seemed to "fluster" her, perhaps owing to the fact that talking to Serena about the case was a violation of juvenile hall "transport instructions," and her job might be affected.

Ballachey believed that he spoke with Bailey once or twice more about the incident, most likely during class. "I don't pretend to have a good short-term memory," he noted. He did remember asking Bailey for her phone number to pass on to Golde. Bailey tore off a corner of a check deposit slip and handed it to him. Again, his best recollection was that this was during class.

Asked when he initially spoke with Matt Golde about the matter, Ballachey replied, "My memory, and I don't trust this memory very much, is that it was before the new trial motion."

Danine Bailey was eager to tell her story to Kohler, adding that she had already spoken with Matt Golde, who was "trying to make something out of nothing." Her interview with Kohler, unlike Ballachey's, was filled with details as to time and place.

Like Ballachey, Bailey was "emphatic" about her conversations with the judge. "I have no ties to Serena," she told Kohler. "I have no ties to the family. I would tell if she said something. Serena never told me anything of the sort." Bailey traced the "misunderstanding" to comments she made to other students in September 1993 during an Evidence Advocacy workshop taught by the judge on Thursdays. While packing up their books after class, the students' discussion turned to the "Diary Girl" case. According to Bailey, she told her colleagues that she knew Serena and made a remark to the effect that, "The girl is a trip. She did it. First she said she did it, then she said she didn't. I know she did it." Bailey made it clear to Kohler that the basis for her remark was a mixture of public knowledge and personal opinion, and not a conversation with Serena. At that time, Bailey estimated, Judge Ballachey was standing eight to ten feet away and apparently heard the comment, but did not pull her aside or pursue the matter "in a fashion that foreshadowed what was to come."

It was two to three weeks later that Bailey spoke with Ballachey during a court recess. At that time, he told her, according to Bailey's quote, "I think I got you into trouble. I spoke to the D.A. handling the Moore case and he may want to speak with you." The judge added that Golde was an "ethical guy" and she should not have any trouble speaking with him.

On the last day of the Evidentiary workshop, December 2, Bailey responded to Ballachey's request for a phone number by tearing off the deposit slip corner.

Bailey admitted to Kohler that she and Serena "talked a lot about this case." Bailey "poked at evidentiary things" and asked questions. "I tried on a lot of occasions to allow her to tell me if she did it," Bailey said. "I pushed her because I wanted to know." But, according to Bailey, Serena made no confessions or admissions of any kind. In speaking with Serena, Bailey acknowledged violating the terms of a memo circulated at juvenile hall over a year before that instructed personnel not to converse with Serena about her case. Realizing that she "probably should not have talked with Serena," Bailey nevertheless expected no administrative response or discipline.

Bailey was upset over being "interrogated" by Golde and Samuelson for "roughly" two hours, describing the tenor of Golde's responses to her as "doubting."

Summing up her interview with Kohler, Bailey concluded, "I don't believe that the judge is lying or trying to set me up. Just that he is saying what he may believe happened, and that he is trying to help his friend (Golde)."

Bailey earned an "A" in her course under Judge Ballachey.

The March 2 hearing was brief. Arguing pretrial motions was set aside as Judge Sabraw stated mildly that "circumstances had come to the court's attention" that necessitated the county of Alameda to recuse—or remove—itself from hearing the case against Serena M. An out-of-county judge would have to be appointed. Sabraw did not explain the reason for the recusal, leaving reporters bewildered and full of questions after the session, which none of the attorneys would answer.

Horngrad and Golde agreed to a trial date of April 25, and requested that the judge be scheduled for that day.

While counting the days toward Serena's criminal trial, Sharri and Michael decided on a plan that would spawn further, and most likely fiery, civil legal proceedings. Quietly, they retained Tanya Starnes, a civil attorney recommended by Penny Cooper, to begin the paperwork for a malpractice case in Serena's name against Belli, Antonio, and the law firm at large. Starnes fully expected a nasty fight from Belli, although she believed Serena would have an excellent chance of prevailing based on Judge Margulies's ruling as to his and Antonio's ineffectiveness of counsel.

It wouldn't be the first time Belli served as a defendant. According to records in San Francisco County alone, since 1966 Belli had been slapped with over eighty civil law suits of various complaints. Twenty-seven cases had been recorded in that county since 1985, including alleged breaches of contract, small claims, negligence, wrongful discharge, and seven malpractice suits. Starnes was uncertain whether Belli still carried malpractice insurance. "Through the grapevine" she'd heard he had been sued so many times that by 1982 he could no longer obtain it. If that were true, his personal assets could be on the line.

Starnes began gathering background information, but the time to file the lawsuit was not yet at hand. As with other aspects of the Moores' lives, it was put on hold. Starnes and the Moores had agreed to wait until Serena's trial was over, at which time Starnes would file immediately, capitalizing on the publicity from Serena's expected acquittal.

Forty

THE "DIARY GIRL'S" final trial, expected to last about two weeks, took place in the dusted-off courtroom of Department 61 within the police department building on Sixth Street in Oakland. Small, with wood-paneled walls and no windows, the room had a certain claustrophobic air, yet, thanks to its plainness and size, seemed far less intimidating than Sandra Margulies's Department 39 in Hayward. The padding in the rust-colored chairs of this rarely used courtroom had long since worn out, causing spectators' rear ends to grow numb well before a recess would be called. The microphone and sound system for the witness chair were broken. Not that they were needed all that much.

James Kleaver was a retired judge from tiny Siskiyou County. He occasionally agreed to take on cases which had been nudged out of various county court calendars because of overload or other circumstances. He had, in his own words, "always been fussy about lawyers' conduct."

Heavy rain sputtered on and off over the Bay Area as Judge Kleaver, in a short-sleeved blue shirt, chatted amicably with Horngrad and Golde just before 9:00 A.M., April 25.

Penny Cooper soon arrived, pulling a cart loaded with a large box of files and papers.

Her stomach churning, Sharri entered the courtroom alone. Reluctantly bowing to the defense attorneys' wishes, Michael had agreed not to attend. As Cooper had explained to them, it would be "awkward" and "inappropriate" to present the necessary but unsavory line of defense that, in accordance with Dr. Herrmann's beliefs, the stepfather was the most likely perpetrator when Michael himself was seated in the courtroom. In addition, Michael's silent, staunch presence beside his wife might seem incongruous to the same judge whom they wanted to mull over his possible guilt.

Sharri wasn't sure which was worse—having to face the trial alone or forcing herself to remain noncommittal amidst the curious inquiries from reporters as to Michael's whereabouts. "We can't afford for him to take more time off work," quickly became her standard answer to The Question. In actuality, Michael *did* plan to take the first three days of the trial off work. He was far too tense to concentrate on anything at his job, and he was determined to fix up their 1964 cherry red Chevrolet convertible. When Serena was freed, he planned to take her for a heady "victory spin."

Taking a seat on the left side of the courtroom, Sharri glanced to her right. The "regulars" from the media were present—Bob Salladay, Raoul Mowatt, Harry MacLean, Joan Lynch, and the rest. Sharri no longer felt threatened by them, in fact, looked upon them as supporters, believing that they were finally realizing that Serena was innocent. The television cameras were a different story; her head still ducked automatically at the sight of them in the hallway. She had been glad to see only two.

Pastor Doug made an appearance, hugging Sharri and assuring her that this time justice would prevail. As a witness for the defense, he was not allowed to stay. A group of Serena's friends from church skipped school to attend the trial, anxious to lend support by their presence. Straggling into the courtroom, they sat in one of the back rows.

At nine-thirty-five, court was called to order. Kleaver, with his round face, thinning brown hair, and glasses, and now robed in black, looked the picture of a learned judge. Serena wore a green pantsuit, pushing Hornrad's dressing instructions to the limit. She was not supposed to wear dark clothing, and was to lighten the color of her outfit each day. Sharri and Michael thought it a little silly, but had complied by rushing out to buy her a few last-minute pants and tops.

Pretrial motions were discussed and easily dealt with. The defense's right to all exculpatory evidence was granted; the People's motion for discovery from defense was granted only in regard to documents and tests used by medical experts. In chambers, Horngrad had requested an advisory jury, an appointed panel of six who had no power other than to "advise" the judge on what its verdict would be. Kleaver ruled that such a jury served little purpose and denied the motion. Defense then asked for the public to be excluded from proceedings, a motion that sent the antennae of every reporter in the room waving furiously. All spectators were asked to step outside as reasons for the motion were discussed.

Shortly before the trial, Serena, who had been the target of oral and written threats before, had received a two-page "death threat" letter apparently written by a gang member. Horngrad and Cooper expected to win their case, and feared that any more press would make it all the more difficult for Serena to return home and resume a normal life. For the record, they raised the motion, with no expectations of its being granted.

Milling about in the hallway, reporters mumbled to each other about phoning their attorneys. After ten minutes, everyone was called back inside, the judge announcing that he was denying the motion, but was ruling that the media not print the minor's last name nor any recognizable photos of her. That ruling extended to after the trial as well.

Reporters calm again and motions done by 10:00 A.M., it was time to begin the actual trial.

Golde, his hair once again grown to slightly below his collar, seemed nonplussed. "I'm sorry, Your Honor," he apologized, "but I thought the motions would take longer. I have witnesses lined up for tomorrow. I don't even have any of my files with me now."

For opening day of a case that Golde had insisted on pursuing to the bitter end, his attitude seemed lackadaisical at best.

Kleaver recessed until 1:30 P.M., giving the Deputy D.A. time to rally.

*   *   *

One-forty P.M. As he stood in the courtroom, reciting nearly the same opening argument given eleven months before, Golde seemed for all appearances the tired actor in an over-run Broadway play. He would later explain his attitude during Serena's second trial in terms of a "moral obligation" to prosecute a defendant whom he believed to be guilty, even though he expected to lose. Nothing had changed, from the prosecutorial point of view, in the past year. But the defense had changed a great deal. Golde contended that Dr. Herrmann "obviously" believed Serena was innocent and "felt bad" and partly responsible for her conviction. As Golde put it, the doctor the second time around would "do everything he could do for the defense, going to the edge" of what the pathologist should say. What he himself did, Golde thought, would be of little consequence in the trial. He would put forth the same evidence and leave it at that.

Through the medical findings, the discovery of the diary, the accusations of molestation, Golde's voice was quiet, his tone flat. "If you look at the entire situation," he concluded limply, "you'll find that this defendant is guilty of murder."

As Golde resumed his seat, Penny Cooper rose, bristling with energy. According to her agreement with Horngrad, she would cross-examine prosecution witnesses and he would question those for the defense. Cooper had toiled over her opening statement until it had taken shape as a tightly crafted overview depicting, she hoped, just enough of her outrage over Serena's case being tried a second time, and, in fact, ever being pursued in the first place.

The line of defense that she and Horngrad had opted to present was disturbing, but powerful. Despite her personal belief that Mallory had died from unknown natural causes, raising suspicion against Michael provided the most airtight case she and Horngrad could build. The necessity for this strategy had become particularly apparent after hearing that Judge Kleaver placed strong emphasis on the testimony of expert witnesses. In light of this proclivity, Horngrad and Cooper had decided to heavily cross-examine Dr. Herrmann, making him their own witness by demonstrating his opinion that Serena's confession did not match medical findings.

Nevertheless, the defense team was prepared to cover all

bases. They had forwarded Mallory's autopsy findings to two other pathologists, one of whom, as a pulmonary specialist, had concluded that Mallory had died of a sudden asthma attack. This conclusion had been reached separately from those of Doctors Warnock and Lawrence, and was supported by medical literature detailing suck attacks, some of the actual cited cases being in addition to those Dr. Warnock had found. In addition, the two pathologists had disagreed with Dr. Herrmann's conclusion of molestation, stating that the anal findings were "of no medical significance."

If they played their cards right, Horngrad and Cooper need never call these witnesses. By accepting, rather than fighting, Dr. Herrmann's testimony and using it to support their defense, they hoped to undercut the prosecution's case without even presenting one witness of their own.

"Your Honor," Cooper began, "this is a rare opportunity to defend a client who is indeed innocent. After the government has put forth its case, we will move for acquittal. This is *not* a close case." The pathologist, Dr. Paul Herrmann, was the government's chief witness and, she predicted, would be the *defense's* chief witness as well. The judge would soon hear Dr. Herrmann testify to the fact that the traumatic asphyxia he found "most likely" was caused accidentally during an act of child molestation, and that the defendant's diary entry did not relate medically to autopsy findings. The stepfather, Michael Moore, Cooper added, had been in the house the night Mallory died, and had been previously arrested for child molestation.

Enter the Fremont Police Department, who according to Cooper, "totally ignored the crucial findings of Dr. Herrmann that Mallory had been molested near the time of her death." They did not question Michael about it, even when he told police that he had "checked" on Mallory around 6:00 A.M., which was after she had already died. Nor did the police "do anything" with a diary entry written by Serena shortly after Mallory's death that was inconsistent with her confession entry in the other diary. This, despite the fact that the police were well aware, due to past dealings with the teenager, of Serena's reputation for lying. Ignoring her "rich history of fabrication," the police arrested and charged Serena Moore and "continued to pursue the case in the absence of any evidence of guilt."

With the exception of Dr. Herrmann, the entire prosecution witness list, Cooper said, was a "sorry lot" and "offered not one shred of evidence" to support the confession diary entry.

The "thorough unreliability" of the diary entry would soon become apparent in light of the defendant's guilt over her sister's death and her history of lying. "Serena had a deep love for Mallory," Cooper concluded. "There is no motive for this crime, no basis for it, and *no evidence.*"

Following the opening arguments was Dr. Herrmann, who had responded to Golde's last-minute call during lunch. Wearing a dark suit and a gold paisley tie, he settled himself in the witness chair with typical humorlessness.

During the break, Sharri had bought earplugs to wear during the pathologist's testimony. She felt she *had* to remain in the courtroom to support Serena, especially since Michael wasn't there, but could not bear to hear Herrmann's recitation once again. When the earplugs failed to work, she stared at her lap and began to cry.

Serena cast her eyes downward also as Golde woodenly led Dr. Herrmann through identification of the autopsy photographs, then on to the doctor's conclusions, his questions a mere synopsis of those in the previous trial. One remark from the witness caused some spectators to roll their eyes. Dr. Herrmann opined that the small amount of anal dilation in Mallory could have been caused by any number of objects, including "the end of a baseball bat."

After only forty-five minutes, the Deputy D.A. was finished.

Striding to the center of the courtroom to lean against a wall that acted as a boundary for the court clerk's desk, Cooper began her brisk cross-exam. Within an hour, she had extracted these important opinions and pieces of information from Dr. Herrmann:

1. This was a "weak medical case," with "aspects that one could argue about," including the cause of death.

2. Of all probable causes, he was "most suspicious of accidental death following molestation." There were other possibilities, but that was "a decided suspicion."

3. The forensic findings could not have been caused by only covering the mouth as noted in the diary confession, since that act by itself would not restrict blood flow and cause the petechial hemorrhages.

4. Dr. Herrmann had discussed the molestation issue with the Fremont Police "more than once."

5. Dr. Herrmann knew *before drawing the conclusion of sodomy on Mallory* that Michael had been accused of molestation in the past. (Since this interesting piece of data did not tend to support Cooper's main defense argument, she did not pursue it.)

6. Epilepsy as a cause of death had been ruled out because of the presence of petechial hemorrhages and the anal findings. (Dr. Herrmann would not move from this position, although he had told Cooper and Horngrad that he "could not rule out epilepsy" during their February meeting.)

7. Nevertheless, although he had never seen such a case, it "seemed logical" to Herrmann that an epileptic seizure could cause petechial hemorrhages due to restriction of blood flow during the seizure.

8. Generally speaking, it was possible for cause of death to be medically undeterminable.

The defense team was delighted. Reporters seemed amazed. After sixteen months of following the case, they were hearing for the first time that Dr. Herrmann himself did not support the prosecution's contention of Serena's guilt. They continued scribbling as the pathologist left the courtroom in an effort to transmit the last bits of the eye-opening testimony from their memories to paper.

Following Dr. Herrmann's testimony was Fire Captain Mike Sanchez. Golde moved through his questions as if by rote, knowing his performance would make little difference. When court recessed for the day, he turned to Cooper in resignation and conceded defeat.

"This case is over."

*   *   *

Tuesday morning, April 26. In his garage, Michael cut and fitted new red carpet into his Chevrolet convertible as, in the Oakland Police Building, Serena was led into court for her second day at trial. Sporting a short-sleeved beige flowered dress made by her mother, Serena took her seat calmly beside Penny Cooper. Dr. Herrmann dispensed with, as far as Serena was concerned, the worst testimony was over.

Sharri was anything but calm. Today, she would be called to the stand. She hated testifying, hated having to face Golde and his "insidious" questions. Most of all she dreaded having to recite the circumstances of finding Mallory dead, knowing she would relive the memories.

Russell Peterson, the young dark-haired paramedic who had examined Mallory the morning of her death, first took the stand. He was followed by the orthodontist Dr. Wong, who was allowed to testify over Cooper's protestations that his testimony was "remote in time, irrelevant, and almost ridiculous." As with the other witnesses for the prosecution, Wong's turn on the stand was far more succinct than in Serena's first trial.

The "Where's Waldo" stick was not mentioned.

Sharri, dressed in a pink blouse and black pants, began her testimony midmorning. Without a microphone, her soft voice barely carried across the small courtroom, and the judge asked her to speak up.

"I don't intend to belabor this like at the first trial," Golde commented, noting her obvious sense of feeling ill at ease. Judge Kleaver told her to "relax" and gave her a smile.

The encouraging words did little good. Sharri's tension soon began to spread across the courtroom like a dense thundercloud. Cooper slid forward in her chair to sit stiffly at attention, quick to object whenever Golde strayed into issues surrounding the Moores' family life. Sharri balked at certain questions, complaining that they were too general to answer, only to respond to others with a flow of unwanted extraneous and explanatory information. Once, Judge Kleaver told her irritably to "please not talk" when an objection from her attorney was pending before the court.

When the testimony turned to the morning of August 18, 1992, Sharri broke into tears, dabbing at her eyes with white tissues from a nearby box. Serena sat with her eyes downcast, but dry.

After a lunch break during which Sharri managed to swallow half a vanilla milk shake, she was back on the stand. To Golde's questions about Serena's accusations of molestation, Sharri reacted slowly, carefully, as one would move across a balance beam shrouded in fog. She could not exonerate Michael in front of the judge; neither could she bear to exude belief in the allegations as reporters jotted in their notepads. But she could defend herself. When Golde pressed her about threatening Serena after the Carson City police report—"Recant, or you'll have no family!"—Sharri vehemently denied saying any such thing.

Golde gave an almost-imperceptible shrug and left it alone.

In cross-examination, Cooper covered Mallory's asthma and a fact not discussed in the first trial—that Mallory had slipped on the Moore's concrete patio the evening before her death and had hit her head. She had cried awhile, then seemed okay. It was a fact of which Dr. Herrmann had been unaware.

When Cooper asked about Diary #1 and the lies it contained, Golde objected. A discussion ensued regarding whether or not the diary could be placed into evidence, Kleaver noting it sounded as though it would be a "character issue" to rebut the alleged confession. Cooper fully intended to submit the diary, while Golde, though he had little fight in him left, continued to protest. Kleaver set the issue aside momentarily, indicating he would hear arguments "at a later time."

At 3:10 P.M., a relieved Sharri was released from the stand.

After a short break, Sarah Moore testified briefly, Golde extracting from her the same information he had found useful in the first trial—that Serena could sneak out of the Moores' house without being heard and that she had participated in anal sex. Cooper's "Objection!" to the latter question was immediate and emphatic. Golde responded that the question was relevant because of the "anal findings" on Mallory. Kleaver agreed, to a point. "However," he added, "the details are not relevant."

Golde had no more questions.

Next up, Officer Uhler. When he settled into the witness chair, he did so with ease. Under Golde's prompting, he detailed Serena's now well-known "My-sister's-better-off-in-heaven" remark. As Shelley Antonio had done, Cooper worked to place the statement in context with Serena's anger over her police interrogation. Then she asked Uhler about something new. Had Serena not *also* told him while in his vehicle that night that she had been in the "getaway car" from a shooting in Oakland? Yes, answered Uhler, and he had dutifully "recorded that information," but didn't know what came of any subsequent investigation.

From the safety of her courtroom seat, Sharri couldn't repress a smirk. So much for Golde's allegations that Serena had never before confessed to another crime!

Following Officer Uhler, a testy argument arose over Golde's intention to call Danine Bailey. Golde briefly explained the circumstances behind Bailey's testimony, saying that he planned to impeach Bailey's denials of hearing a confession from Serena with testimony from Judge Ballachey. Cooper contended that the alleged confession—in effect, "I did it; I didn't do it"—was "not an admission or a clear statement" and therefore of little value. Horngrad broke in, adding that, in her job capacity, Bailey was a sworn police officer, and had not offered Serena any Miranda rights. For that reason, any statement Serena may have made to Bailey was inadmissible. Golde retorted that there was "a difference" between Bailey's capacity and that of actual police officers.

Horngrad threw him a withering look. "I think she's even brought her badge," he remarked.

Kleaver waved away the arguments, saying he would have to hear Bailey testify in order to ascertain whether or not she was a "sworn police officer."

Bailey, carrying a backpack, her hair in a French twist, took her seat in the witness stand and glared at Golde. She highly resented his intent, as she put it, "to make me out a liar" and, in the midst of all the flak, had just about decided that, even with two years of law school behind her, she'd rather be a *nurse*. "If I'm the best witness he's got," she would declare in the hallway after testifying, "his case is *shot*!"

It soon became clear that Bailey had carried police officer status when transporting Serena to and from her trial the previous year. When Golde continued with questions, Horn-grad interrupted, asking that he "cut to the chase" regarding the defendant's Miranda rights. "If the minor's statement doesn't survive Miranda," Horngrad said, "this testimony won't be allowed."

Bailey responded that she had never read Serena her Miranda rights. She had, however, discussed "many different things" while driving to and from court, everything from "hair ribbons" to attorney trial tactics, which Bailey found interesting. She had asked numerous questions of Serena, such as how Serena felt about the press, how she felt about the case, and "if she thought her mom was mad." Golde wondered if Bailey remembered stating any specific opinion to Serena.

"I remember telling her that I didn't think the D.A. had a case," she declared, her expression defiant.

A titter ran through the courtroom.

Kleaver had heard enough. Defense's objection was sustained; he was satisfied that in her capacity as a peace officer, Bailey had been "equivalent" to law enforcement personnel, invoking the necessity of Miranda.

Golde pressed his case, saying that he was prepared to call his investigator, John Samuelson, who would testify that Bailey told him she had *not* questioned Serena, that the defendant had offered an unsolicited statement, which would not invoke Miranda. Were this not so, Golde said, he could not have called Bailey to testify.

Horngrad jumped up, hands shoved in his pockets as he fought with excitement to save the judge's ruling sustaining the objection.

"Counsel!" the court reporter called, "you *have* to slow down!"

Horngrad complied, but continued his argument. Kleaver again agreed. Objection still sustained, Bailey was allowed to leave.

Golde would not give up. Bailey was lying, he declared, and the prosecution should not be precluded from demonstrating her perjury.

Golde was putting two carts before the horse, Horngrad threw out. Perjury or not, the Miranda foundation was lacking.

Kleaver thought a moment. "On the other hand," he responded, "if the prosecution can show that the witness is committing perjury and that there were no questions of the minor, then there is no Miranda problem." Kleaver would "trust Golde's good faith" in the matter and allow him to make an offer of proof to the court.

More arguments followed, Golde threatening to call his investigator, John Samuelson, and Bailey's superior, Herman Bosset, as witnesses to back up his contention that Bailey was lying.

Defense could call its investigator as a witness too, Horngrad retorted, and he and Kohler had also spoken with Bosset, who had said Danine Bailey was a good employee and in no danger of losing her job over the alleged incident with Serena. "Calling all these different witnesses," Horngrad emphasized, "would just snowball the issue." Regardless of the outcome of such testimony, the Miranda issue remained.

Finally, Kleaver sustained the defense's initial objection once more. This time he would hear no further argument from the prosecution. There was "no more to say." His ruling was based on the "Miranda problem," and, in addition, was merely "common sense." Even if all the witnesses were called as offers of proof on either side, there was no real value to the minor's statement anyway, since it was an alleged admission followed by a denial.

Horngrad shook his head in relief. *Three times* they'd had to win that objection, he would later remark, *three times.*

With the disallowance of Bailey's and Ballachey's testimony, Golde's case came to an unexpected, screeching halt.

Still pending, Kleaver noted before recessing for the day, was the matter of introducing the so-called Diary #1 into evidence. They would take up that subject in the morning.

Sharri could barely contain her elation as she drove home. No more witnesses from Golde! And no Bailey/Ballachey, she spurted to Michael, who was still working on the Chevrolet, when she drove up. The Deputy D.A. had hardly put on a case, and now the defense would hit hard, calling the same list of Serena's friends that had testified in the hearing regarding her past lies. How could they not win now?

As Sharri pounded up the old wooden steps into their house, Michael turned back to the convertible. Best get it in tip-top shape, he told himself. It looked like they might need it soon.

In juvenile hall that evening, Serena watched a television show with other inmates in the lounge area. At nine o'clock, her mandatory bedtime, she slid into bed and pulled the covers up to her chin, exhausted from the day's tension. Lying on her back, she stared at the ceiling for a few moments, then closed her eyes to pray before drifting off to sleep.

"*Please*, God," she breathed, "please make a miracle so I can go home when this is all over."

She never dreamed it would be her last night in juvenile hall.

Forty-one

WEDNESDAY, APRIL 27, 1994, sixteen months to the day since Serena was arrested for the murder of her sister.

Court was expected to be a short session. Horngrad and Cooper had subpoenaed Serena's friends to appear the following morning as the kickoff for the defense's case-in-chief. In the meantime, that Wednesday Cooper and Golde came prepared to argue before Judge Kleaver whether the Diary #1 entry of Serena's finding Mallory's body could be admitted into evidence. Among other reasons, Cooper petitioned that it be admitted under Evidence Code 1202 as a "prior inconsistent statement" used to impeach the confession, while Golde, as at the motion for new trial hearing, responded that the two diary entries "were not inconsistent."

Sharri, clad in a gray suit and red blouse, sat alone in the courtroom, unconsciously clutching her fingers. Pastor Doug was in the building for moral support, but still relegated to waiting in the hallway pending his testimony. If the judge denied Cooper's petition, Sharri knew, it would deal a solid blow to the defense. But the judge's quick response left her little time to worry. With his granting under 1202 of the defense's motion, she emitted an audible sigh of relief.

Golde's next move would seem inexplicable to spectators and the defense attorneys alike. Before resting the prosecution, Golde recalled Sharri to the stand to ask her about entries in Serena's diaries, explaining over Cooper's objections that he intended to impeach her testimony that the diaries contained lies. Judge Kleaver allowed him to continue.

Handing her Serena's blue-covered journal, which, containing only one entry, had not even been mentioned in the first trial, Golde asked if that entry contained any lies. Sharri took a moment to read it.

The Deputy D.A.'s mistake was as basic as the legal axiom designed to prevent it—"Don't ask a question unless you know the answer."

"There's a lie right here," Sharri exclaimed, looking up from the diary to eye Golde.

"And what's that?" he wondered. He would later admit that whether she found lies in Serena's diary or not, it mattered very little. By that time in the trial, he knew he "was history," that whatever happened would happen. His objective was to introduce into evidence the entire contents of Diary #1 rather than just the entry in question. There was some "very strange stuff" in there, he thought, and he wanted the judge to read all of it in order to better understand the nature of Serena.

"That we were allowing her boyfriend to come to her baptism," responded Sharri, referring to Serena's relationship with Troy in December of 1992. *"Wrong."*

Handing her Diary #1, Golde pressed on. When it became clear he was prepared to ask her, entry by entry, totalling 161 pages, if each one contained a lie, Judge Kleaver granted a fifteen-minute recess so that Sharri could page through the diary to note any lies, then point them out to the Deputy D.A. Golde had no way of knowing that Sharri had previously been through a similar exercise with the diary, both for Shelley Antonio and later for Horngrad. Within twenty minutes, she had noted eight lies, which she explained to the court when back on the witness stand.

Page 9, November 30, 1989. Sharri had caught Serena in her bedroom with a boy. Serena had been only eleven at the time, Sharri insisted. No way that could have happened without her remembering it.

Page 15, March 17, 1990. "I'm pregnant." Serena was still a virgin at the time.

Same page. One boyfriend was going to "put" another "in the hospital" for getting her pregnant.

Page 66, October 18, 1991. That Serena's biological father had called her. She had not had any contact with him for years and was hurt by that fact, said Sharri.

Page 106, November 21, 1991. An ex-boyfriend's father told Serena that his son had just died of AIDS.

Page 135, August 6, 1992. Serena wrote that she was a virgin, then two days later stated that she "thought she was pregnant." Golde argued that about that time Serena had also written of "having sex all the way," mitigating Sharri's point.

"Well, something just doesn't sound right here," Sharri retorted. "First she says she's a virgin and then two days later that she thinks she's pregnant. You can't know that in two days."

Page 150, August 24, 1992. While visiting her Aunt Roxanne after Mallory's death, Serena had written that Troy was "coming over for dinner." Ridiculous, said Sharri, since Roxanne lived in Tahoe, four hours' drive away. In addition, the family did not approve of Serena's relationship with Troy.

Page 157, September 13, 1992. "I just found out I'm pregnant with Troy's baby." This entry was written just after receiving negative results from a mandatory pregnancy test taken in order to place Serena on birth control pills.

Golde's troubles were not yet over. When he moved to place Diary #1 into evidence, Judge Kleaver agreed with the defense that only those entries just spoken about, rather than the entire volume, should be allowed.

The Deputy's D.A.'s ploy had backfired twice.

Incredulous over their good fortune, Cooper and Horngrad managed to keep their expressions impassive. Next on the agenda was their motion to dismiss. Not only had they managed to tear apart the prosecution's case-in-chief, Golde himself had just argued half their case! With all the evidence of other lies in Serena's diary now before the judge, the validity of the so-called confession was left in shreds.

Golde would have argued that eight lies of 161 pages were "minimal." Judge Kleaver foresaw the contention brewing in Golde's mind but took a different outlook. Up to that point, he'd heard only references to lies in Serena's diaries; now he knew the extent of them. And to his thinking, some of them were indeed "wild." All told, Kleaver felt they supported the defense, casting a suspicion on the truthfulness of *any* of Serena's entries, including the confession.

On that note, Doug Horngrad rose to make his motion to dismiss. Walking solemnly to stand at the clerk's wooden divider directly before the judge, Horngrad reminded the court that according to the law in juvenile trials, the prosecution's case-in-chief must meet the standard of guilt "beyond a reasonable doubt" in order for the trial to proceed.

"You've just heard the government's case," he declared, hands clasped in front of him. "It's done. You can stick a fork in it. That's it."

As Penny Cooper had stated in her opening remarks, Horngrad continued, all of the prosecution's witnesses, excluding Dr. Herrmann, were "indeed a sorry lot." Officer Uhler's testimony was of no probative value. The defendant's statement to him was nothing more than an expression of her feelings after being interrogated. "Not to mention the fact that Serena also told Officer Uhler she had been the wheel person in a getaway car after some shooting." As for Sharri Moore's testimony, she had done absolutely nothing for the government except to explain how the confession diary had been found and turned over to the police. And how odd it was that *not one* of the police officers at the scene the morning of Mallory's death had been called as a witness.

Horngrad spread his hands. "It all boils down to the confession and Dr. Herrmann's testimony. With respect to the diary entry, Diary #1 is in no way consistent with that. And Dr. Herrmann himself said this was a weak medical case. Dr. Herrmann told us that he considered for many weeks the possibility of a natural death. He didn't rule out epilepsy until reaching his conclusion of anal molestation. Only then did he conclude traumatic asphyxia. Even then, he said the asphyxia was from compression to the chest caused by weight on the chest. He said it was consistent with the weight of a 160-pound man."

The attorney's voice intensified. "Dr. Herrmann said, and I quote, that 'this was most likely an unintentional death secondary to an act of child molestation.' That was his 'decided suspicion.' *That* came from the government's *main witness*. Dr. Herrmann also said that death by covering the mouth was an 'unlikely mechanism.' When you have Dr. Herrmann telling you death by compression of the chest, and the diary says death by covering the mouth, it's like someone saying they shot the victim when in fact the victim was stabbed."

As to the prosecution's theory of motive, Horngrad continued, "you would have to weave your way through this maze to find any comprehension." The prosecution maintained that the defendant "killed Mallory to put her out of misery from their mutual tormentor. Yet yesterday, he intimated that she anally molested her sister first. He said the defendant loved her sister so much that she killed her, yet Dr. Wong's testimony was to show that she hated her."

Horngrad reiterated the evidence just heard—that Serena wrote many lies in her diaries. He shook his head, keeping his eyes on the judge. "The government is asking you to convict based on a diary entry when their own coroner tells you it was an accidental death. When he says that death was caused by chest compression and not by covering the mouth. They're asking you to convict on a diary entry when the coroner says molestation occurred at or near the time of death. There is *no reference* to anything like that in the diary. Finally now, the government asks you to accept the theory that the minor molested her sister while killing her out of love *and* hate to prevent further molestation by Michael Moore."

"Only unless," Horngrad emphasized, "you will *never* believe that it's a reasonable possibility that Michael Moore molested and killed Mallory, can you convict the minor."

Rocking on his heels, Horngrad commented, "This was all in due respect a shabby prosecution case. I ask the court to end Serena Moore's sixteen months of incarceration. It is entirely appropriate to grant this motion based on the coroner's statement alone. Serena and the system should not endure *one more day* of proceedings. The government has utterly failed to prove their case beyond a reasonable doubt."

Horngrad's tone softened as he apologized for any aggression on the part of the defense counsel. "If we've been offensive in any way," he concluded, "we do that out of our passion and belief that the minor is innocent."

As Horngrad resumed his seat, Kleaver jotted a final note and turned to Golde. At the judge's invitation, the Deputy D.A. rose and stood behind his table, hands in his pockets. In a *déjà vu* of his closing arguments at Serena's first trial, he stressed, "What we have here is a confession to murder." Although the defense was treating it as "inconsequential," there was "nothing in the record to suggest it was not true." Serena's entry was a "personal, heartfelt confession, a story about how it happened."

Golde shifted his weight. "In terms of the defense's contention that the pathologist testified that the manner of death was inconsistent, I disagree. Dr. Herrmann said death by asphyxia. Because there was no damage to the throat, he concluded compression to the chest. That doesn't preclude covering the mouth. The diary entry doesn't mean she *didn't* sit on the chest *and* cover the mouth."

As for the entry in Diary #1 about finding Mallory's body, Golde called it "very strange," ranging from talking about Mallory to "trying to achieve penetration" during sex. "It was not a tearful statement from a grieving sister."

Regarding motive, the prosecution was not required to prove that. With such a "psychologically damaged teenager," it was "hard to say."

For the first time, Golde admitted, "There's a question about the extent of the molestation, when and how it happened. I'm not abundantly certain at this point. But I do think there was molestation in that house. There was molestation at the time of death." Based on the fact of the confession, he summed up, there was "credible evidence to suggest that Mallory's half sister" had committed the crime.

Defense was allowed the last word. Horngrad kept it short.

Contrary to Golde's statement, he declared, the "so-called confession" was "wholly contradicted." Furthermore, even the Deputy D.A. admitted he didn't know if molestation had occurred or not. "I think we can all agree," Horngrad remarked, "that Serena Moore is not the world's most accurate historian. It's not our job to explain to you what happened beyond a reasonable doubt." The government, in asking the court to convict, had not "discharged that burden" itself.

The courtroom was quiet as the judge prepared to speak. Sharri, sitting alone on the left side of the courtroom, felt her heart quicken, and chided herself. Rationally speaking, she hadn't the slightest expectation of the motion's being granted. And yet, in Horngrad's words, "hope springs eternal."

At first, it was unclear where Judge Kleaver was headed. He noted that the "possibilities" mentioned by Dr. Herrmann as to cause of death were not important. However, the "probabilities and likelihoods" the doctor spoke of *were* important. Those must be coupled with the confession diary entry. "Dr. Herrmann says," Kleaver declared, "that what the diary stated wasn't likely. It probably didn't happen that way. The likelihood of that simply wasn't so." As a result, the court was left with a "really significant doubt" as to the minor's guilt.

Sharri's ears registered the words, but she could hardly assimilate their meaning. Was the judge going to let Serena go?

Serena turned, bug-eyed, to Penny Cooper. Grasping the edge of the table, she began to shake, just as her mother had done months before at her first trial. Silently, Cooper slipped her left hand into the teenager's and hung on tight as her right hand found Horngrad's. So united, the three of them awaited the two words that, after sixteen months, could set Serena free.

Kleaver continued in a quiet, matter-of-fact tone. According to Dr. Herrmann, he said, there was a "clear indication of long-term sexual abuse of Mallory." Michael Moore was the "most likely" culprit. "That," he stated finally, "leads me to the conclusion of serious doubt. For that reason I am granting the motion.

"Case dismissed."

The courtroom erupted, everyone reacting at once. Sharri's gasp was nearly a scream as she broke into heaving sobs. Serena and Penny Cooper clutched each other, Serena crying wildly. Horngrad embraced them both.

Television reporters slammed out of the courtroom. "Get in here!" one yelled at his cameraman as he burst into the hallway. Hearing the cry, Pastor Doug jumped up, heaved his way through the courtroom's creaky doors, and ran to Sharri, his face tight with fear.

"What happened, what happened?!"

She turned and fell against him, arms wound tightly around his neck. "It's over!" she wailed into his shoulder. "It's *over*." He hugged her as he, too, began to cry.

Immediately following the judge's words, Golde's stoicism slipped for a mere split second as he cast his eyes toward the floor. Then, looking resigned, he rose and silently began stacking the files that, after so many months, he would no longer need.

Kleaver slipped out of his robe, and, unlike most judges, who beat hasty retreats after a verdict, stayed to survey the scene.

Serena could have sworn she floated as she was escorted out the rear door by her transport officer. "Come on, let's get you *out* of this place!" the officer sang as she locked Serena in shackles for the last time. During the two-block ride to a county building at Fourth and Broadway where her release papers would be signed, Serena jumped and wiggled as much as her constraints would allow.

As television reporters interviewed the attorneys in the courtroom, Sharri pounded to a hallway pay phone to call Michael. Then, oblivious to onlookers, she fairly danced down the two city blocks to await Serena. Pastor Doug ran across the street to a self-parking lot, retrieved his car, and headed in the same direction. Sharri was too emotional to drive Serena home. He intended to provide them a "getaway vehicle" of his own.

Gray morning clouds were just breaking as, shortly before noon, cameras, reporters and onlookers gathered on the sidewalk in front of the county building at Fourth and Broadway. With an understanding smile, Bob Salladay was patting an emotional colleague on the back. Within five minutes, more television crews had heard the news and came to join the sprawling group. Pastor Doug, as though by divine intervention, found an empty parking space at the curb and rolled into it, engine running and right passenger doors open.

The crowd milled expectantly while inside the building, Serena hopped up and down as her transport officer hurried to unlock her wrist and leg chains. With a flourish, Sharri signed the release papers. Then, as the shackles fell away, Serena took her first free step in sixteen months into the open air. Watching her with glistening eyes, Sharri ran to meet her and, arm in arm, they scurried joyously, uncaring, through the throng of whirring cameras.

"What are you gonna do now?" one reporter shouted.

"Party!" Serena cried.

Skipping down the sidewalk, Serena grabbed a friend in a bear hug, then broke free and jumped into the back of Pastor Doug's car. Sharri clambered in front. Perching excitedly on the edge of her seat, Serena leaned over to wave and flash victory signs at the cameramen scuttling alongside for one last shot of the "Diary Girl" as she pulled away toward home.

On the news that evening, Channel 7 would replay the moment in slow motion, as at the long-awaited conclusion of an epic saga.

Just then, two pedestrians rounding the corner spotted the boisterous crowd and stopped in surprise. "Whoa!" one of the women exclaimed, "what's happening here?"

"I don't know," her friend replied slowly, voice tinged with skepticism as she watched two reporters raise their hands toward the disappearing car in farewell.

"But I thought I heard somebody say something about a murder."

◆

Epilogue

APRIL 27, 1994 was a big news day worldwide as well as for the Moores. The story of "The Diary Girl's" acquittal ran on all local network stations and CNN that evening, along with coverage of former President Nixon's memorial service and the first black vote in Africa. The following morning, Bay Area papers carried the story as front-page news.

For the first few weeks after her release, Serena kept up a frenetic pace, including attending a party in her honor at Pastor Doug's house on Friday evening, reuniting with scores of friends, and going to church Sunday. She also made arrangements to visit Grandma Tessie the following month. Sharri and Michael knew they must allow Serena that relationship, but remained wary of and estranged from Tessie Dornellas themselves.

In the meantime, Sharri made numerous appointments to take care of Serena's various medical and dental needs. Two issues were also of priority—to plan for Serena's education for summer school and the fall, and to find an experienced child psychiatrist to begin the long process of counseling Serena and her parents. Despite the joy over her newfound freedom, Serena was already displaying symptoms that appeared to stem from her sixteen-month incarceration. Used to sleeping under guard and with a light on, at home she was afraid to shower without her mother nearby or enter a dark room alone. These discernible symptoms soon abated; what remained unclear was the extent of psychological trauma Serena retained on a more subconscious level. Not to mention the many unresolved issues regarding her mental health that had arisen before she was ever arrested. For a histrionic teenager bent on gaining attention, Serena certainly had received her wish, albeit not in the manner she would have chosen. Pursued during and after her trial by reporters, journalists, famous talk show hosts, and movie producers, how would Serena respond, say, a year later when the attention abated?

Five days after Serena's release, civil attorney Tanya Starnes held a press conference on the wide stone steps of San Francisco's City Hall to announce a malpractice suit against Melvin Belli, Shelley Antonio, and the Belli firm at large. It would be the eighth malpractice suit filed against Belli since 1985. The plaintiff—"Serena M."—was suing for an undisclosed amount of compensatory and punitive damages due to the attorneys' "consciously disregarding the rights" of their client, charging that they were "guilty of oppression, fraud and malice as defined in Civil Code 3294." As a result of the attorneys' "negligence" and her sixteen-month incarceration, charged the suit, Serena had "suffered severe emotional distress and anguish." To protect the interests of their daughter, Sharri and Michael had appointed another attorney, Virginia Palmer, as Serena's legal "guardian ad litem," responsible for deciding any settlement in the case.

Asked by a reporter the loaded question of how she felt the malpractice suit against the famed "King of Torts" himself would proceed, Starnes responded with a loaded answer. "It shouldn't be much different (from other cases)," she remarked, "except that it's against Mr. Belli."

Channel 7's coverage of the press conference that evening labeled the suit "just another in a series of problems for Belli," who was still steeped in the lawsuit by his ex-partners over the breakup of their firm. Also hanging over his and Antonio's heads was the investigation by the California State Bar into their handling of the "Diary Girl" case. (At press time, the investigation was still pending.)

Belli's formal complaint against Judge Margulies was yet to be resolved as well.

Other controversy about the case lingered, this between the Horngrad/Cooper team and the prosecution. When the defense attorneys criticized Golde for exposing Serena to such a long incarceration by doggedly pursuing the case after Margulies set aside the conviction, an irritated Golde responded that they were attacking him with "unclean hands," that Serena's protracted stay in juvenile hall was a result of Horngard's and Cooper's continuing the case while they "took care of their paying clients." If it had been up to him, he claimed, Serena would have had her second trial within a month.

Cooper and Horngrad went further, maintaining that Golde was wrong ever to have prosecuted the case in the first place, given the strong pieces of evidence that mitigated Serena's diary confession. When challenged why he chose to prosecute knowing that Dr. Herrmann had strong doubts as to Serena's guilt based on the medical evidence from the beginning, Golde replied that "the doctor's opinion was not relevant."

Cooper labeled the remark "unbelievable."

"Even if Matt Golde believed Serena was guilty," she said, "he still should have seen that he had insufficient evidence to prosecute." She also questioned why the Deputy D.A. pushed the case "in view of the positive relationship between the sisters." His theorized motive, in Cooper's words, was "ridiculous."

Judge Kleaver's response to the issue of whether or not the case should have been prosecuted was carefully balanced. The call lay with the D.A.'s Office, he noted. "Some would go ahead with the case because of the confession; others would evaluate further in light of the medical findings and not proceed. If you polled fifty D.A.s, you'd probably get a 25/25 split."

Golde adamantly defended his actions, insisting that his high standards of integrity had not been compromised by his pursuing a case in which he firmly believed—and still believes—the minor to be guilty. "I am perhaps the only unbiased person investigating this case," he stated after Serena's acquittal. "Based on the information I have about the family, I believe she did this. And I believe the whole family is emotionally disturbed."

All three attorneys did agree on one issue—that the Fremont police "flubbed" their handling of Mallory's death from the beginning. The Moores joined them in this opinion.

Golde, viewing the police's actions with a prosecutorial eye, "couldn't agree with much of anything" they did. He pointed first to the initial "haphazard" survey the morning of August 18, 1992, of a scene that later would be labeled that of a homicide. Furthermore, based on Sharri Moore's testimony, it remained apparent that the police report noting a return to the scene a few days later to "seize the bedsheets" was not correct, in that Sharri found the dried spot on Mallory's sheet a day later and informed the police at that time. Whether this was a deliberate "cover-up" as Sharri charged, or an unintended error made in summarizing the investigation to date remained in question.

Captain Mike Lanam, while striving to minimize the blow of accusations against the Fremont police, admitted, "Quite honestly, there were some initial mistakes made, and the rest was catch-up." Regarding allowing various officers to be questioned about specific actions they took in the case, Lanam balked, noting that he would have to "check with the city attorney." In time, a list of specific questions was sent to the Fremont Police Department, but received no answer.

As to Lanam's statement that "initial mistakes" were made, officers on the scene that morning would contend that they made no mistakes, since no sign of foul play had been apparent. As Stuart Kohler's report says of Dejoy, "He stands behind his investigation of Mallory's death."

Asked if he thought Captain Lanam's press conference following Serena's being charged was intended to deflect attention away from the handling of the case up to that point, Golde responded cryptically, "I don't believe they do that much thinking." The diary display at the conference to him was "normal cop behavior," an innate reaction to finding evidence that could break a case.

Golde also was disgusted with the "ineffective" interrogations of Serena by "inexperienced" detectives. He mitigated his charges against the overall police force somewhat by adding that he had spoken with some members of the police department who were "mad" at certain officers involved in the case for "making the department look so bad."

Cooper posed two rhetorical questions regarding the early investigation of the case. Given Dr. Herrmann's conclusion of molestation, why didn't the police question Michael about it and why didn't they give him a polygraph—a standard procedure in police investigations? Based on the police's failing to pursue the avenue of Michael's possible involvement, and based on Dr. Herrmann's indication that the police were suspicious of Serena from the beginning, Cooper and Horngrad could only deduce how the case snowballed. Mia

Black's initial finger-pointing at Serena, and perhaps previous reports of Serena's uncontrollable behavior, seemed to have had a major effect on the police, as did Serena's "parting shot" during her interview with Detective Whiteley that the police should "probably look into maybe suffocation at night." Four months later, when the Confession Diary was discovered, a detective checked the case file on Mallory, saw "traumatic asphyxia" on the coroner's report, and quickly determined a match. "With the notion that the diary was true," Cooper said, "the police never looked back."

Start to finish, the entire case was, in Cooper's conclusion, "tragic."

The tragic case of Serena Moore is riddled with irony. And coincidence.

Or is it a coincidence?

Could a father be falsely accused of molestation both by his stepdaughter *and* by a respected local pathologist? Dr. Herrmann, standing behind his medical findings, would maintain that it is no coincidence at all—the molestation happened. At the same time, four other pathologists—two in the first trial and two for the second—reviewed the autopsy results and concluded that Mallory's anal dilation and small rectal tear were of no medical significance. (The latter two never testified.)

Dr. Herrmann's response to those pathologists is that "the only one good time to see the materials is at the time of autopsy" rather than from viewing slides at a later date. However, his testimony during the second trial could place his conclusions regarding this issue in a different light. Under cross-examination, he stated that he had reached the conclusion of sodomy *after* hearing from the police that Michael Moore had been accused of child molestation in the past. Could that information have nudged him to reach his conclusion while the other pathologists, without that information, deemed the findings "insignificant?" While admitting that he "couldn't say [he] completely ignored what [he] heard about the family situation," Dr. Herrmann also maintains that the anal findings were "just there" and that the dilation in particular disturbed him as soon as he began to examine Mallory's body, at which time he had no information about the Moore family.

If Dr. Herrmann's subsequent knowledge of accusations against Michael in any way played a part in his conclusions, his findings could move from the realm of coincidence into the realm of cause and effect. Sadly, then, for Serena, that cause and effect would point back to her initial charges against Michael, which she insists were false. Her response to any lingering suspicion of Michael is emphatic. "Everybody knows I lied in the past. But I've stopped. I've told people, 'no more, that's it.' And I'll say the truth now—my stepfather did not molest me. He *never touched* me."

Appearing on the Phil Donahue show two weeks after her release, Serena vehemently told the audience, who had quickly turned against Michael, the same statement. To which, one woman yelled back, "Why should we believe you now?"

The harsh reality of that cynical question will haunt Serena for a long time to come.

Serena's "other side of the family"—Aunt Laura, Grandma Tessie, and Roxanne—would agree with the woman's question. Adhering to the belief that both girls were molested, Laura maintains that Serena's defense of Michael is simply another ploy to gain her mother's approval and love. The truth, according to Laura, is that Sharri, Michael, and Serena are all "pathological liars." Laura feels that Mallory and Serena were "totally destroyed by Sharri," and there remains no doubt in her mind that Michael accidentally killed Mallory while molesting her.

Golde continues to believe in Michael's guilt of molestation, but just as strongly maintains that it was Serena who committed murder. "There's still a secret locked up in that house," he charged after Serena's release, "a secret between Serena and Michael. That girl was killed."

The Moores' friends, however, including Serena's teenage chums, remain convinced that molestation did not occur, either with Serena or Mallory. Chris Pauling, who diapered and helped potty train Mallory, saw no emotional or physical evidence of such trauma on the little girl. Even Mia Black, now estranged from the Moore family because of her initial suspicion of Serena, says she "knows nothing" about abuse in the family. This, coming from a woman who spent time with Mallory in

Black's own home. More convincing, perhaps, is Serena's Diary #1, the three-year journal written from her eleventh to fourteenth year, which contains numerous passages about sex with her boyfriend, but no mention of molestation.

The ironies remain. That the case fell into Shelley Antonio's lap, and that this event, in turn, later helped set aside Serena's conviction. That the love Serena felt for Mallory would become the basis of the prosecution's alleged motive for murder. That Michael, disillusioned with his failure to help his stepdaughter, ultimately became the "fall guy" in procuring her acquittal. That the same two damning pieces of evidence responsible for the charges against Serena—the diary confession and Dr. Herrmann's findings—would eventually exonerate her. That after sixteen months, Serena's case would be dismissed for lack of evidence.

These are only a few.

And the biggest irony of all. That, after all is said and done, the tragic question that spawned the case against Serena still remains.

What caused the death of Mallory Moore?

Serena's innocence is no longer legally in question. To hold Michael responsible, one must agree with Dr. Herrmann's opinion of anal molestation, an opinion hotly contested both medically and by those closest to Mallory and her family. And, because of Sharri Moore's testimony that she was awake with an earache and heard nothing during the early morning hours of August 18, 1992, when Mallory apparently died, one also would have to believe that she knew her husband was molesting Mallory but did nothing to stop it, and continues to cover for him even after it led to Mallory's death. Sharri's desperation to find out why her daughter died, depicted at its height in her August 20 interview with Detective Whiteley, casts serious doubt on this theory.

With no real evidence to support the "other perpetrator" scenario, the inaction of the District Attorney's Office speaks for itself. It has not and will not bring charges against Michael Moore.

To believe in the innocence of both Serena and Michael is to embrace the argument that Mallory Moore died of natural causes, most likely asthma—in an attack so sudden and violent that she had no time to cry out to her parents in panic. This kind of death, many physicians will tell you, is virtually impossible. Nevertheless, three expert witnesses hold firm to that conclusion, based on documented medical cases.

The Moores themselves say they will never know exactly what caused Mallory's death, although they suspect the answer lies partly in her asthma and partly in the mysterious "blue spells." They have for the most part come to terms with their not knowing. It is enough that Mallory is gone. They could not be free to build their future if still haunted by the *why* question that drove them to such despair in the first few months after her death.

Therein, now, lies the rub. The Moores must go on—on to piece together their lives, while Mallory's life is forever cut short. Even as Sharri and Michael celebrate Serena's victory, they continue to grieve their loss.

A happy ending? Not entirely.

In my office hangs a finger painting by Mallory, a gracious gift from her mother. Gazing at its freely rendered circles and squiggles of bright red, blue, and green, I can almost see the little hand that created it. Above the design, painted in red letters by a preschool teacher, is her name. MALLORY.

This book done, I turn to new challenges. Yet as I immerse myself in another writing project, Mallory's art work, matted and cherry wood–framed, is a daily reminder of a life lived and lost. Memories of Mallory remain—to those fortunate enough to have known her—forever frozen in time, a time when the world was still a wonderland of dancing, Disney, fireworks, and flattened pennies.

I look at that painting often. Then I think of Mallory's bronze grave marker, and I find solace in believing, as does her family, the words that are inscribed upon it.

SHE DANCES WITH THE ANGELS.

Compelling True Crime Thrillers
From Avon Books

DEATH BENEFIT
by David Heilbroner
72262-3/ $5.50 US/ $6.50 Can

FREED TO KILL
by Gera-Lind Kolarik with Wayne Klatt
71546-5/ $5.50 US/ $6.50 Can

TIN FOR SALE
by John Manca and Vincent Cosgrove
71034-X/ $4.99 US/ $5.99 Can

"I AM CAIN"
by Gera-Lind Kolarik and Wayne Klatt
76624-8/ $4.99 US/ $5.99 Can

GOOMBATA:
THE IMPROBABLE RISE AND FALL OF JOHN GOTTI AND HIS GANG
by John Cummings and Ernest Volkman
71487-6/ $5.99 US/ $6.99 Can

The Best in Biographies from Avon Books

IT'S ALWAYS SOMETHING
by Gilda Radner   71072-2/ $5.95 US/ $6.95 Can

RUSH!
by Michael Arkush   77539-5/ $4.99 US/ $5.99 Can

STILL TALKING
by Joan Rivers   71992-4/ $5.99 US/ $6.99 Can

I, TINA *by Tina Turner and Kurt Loder*
                           70097-2/ $5.99 US/ $7.99 Can

PATTY HEARST: HER OWN STORY
by Patricia Campbell Hearst with Alvin Moscow
                           70651-2/ $6.99 US/ $8.99 Can

SPIKE LEE
by Alex Patterson   76994-8/ $4.99 US/ $5.99 Can

OBSESSION: THE LIVES AND TIMES OF CALVIN KLEIN
by Steven Gaines and Sharon Churcher
                           72500-2/$5.99 US/$7.99 Can